Bruce Carley
Scarborough
1991

The People of God:
Essays on the Believers' Church

THE PEOPLE OF GOD

Essays on the Believers' Church

PAUL BASDEN
DAVID S. DOCKERY
editors

BROADMAN PRESS
NASHVILLE, TENNESSEE

Scripture quotations marked KJV are from the *King James Version of the Bible.*

Scripture quotations marked RSV are from the *Revised Standard Version of the Bible,* copyrighted 1946, 1952, © 1971, 1973.

Scripture quotations marked NASB are from the *New American Standard Bible.* © The Lockman Foundation, 1960, 1962, 1963, 1968, 1971, 1972, 1975, 1977. Used by permission.

Scripture quotations marked NEB are from *The New English Bible.* Copyright © The Delegates of the Oxford University Press and the Syndics of the Cambridge University Press, 1961, 1970. Used by permission.

Scripture quotations marked NIV are from the Holy Bible, *New International Version*, copyright © 1973, 1978, 1984 by International Bible Society.

Scripture quotations marked GNB are from the *Good News Bible:* the Bible in Today's English Version. Old Testament: Copyright © American Bible Society 1976; New Testament: Copyright © American Bible Society 1966, 1971, 1976. Used by permission.

Scripture quotations marked Moffatt are from *The Bible: A New Translation* by James Moffatt, (New York: Harper and Row, Publishers, Inc., 1954).

Library of Congress Cataloging-in-Publication Data

The People of God : essays on the believers' church / [edited by] Paul
  Basden and David Dockery.

    p. cm.

Includes bibliographical references.

ISBN: 0-8054-6023-3

1. Free churches. 2.Church--History of doctrines. I. Basden,
Paul A., 1955- . II. Dockery, David S., 1956- .
BX4817.P46 1990
262--dc20

                90-34731
                CIP

To

James Leo Garrett, Jr.

scholar, teacher, churchman, and friend
on the occasion of his sixty-fifth birthday

Contents

Editors' Preface

In the initial stages of planning this volume, several topics were considered, but the idea of the church as "the people of God" seemed appropriate for several reasons. First, there is hardly an issue that is more fundamental to Baptists than the concept of the Church. Second, this theme has ranked foremost in the thought of James Leo Garrett, Jr. He, perhaps more than anyone else in recent memory, has led this current generation of Baptists to focus on the church. Third, in light of the issues surrounding Scripture and hermeneutics in Baptist life during the past decade it seemed appropriate once again to focus our attention on some of the unique aspects of Baptist foundations. Finally, the topic was chosen because of its crucial importance to biblical, historical, and theological studies.

The title, *The People of God*, communicates the theme that gives continuity to God's work in redemptive history. The essays trace this theme through both the Old and New Testament, as well as through the important periods in church history. The theological and pastoral implications have also been developed. "People of God" is also a term which is broad enough to include other concepts such as "Orthodox," "Reformed," "Catholic," "Believers' Church," "Given Church," or "Free Church," the latter being the label often applied to the Baptistic strand of Christianity. While the emphases of the contributors has centered on the idea of "Believers' Church," we thought that the idea of "People of God" more appropriately and inclusively described this volume. We have indicated the emphases of the chapters with the subtitle, "Essays on the Believers' Church."

The contributors are all former students, colleagues, or teachers of James Leo Garrett, Jr. Each one joins with the editors in expressing our deepest affection and respect for his scholarship, his devotion to the church, his personal concern for his students, and his deep love for our Lord. We offer this volume to our mentor with thanksgiving for who he is and all that he has done for us.

We wish to express appreciation to many who have made this project possible. First, we thank Mrs. Myrta Ann Garrett for her assistance in shaping this volume and suggesting contributors. Also, we thank the contributors for their willingness to join us in putting this volume together. We thank Stan Norman for his work in compiling the useful indexes. To our families, for their love and understanding during the editorial process, we express our deep gratitude. Finally, to our Lord, who graced us with the privilege of knowing and learning from our teacher, James Leo Garrett, Jr., we offer our praise and thanksgiving.

Soli Deo Gloria
Paul A. Basden
David S. Dockery

Dedication to James Leo Garrett, Jr.

by Robert A. Baker

Born on November 25, 1925, in Waco, Texas, James Leo Garrett, Jr., was the only child of Grace Hasseltine Jenkins and James Leo Garrett, Sr., both graduates of Baylor University and both faithful Baptists. During his childhood, Leo was insulated from the economic, social, and religious turbulence of the times by a stable family and regular participation in Sunday School, church, and other Christian activities.

In elementary school and high school, he was accorded numerous honors, graduating from Waco High School with the highest grade average in his class. He entered Baylor University as a law student, but during his sophmore year he committed himself to Christian ministry. On April 4, 1944, the First Baptist Church of Waco licensed him to preach and on November 21, 1945, ordained him after he was called as pastor of the Rankin Baptist Church in Ellis County. His many honors at Baylor included the prestigious editorship of the centennial issue of the *Baylor Yearbook* in 1945 and the permanent presidency of the senior class.

Graduating from Southwestern Baptist Theological Seminary in 1948, he began his life's vocation—teaching. That summer he was interim instructor of Greek at Baylor. On August 31 he married Myrta Ann Latimer, whom he first met at a Baptist Student Union meeting. They have three sons, James Leo III, Robert Thomas, and Paul Latimer.

Garrett continued his studies at home and abroad. He received the Master of Theology degree from Princeton Theological Seminary in 1949, the Doctor of Theology from Southwestern Seminary in 1954, and the Doctor of Philosophy degree from Harvard in 1966. His teaching ministry centered in three institutions: Southwestern Seminary (1949-59, 1979-present), the Southern Baptist Theological Seminary (1959-73), and Baylor University (1973-79). He has written or edited numerous books and articles. He has lectured in the United States, South America, and Europe and has served in many capacities: as a guest at Vatican II; as treasurer of the Machaerus Archeological Excavation in Jordan; as Coordinator, First Conference on the Concept of the Believers' Church; as chairman of the Commission on

Cooperative Christianity and secretary of the Commission on Human Rights, both for the Baptist World Alliance; as managing editor of the *Journal of Church and State*; as associate dean for the Ph.D. degree, Southwestern Seminary; as a member of the Advisory Committee of the Christian Life Commission, Baptist General Convention of Texas; as a member of the editorial board of the journal, *The Second Century*; as an active member of several scholarly societies; and in countless other activities. May God grant him many more years of faithful service.

Contributors

Robert A. Baker
Professor of Church History, Emeritus
Southwestern Baptist Theological Seminary
Fort Worth, Texas

Paul A. Basden
Pastor, Valley Ranch Baptist Church
Irving, Texas

Gerald L. Borchert
J. Rupert Coleman Professor of New Testament Interpretation
The Southern Baptist Theological Seminary
Louisville, Kentucky

Beverly C. Brooks
Assistant Professor of Field Education
Bethel Theological Seminary
Saint Paul, Minnesota

James A. Brooks
Professor of New Testament
Bethel Theological Seminary
Saint Paul, Minnesota

David S. Dockery
Editor of Academic Books, Broadman Press
Nashville, Tennessee

Millard J. Erikson
Executive Vice-President and Dean
Professor of Theology
Bethel Theological Seminary
Saint Paul, Minnesota

William R. Estep, Jr.
Distinguished Professor of Church History
Southwestern Baptist Theological Seminary
Fort Worth, Texas

Timothy George
Dean
Beeson Divinity School
Samford University
Birmingham, Alabama

Sharon Hodgin Gritz
Writer and Speaker
Fort Worth, Texas

William L. Hendricks
Professor of Theology
Director of the Center for Religion and the Arts
The Southern Baptist Theological Seminary
Louisville, Kentucky

Glenn O. Hilburn
Professor and Chairman, Department of Religion
Baylor University
Waco, Texas

E. Glenn Hinson
David T. Porter Professor of Church History
The Southern Baptist Theological Seminary
Louisville, Kentucky

Fisher Humphreys
Professor of Divinity
Samford University
Birmingham, Alabama

Walter C. Kaiser, Jr.
Senior Vice-President and Academic Dean
Professor of Semitic Languages and Old Testament
Trinity Evangelical Divinity School
Deerfield, Illinois

John J. Kiwiet
Professor of Historical Theology, Retired
Southwestern Baptist Theological Seminary
Fort Worth, Texas

Franklin H. Littell
Professor Emeritus
Temple University
Philadelphia, Pennsylvania

J. W. MacGorman
Distinguished Professor of New Testament
Southwestern Baptist Theological Seminary
Fort Worth, Texas

Dale Moody
Professor of Christian Theology, Emeritus
The Southern Baptist Theological Seminary
Louisville, Kentucky

Dwight A. Moody
Pastor, North Park Baptist Church
Adjunct Professor of Religious Studies
La Roche College
Pittsburgh, Pennsylvania

Carey C. Newman
Assistant Professor of Religion
Palm Beach Atlantic College
Palm Beach, Florida

John P. Newport
Vice-President for Academic Affairs and Provost, Retired
Distinguished Professor of Philosophy of Religion, Emeritus
Special Consultant to the President for Academic Research
Southwestern Baptist Theological Seminary
Fort Worth, Texas

William L. Pitts
Professor of Religion
Baylor University
Waco, Texas

Marty L. Reid
Professor of Greek and New Testament
Southeastern Baptist Theological Seminary
Wake Forest, North Carolina

Robert B. Sloan
Associate Professor of Religion
Baylor University
Waco, Texas

C. Penrose St. Amant
Senior Professor of Church History
The Southern Baptist Theological Seminary
Louisville, Kentucky

Wayne E. Ward
Joseph Emerson Brown Professor of Christian Theology
The Southern Baptist Theological Seminary
Louisville, Kentucky

George Huntston Williams
Hollis Professor of Divinity, Emeritus
Harvard University
Cambridge, Massachusetts

Doyle L. Young
Assistant Professor of Church History
Southwestern Baptist Theological Seminary
Fort Worth, Texas

Part 1
Theological Foundations

Scripture presents the church as the people of God, the community and body of Christ, and the fellowship of the Holy Spirit. Historically, the Christian church is a community founded on the teachings of Jesus Christ, His redemptive death and resurrection, and the gift of the Holy Spirit, seeking to be a holy priesthood (1 Pet. 2:5), and declaring the wonderful deeds of God, who called the church out of darkness into His wonderful light (1 Pet 2:9). Since the confessionals made at the Councils of Constantinople (381), Ephesus (431), and Chalcedon (451), the church has continually reaffirmed itself to be "one, holy, catholic, and apostolic." These characteristics have existed in tension with one another as the church in various places and at different times has attempted to work out the theological significance of what it means to be the church, the people of God.

In this foundational section of the book, six noted Baptist theologians articulate their understanding of the purpose of the church, the ordinances/ sacraments of the church, the worship of the church, the discipline of the church, and the importance of the priesthood of believers. John P. Newport lays the groundwork for the following essays in his capable discussion of "The Purpose of the Church" as it exists in the "already/not" yet tension awaiting the eschatological consummation. Dale Moody tackles the implications of the theology and practice of baptism within the Believers' Church tradition. Millard J. Erickson offers his perspective on the Lord's Supper. He raises questions regarding pressing issues in the life of the church and uses the subject of the Lord's Supper as a source of theological agenda.

Recognizing that worship is central to the essence of the church, Wayne E. Ward provides a practical and penetrating look at the distinctives of Free Church worship. Ward protests the inconsistencies between Free Church theology and Free Church worship. New Testament scholar J. W. MacGorman examines the issue of "The Discipline of the Church" with a careful exegesis of 1 Corinthians 5 and calls for the reinstitution of church discipline in our churches today. The final essay in this section investigates the controversial subject, which is nevertheless at the heart of Believers'

Church theology—"The Priesthood of All Believers." Timothy George, from a biblical, theological, and historical perspective explains the significance of this important theme for Christian ministry.

All of these essays, while not touching the theme of church government directly, are written from the perspective that the authority of Christ is expressed through the congregation. This opening section lays the theological foundation for understanding the church as one of the most important realities of the Christian faith.

1
The Purpose of the Church

by John P. Newport

Definition of the Church

In recent years there has been a resurgence of interest in the church. It is agreed among evangelicals that discussions concerning the church should always be rooted in normative guidelines based on a study of the New Testament descriptions and teachings.[1]

The apostle Paul used the word *ekklesia* (church) more than any other New Testament writer. The majority of his writings were addressed to a group of believers in a specific city. However, we should note that the individual congregation, or group of believers in a specific place, is never regarded as only a part or component of the whole church. The church is not a sum or composite of the individual local groups.[2] A better statement would be that the local congregation is the church in local expression. The one church of God expresses itself locally in the fellowship of believers. The church in Ephesus is *the* church of God, not merely a part of the church of God.

It should be noted, however, that unity was not expressed in external organization or ecclesiastical structure. The early church was made up of local groups of believers scattered throughout the Mediterranean world with no external or formal organization binding them together except apostolic authority. Such authority today is found in the Scriptures properly interpreted. This apostolic authority was exerted through spiritual and moral persuasion. It was not formal and legal.[3]

From a broad theological perspective, the church can be defined as the whole body of those who through Christ's death have been savingly reconciled to God and have received new life. While it is universal in nature, it finds expression in local groups of believers.[4]

The Biblical Context for Understanding
the Purpose of the Church

For the Hebrew prophets and the later Hebrew leaders after the exile, the "age to come" would mean the cessation of this present age, and the kingdom of God would take the place of the kingdoms of this world. In contrast, the New Testament testimony is quite clear that the "age to come" has dawned in Jesus Christ, and the kingdom of God has come with power. But here is the paradox. Sinful history still goes on, this present age still continues, and the kingdoms of this world still exercise power. This was the situation which faced the first Christian witnesses. They still anticipated a final consummation in which the process of sinful history would be wound up chronologically. They were equally sure that the "age to come" had dawned and that the powers of that age were already at work in their lives. The death, resurrection, and ascension of Christ had released those powers, and the Spirit of Christ was operating in the Christian fellowship as an earnest or down payment of their future inheritance. Thus the kingdom of God was both present and future.[5]

In other words, the New Testament insists that the "age to come" is not, as Judaism thought, an era of earthly tranquility and righteousness following the Messiah's arrival, when present earthly conditions will be renovated, but it is already coexisting with and penetrating this present "age." This "age to come" has already intruded into and is now being established in this "age" through the incarnation, atonement, and resurrection of Christ and the extension of His work by the Spirit. Thus, any doctrine of the purpose of the church that is biblical is necessarily rooted in this eschatological view.[6]

It is important to observe, however, that though the ages are experienced together, their essential characters remain unchanged. The "age to come" is that realm of divine, redeeming existence, that sovereign rule of the Triune God, that heavenly form of existence which has come in and through Christ. "This age" is life characterized by rebellion and sin that in all of its dimensions—existential, social, political, and natural—is doomed to pass away under the judgment of God. The unbeliever who lives in "this age" does not need merely to improve in order to enter "the age to come," but to die to self and be resurrected through union with Christ. Hence the antithesis between the ages is always preserved (Eph. 1:21; cf. Rom. 12:2; 1 Cor. 1:20; 2:6-8; 3:18,22; 2 Cor. 4:4; Gal. 1:4; Eph. 2:2; 1 Tim. 6:17; Titus 2:12; Rom. 8:30).[7]

This "age," this divine future, is one that only God can bring into existence. Since this new "age" requires, as a condition of its existence, the destruction of sin, death, and the devil, the only ground on which this can be done is the incarnation, death, and resurrection of Christ. For that reason, the "age to come" could only arrive, and has only arrived, in and through Christ. This is, in fact, one of the strongest arguments for Christ's divinity. He must have been divine to do what only God could do in establishing the kingdom and bringing into history the conditions of the messianic "age to come."[8]

The classic presentation of this context is presented by Paul who saw the Christian standing in an interval between two ages. The whole redemptive work of God moves toward the perfect realization of the kingdom of God in the age to come and includes all creation. Until then the old age continues with its burden of sin, evil, and death. However, in the mission of Christ and the coming of the Spirit, the blessings of the new age have reached back to those who are in Christ. Meanwhile, the world and mankind as a whole remain in the grip of the old age.[9]

The church, as God's new creation in Christ, is not to be equated with the kingdom. The kingdom is to be thought of as the reign of God. The church, by contrast, is a realm of God, the people who are under His rule. The kingdom is the rule of God, whereas the church is the human community under that rule.[10] George Ladd states that the church is *created* by the kingdom and is a *witness* to the kingdom, an *instrument* of the kingdom, and the *custodian* of the kingdom.[11] In that sense the church is the presence of the future in the midst of the old. Although the old creation is dying and will be destroyed (at the second coming), a new creation has been born and is growing up in the midst of the old. A new thrust was released in the death and resurrection of Christ. It is here now, present in this life, and will be fully realized in the new heaven and the new earth. For this reason the major emphasis of the church as the new creation is that the church is to be the visible presence of the new creation in the world now. The church is thus the visible society or societies of God's people who are called to act as the presence of the future, the eschatological community in the world made new through Christ.[12]

This "already-not/yet" context undergirds what Ernst Troeltsch calls the "sect-type" view of ecclesiology. If the church is to be what it is called to be, it must emphasize radical obedience to God's will. The church is to seek to be the company of those truly committed and therefore separated from fallen humanity. Unless the demands of this *sect principle* are honored in ecclesiology, the church is tempted to settle comfortably into its environment, taking its cues from the surrounding culture and losing its ultimate vision.[13]

However, as Robert Webber points out, for evangelicals there are problems in the "sect" view. First, some evangelicals are characterized by a moral rigorism which demands too much of the church. This attitude is evident in the inflexibility of the contemporary rigorists who, having set high personal standards for church members, act with intolerance and a lack of love toward those who fail to meet these standards. This rigorism fails to recognize the sinfulness of the members of the church, expecting too much by way of personal holiness. The second problem is that the same group which demands moral holiness often expresses a self-righteous attitude toward other denominations (they are apostate).[14]

According to Webber, evangelicals need to recover an understanding of the church as *simul justus et peccator* ("at the same time righteous and sinner"). This recognition of the church's sinfulness in no way supports an attitude of laxness in the church. The Reformers urged their fellow Christians to seek to bring the earthly church into conformity to the church which exists in the mind of God.[15]

This recognition of the *simul* will help us become more aware of the humanness of the church. Because of her humanity she is subject to worldliness and even heresy. Throughout history the church has repeatedly accommodated herself to the outward forms of culture. There has always been a tendency to identify the visible church with a particular ecclesiastical structure, drawn more from culture than the Scriptures. This was certainly the case with the Roman Catholic Church. This is the reason why the Reformation *had* to take place. And because the Reformers recognized the tendency of the church to become influenced again and again by the standards of the world, they insisted that the earthly church must always be *ecclesia semper reformanda* (the church always reforming itself).[16]

The *simul* emphasis will help evangelicals to become more tolerant of the weaknesses of the church. By recognizing that the church is caught in that tension between the "now" and the "not yet," we can learn to live with a true historic perspective in mind, anticipating the completeness and fullness of the church's holiness in the eschaton and working now on earth toward a tangible and visible demonstration of what the church is called to be.[17]

This, of course, does not deny the importance of reform groups and emphases which through their fervent witness call the church away from its easygoing accommodation to the world. The renewal movements of the present Christian community (including the holiness and charismatic movements when they have learned to relativize their role and are open to other gifts given to the body, 1 Cor. 12—14) serve this purpose. This renewal and reform role is always exercised as a part of the body and is not to be mistaken for the whole, as in the case of some whose reductionism excludes those with other gifts and ministries.[18]

Groups such as Baptists, for example, have seen that an important part of their function is the emphasis on the restitution of the New Testament understanding of the church as a gathered and regenerate community. Baptists point out that it is important to remember the biblical teaching that believers in Christ are saved solely by God's grace in the blood of Jesus Christ (Rom. 3:24f.; 2 Cor. 5:18; Eph. 2:5; Titus 2:14; 3:7), but they are also to be sanctified by the Holy Spirit to lead a holy life (cf. 1 Thess. 4:3-8; Rom. 6:12f., 19).

The Purpose of the Church Seen as an Expression of Christ's Lordship in the Church

Robert Webber suggests that one way to describe the purpose of the church is to explicate the images of the church found in the New Testament such as the people of God, the new creation, the fellowship in faith, and the body of Christ.[19] Because the New Testament is primarily rooted in the Hebraic world rather than the Greek, the purpose of the church is better captured through images than through logical propositions. These images point to the reality of the church as many-sided.[20]

An alternate method, chosen here, is to utilize these images in describing the purpose of the church but to place the images in a twofold framework. We can state the purpose of the church as expressing Christ's lordship in the life of the church and Christ's lordship in the life of the world.

The first part of the purpose of the church is to express Christ's lordship in the life of the church. This can be called an inreach-and-nurture emphasis.

The Purpose of the Church Is to Encourage and Regulate Worship

The initial statement of the importance of this emphasis is found in Acts 2:41-42,46-47. Here we see the early church emphasizing prayer and praise, the waters of baptism, and the bread of the Supper. Corporate prayer and praise in its multifarious expressions, meditative and celebrative, are vehicles of the Spirit in maintaining and strengthening the body of Christ. The prayers and hymns of the church keep the people of God in communion with the vision of God. In worship we are put in touch by the Spirit with the age to come. Our anchors are lodged in the not yet and our lives are given direction and stability. We are also dislodged from the present, made restless with the givens, and thus are strangers and pilgrims in the now.[21]

No detailed prescriptions for worship are given by Paul. In his epistles he writes of worship incidentally.[22] However, even in the epistles to the church at Corinth, which was apparently inclined to spiritual excesses and licentiousness, Paul gives us some guidelines. Worship should involve the following elements.

The proclamation of the Word in the assembly of the church.—The church has not only to thank the preaching of the gospel for its origin, but its continued existence is dependent on the inviolate preservation of this preaching (cf. 1 Cor. 15:1-2; Col. 2:7; 1 Tim. 6:14, et al.).[23]

The narration of the story of the deeds of God, the telling of the story, is a sign of the presence of the Spirit and a tool the Spirit uses to build the church. The reading of Scripture was part of worship in the churches founded by Paul (cf. Acts 13:15; 2 Cor. 3:14). Among the instructions given to Timothy were such things as "the public reading of scripture" along with preaching and teaching (1 Tim. 4:13). Scriptures were read in the home as well as the churches because they were accepted as inspired and authoritative (1 Tim. 3:14-17).[24]

It should also be noted that God gives the church the responsibility of interpreting the Scriptures and provides means for that task. Fruitful stewardship means that the church is constantly commissioned to translate the faith into terms connecting it with the issues and idiom where it lives. This aspect also carries the promise that the Spirit will be present in the church to make good this fruitfulness.[25]

A weakness of the church is its difficulty in keeping balance in relation to the preservation of scriptural purity and applying it to contemporary life. Some construe the Spirit's primary commission to be that of preserving the purity of the gospel in its original code language. Others understand the charge to mean the task of contemporizing the faith in the language and thought forms of our modern culture. Depending on the temptation and challenge, it may sometimes be more important to attend to the text (in periods of acculturation and accommodation), or at other times to the context (periods of retreat and repristination). But finally the Spirit's promise of illumination is bound to both text and context and their right interrelationship.[26]

We should always remember, however, that the Bible can and must function as a reference and judge of our efforts at contextualization. But all kinds of people in the church must join together to seek its meaning together, enriched by the varieties of perspective that constitute the body of Christ.[27]

Baptism and the Lord's Supper.—In the ordinances of baptism and the Lord's Supper an "outward and visible sign" of the Spirit complements the verbal one of proclamation. Word and ordinances keep company in sustaining the life of the church.[28]

Baptism, as the initial ordinance, is a sign of our incorporation into the one body of Christ. Baptism includes both faith and immersion, but it is faith that is the controlling principle. The confession of faith may lead to salvation without immersion in water, but immersion in water does not lead to salvation without the confession of faith in the saving event of Christ's death and resurrection.[29]

Baptists do not accept household or infant baptism. They do use the rite of dedication of children to stress the importance of the family influence.

They are glad to see the growing stress upon the decisiveness of confirmation where household baptism is practiced as a recognition of the importance of the personal act of faith at the age of discretion.[30]

The Lord's Supper is a remembrance of Christ's death and resurrection and an anticipation of the heavenly banquet. The Supper points back to the crucifixion. It is a remembrance of "the blessed sacrifice of his Son." The participant remembers the formative event of the community's history and of his or her personal pilgrimage. The Lord's Supper then and now is portent of the eschatological banquet with its celebration of the final coming together of all things. This is the ordinance of mourning and joy, memory and hope (1 Cor. 11:24-26).[31]

The Supper is also a communion now with Christian people in anticipation of life together in the new heaven and the new earth. Observance calls for penitence and faith in preparation. We remember that in accordance with the general practice of the early church, the Corinthians observed the Lord's Supper with a communal meal. In their case the meal seems to have preceded the institutional rite of bread and wine, and it became the occasion for abuse (1 Cor. 10:21).[32]

Paul's correction appears to have initiated, quite unintentionally no doubt, a process that in time would eliminate the meal altogether from the observance of the Supper. Unfortunately, this result tends to minimize for the future church the joyful aspects of the service that center on the meal, that is, the believers' present communion with one another and with the risen Lord and their anticipation of the messianic banquet at the second coming of the Lord. Another tragic development was the removal of the administration of the ordinances, together with the ministries of the Word, from a congregational context to the exclusive control of a clerical and priestly class.[33]

Music, prayer, and praise.—In addition to the ministry of the Word in its various forms of reading, prophecy, teaching, and the administration of baptism and the Supper, we find mentioned in the Pauline Epistles the singing of psalms, hymns, and spiritual songs as an element of the worship of the assemblies (Col. 3:16; cf., Eph. 5:19).[34] Priority must be given to prayer and praise, for biblical worship seems impossible without these two elements. *Amen* and *Alleluia* are perhaps the most basic words in biblical worship.[35]

The relatively lax church order at the meetings of some Pauline congregations becomes apparent rather quickly at Corinth, a church richly endowed with spiritual gifts (1 Cor. 12:5ff.). The most detailed portrait of the problem is posed and Paul's response to it is found in 1 Corinthians 11 and 14. The picture is one of almost carefree abandon, occasioned, it seems, by exuberant ill-mannered charismatic congregations. It reflects a spiritual animation and power that the apostle recognizes to be from the Holy Spirit. Yet he does not hesitate to criticize the Corinthian practices and to give instructions, a kind of "order of worship," to modify them. As he did later and more broadly in the Pastoral Epistles, Paul here clarifies and tightens the regulation of worship in order to meet problems that have arisen in the churches.[36]

The apostle was particularly concerned with two glaring problems in their worship, its egocentrism and its lack of order and social decencies. He regarded these defects not as mere matters of cultural taste or custom but as the result of ethical and doctrinal error.[37]

The restrictions placed upon the manifestation of tongues reflect Paul's understanding of the purpose of the gifts and of the nature of public worship. Everything is to be done "decently and in order" (1 Cor. 14:40) and for "upbuilding" (v. 3) the hearers. This is proper because "God is not a God of confusion" (v. 33), and His Spirit impels no one to speak in a disruptive way (vv. 26,32f.).

The restrictions placed upon the exercise of prophecy in the Pauline church are similar to those placed upon the use of tongues. The prophets are to subject their messages to the evaluation or "discernment" of the community of gifted persons who are apparently to determine the extent of the "word of God" in a prophet's message (see v. 29). Although prophecy is to be regulated in public worship, it is nevertheless given priority over speaking in tongues. It is an inspired message in the language of the hearers, and in content it is intended for their "upbuilding and encouragement and comfort" (v. 3).[38]

Prophecy was much broader than "prediction," the strict meaning of prophecy as it is popularly conceived today. The remarkable impact of the charismatic movement on the contemporary church requires the modern Christian to relate the New Testament gifts of prophecy and tongues to the current ministry and order of the church. Participants in the charismatic movement may tend to assume, uncritically, that all tongues speaking is from the Holy Spirit. Christians outside the movement may be inclined to ascribe the total phenomenon to psychological causes. The apostle Paul offers criteria for distinguishing divine from emotional, pathological, or demonic phenomena. He judges the charismata in terms of the effects that accompany them and in terms of the spiritual power, the character, and ethics of those who manifest the charismata.[39]

According to Webber, there needs to be a balance between the intellectual and emotional in worship. Webber also notes that evangelicals have a tendency toward a private and individual approach to worship through prayer and Bible study. Thus they need to rethink the order of worship toward a more inclusive rehearsal of the entire faith, an increased use of the Lord's Supper as the focal point of worship, and a return to a creative use of the church year. Perhaps in this way evangelicals will be able to overcome a tendency towards human-centeredness and the lack of comprehensive content in worship which has helped to create among many evangelicals the yearning for a more fulfilling experience of worship.[40]

A Second Part of the Church's Purpose Is to Serve Those in Physical Need Within the Christian Fellowship

According to Acts 2:44-45, the early Christians served the neighbor in need within the Christian community. In that particular context they displayed a very radical act of physical support, a pooling of property and possessions and redistribution on the principle "to each according to his need" (v. 45). The church demonstrated the meaning of *agape* in its internal life, *doing* the story, and thus intuitively modeling the quality of life in the kingdom to come.

Such servanthood comes naturally as a gift of the Spirit. How service is enacted changes with each new occasion. But it continues in each new setting to be a mark of an authentic church. The care in body as well as spirit for the brothers and sisters in Christ is a constitutive factor of the Christian community.[41]

A Third Part of the Church's Purpose Is to Provide Fellowship

In verses 42 and 46 we find the early church sharing the common life and meals. This was more than a ministry of material benevolence. In and through the service was to be seen and felt the throb of fellowship. A purpose of the church, therefore, is to provide a support system. Here joys are shared and burdens are borne.[42]

Paul speaks of sharing one another's experiences: "If one member suffers, all suffer together; if one member is honored, all rejoice together" (1 Cor. 12:26). While hurt is reduced, joy is increased by being shared. We are to encourage and sympathize with each other (Gal. 6:2).[43]

There is always the danger of a ghetto gospel and a minority complex when fellowship is isolated from witness and service in the world. However, fellowship is crucial for the church. According to the Bible, community and fellowship mean shared life together based on our new being in Jesus Christ. To be born again is to be born into God's family and community. Any group of believers which fails to experience intimate life together has failed to experience the church as Christ's living body.[44]

The Fourth Part of the Church's Purpose Is to Exercise Discipline

The church is not a chance collection of people but a community of believers called and united together by the grace of God—a covenant people. Christian believers therefore accept responsibility for each other and agree to exercise such discipline as is necessary to remain faithful to God's covenant. The church should take seriously the Bible's many injunctions to warn, rebuke, exhort, encourage, and build one another up in love.[45]

Jesus laid down a pattern for discipline in Matthew 18:15-17. In severe cases, there may even be a need for excommunication from the group, as in the case of the immoral man mentioned in 1 Corinthians 5:1-2. The primary aim of such disciplinary action is not to rid the group of the erring member, however, but to restore such a person to righteous living and thus to fellowship with believers.[46]

In urging the churches at Corinth and Thessalonica to exercise discipline over the membership, Paul implicitly claimed for them a prerogative granted to synagogues and other secular clubs (1 Cor. 5:5,9ff.; 6:1-6; 2 Thess. 3:6,10,14). Paul's warnings against an argumentative spirit and the abuse of wine at the Supper may have been occasioned in part because some were following a pattern known to characterize the clubs.[47]

Donald Bloesch states that once it was possible to speak of a Christian style of life—this is no longer meaningful for many church people. Yet we can speak of a Muslim style of life or a Communist style of life. The reason is that Islam and Communism represent disciplined communities, while discipline is no longer in effect in most of our churches.[48]

The New Testament is adamant that church members who openly flout the moral law of God or who promulgate doctrines antithetical to the truth of the gospel are to be censured and even excommunicated if they show no signs of repentance. The church thus has an obligation to exercise discipline, but it must do so in love. It is imperative that we recover the idea of the church as a covenantal community. We as the people of the church need to covenant with God and also with one another in order to fulfill our holy vocation.[49]

The Church's Purpose Includes Developing an
Appropriate Organizational and Leadership Balance

The form of government and the exercise of authority in the church are long-disputed questions.[50] The congregation as the basic community expression of the Christian religion gives force to the argument for congregational polity or, at the very least, a place in church governance for the congregation.[51]

Paul regarded Christians as living in a corporate sphere of existence that may be termed "the body of Christ." In 1 Corinthians 12:12-27 the body of Christ is compared with parts of the physical body which represent and by implication are allegorically identified with gifted individuals in the church (for example, vv. 6, 21). Within this framework the apostle set forth two important principles for the use of the gifts of ministry in the body of Christ. The first is the principle of diversity. As the bodily organs differ in status, importance, and function, so also believers differ in accordance with their particular spiritual gifts. When a gift is granted it is not, Paul emphasized, simply at the disposal of the recipient but is to be used as a means of building up the body of Christ. If the charismata become a source of boasting or a means merely to indulge a desire for self-assertion or for an emotional "high," as they apparently did in the church in Corinth, they are being misused.[52]

There is evidence that, along with an unstructured or "free" charismatic ministry, an appointed ministry was also present in the Pauline churches. This type of ministry had its basis and authority in the gifts of the Holy Spirit no less than that which was exercised informally, but in several respects it was distinct. Specifically it was identified with persons who were recognized to have established and continuing responsibilities and who were entitled to esteem and/or to financial support. Most prominent among this group were, of course, the apostles of Jesus Christ. But others are mentioned who also fall into this category. They come into view primarily in two areas: the local administrative leadership and the missionary enterprise. They also appear in ministries of teaching and leadership in worship. In two respects church order in the Pastoral Letters of Paul differs considerably from that reflected in the other Pauline letters. First, the Pastorals give more attention and prominence to appointed ministries. Second, and less significantly, the Pastorals introduce the term "elder" as an alternative title for overseer or bishop.[53]

As Christian history unfolded, the notion developed that ministry belongs to the ordained clergy. The clergy were conceived as the ministers, and the rest of the Christian community as the laity. In practice this meant that some were subjects and others objects in the life of the church. In the past few decades this view of ministry has come under sharp attack in both theory and practice. It has been challenged by a conception of "the ministry of the laity." A new vision of the ministry of the laity has had a helpful effect in many areas of the church's life, but it has also contributed to the loss of a sense of identity among clergy who have attempted to honor this enlarged perception of ministry. And the reaction against the oversimplifications of some of the more recent theories of the ministry of the laity has prompted a too quick return in some places to authoritarian clergy models. In the midst of these tendencies and countertendencies is a rising generation of women seeking ordination and equal participation in the church as pastors.[54]

Gabriel Fackre calls us back to Acts and Paul to view ministry in both its wholeness and particularity. The gifts of proclaiming and celebrating facilitate the identity and memory of the body of Christ. Without these gifts the church does not know who it is or where it has come from. There must be some within the church who are the custodians of the gifts of proclamation and celebration (1 Cor. 3:5; Acts 6:1-6; 2 Tim. 1:11). They do not monopolize these gifts or purposes of the church, but they do guard and facilitate them. This is a special ministry within the general ministry of the whole people of God, "to fan into flame the gift of God" (2 Tim. 1:6, NIV), set apart from the general ministry for that unique purpose. As a particular ministry signaled by the act of ordination, its gifts and functions are essential to the health and wholeness of the church.[55]

Other purposes of the church include service, fellowship, and outreach. The laity constitute the presence of the church in the rhythms and structures of society, the places of work and leisure, governance, education, science, social change, marriage, and the family. They turn occupation into vocation as they live out their own priesthood. Many suggest that there should be a setting apart through special consecration by the church of its gift-ministries through the laity. The emphasis on different responsibilities for ministry should not be hardened into a rigid division of ministry. A living organism is an interrelated whole. Even more so is the body of Christ.[56]

It should be noted that to be *responsible* for the kerygmatic and liturgical gifts does not mean the exclusive monopoly of proclamation and liturgy. The clergy are the guarantors of these organs functioning within the body.[57]

Webber contends that many evangelical pastors and leaders of church organizations have fallen into the worldly model of authority—domination. The answer, he urges, is found in the model of Jesus: "Rather than being lords, disciples are to be servants of one another. The greatest would be servant of all" (Mark 10:42-43, author).[58]

All the gifts are given by the Spirit for the whole body. The dispersion of the power of the Spirit among all the people includes universality in the opportunity of the people of God to enter into any ministry for which personal call and publicly validated equipment have prepared them. The debate about the ordination of women to the ministry of proclamation and worship celebration has sharpened this question of the universality of option. We should remember Peter's words in Acts 2:17-18.

> God says, 'This will happen in the last days: I will pour out on everyone a portion of my spirit; and your sons and daughters shall prophesy. . . . Yes, I will endue even my slaves, both men and women, with a portion of my spirit, and they shall prophesy'(NEB).

Thus, according to Peter, no aspect of the ministry of the church is denied to any part of the people of God, least of all that unique ministry in which mysteries of God are seen and celebrated.[59] Paul affords guidelines and emphases. Some of these are related to local problems and others are transcultural.

The Church's Purpose Includes Edification and Education

That a deeper education in the faith began immediately after conversion and an incorporation into the new community through baptism is suggested by Acts 2:42. Here the new Christians "devoted themselves to the apostles' teaching. " It is most natural that this pattern should develop since the Jewish synagogue was a place of instruction and worship. According to verse 46, it appears that this postbaptismal instruction was on a daily basis.[60]

It should be noted that baptism provides the context in which a person comes to grips with the Christian faith. The heart of the Christian faith is represented in baptism. The new convert to Christianity must be brought into the church community immediately. The convert has been born into a new family, and it is in this family that the new Christian is nurtured and brought into a mature Christian faith. Furthermore, the church must recognize that there are stages of growth.[61]

One of Jesus' commands in the Great Commission was to teach converts "to observe all that I have commanded you" (Matt. 28:20). Paul repeatedly spoke of the edification of the body. In Ephesians 4:12, for example, he indicates that God has given various gifts to the church "[for the equipment of] the saints, for the work of ministry, for building up the body of Christ." Moreover, in Paul's discussion of certain controversial spiritual gifts, he brings up the matter of edification. He says, for example, in 1 Corinthians 14:4-5: "He who speaks in a tongue edifies himself, but he who prophesies edifies the church. . . . He who prophesies is greater than he who speaks in tongues, unless some one interprets, so that the church may be edified." In verse 26 Paul sums up the matter: "Let all things be done for edification."[62]

Education may take many forms and occur on many levels. It is incumbent upon the church to utilize all legitimate means and technologies available today. Beyond the local level the local church cooperates with other churches to carry on specific aspects of their instructional task. For example, theological seminaries and divinity schools equip pastor-teachers and others to instruct people in the Word. This is a fulfillment of Paul's command to Timothy: "And what you have heard from me before many witnesses entrust to faithful men who will be able to teach others also" (2 Tim. 2:2).[63]

The Church's Purpose Seen as an Expression of Christ's Lordship in the World

Christ's Lordship in the World Is Exercised First Through the Church's Proclamation and Testimony

When our Lord sent forth the twelve (Mark 6:7-13), He prefigured the task of the church. As we have seen, the church stands between the dawning of the kingdom with power in the cross and resurrection and the coming of the Holy Spirit and its full consummation in the *Parousia*. Further, the church's preaching is not just a demonstration that the kingdom has come with power. It is a precondition for the final glorious unveiling of the kingdom. The Gentiles must be gathered in before the Lord comes in glory. The full consummation cannot be made manifest until all nations have heard the good news. Oscar Cullmann brings this out very forcefully. The kingdom is already being realized in history. However, the full realization waits on the accomplishment of the world mission.[64]

This is the theme of Paul in Romans 9—11, in many ways a commentary on Mark 13:10: "The gospel must first be preached to all nations." In Romans 10:14 Paul contended that God is following an exact plan. There must be offered to all an opportunity to hear the gospel. The Jews have already heard it, but not all have received it. Therefore, the call now goes to the Gentiles, before finally, at the end, the Jews do enter. For Paul, who was called especially to preach the gospel to the Gentiles before the present time ceased in the second coming, this was all in God's purpose. The full plan is surrounded with mystery, but within that mystery he clearly saw his own calling as apostle to the Gentiles (Rom. 11:13). Paul is an element in the working out of the mystery among the Gentiles and thus in the final consummation. So also, Paul feels compelled to preach the gospel (1 Cor. 9:16) and declares that he is a prisoner of Christ for the Gentiles (Eph. 3:1). Paul and his fellows are ambassadors for Christ. They are pleading with men and women that they should be reconciled to God (2 Cor. 5:20). Because the full number of the Gentiles must be made up (Rom. 11). This understanding of Paul is supported by Johannes Munck in his study of the apostle.[65]

The church's evangelistic and missionary task is thus a crucial part of its purpose. Its preaching is God's act through the testimony of His people. The nations are now being invited to the eschatological feast by God's gracious activity in Christ and in the Spirit through the church. This "now," this "endtime," is the period of grace for the nations. The church by its preaching has the last word to the sons of frail humanity. Men are judged or saved by their attitude to this proclamation.[66]

The primacy of proclamation is also seen in the fact that the birth of the body of Christ described in Acts 1 and 2 is followed by the movement outward in mission narrated in Acts 3 and 4.[67]

That evangelism is the hallmark of evangelical Christianity, no one can question. In this century alone evangelicals have circled the globe and penetrated into the obscure parts of the world to present Christ's saving message to millions of people. Many evangelical leaders have come to recognize that the major fault of evangelism among evangelicals has been the tendency to oversimplify the Christian message. There are at least two ways in which an oversimplification of the gospel is expressed: the first occurs when evangelism is divorced from theology; the second occurs when Christian obedience as the result of faith is neglected.[68]

Evangelicals have also learned the importance of a careful, thoughtful, and precise cross-cultural communication which speaks in such a way that the biblical gospel is understood within the culture and native framework of thought. Western-culturized Christianity should not be imposed upon a non-Western culture.[69]

Fackre contends that evangelism in its apostolic sense as practiced by Peter and John, *acts evangelism*, is the conjoining of word and deed. It is neither a deedless word nor a wordless deed but word *in* deed. He also points out that Peter's narrative concludes, "Repent, then, and turn to God, so that your sins may be wiped out" (Acts 3:19, NIV). The teller of the story comes with a call to decision.[70]

Christ's Lordship in the World Is Exercised By the Church as It Develops a Proper Relationship Between the State and the Common Life

That the state should become demonic and rebel against God did not, for Paul, do away with the divine control (Rom 13:1-7, 1 Cor. 2:8). The state and the law still serve God. The angelic powers serve God in being, along with their civil and earthly counterparts, the instruments of His redemptive plan. They play their part in the drama of redemption (Acts 4:25ff.; cf. 1 Cor. 2:8) and they also serve God's purpose in this period when the ages overlap. They serve the task of restraining evil, preserving order, and making the church's proclamation possible. The gospel can be preached and received because the powers that be serve God in maintaining peace and some measure of social justice. Because of Christ's triumph they now unwittingly serve God's plan.[71]

Despite this victory of Christ over the cosmic powers and their earthly instruments, the latter do not openly exhibit signs of His triumph. They remain rebellious, even though they maintain order. They serve God in spite of themselves. Indeed, the state and its guardian powers have pretensions to power and rebellious inclinations which may become demonic. They may become the "beast," envisioned by the Book of Revelation. They may persecute the church, even while they make its proclamation possible. An unleashing of the demonic power is still possible. We need to remember that Christ's triumph on the cross is a decisive triumph, a once-for-all victory, but that it does not immediately issue in the abolition of rebellion at the human or cosmic level. As John saw, the powers of this world were passing away, but they still are powers to reckon with. Something of this insight can be found in the Apocalypse, where the demonic powers are pictured as bound and yet released to exercise a catastrophic final bid for power before the final consummation.[72]

Hence we have the unusual tension of the Now. The cosmic powers have been subjected (Col. 1:16ff.; 2:15; Phil. 2:10; 1 Pet. 3:22); they will be subjected (1 Cor. 15:24-25; Acts 10:13)—just as the end has come and will come. Between the cross and the *Parousia*, the cosmic powers serve their purpose and yet still exercise their rebellion. Insofar as the cosmic powers and their earthly counterparts serve God's purpose and maintain law and order, the Christian must acknowledge their authority under God. To pay to the state its taxes and dues (Rom. 13:7), to honor its officers (Rom. 13:7; 1 Pet. 2:17), to pray for its welfare (1 Tim. 2:1ff.), are Christian responsibilities.[73]

When the state's demonic nature becomes uppermost and it becomes beastlike, the Christian must refuse acknowledgment, for he serves the Lord Christ. Thus, for the author of the Apocalypse, the state's claims for the imperial cult and the worship of Caesar, its manifestation as the beast, call down the wrath of the Lamb. The saints resist and become martyrs. When the state leaves the area that is Caesar's and penetrates into the area of overlordship which belongs to Christ alone, the attitude of the Christian is unequivocally determined. Only Christ is Lord. The Christian must obey God rather than men and suffer in so doing (Acts 5:29).[74]

Christians have conquered the cosmic powers. They sit with Christ in heavenly places far above principalities and powers. They serve the state as a service to God, acknowledge its restraining power, and pray for its welfare. But they do not fear it, for they rule it invisibly. The state's power of death, its persecution, its demonic manifestation, can have no final influence in the life of Christians. Indeed, the church judges the cosmic powers and their earthly instruments, while acknowledging their earthly assistance to the progress of its mission. In persecuting the church instead of providing a framework of order, the state spells its own doom. The blood of the martyrs cries to heaven and the beast is headed for final destruction. This is the theme of the Apocalypse.[75]

If a person is in Christ, he or she is committed to the proclamation of the gospel to all peoples. But the whole cosmic order was created in Christ and subjected in Him to the same end. Hence to believe in Christ means to support that world order which also supports the end for which the cosmos existed. Obedience to the guardian powers means cooperation with them in a common end which they serve in their own way. Such obedience is a matter of conscience and not a way of avoiding trouble.[76]

The Christian should be more sensitive to injustice and tyranny than the non-Christian. When the demands of the state will no longer support the church's mission under Christ, the church rebels. Until then the two cooperate. Indeed they are mutually complementary. God's purpose can be actualized in this age in the church, because the state provides a framework of order.[77]

Fackre contends that as the eschatological expectations of the early church lengthened, the sense of responsibility for the secular systems and processes increased. That expanded perspective, at worst, has led to the captivity of the church by the authorities and powers in its attempt to penetrate them, and at best to the prophetic challenge to these structures in obedience to the lordship of Christ.[78]

Donald Bloesch maintains that our choice today is between a prophetic religion and a culture religion.[79] The first is anchored in a holy God who infinitely transcends every cultural and religious form that testifies to Him. The second absolutizes the cultural or mythical garb in which God supposedly meets us. A prophetic religion will keep a nation humble, but at the same time hopeful, knowing that its destiny is in the hands of a living and sovereign God. A culture religion makes a nation vain and ultimately foolish, tempting it to yield to the deception that the gods are in its power and service.[80]

Christ's Lordship Is Exercised by the Church Indirectly
Through Its Members' Ethical Activities in the World

This purpose means that God is first encountered redemptively by passage out of the world and into the church. We must not ignore the role of faith in Jesus Christ as the essential prerequisite for salvation and the indispensable means by which one is transferred from the sphere of Adam to the sphere of Christ. It should also be remembered that according to Paul the Adamic world order will remain in opposition to God until the Parousia of Jesus Christ.[81]

However, while Paul regards the Christians' true commonwealth as the kingdom "in [the] heaven[s]" (Phil. 3:20), he is not indifferent to their obligations to the present world. Paul recognizes that his own ministry of exhortation will have its effects on the behavior of believers. This behavior will itself have effects on society. The Christian's obligation to society belongs to Paul's theology of ethics, specifically to the command to love one's neighbor (Rom. 13:8ff).[82] Jesus suggests in Matthew 25:31-46 that the one sign by which true believers can be distinguished from those who make empty professions is acts of love which are done in Jesus' name and emulate His example. Emphasis on social concern carries over into the Epistles as well. James is particularly strong in stressing practical Christianity. Such acts can bring and have brought significant transformations in both personal and societal relationships within the present age. For Christians this neighbor love is part of what Paul called "the fruit of the Spirit" (Gal. 5:22f.). Clearly, Christians will fulfill their social role in the secular society with more realism and therefore with more true optimism when they recognize the true nature of the present world order as it is taught us by Christ's apostle.[83]

In contrast to the dominant biblical approach which can be described as God-church-world, in recent years the emphasis has been on God-world-church. There has been more stress on God's immanence than on His transcendence. God is seen as working directly in the world, outside of the formal structure of the church, and as accomplishing His purpose even through persons and institutions that are not avowedly Christian.[84]

In response to this recent emphasis, Ellis contends that when Christian social action is given first place, as it often is in modern secular society, it can be debased into idolatry or sentimentalism. Only when love for neighbor is defined in terms of love for God, and God's love for us and in us, does it conform to the New Testament teaching and become a transforming power in every relationship that it touches. Of course, the church is inevitably related to the society around it. In the apostolic church Paul and others used the societal structures that were at hand in order to facilitate their mission.[85]

The church works within the world, is assigned a social "place" by the world, and gives benefits to the world. Yet, when it is true to itself, it does not belong to this age, cannot really fit its structures, and remains a stranger in the society of the world. Nevertheless, Paul had no doubt that it was within such a social context that Christ had called him to fulfill his ministry. We who are part of the distant harvest of his labors are also witnesses to its effects both in individual lives and, to some degree at least, upon the social order.[86]

Gabriel Fackre insists that the church should be more directly active in the world. For him this is made clear in Christ's declaration of war against the powers and principalities at the inception of His ministry as described in Luke 4:8-19. In this battle He engaged structures of power, a political-economic-military-ecclesiastical complex that saw His claims of lordship as a threat to its own tyrannies and that finally brought Him to court and to death. He also drove the moneychangers out of the temple. This forewarns us of the corruptions of economic power, and, through His confrontation with Caesar, puts us on notice to the onslaught of political power.[87]

Jurgen Moltmann contends that liberation theology has recovered biblical emphases on economic, political, and racial injustice.[88] Fackre also states that liberation theology has heightened the awareness of the church in our time to the presence of systemic evil and has given Samaritan sight to see the invisible poor and plundered. Fackre admits, however, that many liberation groups do not personally know Christ as the Liberator from sin and guilt and have yet to participate in the fullness of His atoning work. Herein lies the Church's evangelism mandate.[89] Gustavo Gutierrez, a prominent liberation theologian, also identifies Christ's granting us freedom from sin as basic in practice; however, his emphasis seems to be placed particularly upon the economic and political aspects.[90]

Donald Bloesch is opposed to certain strands within liberation theology and Protestant liberalism. He insists that the church of God is primarily neither a humanitarian agency nor an ethical culture society. Instead, it is the social embodiment of the new reality of the kingdom of God. Its gospel is neither the social gospel nor the privatistic gospel of interior peace, but the biblical gospel of reconciliation and redemption through the atoning work of Christ on the cross and His glorious resurrection from the grave. It must never be forgotten, however, that such a gospel has far-reaching social and political implications.[91]

The church has both a spiritual mission and a cultural mandate. Its primary goal is to bring the glad tidings of reconciliation and redemption to all races and nations, but it is also responsible for teaching people to be disciples of Christ in the very midst of the world's plight and dereliction.[92] Erickson agrees that the crucial issue in Scripture is our bondage in sin, and the separation and estrangement from God which sin has produced. Political freedom, economic sufficiency, and physical health, important as they are, are secondary to spiritual destiny. Not nearly enough is said in liberation theology about what the New Testament clearly indicates to be the primary dimension of salvation.[93]

Since we have indicated that the context for the purpose of the church is provided by the eschatological "already-not yet" theme, it should be noted that this theme provides a strong motivation and dynamic context for

Christian ethics. Jesus asserted that His followers would remain in the world. He also declared that all authority had been given to Him and that the god of this world was being ousted. It therefore follows that while Christian ethics has a personal and interior dimension, it must also have a public and exterior proclamation arising from Jesus' authority and based upon His conquest. This proclamation is the gospel of Christ whose rule is not postponed to the chronological end of the ages, but has even now begun. The chief purpose of New Testament eschatology is not to encourage speculative fascination with world politics but rather, to compel a deep and unremitting commitment to both evangelistic and ethical action in the world.[94]

Notes

1. Robert E. Webber, *Common Roots: A Call to Evangelical Maturity* (Grand Rapids: Zondervan, 1978), 41.

2. Millard J. Erickson, *Christian Theology*, 3 vols. (Grand Rapids: Baker, 1985), 3:1033.

3. George Eldon Ladd, *A Theology of the New Testament* (Grand Rapids: Eerdmans, 1974), 353-54, 379f., 531; E. Earle Ellis, *Pauline Theology: Ministry and Society* (Grand Rapids: Eerdmans, 1989), 8.

4. Erickson, *Christian Theology*, 1034.

5. Eric C. Rust, *Salvation History: A Biblical Interpretation* (Richmond, Va.: John Knox Press, 1962), 229-30.

6. David F. Wells, "The Future" in *Christian Faith and Practice in the Modern World*, eds. Mark A. Noll and David F. Wells (Grand Rapids: Eerdmans, 1988), 291; G. E. Ladd, "Apocalyptic and the New Testament Theology," in *Reconciliation and Hope*, ed. R. Banks (Grand Rapids: Eerdmans, 1974), 285-96.

7. Wells, "The Future," 292; cf. Emil Brunner, *The Misunderstanding of the Church*, trans. Harold Knight (Philadelphia: Westminster Press, 1953), 55-59.

8. Ibid., 293-94.

9. Ladd, *Theology*, 396-97.

10. George E. Ladd, *Jesus and the Kingdom* (New York: Harper and Row, 1964), 259-60.

11. Ladd, *Theology*, 105ff.

12. Webber, *Common Roots*, 45, 47.

13. Gabriel Fackre, *The Christian Story: A Narrative Interpretation of Basic Christian Doctrine* (Grand Rapids: Eerdmans, 1978, 1984), 171-72.

14. Webber, *Common Roots*, 60-61.

15. Ibid., 61.

16. Ibid., 62.

17. Ibid.

18. Fackre, *Christian Story*, 173.

19. Webber, *Common Roots*, 41-42; Paul S. Minear, *Images of the Church in the New Testament* (Philadelphia: Westminster Press, 1960).

20. Ibid., 52-53; Ladd, *Theology*, 537-47.

21. Fackre, *Christian Story*, 160.

22. Herman Ridderbos, *Paul: An Outline of His Theology* (Grand Rapids: Eerdmans, 1975), 482.

23. Ibid.

24. Fackre, *Christian Story*, 160; Dale Moody, *The Word of Truth: A Summary of Christian Doctrine Based on Biblical Revelation* (Grand Rapids: Eerdmans, 1981), 478.

25. Gabriel Fackre, "God the Discloser," in *Christian Faith and Practice in the Modern*

World, eds. Noll and Wells (Grand Rapids: Eerdmans, 1988), 105.

26. Ibid.

27. Ibid., 109.

28. Fackre, *Christian Story*, 160.

29. Moody, *The Word of Truth*, 463, 466.

30. Fackre, *Christian Story*, 190.

31. Ibid., 191-92.

32. Ellis, *Pauline Theology*, 112.

33. Ibid., 113, 121.

34. Ridderbos, *Paul*, 485.

35. Moody, *The Word of Truth*, 478.

36. Ellis, *Pauline Theology*, 112.

37. Ibid.

38. Ibid., 115-17.

39. Ibid., 117, 119.

40. Webber, *Common Roots*, 111.

41. Fackre, *Christian Story*, 161-62.

42. Ibid., 162; Paul D. Hanson, *The People Called: The Growth of Community in the Bible* (San Francisco: Harper & Row, 1986), 501-3.

43. Erickson, *Christian Theology*, 3:1055.

44. Moody, *Word of Truth*, 431-32; Robin Keeley, ed., *Eerdmans' Handbook to Christian Belief* (Grand Rapids: Eerdmans, 1982), 397.

45. Keeley, *Eerdmans'*, 397.

46. Erickson, *Christian Theology*, 3:1055.

47. Ellis, *Pauline Theology*, 138.

48. Donald G. Bloesch, *The Reform of the Church* (Grand Rapids: Eerdmans, 1970), 73.

49. Ibid., 74-75, 85; Carl F. H. Henry, ed., *Basic Christian Doctrines* (New York: Holt, Rinehart and Winston, 1962), 252.

50. Fackre, *Christian Story*, 182.

51. Ibid.

52. Ellis, *Pauline Theology*, 40, 45, 48-49.

53. Ibid., 92-93, 102-3.

54. Fackre, *Christian Story*, 175-76.

55. Ibid., 176-77; Henry, *Basic Christian Doctrines*, 245.

56. Ibid., 178.

57. Ibid., 179.

58. Webber, *Common Roots*, 69.

59. Fackre, *Christian Story*, 181.

60. Webber, *Common Roots*, 183.

61. Ibid., 189, 193-94.

62. Erickson, *Christian Theology*, 3:1054-55.

63. Ibid., 3:1055-56.

64. Rust, *Salvation History*, 259, 263-64; Oscar Cullmann, *Christ and Time* (Philadelphia: Westminster Press, 1950).

65. Ibid., 264; Johannes Munck, *Paul and the Salvation of Mankind* (Richmond, Va.: John Knox Press, 1959).

66. Rust, *Salvation History*. 266-67.

67. Fackre, *Christian Story*, 166.

68. Webber, *Common Roots*, 155-57.

69. Ibid., 170, 177.

70. Fackre, *Christian Story*, 168.

71. Rust, *Salvation History*, 268, 271-72.

72. Ibid., 272.

73. Ibid., 273.

74. Ibid., 273-74; cf. Hanson, *The People Called*, 495-96.

75. Ibid., 274.

76. Ibid., 275-276.

77. Ibid., 176; Suzanne De Dietrich, *The Witnessing Community: The Biblical Record of God's Purpose* (Philadelphia: Westminster Press, 1958), 171-75.

78. Fackre, *Christian Story*, 170.

79. Donald Bloesch, "God the Civilizer," in *Christian Faith and Practice in the Modern World*, eds. Noll and Wells (Grand Rapids: Eerdmans, 1988), 196.

80. Ibid.

81. Ellis, *Pauline Theology*, 22.

82. Ibid., 23-24; Erickson, *Christian Theology*, 3:1058.

83. Ibid., 25; Hanson, *The People Called*, 503-18.

84. Erickson, *Christian Theology*, 3:1028; Colin W. Williams, *New Directions in Theology Today*, Vol. IV: *The Church* (Philadelphia: Westminster Press, 1968), 133-149; Robert McAfee Brown, *Frontiers for the Church Today* (New York: Oxford University Press, 1973), 81-90.

85. Ellis, *Pauline Theology*, 158-59; Richard J. Coleman, *Issues of Theological Conflict* (Grand Rapids: Eerdmans, 1972), 212-17.

86. Ellis, *Pauline Theology*, 159; Coleman, *Issues*, 223-39.

87. Fackre, *Christian Story*, 205; Orlando E. Costas, *The Church and Its Mission: Shattering Critique from the Third World* (Wheaton: Tyndale House Publishers, 1974), 240-64.

88. Jürgen Moltmann, *Religion, Revolution, and the Future*, trans. M. Douglas Meeks (New York: Scribner, 1969), 38-40; 131-43; Gustavo Gutierrez, *A Theology of Liberation: History, Politics, and Salvation*, trans. Sister Caridad Inda and John Eagleson (Maryknoll, N.Y.: Orbis Books, 1973), 4f., 36, 215; Juan Luis Segundo, *The Liberation of Theology*, trans. John Drury (Maryknoll, N.Y.: Orbis Books, 1976), 7-38.

89. Fackre, *Christian Story*, 205, 209.

90. Erickson, *Christian Theology*, 3:1006.

91. Bloesch, "God the Civilizer," 193; cf. also Donald G. Bloesch, *Essentials of Evangelical Theology*, Vol. 2: *Life, Ministry, and Hope* (San Francisco: Harper & Row, Publishers, 1979), 167-71.

92. Bloesch, "God the Civilizer," 193-94; Carl F. H. Henry, *God, Revelation and Authority*, Vol. IV: *God Who Speaks and Shows—Fifteen Theses, Part Three* (Waco: Word Books, Publisher, 1979), 537-41.

93. Erickson, *Christian Theology*, 3:1007.

94. Wells, "The Future," 300-1.

2
Baptism in Theology and Practice

By Dale Moody

Baptism and Purification

As far as can be determined the oldest meaning of baptism was that of *purification*. As far back as Moses and Joshua the washing of clothes, the body, and abstinence from sexual intercourse were required of those who would make a covenant with the Lord (Ex. 19:10-15; Josh. 3).

Orthodox Judaism required proselyte baptism of unclean Gentile converts (*yeb*, 47*a,b*). This also symbolized passage through the Reed Sea, (*yam supf*, Red Sea in Greek), at the time of the first Passover in the exodus from Egypt.

The community of Qumran, which is located within sight of the place where Israel crossed the Jordan, initiated new members into the sectarian community in a manner described in the *Manual of Discipline* 5-6. Over the period of three years, daily washings were required after the return from field work at 11 A.M. At the end of the three years, full membership required the ceremony of the Great Purification.

Although it is a disputed point in New Testament studies, it is almost certain (in my mind) that John the Baptist was adopted and reared at Qumran after the death of his aged parents. As he pondered the words of Isaiah 40:3, he heard the call to be the voice crying in the wilderness (Mark 1:1-8; Matt. 3:1-12; Luke 3:1-20; John 1:6,15,19-28). Great throngs came to John to flee the coming wrath by "confessing their sins"(Matt. 3:6; Mark 1:5). Perhaps after they removed their robes and sandals on the east bank, they crossed the Jordan at the very place where Israel crossed in the days of Joshua. The submersion in the Jordan, and at other places later, was indeed "the baptism of repentance" (Acts 19:4).

Purification continued to be a major meaning in the Epistles of Paul. There are three most instructive "washing" passages in the Pauline Epistles. First Corinthians 6:11 is often made explosive because of the context. The very literal translation of the *New American Standard Bible* of 1 Corinthians 6:9-11 explains in part why.

> Or do you not know that the unrighteous shall not inherit the kingdom of God? Do not be deceived; neither fornicators, nor idolaters, nor adulterers, nor effeminate, nor homosexuals, nor thieves, nor the covetous, nor drunkards, nor revilers, nor swindlers, shall inherit the kingdom of God. And such were some of you; but you were washed, but you were sanctified, but you were justified in the name of the Lord Jesus Christ, and in the Spirit of our God.

In a society much like our own, the apostle Paul seemed to think that the kingdom of God would not be overcrowded! The five sexual sins condemned in verse 9 should be understood in the context of Roman culture in which most of the Roman emperors were homosexuals. According to Seutonius (6.78) Nero actually married the boy Sporus in a wedding of great pomp and circumstance. Many today condemn Paul but, alas, not such sexual sins.

Five social sins added to the list (v. 10) are not rare in our culture today. Being washed is both ceremonial in baptism and spiritual in sanctification. Sanctification is past and punctiliar, as here, or progressive, in the present, as in 1 Corinthians 1:2 where believers are called saints who are made perfect in the future (1 Thess. 5:23). First Thessalonians uses two different words to distinguish present and future sanctification. *Hagiosune*, perfect sanctification, is the condition of saints when God establishes their hearts "in holiness before our God and Father at the coming [*Parousia*] of our Lord Jesus with all his saints" (3:13). On the other hand *hagiosmos*, progressive sanctification, describes the state of sexual fidelity in marriage (4:4). This was all initiated in the past sanctification of 1 Corinthians 6:11 which is stated with the aorist punctiliar tense (*hegioasthete*).

In the process of historical development, this emphasis on ceremonial purification led to changes in the mode. Increased emphasis on total depravity taught that unbaptized people were unsaved. Even unbaptized infants were in need of baptismal regeneration to escape the condemnation of hell. This was modified to mean the edge of hell, *limbo*, but they were nevertheless deprived of the beatific vision. This was a special concern for Cyprian of Carthage (Eph. 64.2) who wondered if an eight-day delay were permissible, as in the ceremony of circumcision.

Tertullian believed that children were born in the paradise of innocence and lived there until puberty, so he rejected infant baptism (*De baptismo* 18) but Cyprian's concern was confirmed in the writings of Augustine (*De pecatto originali* 44).[1]

Very early clinical baptism was allowed for the sick who were permitted to received threefold pouring on the head instead of the threefold immersion that developed from the second century.

By the Council of Vienne (1311-12) a decision was made in which threefold pouring on the head became an option with threefold immersion. Saint Thomas Aquinas justified this change with the argument that, since the intelligence is in the head, pouring water on the head would do as much good as the immersion of the whole body! (*Summa Theologica* 66.7)

By the time of the Reformation Martin Luther insisted on a return to immersion, even infant immersion, for that was the clear meaning of the word. In his *Treatise on Baptism* (1519) Luther began with the statement: "Baptism (German *die Taufe*) is called in the Greek language *baptismos*, in Latin *mersio*, which means to plunge something entirely into the water, so that the water closes over it."

The second "washing" passage in the Pauline Epistles that perhaps has reference to baptism is Ephesians 5:26 which refers to the perfect sanctification of the church as the bride of Christ after she had been cleansed "by the washing of water with the word." F. F. Bruce appeals to the bridal language of Ezekiel 16:6-14 where Yahweh purifies Jerusalem as a foundling. He says: "I bathed you with water. . . . I clothed you also with embroidered cloth. . . . And I decked you with ornaments."[2]

To wash with water "by the Word" has been interpreted in terms of the Eastern *epiclesis*, invocation upon the baptismal water, but the *epiclesis* is usually associated with the bread and wine of the Eucharist which followed immersion in water.[3] Some Baptists have emphasized the preaching of the gospel always at the baptismal service. Just what *en hremati* (with the word) means I do not know, but the use of water and the word is a good balance as well as water baptism and Spirit baptism. This is perhaps why 1 Corinthians 6:11 adds "in the name of the Lord Jesus Christ and the Spirit of our God" after justification. There the German Lutheran scholar Heinrich Schlier, now become Roman Catholic, has seen references to the idea of the sacred marriage in heaven. Bruce is obviously fascinated by this interpretation. John Calvin's commentary on Acts 8:38 says much the same. John Wesley's insistence on the practice of immersion got him involved in serious controversy (*Journal*, August 1737).

The third "washing" passage in the Epistles of Paul is in a baptismal hymn at Titus 3:4-7.

> But when the kindness of God our Savior
> and his love toward man appeared
> but according to his mercy he saved us
> through the washing of regeneration
> and the renewing of the Holy Spirit
> which he poured out upon us richly
> through Jesus Christ our Savior,

that being justified by his grace
we might be made heirs according to the hope of eternal life.[4]

Purification is a pervasive theme in the Epistle to Titus. The hymnody makes melody with theology. A "puritan hymn" is the climax of the first chapter (vv. 15-16). The "epiphany hymn" at the end of chapter 2 says that God's purpose between the epiphany of His grace at the first coming of Christ and the epiphany of His glory at the second coming is to "purify unto himself a people for his own possession, zealous of good works" (vv. 11-14, ASV). Then the third chapter includes this baptismal hymn about "the washing of regeneration and renewal in the Holy Spirit" (3:5). Here as always in the New Testament there is a beautiful balance between the visible sign in water baptism and the invisible grace in Spirit baptism.[5]

Behind all of these "washing" passages may be the remembrance of Paul's own baptism when Ananias of Damascus said to Paul: "Rising up, be baptized, and wash away your sins, having called upon his name" (Acts 22:16). This rather literal translation indicates that baptism in the name of the Lord (A.V.) followed after calling upon His name in conversion.

Baptism and Identification

A second major meaning of baptism in the New Testament may be called *identification*. A very old baptismal formula is first used in the well-known and much debated passage in Acts 2:38.[6] It calls on all who believe to: "Repent, and be baptized every one of you in the name of Jesus Christ [*epi toi onomatic Jesou Christou*] for [*eis*] the forgiveness of your sins; and you shall receive the gift of the Holy Spirit." The endless controversies between the sacramental and evangelical interpretation of *eis*, which can mean either "for" or "because of," should not obscure the normative importance of this verse.

This does not restrict the gift of the Spirit to a submarine salvation in which regeneration can take place only under water. One may receive the baptism in the Spirit either after baptism, in water, or before. It is very clear in Acts 8:16 that the Samaritan believers did not receive the Spirit at the time they were "baptized in the name of the Lord Jesus" (*eis to onoma tou kuriou Jesou*).

The apostolic laying on of hands is also secondary for the reception of the Spirit. The household of Cornelius received the Spirit *before* water baptism in Acts 10:48. Laying on of hands is not even mentioned. However, Acts 19:1-5 mentions baptism *eis to onoma tou kuriou Christou* and the laying on of hands. Water baptism, laying on of hands, the baptism of the Spirit, and speaking in tongues may belong to the *bene esse* (well-being) of salvation, but the *esse* (essential) of salvation is repentance and belief.

It seems that Alexander Campbell (1788-1866) during all of his ministry took a view very much the same when he distinguished between the *real* and the *formal* forgiveness of sins. He argued that Paul's sins were *really* forgiven when he believed but they were *formally* forgiven when he was baptized. Otherwise why did Ananias say to him: "And now why do you wait? Rise and be baptized, and wash away your sins, calling on his name" (Acts 22:16)? This he argued in his debate with the Presbyterian Macalla, and he did not later change.[7] Nearly thirty years later, at the age of sixty-four, he finally wrote his book on *Christian Baptism* in which he repeated the argument with emphasis when he said:

> Nor, indeed, that there is anything in the mere element of water, or in the form of placing the subject in it, or in the person who administers it, or in the formula upon the occasion, though both good taste and piety have something to do in these particulars, but all its virtue and efficacy is in the faith and intelligence of him who receives it.[8]

It may be that the heat of debate has clouded his view, but it seems unwise for Baptists to reject such an argument.

Neither the magic sacramentalism often set forth by many zealous followers of Campbell nor the "mere symbolism" heard from many Baptists does justice to the dynamic balance of the Acts and the rest of the New Testament. If Campbell was weak, it was his lack of emphasis on the work of the Holy Spirit in the initiation of salvation in the true believer. His rationalism was too shy on the Christian experience emphasized in the Separate Baptists in general and the Great Kentucky Revival in particular. The remedy for rationalism is to be found in faithful exposition of the New Testament as a whole and the Acts of the Apostles in particular. This statement came into full focus in dialogue with three branches of the Stone Campbell Movement and the exposition of the Acts of the Apostles over thirty times in the same year. The conservative J. W. McGarvey, who wrote a commentary on Acts (1892) which may be considered standard for the Movement, regarded the manifestations of the Holy Spirit in Acts as abnormal, while W. O. Carver the Baptist (1916) viewed the work of the Holy Spirit in the same passages as quite normative and usual in the continuation of the apostolic mission.

Baptism "in the name" is the central concept for identification with Christ in the Acts of the Apostle. It continues in an interesting way as Paul rebuked factions in the Corinthian church for acting as if they belonged to Paul or were baptized in Paul's name (1 Cor. 1:10-17). They belonged to Christ who was crucified for them and in whose name they were baptized.

A special case on baptism "in the name" is found in the Great Commission of Matthew 28:19. However, it is possible that baptism "in the name of the Father and of the Son and of the Holy Spirit" is a second-century formula used to emphasize the developing debate on the Holy Trinity. At least the Acts of the Apostles says nothing about Trinitarian baptism. As late as Eusebius (c.260-c.340) the formula for baptism in Matthew 28:19 is usually the short form "in my name."[9] In both formulas the main point is the making of disciples.

The theology and practice of baptism in the Acts of the Apostles were influenced not only by the gift of the Spirit from Pentecost onward but also by the concept of the Christian household, first emphasized in the promise of the Spirit in Acts 2:39 which says: "For the promise is to you and to your children and to all that are far off, every one whom the Lord our God calls to him."

This promise continues in the later practice of household baptisms (Acts 16:15,31; 18:8). Much ink has been shed between those who advocate believer's baptism only and those who practice infant baptism, the first insisting that all who were baptized and received the Spirit were individual believers and the other declaring that infants in a Christian household were baptized also.

In the early Greek churches there is not a single instance of infant baptism until the question is raised in the fourth century. Even today the Eastern church is not certain why they baptize infants within the first three years of their lives. In the Latin church the debate is first raised in the third century with infant guilt as the basis for the practice, Tertullian (De baptismo 18) opposed the practice and Cyprian advocated it. Not even Augustine was baptized in infancy, even though he had been "salted," as was the practice, from the womb of his Christian mother. Augustine's view of original sin established the uniform practice of infant baptism (immersion). Anabaptists and the Baptists protested against this theology. Even now those who reject Augustine's view of original sin have no real theological basis for the practice of infant baptism (immersion, pouring, or sprinkling), but those who raise the question are considered schismatic. Those who reject Augustine's doctrine of original sin are declared heretics by those who affirm it.

Evidence for household baptism is found in Paul's Epistles (1 Cor. 1:16), but the theological basis is widely debated on the issue of holiness (1 Cor. 7:14). However, Paul's theology and practice of baptism is based primarily on a belief found only in Paul's Epistles. To this we now turn.

Paul's pillar Epistles (1 and 2 Corinthians, Galatians, and Romans) have profound statements on the theology and practice of baptism. The response to the question about eating meat sacrificed to idols in 1 Corinthians 10—11 reveals very early beliefs about baptism as well as about communion and the

Lord's Supper. The typological discussion on baptism has a comparison of baptism into Moses at the exodus from Egypt and baptism into Christ in the church which recalls five of the seven warnings about rebellion in the wilderness so profoundly discussed in recent studies of the Old Testament.[10] The normal pattern of water baptism and communion followed by the gift of the Spirit is seen in the sequence of crossing the Red Sea in baptism and the gift of manna and water from the rock (Ex. 15—17).

Paul's response to the question about spiritual gifts (*charismata, pneumatika*) in 1 Corinthians 12—14 states the relation between baptism and the Spirit in what seems to be a spiritual song (1 Cor. 12:13).

> For in one Spirit were we all baptized into one body—whether Jews or Greeks, whether slaves or free, and we were all made to drink of one Spirit (NASB).

The verb "drink" is used to emphasize the typology between Moses and Christ.

The reference about baptism *hyper ton nekron* (on behalf of the dead) in 1 Corinthians 15:29 seems to indicate a practice that was not continued in the church until modern Mormonism revived it. Like prayer on behalf of the dead in 2 Maccabees 12:42-44 in the Greek Bible, the Septuagint, this should be regarded as a secondary Christian practice, deutero-canonical but not canonical.

The church as the body of Christ is not mentioned in Paul's polemical epistle to the Galatians, but one of the pregnant passages on the authentic theology and practice of baptism is Galatians 3:27f. This too is perhaps another one of Paul's spiritual songs with profound implications then and now.

> For as many of you as were baptized into Christ have put on Christ. There is neither Jew nor Greek, there is neither slave nor free, there is neither male nor female, for you are all one in Christ Jesus (vv. 27-28).

This is about as near to the center of the New Testament canon as possible. Paul's first ten letters were perhaps the first New Testament.

If there is a theology and a practice of baptism that has been central for the meaning and mode of baptism among Baptists it must surely be the response to Paul's rhetorical question in Romans 6:3-4.

> Do you not know that all of us who were baptized into Christ Jesus were baptized into his death? We were buried therefore with him by baptism into death, so as Christ was raised from the dead by the glory of the Father, we too might walk in newness of life.

The fact that Paul could appeal to the knowledge which the Romans, whom he had not instructed, were assumed to know already shows how widely this view was accepted among the disciples of Jesus Christ.

It was this passage that convinced the first Particular Baptists around 1639 in London, England, to restore immersion as the mode for baptism, but it was not until Robert Robinson (1735-90) traced the history of baptism through the centuries that an effort was made to restore forward baptism rather than backward baptism as the original apostolic mode. Few today have profited from his great learning, perhaps because he was accused of Unitarian tendencies.[11]

One of Paul's Prison Epistles, whether from Rome or from Caesarea, continues to stress baptism as the lopping off of the sins of the flesh, as the foreskin is lopped off in circumcision, in what also has the marks of a Christian hymn (Col. 2:11f.). Another hymn does not use the word *baptism*, but the idea is stated in classic form (Eph. 2:4-10). Ephesians has at least seven references to the church as the body of Christ (1:23; 2:16; 4:4,12,16; 5:23,30).

Many who love to call themselves "evangelical" invoke the name of F. F. Bruce, a member of a Brethren group. I too hold Bruce in high esteem on most New Testament matters, especially when he affirms the incipient catholicism in 1 Corinthians, Romans, Colossians, and Ephesians as the genuine production of Paul's personal pilgrimage as he works out the implication of the church as the one body of Christ composed of "all the redeemed through all the ages." This is true ecumenicity, not narrow and rigid sectarianism.

Baptism and Incorporation

A spiritual song in 1 Corinthians 12:12f. introduced the idea of baptism into the body of Christ in relation to baptism in the Spirit, but this remained in the background until the compilation of the queen of the Prison Epistles, the Ephesian Letter. This means that Romans and Ephesians are the "twin towers" of the Pauline Corpus.

The climax of the baptismal theology of Paul and the very heart of Ephesians is the declaration of the sevenfold unity of the church without which any claim of Christian catholicity or ecumenicity is a vain boast. The Christian *credo* in Ephesians 4:4-6 confesses: "There is one body and one Spirit, just as also you were called in one hope of your calling; One Lord, one faith, one baptism, One God and Father of all who is over all and through all and in all" (NASB).

Bruce is correct in saying that "it is beside the point to ask whether it is baptism in water or baptism of the Spirit: it is Christian baptism. "

Baptism and Regeneration

There remains only one other passage in the Pauline Epistles on baptism. That is in the Pastoral Epistles. Both Roman Catholicism and Protestant Calvinism have made the relation between baptism and regeneration a controversial point. Infant regeneration through baptism has been taught in Roman Catholicism since Cyprian and Augustine. With the emphasis on justification by faith in Lutheranism, the practice of infant baptism is defended with the theory of infant faith.[12] Most Baptists reject the idea of infant damnation so neither infant regeneration nor infant justification is thought necessary. The need for both regeneration and justification come after "the age of accountability" is reached. *The Baptist Faith and Message* of 1963 wisely reversed the order in the Abstract of Principles of The Southern Baptist Theological Seminary of 1858 which was rooted in Calvinism which has a doctrine of infant condemnation and infant regeneration based upon Calvinism's concept of the Children of the Covenant.[13] The baptismal hymn in Titus 3:4-7 has the same balance as do all the other New Testament passages on the relationship between water baptism and Spirit baptism.[14]

Baptism and Illumination

There is another minor meaning in the New Testament that should at least be mentioned to supplement the three major meanings of purification, identification, and incorporation.

Illumination is a distinctive doctrine in the Epistle to the Hebrews. Illumination perhaps has reference to baptism in Hebrews 6:4-6 and 10:32. At least it was so interpreted in second-century Rome (Justin Martyr, *Apology* 61). This makes the cognitive element in baptism essential as both Karl Barth and his son Markus have rightly emphasized, especially when they conclude that it makes infant baptism invalid.

Notes

1. See my book, *Baptism: Foundation for Christian Unity* (Philadelphia: Westminster Press, 1967), 14-32, for developments in the Roman Catholic tradition. The English Baptist, Robert Robinson, *The History of Baptism* (London: Couchman and Fry, 1790), has an illustration of threefold forward immersion on the *title page* of this classic book not yet absorbed by Baptists, even though J. R. Graves reprinted the book with notes in 1866.

2. F. F. Bruce, *The Epistles to the Colossians, to Philemon and to the Ephesians* (Grand Rapids: Eerdmans, 1984).

3. "Epiclesis" in *Oxford Dictionary of the Christian Church*, 2d ed. (New York: Oxford University Press, 1974).

4. Unless otherwise stated, translations are the author's.

5. See my book *Spirit of the Living God* (Nashville: Broadman Press, 1976), 140-41.

6. W. O. Carver, *The Acts of the Apostles* (Nashville: Sunday School Board, Southern Baptist Convention, 1916), 219.

7. Wilhelm Heitmuller, *Im Namen Jesu* (Gottingen: Vandenhoeck and Ruprecht, 1903) is a comprehensive study of this formula.

8. Leroy Garrett, *The Stone Campbell Movement* (Joplin, Mo.: College Press, 1981), 194-96.

9. *Christian Baptism* (Nashville: Gospel Advocate Company, 1951), 219.

10. See Dale Moody, *Spirit of the Living God* (Philadelphia: Westminster Press, 1968), 44. Also see my *The Word of Truth* (Grand Rapids: Wm. B. Eerdmans Publishing Company, 1981), 115-26.

11. George W. Coats, *Rebellion in the Wilderness* (Nashville: Abingdon Press, 1968); Philip J. Budd, "Numbers," *Word Biblical Commentary*, 5 (Waco, Texas: Word Books, 1984).

12. See *The History of Baptism* (1790) and *Ecclesiastical Researches* (1792).

13. Bruce, "The Epistles to the Colossians, to Philemon and to the Ephesians," 237-40.

14. See the statement of the Southern Baptist Convention in the *1963 Annual*, 275, when the slogan was "To make men free"!

3
The Lord's Supper

by Millard J. Erickson

Recently, while my wife and I were visiting our daughter in West Germany, we traveled to the city of Marburg, not far from where she lives. We climbed the hill to the castle, from which one has a panoramic view of the city. Looking at the huge structure, I recalled the discussion which took place within those walls between Martin Luther and Ulrich Zwingli, October 1-3, 1529. The leaders of these two branches of the Protestant Reformation had come together to explore the possibility of some merger of their two movements. They had fifteen doctrinal articles to discuss, and were successful in reaching agreement on fourteen of them, and most of the fifteenth, which dealt with the Lord's Supper. On the last half article, however, the question of the real presence of the body and blood of Christ within the elements of the Lord's Supper, agreement broke down. They were unable to reach a consensus, and went their separate ways, Luther saying to Martin Bucer, "You have a different spirit than we." Because of a difference of conviction upon this one matter, the two churches were unable to work together. This was a reminder that the doctrine of the Lord's Supper has at times been a topic of intense discussion, and even of sharp disagreement.[1]

More than 400 years have passed since that historic discussion. The Lord's Supper is still a matter of discussion and even controversy. Yet, with the elapsing of this much time, the debated issues have changed somewhat. While the issue of the real presence is still of concern, it has faded a bit in the light of new issues occasioned by changes in our world. This chapter examines some of the issues under discussion today in the doctrine of the Lord's Supper.

It will also be the case that some of the issues are the same as in earlier periods, but the specific reasons for discussing them, or the specific causes which bring them to attention, are different. Thus, for example, at various times in the history of the church, the issue of one communion cup versus many individual glasses has been of concern. With the advent of AIDS as a threat, however, the issue has taken on a new dimension.

To some extent, examining what issues are currently under discussion in this area will be a clue to understanding the dynamics of theological development in general. For the factors that affect which issues come to the forefront in this doctrine are also operative in the wider theological arena. Thus the agenda for theology in the present and the immediate future can perhaps be partially discerned by examining current issues in the doctrine of the Lord's Supper.

What issues have traditionally been of concern to Christian theologians, and specifically to Baptists? The following may be enumerated.

1. As we noted above, the issue of the presence of Christ in the elements of the sacrament/ordinance has historically been a major topic of discussion. The range of convictions has been from the real presence and transubstantiation view of Roman Catholicism through the spiritual presence to the merely symbolic view of the elements, as held by many Baptists and similar groups.

2. Closely related to this is the issue of transubstantiation. Although Luther and his followers held that the bread and wine were literally the body and blood of Christ (or more correctly, contained the body and blood), they rejected the Roman Catholic view that at a point in the mass, when the priest pronounced certain words of the ritual, a change was effected from bread and wine to flesh and blood.[2] The underlying issue was the role of the officiant, the Roman Catholics insisting upon the necessity of an ordained Catholic priest. Thus, sacerdotalism is really at the core of the dispute.

3. A further issue separating Roman Catholicism from Protestantism of various kinds was whether the laity could receive the Lord's Supper in both kinds, or only the bread. This was one factor mentioned by Luther in his treatise on the "Babylonian Captivity of the Church."[3]

4. The frequency of observance of the Lord's Supper was a cause of some dispute, sometimes within a given congregation. Some denominations administered the ordinance/sacrament every week, others once a month, still others only once per quarter.[4]

5. A special set of issues concerned Baptists. Some of these were intra-denominational in nature:

a.) Open or closed communion was a major issue a century ago and even into the twentieth century. Some churches allowed any confessing believer to partake of the Lord's Supper,[5] while others restricted the ordinance to those who had been immersed, and others to those persons who were members of that particular church.[6]

b.) Related to this was the question of the administrator. In churches influenced by the landmark movement, the administrator must be someone whose baptism and ordination were valid (i.e., could be traced back to John the Baptist). This is a unique Baptist version of apostolic succession.[7]

c.) A further issue was the role of the Lord's Supper in the administration of church discipline. This was frequently one way in which a spiritually or morally unruly member was disciplined by withdrawing the right of access to communion. This, of course, proved most successful among those congregations which practiced closed communion, since larger congregations practicing open communion would have difficulty identifying those eligible to receive the ordinance.[8]

With the passing of time, issues change. In part this is due to the fact that new cultural and intellectual factors in society in general produce new situations to which theology and the theology of a particular denomination or group must respond. The response takes its shape in part from the situation. In some cases, the same general topic is of concern, but particular form of expression may be quite different. It will be our concern in the remainder of this chapter to take note of three issues in current discussions of the Lord's Supper. In some ways, each has been with us for some time. Yet, they have special urgency and address special questions at the present. As we examine these, we shall first observe the discussion in the broader theological setting and then note the special form which these questions take in Baptist discussion, or where Baptists have not currently been discussing them, the special implications that they would have within the context of Baptist theology.

We will note, in each of these areas, how the doctrine of the Lord's Supper relates to other areas of doctrine. For as we have pointed out elsewhere, Christian theology is organic in character.[9] By that is meant that the part is intimately connected with the whole. Its particular manifestation is affected by the character of the whole system of theology. Similarly, it contributes to the character of the whole and thus to the content of other specific doctrines within it. We will find that the issue related to the Lord's Supper is actually one manifestation in this area of a more general doctrinal tendency or part of the whole theological milieu. The issues which we will examine are practical problems. Yet, to the extent that they rest upon theological factors, they may point us to part of the theological task which needs to be pursued in the present and the future. They thus help supply us with the agenda for theology.

The first issue which we consider part of the agenda for the present and the future is the presidency of the Lord's Supper, or to put it differently, the issue of who may administer the Lord's Supper. This, we will note, is part of the larger issue of the nature of ordination.

The issue is becoming most pressing in the Roman Catholic Church.[10] This is true because of two considerations. The first is the growing shortage of ordained priests. While portions of the liturgy of the mass may be performed by laypersons, the Eucharist or the consecration of the host requires the presence and functioning of a priest. Increasingly, Roman Catholics are facing the issue of whether the sacrament will be available to all Catholics who wish to partake of it, and with the frequency which they desire. The other issue concerns the role of women. As their ineligibility to perform this sacramental rite increasingly conflicts with the growing Christian feminist movement, tension centers upon the Eucharist. A majority of those present-ing themselves to receive the sacrament are women, in the Roman Catholic Church as in other fellowships, yet all who administer the rite are men.

Some of these same phenomena are found in much less sacramental de-nominations. In theory, Baptists draw no strong distinction between laity and clergy. Ordination is frequently understood as merely a public recogni-tion of a divine calling. It does not convey any special power or special authority for ministry that would not be present without it. Yet many a Baptist church has faced the dilemma of what to do about celebrating the Lord's Supper on a Sunday morning when neither its pastor nor any other ordained minister is available.

Related to this is not only the nature of ministry and of ordination, but of the church itself. Christ gave the Lord's Supper to the church, according to the teaching of most Christian denominations. But is it legitimate to observe the ordinance in a meeting which is not a session of a properly organized local congregation? Specifically, it is not merely a question of meetings of a group of people who may be drawn from several local congregations of the same denomination, as a camp for example. More than that, it is a question of the status of parachurch organizations. Are such to be considered a church, or in some sense a part of the church?

In a sense, the problem is simpler for the more sacramental churches than for free church groups such as Baptists. The former have rather carefully developed doctrines of ministry and of ordination, as well as of the sacra-ments. They know rather precisely why one person cannot preside at the Eucharist and another can. It is then a matter of justifying why this concep-tion should be maintained, or in other words, of its validity. For Baptists the problem is frequently the lack of a developed theory of ministry, ordination, and ordinances.

The other problem facing free churches such as Baptists is also related to the role of women. In many churches struggling with the place of women within the local congregation's functioning, the problems relate to three is-sues: their right to preach to or teach men; their right to hold positions of leadership that are deemed to be exercise of authority over men; and their right to participate in serving the Lord's Supper. In the latter case, not sim-ply the presidency of the Supper, but even the distribution of the elements to the partakers, is at issue. At times, the distinction becomes quite closely refined. In one church, women are permitted to serve as ushers, but only on the side aisles, the center aisle being reserved for men.

It appears that Baptists will need to develop thoroughly their doctrine of ordination if they are to deal adequately with the issue of presidency at the Lord's Supper, whether concerning women or unordained males. Here we may note that there is no uniform history of Baptist thinking and practice. Some hold a simple theory that prior to the nineteenth century there was uniformity of thinking and that the rather radical changes in Baptist belief in the nineteenth century represented a reaction to the Catholic revival. This does not really accord with the facts, however.[11] The role of ordination among nonsacramentarians is always something of an enigma, for sacerdotalism tends to be a natural corollary of sacramentalism. In the case of sacramentalists, ordination is clearly a necessity, for without it, there literally cannot be a valid observance of the Lord's Supper. What, however, is the requirement for an effective observance among nonsacramentarians such as Baptists? Is it simply someone possessing the necessary physical and communicational skills to preside in an effective manner? If so, are the spiritual qualifications of the administrant irrelevant? Could it by done by someone who is in no sense a Christian believer, such as an atheistic actor trained to preside at a Lord's Supper scene in a play?

What is frequently said in these situations is that it is necessary for the presiding person to be someone whom the church has selected, authorized or approved.[12] This lays the primary responsibility and authority for the observance of the Lord's Supper upon the church, or more correctly, upon the congregation. This is a position logically consistent with the overall doctrine and polity of the congregational type of churches. The further question, however, is the nature of this recognition of approval. How formal and permanent need it be? Could it be simply the decision at a given assembly of the congregation that a certain person should preside that day? Need it require action by the entire congregation as a whole, or could it be accomplished simply by some officer of the congregation asking one person to preside? Does it require some permanent, public, and official authorization, such as that usually associated with ordination? It would seem that where the question of the qualification of the administrant has been a large issue, Baptists have usually placed more emphasis upon the ordination than upon the administrant's actual membership within the group, since it is then more acceptable to bring in an ordained minister to serve the Lord's Supper than to have a nonordained layperson from within the group preside. In any event, this presents Baptists with an item for their theological agenda.

Perhaps the question also forces us back into the old question which divided Luther and Zwingli, as well: What is the nature, if any, of the presence of the body and blood of the Lord within the Lord's Supper? If it is appropriate to refer to this rite as the Lord's Supper, in what sense is it that? In what way is He present at or within the ceremony? Is His presence real or substantial, and if so, is it within the elements of the bread and wine, per se? Here, unfortunately, Baptists have been less than completely clear and cogent. In large part, this is related to the fact that Baptist thought on this subject has been largely negative. Whatever their view, they were certain that they did not believe that the actual substance of Christ's body and blood were present within the bread and wine. They have not been equally clear regarding the sense, if any, in which it is appropriate to refer to His presence.

Baptists have been quick to affirm that the bread and wine are symbols of the body and blood of Christ,[13] but have not really wrestled with the question of whether they are symbols or signs, in Paul Tillich's usage of those terms.[14] Do the symbols participate in the reality which they represent? Is there a spiritual presence of Christ at the Lord's Supper which is in some way different from His presence anywhere else? For that matter, what is the nature of His presence with the Christian and in the church? What is the difference between the Lord's Supper and a simple meal of bread and wine (or grape juice) among Christian believers, with no declaration that the Lord's Supper is being observed, no reading of the Lord's Supper passages, in other words, a congregational bread-and-grape-juice supper? By failing to deal adequately with these issues, Baptists have sometimes conveyed the impression that they hold to what one Baptist leader referred to as the "doctrine of the real absence."

Even if there is agreement upon the nature of the divine presence (the issue which divided Luther and Zwingli), there is still the issue which divided Luther from the Roman Catholic Church, namely, what brings about this presence? For his quarrel with the Catholics was not over the real presence, but over transubstantiation. He rejected the idea that when the priest pronounced certain words, and performed certain actions, the bread and wine were transformed (or more correctly, transubstantiated) into the body and blood of Christ. If there is agreement that Christ is present at the Lord's table in some fashion different from His presence at a church potluck or a softball game, or even more, by such an event not involving believers, what is this difference? Here it will be seen that the issue is broader than merely the nature of ordination, per se.

A second major issue which has gained recent prominence is the question of the common communion cup. In a sense this is not a new issue, having been a source of some concern at various times in the past. In one Baptist congregation in Chicago this issue had, during the early 1940s, produced strong disagreement, threatening to result in schism. It has frequently been recognized as at least potentially a health problem. More recently the problem has taken on larger and more dramatic proportions with the growing threat of AIDS. The debate on the subject was prominent in *The Christian Century* in 1985. At Luther-Northwestern Theological Seminary, the practice of using the common communion cup was discontinued.[15] Congregations in high-risk communities (such as San Francisco), have been especially concerned.

Two factors seem, at least on the surface, to be in conflict with one another. One is the sense of significance involved in the use of one communion cup by all participants in the Lord's Supper. This may stem from a desire to recreate as closely as possible the circumstances of the original meal at which Christ instituted this ordinance (or sacrament, depending upon one's theological interpretation). Or it may be simply a question of the symbolism of the body of Christ by using a common communion cup. Where this is done, there is also one loaf of bread, from which the partakers tear pieces. The other factor is the health and safety of the partakers. For certainly congregational love for one another includes concern for the physical health of fellow members. Observe, for example, how frequently the prayers of church members for one another are for physical health.

The underlying issue seems to be what aspects or components of the Lord's Supper are significant for preserving the symbolism of the rite. For presumably virtually all denominations believe in the symbolic and commemorative values of the Lord's Supper, whether they also believe it to be more than that. The question is then what is required to preserve the necessary meaning of that practice. There is some justification for arguing that the Lord's Supper, among other things, is supposed to symbolize the unity of believers. Paul's extensive discussion of this in 1 Corinthians 11 supports such a contention. But does this require the use of one cup, or can other actions, either verbal or nonverbal or both, accomplish the same thing? Even such a common practice as singing a hymn together would appear to help convey that meaning.

This brings us back to the other question, of the degree to which it is desirable and even necessary to replicate the exact circumstances of the original event. No one does that in all details, and indeed such could lead to absurdities, such as requiring the partakers to recline rather than sit or stand, and even limiting the number of participants to twelve. A test of the fervency of concern for replication can be roughly gauged by whether a congregation holds its observance of the Lord's Supper on Thursday or Friday of Holy Week. A Maundy Thursday observance argues for re-creation of the original event of institution, whereas a Good Friday observance correlates more closely with preservation of the event proclaimed. (In a sense, observance of the Lord's Supper on Thursday should logically be followed by a crucifixion, at least a mock one, on Friday, but then we have redundancy of symbols.) The crucial issue is the significant or indispensable components of what is being commemorated.

The other question relates to the other side of the conflict, namely the danger of contracting AIDS. There seems to be relatively little evidence that one can be infected with the disease through the transmission of saliva. We should note that this is a matter where a later discovery of error in this casual analysis could literally prove fatal. Further, anxiety over the possible danger, whether founded or not, is what causes the difficulty for the practice of all partakers using a common cup.

The concern is not limited to the question of the possible transmission of AIDS, however. At Luther-Northwestern Theological Seminary, the practice of the common cup was discontinued in large part because of an article written by a a retired University of Minnesota public-health professor, Dr. George Michaelson, who termed the use of the common cup a "filthy" and "unhygienic" practice, and stated that after only few communications have been served, "the cup becomes heavily contaminated with millions of bacteria and viruses." He stated that "well over 100 communicable diseases can be transmitted directly or indirectly by contact between ill and healthy persons . . . for about a dozen illnesses, the major means of disease transmission is the common drinking cup or glass."[16]

There is one additional dimension to this issue. In general, what is involved is not the exclusion of AIDS patients from the Lord's Supper. In many cases, that condition is not known to the congregation, and the information is not obtainable. However, to the extent that departure from the practice of a common cup is motivated by desire to avoid contact with those who have AIDS, this is in a small sense an issue of withdrawing fellowship with them (although it is also withdrawn from all other participants in the Lord's Supper as well). Thus, we have here to some extent the issue again which underlies closed communion. And in a sense, it is the issue which underlay the dispute between Augustine and the Donatists: the purity of the church and the necessity of the church attempting to preserve that purity within its bounds by care in extending fellowship. This is the major point of an article by Gordon W. Lathrop. He insists that there is no scientific evidence for the transmission of AIDS through a common cup.[17] Indeed, he argues that the use of the common cup is the most sanitary of the practices available.[18] Fear of the common cup is not simply a concern about disease, however. Rather, it is fear of "pollution" by contact with those who are different, who are not "holy" and "pure." And it is this which makes abandonment of the common cup so unchristian. He says:

> Then the talk of disease, even when the facts do not support that talk, is a way of talking about a deeper symbolic thing: the fear of the polluted one. From a Christian point of view there is suddenly a great issue at risk: we are not saved by our separation from the sinners. We are all sinners. And the blood of Christ is poured out for us all. In this time of exclusion and fear the gospel clearly points to the great value of the use of the cup, to the Blood of the One-who-was-with-sinners made to be common to us all.[19]

Generally speaking, the use of a single cup is not currently a major issue for Baptist churches. While there was fairly general use of the common cup at an earlier time, that is largely a matter of historical interest at the present.[20] Rather than simply ignoring this issue as a problem for someone else, however, Lathrop suggests that this is an opportune time, in the crisis provoked by the fear of AIDS, to consider adopting (or readopting) it. He says, "your act would recover an ancient biblical and liturgical sign of unity, generosity and grace in Christ at a time pastorally in need of such signs."[21]

The final major issue for today is the nature of the service of the Lord's Supper itself. The term "Eucharist" is used by those who see the key to understanding the nature of the rite as found in Paul's use of the term *eucharisto* in 1 Corinthians 11:24. This sees the primary nature of the Lord's Supper as being an act of thanksgiving. Further, this is then to be undertaken, not in a spirit of sobriety but of celebration. It is a festive, not a somber, occasion, and should be treated as such. The motif is taken from Jesus' having taken the bread and given thanks. In some cases, this is also tied to the Jewish Passover as being a festive time. Others, however, have made and still do, make it a time of quiet reflection, occasioned both by awe in the face of the greatness of the divine sacrifice and of self-examination in light of Paul's words in verses 27-32. For the latter group of people, the ordinance is observed in a quieter, more contemplative mood.

To some extent, this issue is simply whether the mood or tone of the service shall be solemn or joyous. Yet in Baptist churches there frequently are larger issues, for in some cases, underlying these differences, however, are differing general conceptions of the nature of worship. Increasingly, the difference can be understood as that between praise or celebration and worship. In the former the emphasis is upon announcement directed to others, regarding the mighty works of God. In the latter case, the emphasis is upon worship, directed to God. And frequently, there is also an objective-subjective difference. The praise approach has as its locus more the feelings of the one celebrating, while the worship approach focuses more upon the one who has done those things. This is in many cases a generational difference. Although oversimplified, one can observe that many younger people prefer the praise or feeling-oriented type of worship, while their parents may be more oriented toward the more traditional focus upon the object of the praise and worship. In the setting of the Lord's Supper, the older generation might be more concerned about the correct understanding of the ordinance, and upon "rightly discerning the body," while the youth might be more oriented to their own experience and the emotions issuing from this observance.

The ordinance of the Lord's Supper poses for us the dilemma which confronted Friedrich Schleiermacher, and, for that matter, those who sought to criticize or evaluate his thought. Schleiermacher made the feelings, rather than the intellect, the locus of religion. To be pious was not to hold the correct doctrines about God, or even, for that matter, to act in the correct and ethical way. Piety was a matter of feeling, and specifically, the feeling of absolute dependence upon God. The difficulty, however, was the ambivalence between considering these feelings merely in themselves and considering them as intuitions of God. In the former case, the understanding tended to deteriorate not only into subjectivity, but rather subjectivism. Did there really need to be any object of these feelings, or could one be religious just on the basis of the feelings? In the latter case, the question became focused more upon what object of these feelings one should then pursue. The correct description of the object, God, became increasingly important, so that something like doctrinal orthodoxy began to be introduced, at least in incipient fashion. The understanding of the nature of God was involved, as well. To the extent that emphasis was placed upon the feelings, God was seen as more immanent. To the extent that stress was placed upon the object of the feelings, or the cause of the feelings, God was considered more transcendent in nature.

We have been suggesting that the mode or style of worship implies a particular understanding of the nature of religion and of God. This is not to say that these are derived from the type of worship, but rather that they are revealed by it. This is not an ontological, but instead an epistemological implication. How we worship is ultimately a function of what we think religion to be, and what we think God to be like. In the present context of discussion, the issue is whether the primary emphasis shall be placed upon the objective fact of what is being observed or celebrated, or upon the feeling of celebration itself. It therefore appears that some very basic and far-reaching issues may be under contention and that we may need to examine these logically prior to dealing with the practical issues of the Lord's Supper.

Worship has not traditionally been one of the strengths of Baptist local church practice. Yet it would seem that the Lord's Supper provides an unusually good opportunity for growth in the practice of worship. The Lord's Supper can be simply an appendage to a service which may have been strongly evangelistic in nature. It may be hurried through, with an eye on the watch that tells one that the roast is becoming overly well done, or that the televised football game is proceeding. It may be simply an occasion for emotional stimulation. Or it may be a primary means of expressing our wonder and love for God. What we as Baptists do with it will be an indication of the whole direction of our worship, and even of our theology.

Conclusion

We have sought to examine three contemporary issues related to the doctrine of the Lord's Supper: the proper administrant of the ordinance, the use of a common cup, and the nature of the service itself. We have contended that these issues of practice are related to doctrinal issues, not merely pertaining to the Lord's Supper, but to more general doctrinal questions. These therefore give us an agenda which as theologians, and specifically Baptist theologians, we need to address. Some of these are the following:

1. What is the nature of ordination? Who confers it and what power or authority does it carry?

2. What are the distinguishing marks or constituting factors which make a collection of persons a local church? What are its privileges and authority?

3. What is the nature of Christ's presence with the Christian and in the church?

4. What is the nature of theological signs or symbols? What are the essential elements of such symbols? Do they participate in the reality of what they symbolize, and if so, in what sense?

5. What is the nature of worship? To what degree should the emphasis in worship be placed upon the subject and the subject of the worship, respectively?

6. What are the relative places of the subjective and the objective aspects of religion? To what extent is it appropriately a matter of ideas and beliefs, and to what extent a matter of feeling?

7. What is the relationship of divine transcendence and immanence to one another?

Notes

1. William Walker, Richard A. Norris, David W. Lotz, and Robert Handy, *A History of the Christian Church*, 4th ed. (New York: Charles Scribner's Sons, 1985), 456.

2. Martin Luther, "The Babylonian Captivity of the Church," *Three Treatises* (Philadelphia: Muhlenberg Press, 1943), 136-43.

3. Ibid., 127-36.

4. Dale Moody, *The Word of Truth* (Grand Rapids: Eerdmans, 1981), 473.

5. William McNutt, *Polity and Practice in Baptist Churches* (Philadelphia: Judson Press, 1935), 121-23; Gordon G. Johnson, *My Church* (Arlington Heights, Ill.: Harvest Publications, 1982), 90-94.

6. Augustus H. Strong, *Systematic Theology* (Philadelphia: Judson Press, 1907), 970-80; Edward T. Hiscox, *The New Directory for Baptist Churches* (Philadelphia: Judson Press, 1894), 447-63; W. T. Conner, *Christian Doctrine* (Nashville: Broadman Press, 1937), 289-90.

7. Conner, 285.

8. Moody, 472-73; Hiscox, 451; Strong, 978.

9. Millard J. Erickson, *Christian Theology* (Grand Rapids: Baker Book House, 1986), 782.

10. John Austin Baker, "Eucharistic Presidency and Women's Ordination," *Theology*, 83 (Sept. 1985): 350-57.

11. Michael Walker, "The Presidency of the Lord's Table Among Nineteenth Century British Baptists," *The Baptist Quarterly* 32 (Jan. 1988): 208.

12. Walker, 218; McNutt, 123-24; Strong, 962.

13. Strong, 962-65.

14. Paul Tillich, *Systematic Theology* (Chicago: University of Chicago Press, 1951), 1:239.

15. "Common Cup Discontinued," *Christian Century*, Nov. 6, 1985, 994.

16. Ibid.

17. Gordon Lathrop, "Aids and the Cup," *Worship*, March, 1988, 161.

18. Ibid., 162.

19. Ibid., 164.

20. Moody, 472.

21. Lathrop, 165.

4
The Worship of the Church

by Wayne E. Ward

Introduction

Worship opens a window on the theology of the worshiping community. Often, it is a more accurate expression of the beliefs of that community than is its creed or other doctrinal statements. Just as the real beliefs of a religious community are usually demonstrated more clearly by its actions than by its statement of faith, so the style, form, and content of its worship usually illustrate quite clearly its deepest convictions about God, human beings, sin, salvation, church and, most of all, about the worshiper's relationship to God now and in the hereafter.

Purpose

With such an assumption this essay is intended to be an exploration of the relationship between theology and worship in the Believers' Church tradition, giving special attention to the worship practices of Baptists throughout their history and in their churches today. It will also consider in a limited, but hopefully significant way, both the kinship and the distinctiveness of Baptist ecclesiology within the broader context of Protestantism. It may even help to explain the familiar characterization of Baptists as the "protestants" of the Protestants, since they were such an irritant to the major Protestant Reformers that both Continental Anabaptists and the direct forebears of modern Baptists in English Separatism suffered more at the hands of their fellow Protestants than they did from the Pope.

Luther, for example, sought the absolute elimination of those despised "Schwarmergeister" (pesky, swarming insects), the Anabaptist "fanatics" or "enthusiasts" who were too Protestant for him, and supported a harsh campaign against them.[1] His vilification of them is matched only by the language he used to vilify the Jews. This contributed to a reservoir of contempt and hatred for both which endured through the centuries.

Apologia

I write this essay as one who is deeply committed to the Believers' Church tradition. I will not seek to deny the deep indebtedness of our Baptist tradition to the broader Protestant tradition of Luther, Calvin, Zwingli, and the Anglican Reformers; but I will not gloss over the fact that believers carried out the reformation of Catholic ecclesiology with a thoroughness which shocked the great Reformers in their day and still irritates some of those within the mainline Protestant churches today.

Focus of Worship

The English word *worship* comes from the Old English word *weorthscipe* (*weorth*, worthy, worth + *-scipe,* -ship), and it denotes worthiness, repute, respect, or reverence paid to a divine being. It may designate a ritual or religious practice which is intended to bring the devotee into a deeper relationship with God. It may also include praise, thanksgiving, confession, and petition to God, as well as offerings, meditations, readings from sacred texts, and homilies.

In the Believers' Church, however, prophetic proclamation from the Scriptures is the focal point of worship, and it usually culminates in exhortation or invitation to repentance, dedication, or other responses from the worshipers. This radical shift of the central act of worship in the Believers' Church from the celebration of the Mass to the exposition of the Scriptures accounts for most of the distinctive elements in its worship, its educational programs for its church members, and even for the architecture of its church buildings, educational buildings, and "family life" centers.[2]

In the history of religions, worship has involved all of the five senses and a wide range of physical and mental activities, including singing, dancing, acrobatics, instrumental music, self-mutilation, and even sexual rites. These worship rituals have had purposes as varied as their forms. Sometimes they sought only to praise and glorify God. At other times the primary purpose was to inspire the worshipers. Throughout the biblical world of both the Old and New Testaments, the frequent sexual rites in pagan worship were intended to engender fertility in flocks and fields by sympathetic influence from the worshipers. The battle of the prophets of Israel and the apostles of the church against the encroachment of these pagan rites is seen throughout the Bible.

Biblical Language for Worship

The most extensively used word for "worship" in the Hebrew Bible is *shachah*, which literally means to "bow oneself down." It is found in the biblical books from Genesis to Zechariah (it does not appear in Malachi), and in its scores of occurrences it is almost always translated "worship" in our English versions.[3]

In the Book of Daniel the word *segad* occurs twelve times. Its literal meaning is also to "bow down" or "do obeisance," but it is consistently translated "worship" in our older English versions and is the only word for worship in the prophecy of Daniel. The word for "servant," *ebed*, is used five times in 2 Kings and is always translated "worshiper" in the *King James Version*. One time the word *atsab*, "to make an idol," is translated "worship" in Jeremiah 44:19.[4]

In the New Testament the primary word for "worship" is *proskuneo*, to "kiss (the hand) toward."[5] It occurs dozens of times from Matthew through Revelation. The word *latreuo*, to "worship" or "serve" *publicly* is used four times, and forms of *sebomai*, to "venerate" or "adore" are translated into English as "worship" or "worshipers" eight times.[6]

Renewal of Worship

The monotony and emptiness of the worship experience in a great many Baptist churches today has contributed to a revival of interest in the Anglican and Catholic liturgy. Sometimes this has been expressed in a desire to make the Eucharist or "Lord's Supper" the focal point of worship. Although some churches in the Believers' Church tradition have continued the Catholic pattern of making the act of Communion the central act of worship[7] almost all Baptist churches continue to make the "Bible on the pulpit" (or on the *Communion table!*) and the "preaching of the Word" from the Bible the focal point of worship. Indeed, in many of our rural churches and sometimes in our urban churches one will still hear this question at the end of the Sunday School hour: "Are you staying for the *preaching* service?"

Old habits die slowly, especially in the area of traditional religious rituals; but the question which is disturbing some Baptists today is whether the effort to reach back into our richer liturgical heritage in order to strengthen our worship may bring with it the medieval theology which was expressed in that liturgy. Worship patterns will eventually *shape* theology as much as they are shaped *by* theology, and they could, in time, undermine the distinctiveness of the Believers' Church and take it back to the Catholic womb.

Jewish Background of Christian Worship

The most direct and most influential source of Christian worship patterns is the Jewish synagogue. The regular reading from both the Law and the Prophets in Jewish worship is paralleled in the Christian reading from the

Gospels and the Epistles of the apostles.[8] Indeed, this pattern of worship almost certainly guided the formation of the New Testament canon of Scripture into the Gospels and the apostles (Epistles) as it had guided the formation of the Old Testament canon into the Law, the Prophets, and the Psalms.[9] This double reading in the order of worship was followed by the singing of psalms in both synagogue and church. So committed to this pattern of psalm-singing was the Baptist tradition that the effort to introduce hymns and gospel songs brought resistance and conflict well into the nineteenth century.[10] In the formation of the Hebrew canon of Scripture, the Psalter (or hymnbook) formed the stackpole for the third division of the canon, the *Hagiographa* or "Sacred Writings."[11] The Hebrew Psalter was clearly the hymnbook of the early Christian churches, but they sang, in addition to the psalms, certain "hymns and spiritual songs" (Col. 3:16). Biblical scholars believe that they have found scores of stanzas, lines, and phrases from these "hymns and spiritual songs" embedded in the New Testament text from Matthew to Revelation.

Theological Roots of Worship

In order to understand what is happening, or *should* happen in worship, it is necessary to go back to the theological roots of our Christian faith. Because worship is a planned and ritualized expression of that faith, including our understanding of God, the way in which He relates to us, the appropriate ways in which we may approach Him, and what He expects from us in worship, it is imperative that we find the theological core of our faith.

All of the religions of humankind, including many forms of Christianity, are designed to elevate human beings toward union or communion with Ultimate Reality, the Divine. All of these upward-reaching religions are human creations. Everything in them, whether smoking altars, music, incense, prayers, or rituals of any other kind, is designed to lift the devout worshiper out of the human condition of sin, guilt, and brokenness toward a healing, cleansing, redeeming encounter with the living God. It is a worthy goal. What could be more important than a transforming encounter with the One who created us, in whom we live and move and have our being, who gives the deepest meaning to our lives here and now, and who is the only hope we have of anything beyond this earthly journey?

Exactly at this point a great danger looms. Because we believe that God has planted this longing for Him within us,[12] that it is indeed His very *image* in us, we are too eager to "climb up" to Him in the way which seems most appropriate to us. We try to set the conditions and ask God to meet us on *our* terms. We try to treat Him like the genie in the bottle. When we say the right words and go through the proper ritual, we expect Him to pop right up and meet our needs. In other words, we act as if God existed to meet our needs, when, the truth is, we do not even know what our real needs are until God reveals Himself to us and we discover our true selves.

The good news of the gospel of Jesus Christ turns these human religions of works-salvation upside down. Because humankind cannot climb the "golden ladder" to God's heavenly realm by its own efforts, God "comes down" to redeem humanity from the inside. Incarnation! God in Christ comes to us in full human reality, bone of our bone and flesh of our flesh, and experiences all of the pain, suffering, joy, sorrow, and loneliness which we could ever experience, and more. Only by entering into our human experience and even suffering the total abandonment, agony, and death of the cross could God in Christ heal us of our mortal wound. He took our sin and all its destructive power, together with its indelible sign of death, and overcame both sin and death from inside the human race. There are no words, music, or actions through which we may adequately express our gratitude and joy for what God has done for us, is doing in our lives now, and will do throughout all eternity.

Worship must celebrate this overwhelming grace of God in coming to us and transforming both us and our human situation by His redeeming love. We dare not reject His sovereign grace by trying to "make up" something which we think is lacking in His provision for us. We cannot debase His once-for-all atoning sacrifice on Calvary's cross by presuming to re-create that sacrifice upon the altar every Sunday. We give our own lives daily as living sacrifices, not in order to earn a forgiveness which God in His infinite grace has already given, but, because He has forgiven us, we pour out our lives in a thanksgiving of faithful service to Him and others in His name.

The Divine Initiative in Worship

Because the divine initiative in coming to us is the only way we could ever encounter God, it follows that His initiative in coming to us is our only hope of encounter with Him in worship. God does not need our worship. There are, indeed, worship forms and liturgies which seem to be based upon the assumption that God needs to be adored, praised, or placated. The very essence of many worship rituals is the effort to placate an angry deity, gain the goodwill of one who is feared, or ingratiate the worshipers with their God in order to earn specific favors.

In worship we should try to prepare ourselves for the coming of God to us at the time and place and in the way which He chooses. We may bring our conscious needs before God in prayer and worship, but we should be even more concerned to wait for God to reveal Himself to us and make us aware of our real needs as His children. The form and content of worship should be directed toward the goal of receiving the revelation of the Divine Word through reading and exposition of the Scripture, accompanied by the singing of scripturally based hymns and the offering of prayers of praise, intercession, and petition with the constant awareness of our complete dependence upon the power of the Holy Spirit. Even the motivation to worship God and to wait upon His self-disclosure is precipitated by the convicting power of the Holy Spirit, and only the Spirit can interpret and confirm God's Word to our minds and hearts.

Early Baptist Struggle over Worship

From the earliest records of the first Baptist churches in England, in the opening years of the seventeenth century, come the sounds of intense debate, discussion, and disagreement over the proper form and content of worship.[13] They were trying to restore the primitive apostolic form of the church, and, with unerring logic, they understood that worship must be an outward expression of their ecclesiology. Since the "gathered community of believers" was their basic concept of the church, all forms of worship, including baptism, Lord's Supper, prayers, hymns, Scripture exposition, confession, and receiving of forgiveness, involved full congregational participation. Because the focal point of the entire worship experience was the exposition of the Word of God for the purpose of revealing God's truth and God's will for the believers, it followed that the major portion of the worship time was spent in preaching (or *prophesying*, as it was frequently called) from Holy Scripture. In services which regularly lasted from eight in the morning until noon, and from two in the afternoon until five, three or more of the preachers who were deemed to have the gift of interpretation of Scripture would hold forth in exposition, exhortation, and even dialogue with members of the congregation and among themselves. Often, beginning with the youngest preacher among them, they would read and interpret the chosen text of Holy Scripture, endeavoring to deepen their understanding of its meaning by questioning and supplementing each other's exposition. Then, the senior preacher would sometimes summarize the discussion in the manner of a moderator of a panel.

In article nineteen of the 1611 *Confession of Faith* of the Gainsborough Church, formerly led by John Smyth, but at that time led by Thomas Helwys, the main elements of worship are clearly delineated. Each church should meet every first day of the week because it is the Lord's Day, the day of His resurrection. The church was "to assemble together to pray, prophesy (expound the Scriptures), praise God and break Bread . . . ."[14] This certainly meant that this congregation was observing the Lord's Supper each Sunday, and a few congregations continued that practice for a short time.

However, in the Baptist churches the general practice quickly reduced the frequency to a monthly observance of the Supper for at least two reasons: they were afraid of the repetition which might lead them back toward a sacramental emphasis like the Catholic Mass, and they did not want to threaten the centrality of biblical preaching in their worship.[15] The characteristic pattern of Baptist worship was established by 1612, and it has continued with remarkable consistency, in a Free Church tradition, without bishop, creed, or council to impose uniformity, until this day. Only in these latter years of the twentieth century have yearnings for a "richer" worship liturgy led some churches to experiment with beautiful rituals of water, word, and wine which are aesthetically pleasing and often spiritually moving, but which have their theological root in the sacrament of the altar and the baptismal font. Although no Baptist churches declared their return to Canterbury or Rome, several Baptist pastors, professors, and laypersons have publicly announced their "return to Mother Church." Every one of them, whose *apologia* I have read, has given as one of his or her major reasons the longing for the centrality of the Eucharist or sacrament of the Lord's table in the Anglican or Roman Catholic worship experience.

It requires no special powers of spiritual discernment to see in this trend in some congregations and among ministers a concern of increasing urgency and, in some places, of crisis proportions over the barrenness, emptiness, and lackadaisical disorder of some of our Baptist worship experiences. The longing for more meaningful worship must be encouraged and fulfilled in a way which is consistent with our deepest beliefs as Baptists. Our failure to reach and even *indoctrinate* new converts, as well as more mature Christians, in the foundational soteriology and ecclesiology which characterize our Baptist theological heritage is coming back to haunt us now. Having abandoned serious doctrinal teaching, and having forsaken the primary exposition of the written Word as the center of the worship experience (called the "sacrament of the Word" by both Calvin and early English Baptists), it now remains to be seen whether most Baptists will move back toward our Anglican and Catholic roots, filter out into an ecumenical evangelicalism which has little understanding of, or concern for, believer's baptism, or whether they will simply go on muddling through an unsatisfying worship experience which is based upon little or no theology at all.

Only time will tell whether we will treasure and preserve the doctrinal bequest of our forefathers and mothers in seventeenth-century England, who suffered the whip, imprisonment, and even death for their profound belief in soul competency, believer's baptism, the exposition of an utterly trustworthy and authoritative Holy Scripture as the center of the worship experience, and the church as a gathered community of believers under the direct lordship of Jesus. When these early English Baptists met in worship and proclaimed their faith in spite of the brutal persecution by bishop and magistrate, they were convinced that what they believed really mattered. Those bishops who based their authority to punish these dissenters upon the claim to be Christ's vicar on earth often were met with the challenge, "With all due respect, Reverend Sir, Christ needs no vicar, for He is here Himself!"[16] If the bishops and legally appointed clerics really are the authoritative representatives of an absentee Lord, then devout church members have no option but to obey them. But if Christ the Lord is really present as Head of His Church, composed of all true believers of every time and place, gathered in communities of baptized believers to praise, adore, hear, and obey Him, then we must own His lordship by serving Him as Lord and defend His lordship against every bishop, cleric, politician, and authoritarian pastor who would infringe upon it. The issues are as clear today as they were in the seventeenth century: *Bible* or tradition? Legally enforced religious conformity, or *freedom of the conscience?* Political and religious lords over the church, or the *direct Lordship of the Living Christ through His Written Word and by His Spirit?* A worship liturgy shaped by the beautiful and hallowed tradition of the continual sacrifice of the body and blood of Jesus upon the altar, or worship that *adores the Living Lord and listens to His Word for instruction, rebuke, and guidance?*

The issues are clear, and the cost of discipleship will still include the cross. After thoughtful attention to our theological roots, are we ready to go back to an inherited religion, sealed by infant baptism, celebrated in sacramental ritual, and even enforced by political establishment if possible? Or does our Living Lord Who rules over His church still call us to renounce all other lords, political or religious, who would bind the conscience, and follow His command to make disciples in every ethnic group and nation to the ends of the earth, baptizing them in the name of the Father, the Son, and the Holy Spirit, and teaching these disciples His words of truth every time we gather to worship Him?

Where Do We Go from Here?

It is easy to trace the historical and biblical roots of our Baptist theology of worship, and it is easier still to level wide-ranging criticisms at our shallow patterns of worship. But the best criticism is always a constructive alternative which intends to correct the areas which are criticized. In an effort to make a small contribution to the solution of the problem of barrenness in our worship, confusion over its theological meaning, and even uncertainty about our very identity as Baptists, I should like to propose the following courses of action:

1. We should begin a thorough teaching of our Baptist history to all age groups in our churches, from the youngest to the oldest, in order to show them why we have distinctive beliefs regarding the authority of Scripture over church tradition, the soul competency of each individual believer, believer's baptism, the gathered church concept, and the passionate commitment to the concept of a free church in a free state. It is not enough to repeat old doctrines and impose them on children or adults in our churches. They must know *why* Baptists came to hold these distinctive doctrines, *how* they came to understand and define those doctrines as they did, and also how much struggle, disagreement, reversal of positions, and charitable tolerance of other viewpoints characterized this formative period of our history.

The most baneful legacy of the Landmark movement among Southern Baptists in the mid-nineteenth century is probably not its exclusivist views on church, baptism, and the Lord's Supper. It is their artificial reading of "Baptist succession" throughout church history, suggesting that these distinctive Baptist doctrines had always been there, and obscuring the painful struggle of our Baptist pioneers to define them over against the Anglican and Catholic Churches out of which they came. In these days of laudable ecumenical contacts and irenic spirit in relationship with our fellow Christians, it is important to remember that we further ecumenical Christianity by honestly and graciously sharing our distinctive understanding of Christian doctrines more than we do by acting as if there were no differences or as if they do not matter. We also should listen earnestly to our fellow Christians and learn from them. We have no corner on the truth, and we should all be learning from each other as we study God's Word and evaluate our own traditions critically and responsibly. The real break in Christian fellowship, leading to separation and distinct denominations, comes when we cannot agree on the primary source of our doctrinal authority, whether Bible, creed, or church tradition, or when some people claim the authority to impose their own views upon fellow Christians, denying them the freedom which they claim for themselves.

2. We should find a more effective way of teaching Baptist doctrine to baptismal candidates and new church members. The typical way of catechism and indoctrination, in which the answers are already assumed and dispensed upon the authority of the church, should be jettisoned as unworthy of Christians who claim no exclusive ownership of divine truth. Instead, we should lead Christians of all ages and levels of maturity from the biblical text, through the debates of church history, to the contemporary construction of each doctrine in our time and place. We cannot and should not impose doctrinal positions upon others by the use of threat and coercive authority. We must win their minds and hearts and tell them every day that we

have only a partial and limited understanding of God's truth, and we must be open to constant questioning and rethinking of cherished views. This does not mean that we have to live in a state of suspended conclusion and never have convictions about anything. But it does mean that we act upon our firm convictions in the light which we have, knowing that further light and truth from God's Word, interpreted by its Holy Spirit Author, may lead us to a deeper understanding or a new application of the truth we hold dear.

3. Finally, we should rethink and constantly readapt all our worship experiences, including Sunday worship, baptism, Lord's Supper, weddings, funerals, and prayer meetings, in the light of our biblical study, our reading of the history of the church and the broader story of humankind. We can enrich our worship with music, poetry, and art in all its forms but only when we are guided by a clear understanding of who God is, how He comes to us in worship, how we are called, redeemed, and incorporated into the church, and how we may celebrate His constant saving, healing, renewing Presence in our lives. Worship may be lifeless not because God is dead, but because we are. Our every effort to enrich and deepen our worship should be a consecrated offering unto God. That is the meaning of worship. It completes the circle of God's self-giving love, which comes to us, unworthy as we are, and lifts us up into an eternal fellowship with our Creator-Redeemer-God, unbroken by the valley of death and unending in our heavenly home.

Notes

1. See John C. Wenger, *Glimpses of Mennonite History and Doctrine*, 2d ed., rev. and enl. (Scottdale, Pa.: Herald Press, 1947), especially 47ff. for complete documentation of Luther's demand for condemnation, fines, imprisonment, and even the death penalty for Anabaptists.

2. The gathering of the community of believers for the exposition of the Scriptures as the focal point of worship encourages the central pulpit, rather than the divided chancel for the adoration of the elevated host of the Mass, prefers a semicircular or fan-shaped worship center for the "gathering," calls for educational buildings which provide rooms and equipment for small-group or "family" Bible study, and even "family life centers" which emphasize "gathered community" (Matt. 18:20,) or "family" and group-oriented play and exercise activities and equipment.

3. Robert Young, *Analytical Concordance to the Bible* (New York: Funk and Wagnalls Company, n.d.), 1074-75.

4. Ibid.

5. Ibid.

6. Ibid.

7. See especially the disagreements between English Baptists and the Amsterdam Mennonites (who required observance of the Supper every Sunday) in Carlton Turner Mitchell, *Baptist Worship in Relation to Baptist Concepts of the Church, 1608-1865* (Ph.D. diss., New York University, 1962). The lengthy struggle over the frequency of observance of the Lord's Supper is traced in chapters 3 and 4, 42-99.

8. See Justin Martyr, *The First Apology*, trans. Thomas B. Falls (New York: Christian Heritage, 1948), 107.

9. See Wayne E. Ward, *The Concept of Holy Scripture in Biblical Literature* (Th.D. diss.,

Southern Baptist Theological Seminary, 1952).

10. Mitchell, 37, 50, 86, 109ff., 135-36, 165-66, 193ff., and 232-34.

11. Luke 24:44. See the historical treatment in Ward.

12. Augustine's famous prayer in his *Confessions* contains the classic statement of this longing in the human heart: "Thou hast made us for Thyself, and our hearts are restless until they find their rest in Thee!"

13. See Mitchell, 69-99, for citation of primary sources and extensive quotations from them.

14. W. J. McGlothlin, *Baptist Confessions of Faith* (Valley Forge, Pa.: Judson Press, 1974).

15. Mitchell, 56.

16. This Baptist plea for the "crown rights of the Redeemer" over against the claims of bishop or magistrate is traced in virtually all of our histories of early English and American colonial Baptists.

5
The Discipline of the Church

by J. W. MacGorman

Admittedly the biblical concept of discipline included both instruction and training on the one hand and reproof and correction on the other. Its positive features centered on all the concerns pertinent to the constitution and maintenance of an orderly congregational life. How believers were related to each other as an expression of the body of Christ; how they comported themselves in the midst of a pagan society; how the ministries of the churches were organized and the ordinances were observed; how the essentials of the faith were formulated into confessional statements and their history—these were positive features of church discipline.

However, the New Testament reveals numerous instances in which doctrinal or moral errors threatened the integrity of gospel proclamation and compromised the character of believing communities. These evoked the negative disciplinary expressions of reproof and correction. For example, the Judaistic infiltration of the Galatian churches was denounced by Paul as a perversion of the gospel of Christ (Gal. 1:7). Again, the overclaim of glossolalic abusers and the overreaction against them in Corinth elicited from Paul a corrective statement regarding charismatic endowments (1 Cor. 12:1—14:40). It included specific instructions for the conduct of public worship (14:26-40).

With this acknowledgment of the broad scope of church discipline in the New Testament, the present study will focus primarily upon one passage, namely 1 Corinthians 5:1-13. Here the error confronted was a flagrant moral wrong that was being tolerated by the church; thus it required reproof and correction.

The Problem (vv. 1-2)

A man in the Corinthian church was living in an illicit sexual relationship with "his father's wife" (v. 1). That she was described in this way rather than as his mother makes it reasonable to assume that she was his stepmother. Evidently she was a pagan, for Paul did not include her in his instructions. Whether she were widowed, divorced, or separated from her husband is not indicated in the text, and no mention is made of her husband.

That both father and son should have sexual relations with the same woman was regarded as particularly scandalous. The Old Testament expressly forbade it in Leviticus 18:8, "You shall not uncover the nakedness of your father's wife; it is your father's nakedness" (RSV).[1] Moffatt's translation of this verse is more explicit, "You shall not have intercourse with any wife of your father; she belongs to your father." Likewise Roman law forbade such unions, even after the death of the father, as evidenced in the Institutes of Gaius.[2]

Some translations give the erroneous impression that this kind of incestuous relationship was never found in pagan society. For example, the *Revised Standard Version* renders 1 Corinthians 5:1; "It is actually reported that there is immorality among you, and of a kind that is not found even among pagans; for a man is living with his father's wife." (Cf. the NASB rendering of the clause in question, "and immorality of such a kind as does not exist even among the Gentiles.") However, it is doubtful that Paul intended to state that such sexual liaisons never occurred in ancient pagan society, but rather that they were generally condemned. Thus *The New English Bible* renders, "immorality such as even pagans do not tolerate." After all, if this kind of sexual wrong never occurred in the pagan world, it would scarcely have merited prohibition in a Roman code.[3]

And what was the attitude of the Corinthian church toward this flagrant sexual wrong in their midst that had gained such notoriety? Paul charged, "And you are arrogant!" (v. 2). The verb in this clause (*phusioo*) means literally "to be puffed up" with pride. It occurs only seven times in the New Testament, all in the letters of Paul—and six are in 1 Corinthians![4] It seems to be a word that came readily to Paul's mind when he thought of the Corinthians.

The reason for the Corinthians' arrogance was not specified. Some might claim that it derived from the same libertarian bent that Paul would challenge in 1 Corinthians 6:12, " 'All things are lawful for me,' but not all things are helpful. 'All things are lawful for me,' but I will not be enslaved by anything." However, Hans Conzelmann thinks not, saying, "A specific link between this case and the Corinthian slogan of freedom, that is to say a speculative ground for the incestuous man's behavior, is not suggested."[5]

More probably the answer is to be found in the carnality that rendered the Corinthians incapable of feeling either moral outrage or compassion. Earlier Paul had attributed their factionalism to their carnality, "But I, brethren, could not address you as spiritual men, but as men of the flesh, as babes in Christ" (1 Cor. 3:1). And with regard to the shameful immorality in their midst, it was not otherwise; for where a carnal spirit prevails, there is a remarkable insensitivity to sin of any stripe.

Be that as it may, grief, not arrogance, was the desired response of the church toward such shame, "Ought you not rather to mourn?" (v. 2). Who knows how many pagans in Corinth vilified the church and its message for tolerating this situation! As a wise preacher father said to me many years ago, "Some Christians are boasting about a broadened mind who should be weeping over a dying conscience." Besides, the situation was tragic for the two persons most intimately involved. For the Christian stepson it meant that the old fleshly nature had gained the upper hand, destroying his witness and bringing him under the judgment of God. For the pagan stepmother it meant further degradation, this time from the one who should have been God's most immediate person for leading her to experience saving faith.

The church in the midst of a pagan society can become increasingly insensitive to moral wrong. In this instance familiarity breeds complacency rather than contempt. The membership becomes shockproof as it tolerates vice. At any rate, Paul wrote this chapter of indictment to rebuke the church in Corinth for its casual attitude toward sexual sin, and he demanded that they take action against the offending member.

The Demand for Exclusion (vv. 3-5)

Though Paul was in Ephesus at the time he was writing this letter, he did not hesitate to pronounce judgment upon this shameful wrong (1 Cor. 16:8). This is noteworthy, because some church members will leave town to keep from taking a moral stand, whereas Paul didn't allow being out of town to keep him from taking one. He demanded that the church exclude the guilty man from its fellowship: "When you are assembled, and my spirit is present, with the power of our Lord Jesus, you are to deliver this man to Satan for the destruction of the flesh, that his spirit may be saved in the day of the Lord Jesus" (vv. 4-5).[6]

Certain features in this awesome instruction call for further comment. First, church discipline was to be accomplished in the name and through the power of Jesus Christ as Lord of the church (v. 4). Second, it was the responsibility of the entire congregation rather than of the leadership only (v. 4). This was not the kind of problem that could be turned over to a committee for resolution. It was a *body* problem, not simply an arm or a leg problem, and it required the participation of all members. Third, the discipline called for the exclusion of the offending member (v. 5). No corporal punishment was meted out such as Paul had suffered at the hands of the Jews on five different occasions (2 Cor. 11:24). Rather church discipline in the New Testament usually took the form of exclusion or a withdrawal of fellowship. And fourth, the purpose of church discipline was the ultimate reclamation of the offender (v. 5). It was redemptive in its intention and never merely punitive.

Paul's command "to deliver this man to Satan for the destruction of the flesh, that his spirit may be saved in the day of the Lord Jesus" (v. 5) requires some probing. What concept formed the background for his order to hand over the unrepentant wrongdoer to Satan? Evidently the church was a haven where believers enjoyed the protection and guardianship of Jesus Christ during their sojourn on earth. Outside of the church or in the world was the sphere in which Satan held sway. Thus C. K. Barrett comments, "To be excluded from the sphere in which Christ's work was operative was to be thrust back into that in which Satan still exercised authority."[7] Similarly John Calvin, arguing the sense of excommunication, added that "as Christ reigns *in* the Church, so Satan reigns *out of* the Church. "[8]

Now then, what did Paul mean by "the destruction of the flesh?" Some have concluded that the phrase denotes the death of the physical body. For example, Conzelmann writes, "The destruction of the flesh can hardly mean anything else but death (cf. 11:30)."[9] *The New English Bible* supports this sense by translating the passage, "this man is to be consigned to Satan for the destruction of the body." Robert G. Bratcher likewise understands "flesh" as synonymous with "body" and characterizes Satan's realm as one of sickness and death. He acknowledges that "this makes sense only on the supposition that such a death is different from the death that awaits all people, and it is probable that in the background of Paul's command is the belief that the world would end in that generation and Christians would not die (see 15:51-57)."[10]

Yet it seems more probable that Paul was using the term "flesh" metaphorically here to refer to the old nature that is dominated by sin. (Cf. Gal. 5:13,16-21; Rom. 8:5-8,12-13; Eph. 2:3; Col. 3:5-10). This was the nature that had gained the upper hand in the life of the offender and had led him into flagrant sexual wrong. By denying him the protected and protective company of the congregation and by thrusting him out into Satan's realm, it was hoped that the old fleshly nature would be destroyed. Sometimes it takes the *consequences* of sin to destroy the *attractiveness* of sin.

The desired end, of course, was that the man's spirit would be saved in the day of the Lord Jesus, or the eschatological judgment. William Baird comments, "The purpose of this drastic action is disciplinary—the destruction of the flesh and the salvation of the spirit. But since 'flesh' here is probably not to be taken literally, the destruction of the flesh may mean the annihilation of the power of sin."[11]

The Call to Cleansing and Celebration (vv. 6-8)

For the background to these verses one needs to turn to the Old Testament passages dealing with the observance of the Passover and the Feast of Unleavened Bread. The basic material is found in Exodus 12:1-51; Leviticus 23:4-8; and Deuteronomy 16:1-8.

During the original Passover meal in Egypt, unleavened bread was eaten with the roasted lamb and bitter herbs (Ex. 12:8). Simply made and quickly eaten, it was appropriate to the need for a hasty flight from the land of bondage. In subsequent commemorations of God's miraculous deliverance of His people, Israel was required to eat unleavened bread for the seven days following the Passover observance. Any person who ate leavened bread during this time was cut off from Israel (Ex. 12:15). For this reason great care was taken in Jewish homes to search out and dispose of the old leaven. Women examined cracks in their kneading boards to make sure that no undiscovered bit of fermented dough remained that could contaminate the new batch.

With these concepts in mind, Paul rebuked the Corinthians for their casual attitude toward the sexual sin of one of their members. He likened the presence of the immoral man in the church to the old leaven that would contaminate the whole batch of dough. Thus he chided and admonished, "Your boasting is not good. Do you not know that a little leaven leavens the whole lump?" (v. 6).

Chances are that the Corinthians would not have disputed the illustration that Paul used. No one needed to persuade them regarding the power of a small piece of fermented dough or leaven to permeate an entire batch of dough. In their homes they had observed the phenomenon many times. But they probably would have questioned the application that Paul made of the illustration. They might have pointed to the incestuous relationship as an isolated case and one that they themselves did not condone, thus it could not hurt them. But Paul was realistic about the contagiousness of evil. He knew that tolerated sin did not remain isolated sin; it was as pervasive as leaven. For when immorality is condoned in a church, the moral fiber of the entire congregation is weakened. None escapes its contamination, including the leadership of the church. The point of the illustration is that the *whole lump* is leavened.

Thus Paul issued to the morally lax Corinthians the call for cleansing, "Cleanse out the old leaven that you may be a new lump, as you really are unleavened. For Christ, our paschal lamb, has been sacrificed" (v. 7).

With Christ as the paschal lamb that had been sacrificed and with believers constituting the subsequent unleavened loaves that had been freshly cleansed, the call to celebration rightly followed. Thus Paul enjoined his readers, "Let us, therefore, celebrate the festival, not with the old leaven, the leaven of malice and evil, but with the unleavened bread of sincerity and truth" (v. 8).

Note here that the call to *celebration* is contingent upon the demand for *cleansing*. No church can celebrate the deliverance from sin that Christ has made possible through His sacrificial death on the cross while sheltering or condoning evil in its midst. It is no less true today than it was in ancient Corinth.

The Clarification of an Earlier Letter (vv. 9-13)

At this point Paul found it necessary to clear up a misunderstanding of an earlier letter he had sent to Corinth. From this we learn that 1 Corinthians was not Paul's first letter to the church he had founded there (1 Cor. 2:1-5; Acts 18:1-17).[12]

In this former correspondence Paul had urged the Corinthians not to continue in fellowship with immoral church members. However, they had understood him to say that they must withdraw from associations with all immoral persons in the world. Thus Paul corrected their misunderstanding, "I wrote to you in my letter not to associate with immoral men; not at all meaning the immoral of this world, or the greedy and robbers, or idolaters, since then you would need to go out of the world" (vv. 9-10). Then he reiterated his earlier instruction "not to associate with any one who bears the name of brother if he is guilty of immorality or greed, or is an idolater, reviler, drunkard, or robber—not even to eat with such a one" (v. 11). The church had the responsibility of self-judgment (v. 12), but the judgment of those outside the church was God's responsibility (v. 13).

Then for the fourth time in a brief chapter numbering thirteen verses, Paul demanded the exclusion of the immoral church member (vv. 2,5,7, and 13). The *Revised Standard Version* encloses the final injunction in verse 13 in quotation marks, "Drive out the wicked person from among you." Conzelmann describes these words as "a biblical formula from the realm of sacred law."[13] They may be found in passages like Deuteronomy 13:5; 17:7,12; 19:19; 21:21; 22:21; and 24:7.

Summary

It will prove helpful now to venture a summary of what 1 Corinthians 5:1-13 teaches about church discipline as expressed in reproof and correction.

First, It Was Not Exercised Over Trivialities (v. 1)

This passage dealt with an instance of flagrant sexual sin, one that even offended pagans. The wrong had a dimension too great to ignore or tolerate. It had to be recognized and confronted, for the credibility of the gospel message and the integrity of the believing community were at stake.

As Paul could not remain silent in Antioch when Peter withdrew from table-fellowship with Gentile converts (Gal. 2:11-14), so he could not remain silent regarding the shocking moral lapse being tolerated by the Corinthian church. There Peter and the Jewish believers who followed his disastrous example were indicted for not walking straightly toward the truth of the gospel (v. 14). The charge was hypocrisy, as fellowship with Gentile believers was denied by a frightened reversion to an outmoded Jewish traditionalism. Here the breach was moral rather than social, but it also compromised the truth of the gospel. The charge was arrogance or complacency, as fellowship was maintained with an incestuous member who flouted both explicit biblical teaching and pagan code.

Church history is replete with examples of discipline exercised over trifles or mere differences of opinion, more cultural than moral, regarding matters not essential to salvation. Certainly these have contributed to the negative feeling toward all church discipline that prevails in many quarters today.

Second, It Was Exercised by the Whole Church (vv. 4-5)

Paul did not denounce leadership only for the toleration of evil in the Corinthian church. Neither did he instruct leadership only regarding its removal. Rather he called for the entire congregation to assemble to deal with the problem. Though absent in body by virtue of his residence in Ephesus (1 Cor. 16:8), Paul stated that he would be present with them in spirit. Then in the mighty name of Jesus and with His power, the church was to act.

One may point to the difference between the house churches of Paul's day and the many large churches, numbering thousands of members, in our day as a reason why total church involvement is impossible. Yet when doctrinal error or moral wrong call for reproof and correction in our churches, the problem remains a body problem and requires a body solution.

Third, It Was Redemptive Rather than Punitive (v. 5)

As severe as the discipline was that Paul ordered for the Corinthian offender, the end sought was his ultimate salvation "in the day of the Lord Jesus."

This redemptive or restorative aspect of church discipline is found elsewhere in Paul's writings. For example, Galatians 6:1 reads, "Brethren, if a man is detected in any trespass, you who are spiritual, restore such a one in a spirit of gentleness, looking at yourself, lest you also be tempted" (*author's translation*).[14] The "any trespass" is appropriately inclusive and is better than a lengthy enumeration of wrongs that would inevitably omit some. Likewise it disallows a gradation of trespasses into a scale of those that are more and less forgivable. The "you who are spiritual" recognizes that church discipline is a spiritual function in congregational ministry. The singular form of the participle translated above as "looking at" represents a dramatic shift from the plural in the latter part of the verse.[15] It is difficult to indicate this shift in English translations, but the inference is that it behooves each one to be aware of his or her own vulnerability to temptation while administering church discipline. And finally the verb "restore" underscores the primary motivation in church discipline, namely, the restoration or reclaim of the offending member. The same verb is used in Mark 1:19 and Matthew 4:21 to describe James and John, the sons of Zebedee, mending nets in a boat with their father. It means restoring to wholeness that which has been torn, an apt figure to portray the remedial purpose of church discipline.

Here it would be salutary if the penal conceptions that have often attended church discipline could be retired from further use. Too often they conjure up visions of the accused standing before the bar of steely faced inquisitors, who pronounce varying sentences of imprisonment, exile, or even death. How much better it could be if the penal conceptions of church discipline would yield to the imagery of the emergency room of a hospital. No one resents a hospital for having an emergency-room service to take care of those who need immediate and urgent care. Admittedly church discipline regarded as punishment is well-served by the penal categories, but church discipline regarded as reclaim or restoration to wholeness of the offender is admirably served by the hospital imagery.

Fourth, It Was Realistic About the Contagiousness of Evil (vv. 6-7)

No leaven ever regards any part of the batter as off-limits. Though small in comparison to the lump of dough, leaven possesses an extraordinary pervasiveness that eventually permeates the entire mass: "Do you not know that a little leaven [ferments] the whole lump of dough?" (v. 6).

When this figure is applied to the condoning of evil in the life of a church, it is hard to accept. Some may even express an abhorrence of the evil in question as a proof of their invulnerability to its influence. In doing so, they have lost sight of the fact that a church by its very nature is the body of Christ, made up of individual members (1 Cor. 12:27). An interdependence prevails both at the point of function and malfunction: "If one member suffers, all suffer together; if one member is honored, all rejoice together" (1 Cor. 12:26).

As poison in a bloodstream eventually affects all parts of the body, so evil condoned in the life of a church eventually has consequences for all members, including the leaders. Batches of leavened dough do not come with sealed-off compartments.

Fifth, It Generally Called for Exclusion from the Church (vv. 2, 5, 11, and 13)

Four times in the thirteen verses of this chapter, Paul called for the exclusion of the incestuous member. In verse 2 he demanded, "Let him who has done this be removed from among you." In verse 5 he ordered, "You are to deliver this man to Satan for the destruction of the flesh, that his spirit may be saved in the day of the Lord Jesus." Again, in verse 7, "cleanse out the old leaven that you may be a new lump." And finally in verse 13, he reiterated, "Drive out the wicked person from among you."

In this instance Paul deemed exclusion to be necessary for the protection of the integrity of the church. C. K. Barrett concurs, "Any community inculcating moral standards (such as the primitive church and the Qumran sect) is bound to recognize a degree beyond which transgression of its code becomes intolerable because destructive of the foundations on which the community rests, so that exclusion becomes necessary."[16]

But a withdrawal of fellowship does not require a withdrawal of concern for the excluded member. Indeed, it is hoped that eventually the exclusion will serve the best interests of the offender by hastening his or her repentance and reclamation.

Conclusion

Many reasons are advanced today to account for the widespread abandonment of the New Testament practice of church discipline: (1) The well-documented abuses of the past, in which harsh and vindictive punishment was often meted out to those who deviated from established norms, has left a negative legacy. (2) The level of Christian commitment in our churches is so low that the capacity to administer discipline has been lost. (3) Large church memberships have made impossible the pastoral care that is prerequisite to consistent and salutary discipline. (4) The multiplicity of churches and denominations in our communities has made the withdrawal of fellowship improbable, for excluded members would be accepted readily into other congregations. (5) There is the desire to protect the innocent members of an offender's family. (6) In a society that has become increasingly litigious, there may be the fear of a lawsuit with a heavy indemnity.[17]

These observations and others that could be cited may be true, at least in part. However, before all responsibility for seeking and maintaining a disciplined church membership is shelved, some other considerations merit attention. For example, the failure to exercise and accept discipline in our churches encourages hypocrisy, both in those who perpetrate grievous wrong and in those who tolerate it. The shame quotient diminishes. Also, a church's failure to exercise discipline makes more difficult God's work of reclaiming the unrepentant offender. And again, when churches tolerate flagrant wrong in their members, it earns the rebuke of a lost world that is alienated from God and needs the gospel.

Notes

1. Unless noted otherwise, all quotations of the Bible in this chapter are taken from the *Revised Standard Version*.

2. Jean Hering, *The First Epistle of Saint Paul to the Corinthians,* trans. from the Second French Edition by A. W. Heathcote and P. J. Allcock (London: Epworth Press, 1962), 34.

3. The absence of a verb in the relative clause in question in 1 Corinthians 5:1 invites such diversities in translation.

4. The seven occurrences of *phusioo* are found in 1 Corinthians 4:6,18,19; 5:2; 8:1; 13:4; and Colossians 2:18.

5. Hans Conzelmann, *1 Corinthians, Hermeneia—A Critical and Historical Commentary on the Bible,* ed. George W. MacRae (Philadelphia: Fortress Press, 1975), 96.

6. The syntax of the two prepositional phrases in verse 4 is difficult to determine: "in the name of the Lord Jesus" and "with the power of our Lord Jesus." The words in verses 4-5 with which these phrases are to be construed are by no means obvious. This accounts for the variations in different translations of the passage. For an enumeration and critical assessment of the possible constructions, see Conzelmann, 97-98.

7. C. K. Barrett, *The First Epistle to the Corinthians, Harper's New Testament Commentaries,* ed. Henry Chadwick (New York: Harper & Row, Publishers, 1968), 126.

8. John Calvin, *Commentary on the Epistles of Paul the Apostle to the Corinthians,* trans. by the Reverend John Pringle (Grand Rapids: Wm. B. Eerdmans Publishing Company, 1948), 1:185.

9. Conzelmann, 97.

10. Robert G. Bratcher, *A Translator's Guide to Paul's First Letter to the Corinthians* (London: United Bible Societies, 1982), 44.

11. William Baird, *The Corinthian Church—A Biblical Approach to Urban Culture* (New York: Abingdon Press, 1964), 66.

12. Some scholars believe that at least a part of this earlier letter has been preserved in 2 Corinthians 6:14—7:1. They point out that the thought of 6:11-13 picks up nicely with that of 7:2-4.

13. Conzelmann, 102.

14. The verb translated "is detected" may carry the sense of "is overtaken," and is so understood in the *King James Version* and *Revised Standard Version*.

15. This adverbial participle may have an imperatival force derived from its relationship to the verb translated "restore." For examples, both the *Revised Standard Version* and *The New English Bible* render it "Look to."

16. Barrett, 123.

17. Findley B. Edge, *A Quest for Vitality in Religion* (Nashville: Broadman Press, 1963), 223-25, gives four reasons why church discipline is not practiced now: (1) because sin is so

prevalent in the lives of the members that we don't know where to begin; (2) because the practice of church discipline would disrupt the life of the church; (3) because there has been a revolt against the flagrant abuses associated with past efforts to maintain discipline; and (4) because members have a low or lax view of what it means to be the church in the world.

6
The Priesthood of All Believers

by Timothy George

It is ironic that the doctrine of the priesthood of all believers has displaced biblical inerrancy as the hottest item of dispute in the current SBC controversy.[1] Perhaps this is related to the fact that the term "inerrancy" has lost some of its polemical punch as it has become more widely acceptable. Inerrancy, of course, is not a term of recent vintage within the denomination. In a book entitled, *Baptist, Why and Why Not,* published by the Sunday School Board in 1900, J. M. Frost, then the corresponding secretary of the Board, wrote: "We accept the Scriptures as an all-sufficient and infallible rule of faith and practice, and insist upon the absolute inerrancy and sole authority of the Word of God."[2] Many, however, are still reluctant to use the term because of its political connotations or because of its presumed incompatibility with serious biblical scholarship.

The irony of the present dispute is that no one denies the priesthood of believers! What is at stake is how this principle is to be understood and how it is related to other, equally valid, doctrinal concerns. The squabble over pastoral authority, an important but separable issue, has obscured what is— or ought to be—the central focus of the debate, namely the quest for a proper balance between individual responsibility and theological integrity. The strategy of the present essay is first, to examine the relation between the priesthood of believers and the historic Baptist tenets of soul competency and religious liberty; then to probe the tension between confessional identity and hermeneutical autonomy, the so-called "right of private interpretation;" and, finally, to recall the original Reformation meaning of the priesthood of all believers in light of subsequent developments and present applications.

Soul Competency and Religious Liberty

Soul competency and religious liberty are important, historic Baptist principles, but they should not be equated with the priesthood of all believers. Soul competency, as stated by E. Y. Mullins, is based on the premise that all persons have an inalienable right of direct access to God. Put otherwise, all persons created in the image of God stand in a unique and inviolable relation to their Creator and, when quickened by divine grace, are fully "competent" or capable of responding to God directly.[3]

W. T. Conner spoke of "man's capacity for God," and earlier theologians related this dimension of the human self to one's ability to reason, make moral judgments, contemplate immortality and be awed by the grandeur and mystery of the universe.[4] Soul competency, in other words, is part of what it means for a human being to be created in the image of God.

In book 1 of his *Institutes of the Christian Religion*, John Calvin gave a classic interpretation of the innate knowledge of God which has been implanted in all persons. He referred to it variously as "an awareness of divinity," "the seed of religion" (*semen religionis*), and "the worm of conscience."[5] This "natural" capacity of the soul for God is the basis for the incurably religious bent of all human beings. Given the devastating effects of the fall, however, human religiousness can only issue in idolatry and self-centeredness apart from the interposition of God's grace. From the standpoint of soteriology, then, we should speak more accurately of "soul incompetence." However, as Paul declared in Romans 1 and 2, the awareness of God in every conscience is sufficiently clear to render every human being utterly inexcusable before the bar of divine judgment.

Soul competency means thus that *every* individual is responsible to God. This principle undergirds our evangelistic appeals for repentance and faith. There are no sponsors or proxies in the relation of the individual to God. As B. H. Carroll put it, "This is the first principle of New Testament law—to bring each naked soul face to face with God . . . O soul, thou art alone before God!"[6]

Soul competency pertains universally to all persons, not merely to Christians. Baptists, however, do not teach the "*priesthood* of all human beings." Priesthood applies only to those who, through repentance and faith, have been admitted into the covenant of grace and, consequently, have been made participants in the priestly ministry of their Mediator, Jesus Christ (i.e., to believers only). As we shall see, priesthood of believers is really a part of the doctrine of the church. It cannot be stretched into an anthropological generalization without doing great violence to its biblical and historic Reformation meaning.

Baptists have a splendid history as champions of religious liberty and the separation of church and state. Since God alone is Lord of the conscience, the temporal realm has no authority to coerce religious commitments. Seventeenth-century English Baptists were among the first advocates of absolute religious toleration. In his famous treatise, *The Mystery of Inquity*, Thomas Helwys addressed King James in 1612: "Let them be heretics,

Turks, Jews, or whatsoever, it appertains not to the earthly power to punish them."[7]

The Baptist commitment to religious liberty, however, has never been a pretext for doctrinal indifference or moral laxity. In 1689 the London Baptists published a *Second Confession* to show their hearty agreement with "that wholesome protestant doctrine . . . in all the fundamental articles of the Christian religion."[8] When, shortly thereafter, some Baptists abandoned their belief in the deity of Christ and became Unitarians, there was a major split in Baptist ranks. Even earlier, the *Standard Confession* of the General Baptists published in 1660, had juxtaposed a clear call for liberty of conscience with right of each congregation to maintain its doctrinal integrity. Thus article 24 asserts "that it is the will and mind of God (in these Gospel times) that all men should have the free liberty of their own consciences in matters of Religion, or Worship, without the least oppression, or persecution." This follows the admonition of article 17 that the true church should "reject all Hereticks" along with any others who teach "contrary to the Doctrine (of Christ) which they have learned."[9]

In America the Baptist plea for freedom of religion was furthered by Roger Williams who lambasted the "soul-murdering" magistrates of Massachusetts for their efforts to coerce religious uniformity in the Bay Colony. When he founded the colony of Rhode Island, Williams sought and secured laws against religious persecution. Yet there was hardly a more stubborn religious controversialist in all of New England than Roger Williams. He broke fellowship with Separatists of Plymouth because their Separatism was less strict than his; he refused to join the church in Boston because it would not publicly repent of ever having had fellowship with the (false!) Church of England; he excoriated the Quakers because of their doctrine of the "inner light" which, to his mind, undermined the necessity of grace. Edmund Morgan has said of Williams, "Most of his writings were demonstrations that other people were wrong."[10] The great apostle of religious liberty would be shocked to know that in some circles he is touted today as the progenitor of modern theological liberalism!

Religious liberty guarantees the ability of every congregation to order its own internal life, its doctrine and discipline, in accordance with its own perception of divine truth. It requires that there be no external political monitoring of the internal religious life of voluntary associations. Practically, this means that heresy is always possible and that spiritual vigilance is a constant necessity. Thus, priesthood of believers does not mean, "I am a priest. I can believe anything I want to." Among other things, it means rather, "As a priest in a convenanted community of believers, I must be alert to keep my congregation from departing from 'the faith once for all delivered to the saints' " (Jude 3).

Individual Responsibility and Theological Integrity

One of the greatest advances in Christian history was the translation and dissemination of Holy Scripture in the language of the common people. The legacy of an open Bible means that every believer has both the right and the responsibility to search the Scriptures diligently and follow their counsel obediently.

While studying his New Testament, the young Congregational missionary, Adoniram Judson, became convinced that infant baptism was unscriptural. Forthwith he became a Baptist! We applaud Judson's discovery, but the "right of private interpretation" can also lead in the opposite direction. In the nineteenth century, not a few Baptists became convinced, through their sincere study of the Bible, of the eventual salvation of all persons. Many of them became in fact Universalists. More recently, a Baptist leader in another country openly questioned the reality of the incarnation, comparing belief in the deity of Christ to a child's belief in the tooth fairy.[11] In neither of these examples did anyone deny outright the authority of the Bible. In both cases, however, the conclusions arrived at could not be squared with, to quote the preamble to *The Baptist Faith and Message,* "certain definite doctrines that Baptists believe, cherish, and with which they have been and are now closely identified."[12]

The issue is *not* the right of every individual believer to worship God and interpret Scripture according to the dictates of his own conscience. No one has spoken more eloquently to this principle than George W. Truett in his 1939 address to the Baptist World Alliance: "For any person or institution to dare to come between the soul and God is a blasphemous impertinence."[13] No *true* Baptist has ever denied that! What is at stake is the right of a *community* of believer-priests, whether local congregation, association, state or national convention, to define for itself, under the leadership of the Holy Spirit, the acceptable doctrinal perimeters of its own fellowship.

Baptists have never been *creedalistic* in the sense of placing man-made doctrinal constructs above the Holy Scripture. To my knowledge, no Baptist body has ever put forth a confession of faith which claimed to be infallible or beyond revision. The preamble to *The Baptist Faith and Message* states explicitly: "As in the past so in the future Baptists should hold themselves free to revise their statements of faith as may seem to them wise and expedient at any time."[14] If we take seriously the Reformation principle of *sola Scriptura,* we must see our confessional standards as derivative documents. We must be ready always to measure them by Holy Writ as by a touchstone.

Historically, Baptists have often recoiled from the very word *creed* because of its association with the ecclesiastico-political repression of religious dissent. Doubtless this is what W. B. Johnson, the first president of the Southern Baptist Convention, had in mind when he referred in 1845 to "a Baptist aversion to all creeds but the Bible."[15] In fact, it was unnecessary for the nascent Convention to adopt a specific theological standard because of the overwhelming doctrinal consensus which prevailed among the messengers, most of whom belonged to congregations which adhered to the *Philadelphia Confession of Faith*, an American adaptation of the 1689 *Second London Confession*.

A few years later, however, James Petrigru Boyce, in setting forth the rationale for Southern Baptists' first theological seminary, insisted that each professor subscribe to a set of doctrinal principles. Moreover, Boyce insisted, "His agreement with the standard should be exact. His declaration of it should be based upon no mental reservation, upon no private understanding with those who immediately invest him into office."[16] Boyce was well aware that there were those who felt that such a policy of strict subscription was a violation of academic freedom and liberty of conscience, but he urged its adoption nonetheless:

> You will infringe the rights of no man, and you will secure the rights of those who have established here an instrumentality for the production of a sound ministry. It is no hardship to those who teach here, to be called upon to sign the declaration of their principles, for there are fields of usefulness open elsewhere to every man, and none need accept your call who cannot conscientiously sign your formulary.[17]

Boyce related the reluctance of some Baptists to adopt a specific doctrinal standard to the influence of Alexander Campbell whose slogan of "no creed but the Bible" had lured many Baptists away from their traditional confessional moorings.[18] Campbell had decried the use of confessions as an infringement upon the rights of conscience. Boyce, however, in a brilliant rebuttal, traced the history of confessional statements from New Testament times down to his own day. He showed that Baptists in particular had been prolific in promulgating confessions, both as public declarations of their own faith and as a means of testing the true faith in others. He later recalled, "It was with great difficulty, at first, that some of the members of the Convention were led to vote for what they called a Creed. But it was manifest that some such provision ought to exist."[19]

At strategic points in their history, Baptist have not hesitated to identify themselves with the great truths of historic evangelical theology, and to do so explicitly. In the first decades of the twentieth century, radical biblical criticism had led to an undermining of the basic truths of the gospel itself.

Aware of this encroachment in many of the mainline denominations, E. Y. Mullins, who can hardly be labeled a "fundamentalist," declared before the Southern Baptist Convention in 1923:

> We record again our unwavering adherence to the supernatural elements in the Christian religion. The Bible is God's revelation of himself through man moved by the Holy Spirit. Jesus Christ was born of the Virgin Mary through the power of the Holy Spirit. He was the divine and eternal Son of God. He wrought miracles, healing the sick, casting out demons, raising the dead. He died as the vicarious atoning Savior of the world and was buried. He rose again from the dead. The tomb was emptied of its contents. In his risen body he appeared many times to his disciples. He ascended to the right hand of the Father. He will come again in person, the same Jesus who ascended from the Mount of Olives. We believe that adherence to the above truths and facts is a necessary condition of service for teachers in our Baptist schools.[20]

Mullins's call for conscientious adherence to the "supernatural elements" of the Christian kerygma does not violate the priesthood of believers, any more than the New Testament's designation of the denial of the incarnation as anti-Christian (1 John 4:3) nullifies soul competency. Every Christian remains free to interpret the Bible as he believes he is led by the Holy Spirit. The doctrine of religious liberty declares that penal measures must not be used by the civil authorities to enforce belief. But it also implies that the church must be free to define and maintain the boundaries of its own fellowship. A church which is unable to do this or, even worse, no longer thinks it is worth doing, is a church which has lost its soul.

Where and how do we draw the boundaries? Undoubtedly, this is one of the most delicate tasks the church faces. We can err either by drawing the boundaries too tightly, or by refusing to draw them at all. On the one hand, we lapse into legalism; on the other, into relativism. For example, most Southern Baptists would not be willing to make agreement on the details of a particular hermeneutic of eschatology, say, pretribulational premillennialism, a binding test of fellowship. But can—or should—we accept as tolerable the demythologization of the *Parousia* which reduces the return of Christ to a nonevent? Must we allow under the umbrella of acceptable diversity a "process" view of God which denies His very omnipotence, or a radical historicist reading of the Bible which minimizes the miraculous, or a liberationist interpretation of salvation history which levels the lordship of Jesus Christ? It is the role of a proper and faithful theology, that is to say, a biblical and evangelical theology, to help the church answer these questions. The proclamation of the whole counsel of God involves identifying and saying "no" to those forms of teaching which, if carried out consistently, would threaten the truth of divine revelation itself. Karl Barth was surely right when he said: "If we do not have the confidence of *damnamus*, we ought to omit *credimus*, and go back to doing theology as usual."[21] While pastors and teachers have a special responsibility to guard with care that which has been committed to their trust (1 Tim. 6:20), in the final analysis this is the task of the entire community of faith and not merely one segment of it. Indeed, this is one of the salient features of the Reformation doctrine of the priesthood of all believers.

Priesthood of Believers—The Reformation Model

The priesthood of all believers was a cardinal principle of the Reformation of the sixteenth century. It was used by the Reformers to buttress an evangelical understanding of the church over against the clericalism and sacerdotalism of medieval Catholicism. In modern theology, however, the ecclesial context of this Reformation principle has been almost totally eclipsed. For example, in the current Southern Baptist debate on the issue, both sides have referred (uncritically) to the "priesthood of *the believer*." The Reformers talked instead of the "priesthood of all believers" (plural). For them it was never a question of a lonely, isolated seeker of truth, but rather of a band of faithful believers united in a common confession as a local, visible *congregatio sanctorum*.

The modern reinterpretation of the Reformation goes back to the philsopher Hegel who saw Luther as the great champion of human freedom whose stand against medieval obscurantism signaled the dawn of modern civilization. With Friedrich Schleiermacher and "the turn to the subject" in theology, Luther became more and more the hero of modern rugged individualism. Consequently, the doctrine of the priesthood of all believers degenerated into the ideology of "every tub sitting on its own bottom."

In this context the concepts of priesthood of believers and soul competency were conflated, the one become virtually interchangeable with the other. Winthrop S. Hudson, one of the most percpetive interpreters of Baptist history, has pointed to the devastating impact of this development on Baptist ecclesiology:

> To the extent that Baptists were to develop an apologetic for their church life during the early decades of the twentieth century, it was to be on the basis of this highly individualistic principle. It has become increasingly apparent that this principle was derived from the general cultural and religious climate of the nineteenth century rather than from any serious study of the Bible. . . . The practical effect of the stress upon "soul competency" as the cardinal doctrine of Baptists was to make every man's hat his own church.[22]

The appeal to individual experience and private judgment—traditionally both suspect categories in Christian theology!—corresponded to the shift away from biblical authority and the dogmatic consensus of historic Christianity. It also produced a truncated and perverted version of what Luther and the other Reformers intended when they formulated the doctrine of the spiritual priesthood of all believers.

Paul Althaus, the great interpreter of Luther's theology, explains the original Reformation meaning of this term:

> Luther never understands the priesthood of all believers merely in the sense of the Christian's freedom to stand in a direct relationship to God without a human mediator. Rather he constantly emphasizes the Christian's evangelical authority to come before God on behalf of the brethren and also of the world. The universal priesthood expresses not religious individualism but its exact opposite, the reality of the congregation as a community.[23]

Of course, Luther *did* believe that all Christians had direct access to God without recourse to "the tin gods and buffoons of this world, the pope with his priests."[24] But for Luther the priesthood of all believers did not mean, "I am my own priest." It meant rather: in the community of saints, God has so tempered the body that we are all priests to each other.[25] We stand before God and intercede for one another, we proclaim God's Word to one another and celebrate His presence among us in worship, praise, and fellowship. Moreover, our priestly ministry does not terminate upon ourselves. It propels us into the world in service and witness. It constrains us to "shew forth the praises of him who has called [us] out of darkness into his marvellous light" (1 Pet. 2:9).

Priesthood of believers, then, has more to do with the Christian's service than with his status. One function Luther specifies as incumbent upon all believer-priests is that of "a guardian or watchman on the tower" (*warttman odder welcher auff der Wart*).

> This is exactly what one calls someone who lives in a tower to watch and to look out over the town so that fire or foe do not harm it. Therefore, every minister . . . should be . . . an overseer or watchman, so that in his town and among his people the gospel and faith in Christ are built up and win out over foe, devil, and heresy.[26]

According to Luther, then, the priesthood of all believers, far from providing a cover for individual doctrinal error, is a stimulus for defending the church against those forces which would weaken and destroy it.

John Calvin interpreted the priesthood of all believers in terms of the church's threefold participation in Christ's prophetic, kingly, and priestly ministry. Specifically, every Christian is mandated to be a representative Christ in his redemptive outreach to the world. "All believers . . . should seek to bring others [into the church], should strive to lead the wanderers back to the road, should stretch forth a hand to the fallen and should win over the outsiders."[27]

The priesthood of believers is not a prerogative on which we can rest; it is a commission which sends us forth into the world to exercise a priestly ministry not for ourselves, but for others—"the outsiders"—not instead of Christ, but for the sake of Christ and His behest.

For Calvin, the priesthood of all believers was not only a spiritual privilege, but it was also a moral obligation and a personal vocation. Cyril Eastwood, the great Methodist scholar whose book on the priesthood of believers is one of the few comprehensive treatments of the theme, lamented the distortion of this tremendous evangelical imperative:

> The common error that the phrase "Priesthood of Believers" is synonymous with "private judgment" is most unfortunate and is certainly a misrepresentation. . . . Of course, the Reformers emphasized "private judgment," but it was always "informed" judgment, and it was always controlled, checked, and corroborated by the testimony of the congregation. Indeed Calvin himself fully realized that uncontrolled private judgment means subjectivism, eccentricity, anarchy, and chaos.[28]

Given our commitment to religious liberty, Baptists cannot approve Calvin's method of dealing with the excesses of uncontrolled private judgment, as evidenced by his acquiescence in the execution of Michael Servetus who had repudiated the Christian doctrine of the Trinity. At the same time, we can and should recognize the danger which such teaching poses to the life of the church. We should not invite Servetus to become the pastor of our church or a professor in our seminary! To do so would violate the integrity of our Christian faith. It would also be an abdication of our responsibility in the priesthood of all believers.

No one should deny the importance of the doctrine of the priesthood of all believers. It is a precious and irreducible part of our Reformation heritage and our Baptist legacy. But let no one trivialize its meaning by equating it with modern individualism or theological minimalism. It is a call to ministry and service; it is a barometer of the quality of our life together in the Body of Christ and of the coherence of our witness in the world for which Christ died.

Notes

1. The 1988 SBC resolution on "Priesthood of the Believer" provoked a firestorm of controversy. Among the many discussions in Baptist state papers, see Vernon Davis, "Southern Baptists and 'Priesthood,' " *Florida Baptist Witness*, July 14, 1988, and Timothy George, "Priesthood of the Believers—Refocusing the Debate," *Florida Baptist Witness*, October 1988. See also Walter B. Shurden, *Priesthood of Believers* (Nashville: Convention Press, 1987).

2. J. M. Frost, "Introduction," *Baptist, Why and Why Not* (Nashville: Sunday School Board of the SBC, 1900), 12.

3. Mullins referred to soul competency as the "religious axiom" and regarded it as the basis

for the Baptist rejection of infant baptism. E. Y. Mullins, et al., *The Faith and Its Furtherance* (Nashville: Broadman Press, 1936), 51-64.

4. W. T. Conner, *Christian Doctrine* (Nashville: Broadman Press, 1937), 17. Cf. the following statement by James P. Boyce: "The recognition and contemplation of such a [self-existent spirit, infinite, eternal, and unchangeable] . . . awaken reverence and fear . . . and lead men everywhere, when in danger or distress, to call upon God . . . ." *Abstract of Systematic Theology* (Philadelphia: American Baptist Publication Society, 1899), 30. See also Alvah Hovey, *Manual of Christian Theology* (New York: Silver, Burdett, and Co., 1900), 33-40.

5. John Calvin, *Institutes of the Christian Religion,* eds. John T. McNeill and Ford Lewis Battles (Philadelphia: Westminster Press, 1960), 43-51 [I. 3-4].

6. B. H. Carroll, *Baptist and Their Doctrines* (New York: Fleming Revell, 1913), 15-16.

7. Thomas Helwys, *A Short Declaration of the Mystery of Iniquity* (London: 1612), 46. For a fuller treatment of Helwys in the context of the early Baptist literature of toleration, see Timothy George, "Between Pacifism and Coercion: The English Baptist Doctrine of Religious Toleration," *Mennonite Quarterly Review* 58 (1984): 30-49.

8. W. L. Lumpkin, ed. *Baptist Confessions of Faith* (Valley Forge, Pa: Judson Press, 1959), 245.

9. Ibid., 230-32.

10. Edmund S. Morgan, *Roger Williams: The Church and the State* (New York: Harcourt, Brace and World, 1967), 28. Morgan, along with Perry Miller in his *Roger Williams: His Contribution to the American Tradition,* has attempted to rescue Williams from the modern liberal historians who read their own agenda back into his life. Along this line, Conrad Wright has placed Williams's debate with John Cotton in its proper seventeenth-century context. See his "John Cotton Washed and Made White," in *Continuity and Discontinuity in Church History: Essays Presented to George Huntston Williams,* eds. F. F. Church and Timothy George (Leiden: E. J. Brill, 1979), 338-50.

11. H. Leon McBeth, *The Baptist Heritage* (Nashville: Broadman Press, 1987), 517-18.

12. Herschel H. Hobbs, *The Baptist Faith and Message* (Nashville: Broadman Press, 1987).

13. Quoted, J. M. Dawson, *Baptists and the American Republic* (Nashville: Broadman Press, 1956), 221.

14. Hobbs, *Faith and Message,* 3.

15. *Proceedings of the Southern Baptist Convention, 1845* (Richmond: H. K. Ellyson, 1845), 19.

16. James P. Boyce, *Three Changes in Theological Institutions* (Greenville: C. J. Elford's Book and Job Press, 1856), 35.

17. Ibid., 44.

18. John A. Broadus, *Memoir of James P. Boyce* (New York: Armstrong and Son, 1893), 140. Thomas J. Nettles, "Creedalism, Confessionalism, and the Baptist Faith and Message," in *The Unfettered Word,* ed. Robison B. James (Waco: Word Books, 1987), 138-54, has shown how deeply rooted in Southern Baptist history is the appeal to clear confessional guidelines. For example, he quotes B. H. Carroll who declared "The modern cry, 'Less creed and more liberty,' is a degeneration from the vertebrate to the jellyfish, and means less unity and less morality, and it means more heresy . . . . It is a positive and very hurtful sin to magnify liberty at the expense of doctrine." Nettles, 148. Walter B. Shurden, on the other hand, has interpreted the growing confessional consciousness in Southern Baptist life as a threat to traditional Baptist freedoms. See his "The Problem of Authority in the Southern Baptist Convention," *Review and Expositor* 75 (1978): 219-33. A similar opinion is expressed by John J. Hurt: "Should Southern Baptists Have a Creed/Confession?—No!" *Review and Expositor* 76 (1979): 85-88.

19. James P. Boyce, "The Doctrinal Position of the Seminary," *Western Recorder,* June 20, 1874.

20. *Annual,* Southern Baptist Convention, 1923.

21. *Church Dogmatics* I/1, 630. For a fuller statement of the role of theology in this process, see Timothy George, "Dogma Beyond Anathema: Historical Theology in the Service of the

Church," *Review and Expositor* 84 (1987): 691-713.

22. *Baptist Concepts of the Church,* ed. Winthrop S. Hudson (Chicago: Judson Press, 1959), 215-16.

23. Paul Althaus, *The Theology of Martin Luther* (Philadelphia: Fortress Press, 1966), 314.

24. *LW* 36, 140.

25. Carlyle Marney, not known for his traditionalism, understood correctly the communal character of Luther's emphasis: "There, where you and *they* are—you, all of you, are the ministry of the Word. This does not mean that you are competent to deal with God for yourself. It means rather that you are competent and responsible to deal with God and for the neighbor. It was a gross perversion of the gospel that inserted a bastard individualism here and then taught us that the believer's priesthood meant that 'every tub must set [sic] on its own bottom.' " *Priests to Each Other* (Valley Forge, Pa.: Judson Press, 1974), 12.

26. *LW* 39, 154-55. This quotation is from Luther's "Answer to the Hyperchristian, Hyperspiritual, and Hyperlearned Book by Goat Emser in Leipzig" (1521) which contains his fullest development of the doctrine of the priesthood of all believers.

27. *Calvin's Commentaries,* eds. David W. Torrance and Thomas R. Torrance (Grand Rapids: Eerdmans, 1963), 12:144; *Comm.* Heb. 10:25. Compare also Thomas F. Torrance's *Royal Priesthood* (Edinburgh: Oliver and Boyd, 1955).

28. Cyril Eastwood, *The Priesthood of all Believers* (Minneapolis: Augsburg Publishing House, 1960), 80. The renowned Baptist theologian, Russell Aldwinclke, made a similar point in his address on "The Nature and Purpose of Our Freedom," which he delivered at the Baptist World Alliance meeting in 1965. "Yet in our claims to freedom . . . Baptists need to be on guard against a serious misunderstanding of the priesthood of all believers as this was understood by the Protestant Reformers. When Peter applies the phrase 'an holy priesthood' (1 Pet. 2:5) to the whole body of believing Christians, he reminds us that we are priests only as members of the Christian fellowship. The priesthood of all believers does not mean only the right to private judgment and intellectual freedom, which Socrates and Bertrand Russell would also stoutly maintain, but the freedom within the community of believers to be, as Luther said, Christ to our neighbor, to show forth the special kind of love and compassion which flows from Christ and works in those who are members of His body, the church. When we assert freedom from priestly dominance in a sacramental sense, we are not claiming freedom of thought necessarily in a general sense, though this may be important even to Christians. We are claiming freedom to love, as Christ loved, all those for whom He died, and claiming this freedom as members of His fellowship of believers. In repudiating a certain understanding of the church, we are not repudiating entirely the importance of the church as the redeemed community through which God works." Walter B. Shurden, ed., *The Life of Baptists in the Life of the World* (Nashville: Broadman Press, 1985), 214.

Part 2
Biblical Images

The apostle Peter applied to the New Testament Church terms used in the Old Testament for the people of God (1 Pet. 2). This application raises the question of the relationship between the church and Israel. The first essay, written by Old Testament scholar Walter C. Kaiser, Jr., wrestles with the issue of "Israel as the People of God" and the relationship of the church to the Old Testament people. Kaiser examines these issues and discusses dispensational and covenantal approaches, thus providing the groundwork for the following five New Testament essays.

James A. Brooks and Beverly C. Brooks combine to look at "Images of the Church in the Synoptic Gospels." According to Matthew, the only Gospel to use the word "church," the origin of the church goes back to Jesus Himself (Matt. 16:18). The authors focus on the historical issues surrounding this foundational passage and the relationship of the church to Jesus' overall message of the kingdom of God. Gerald L. Borchert also investigates the words of Jesus, describing the "Images of the Church in John." The "upper room discourse" (John 13—17) provides the source for the major section of Borchert's contribution.

The question of the catholicity of the early church remains a pressing concern in New Testament studies. This matter and other historical questions are clearly addressed by Carey C. Newman in the chapter on the "Images of the Church in Acts." The New Testament speaks of the church as a living organism of persons closely related to Christ and to one another. A variety of images were used by Paul and the authors of the General Epistles to describe the life of the church. Among nearly one hundred that can be identified in the New Testament, these images include: "the body of Christ," "the temple of the Holy Spirit," "the fellowship of the Holy Spirit," "the pillar of truth," and "the household of God." Robert B. Sloan and Marty L. Reid illustrate the theological dimensions of these images in their essays on the "Images of the Church in Paul" and the "Images of the Church in the General Epistles."

Since the Bible is the final authority in all matters of faith and practice for those in the Believers' Church tradition, this important section is paramount for the Believers' Church vision. While the metaphorical images surveyed in this section may not be intended to be interpreted literally, it is nevertheless imperative to recognize that their meanings must be taken seriously.

7
Israel as the People of God

by Walter C. Kaiser, Jr.

No statement of the doctrine of the church or the doctrine of salvation can claim to be complete, much less Pauline or even biblical, if it fails to integrate the theme of ethnic Israel into its theology. Israel continues to be one of the greatest stumbling stones for contemporary biblical theologies even after we have mastered the lessons of the post-Marcionite age and Auschwitz. Moreover, two of the most startling events in recent history have given new urgency to the study of the place of Israel in theology and the history of ideas: the holocaust of Nazi Germany and the unprecedented reestablishment of the State of Israel on May 14, 1948.

The Question of Israel

In one form or another, most theologies of the church have wrestled with the question of Israel. All will concede that the roots of our Christian faith are firmly embedded in Jewish origins. The Jewish people are accorded the courtesy of being labeled the "People of the Book." But frequently that is the end of the matter.

What is the proper way to treat Israel, the Jews, and the question of the "People of God?" Shall we clearly distinguish the people of the book from the people of God? Or shall we replace Israel with the church?

The first option is clearly seen in Charles C. Ryrie. He asked,

> What, then, is the *sine qua non* of dispensationalism? . . . A dispensationalist keeps Israel and the Church distinct . . . This is probably the most basic theological test of whether or not a man is a dispensationalist, and it is undoubtedly the most practical and conclusive.[1]

The second option is generally associated with covenant theology (though there are major exceptions even within this group). In this view the church replaces Israel and continues all of the spiritual aspects of the ancient promises made to ethnic Israel. William E. Cox explained it this way:

> The Old Testament records two kinds of promises which God made to national Israel: national promises and spiritual promises. The spiritual promises encompassed every spiritual descendant of Abraham, and were not restricted

to national Israel (Gen. 12:3; 22:18; Rom. 2:28-29; 4:17; Eph. 2:11-16; 3:6-9; Phil. 3:3; Col. 2:11). The spiritual promises still are being fulfilled through the church today. Israel's national promises all have been either fulfilled or invalidated because of unbelief.[2]

A mediating view has proposed what we believe is the solution to the tension raised in the preceding two options. It agrees with dispensationalism's point that God is not finished with Israel as yet, therefore the so-called national promises, so deeply embedded in the spiritual promises, are part of God's design for the present and the future. But this mediating view also agrees with the point made by covenant theology that there is only one "People of God" in both Testaments. George E. Ladd has set this position forth in a new way:

> There is therefore but one people of God. This is not to say that the Old Testament saints belonged to the Church and that we must speak of the Church in the Old Testament . . . The Church properly speaking had its birthday on the day of Pentecost, for the Church is composed of all those who by one Spirit have been baptized into one body (1 Cor. 12:13), and this baptizing work of the Spirit began on the day of Pentecost.
> While we must therefore speak of Israel and the Church, we must speak of only one people of God.[3]

But how does one go about demonstrating that this mediating view is the view that a consistent biblical theology would endorse? It will be necessary to examine the New Testament usage of "Israel," "Israel of God," and "people" or "people of God." We must also examine two of the main teaching blocks of text on this question: Romans 9—11 and the use of Amos 9:11-12 in the Acts 15 dispute over what constituted the people of God.

The Israel of God

Replacement theologians (if we may playfully use that term for most covenant theologians) state quite straightforwardly that the church is the new Israel. In fact, so confident are most in this school that the terms "Israel" and "church" are used interchangeably in their writings. But was the New Testament the source of this confidence?

The New Testament does employ the term "Israel" seventy-three times. However, from this long list, replacement theologians have only pointed to three passages to demonstrate the church equals Israel equation (viz., Rom. 9:6; 11:26; and Gal. 6:16). Only the Galatians passage is appealed to by all replacement theologians, a fact that underscores that the two Romans passages are seen even by many covenant theologians as descriptive of ethnic Israel alone.

Romans 9:6 affirms: "For not all who are descended from Israel are Israel." Paul is not distinguishing between Jews and Gentiles or between Israel and the church. Instead, he is distinguishing between Jews who believe in the Messiah and those who do not! Those descended from Israel include all the physical lineage of Abraham, Isaac, and Jacob (i.e., all Jews). But within the nation of Israel and within the scattered ethnic group of Jewish people around the world are those Jews who believe. This is the "Israel" God had intended. It is the group of believers within that nation who go beyond physical descent only and partake by faith of the promises of God. That is the point of the two illustrations that follow in Romans 9:7-9. Ishmael could claim physical descent from Abraham, but Isaac had more than that: he was the son of promise as well!

What about Romans 11:26? "And so all Israel will be saved." Some are so puzzled by Paul's declaration that "all Israel" will be saved that the only way they feel they can salvage anything that is consistent with the rest of Scripture is to equate "all Israel" with the elect of God in the church. Others misinterpret verse 26 to mean that all Jews will be saved eventually and thus Jewish evangelism and missions to the Jewish people are unnecessary. But Paul did not mean all Jews of all times; he referred only to the Jews living at the time he was discussing in this key passage. This number must also be balanced off against "the full number of the Gentiles" that must first come to Christ. God does have a "complete number" or a set number of Gentiles that He has in mind who will share in the promises first made with the patriarchs. Only after this has been achieved, and after the Jewish people have been provoked to jealousy, will "all Israel" be saved. The "all" of this passage should be handled in the same manner as the "all the world should be taxed" of Luke 2:1 (KJV), or as "all Israel came out of Egypt" in the exodus. It certainly speaks of the overwhelming multitude of those worlds of reference. Thus the reference is to a collective "all" meaning the greater majority, but not every single individual.

The case for finding in the New Testament places where Israel is replaced by the church depends on Galatians 6:16, for none of the other seventy-two passages where "Israel" is used in the New Testament will demonstrate this alleged equation. The text reads, "Peace and mercy to all who follow this rule, even to the Israel of God."

The whole case for the equation of Israel and the Church rests on the Greek conjunction *kai* meaning "and." It is clear that the *New International Version* (NIV) has understood *kai* in its secondary and lesser meaning of "even." However, this seems dubious, for if Paul had wished to identify the Christian church with the "Israel of God," then the best way to accomplish that would have been to omit the *kai* altogether and to allow the phrase "Israel of God" to stand in apposition to the preceding clause. Furthermore, since this is the only instance out of seventy-three New Testament usages where "Israel" is alleged to be equal to the church, it makes it all the more suspect to establish this equation on a verse that may well be translated as "And as many as shall live by this rule, peace be on them and mercy, and on the Israel of God." In verse 15 of Galatians 6, Paul had summarized his case against those Judaizers who were demanding that Gentiles must attain their salvation by adhering to the law of Moses. Salvation would be by faith alone. Paul concluded by pronouncing a blessing on the two groups who would follow this rule: (1) the "them" (v. 16, KJV), Gentile Christians, and (2) the "Israel of God." Therefore, it is impossible to call the church a "spiritual Israel" or a "new Israel." "Israel" in the New Testament is used of the Jewish nation or the Jewish people as a whole, but never of the church or of the Gentile believers.

The People of God

One of the most frequently repeated formulas of the promise theme found in both Testaments in over fifty instances is the tripartite formula, "I will be your God, you shall be my people and I will dwell in the midst of you."[4] It is the middle assertion of this threefold statement that supplies the great continuity term for the single "people of God/the Lord" in both Testaments. This covenant formula is one of the most important confessional statements in the entire Bible. Both Israel in the Old Testament and the believing church in the New Testament are declared to form the one continuous body. Thus, while Israel has not been replaced by the church, believing Israel and a believing church both share incorporation into the "people of God."

The biblical idea of the "people of God" finds its first formal expression in the Book of Exodus. Previously in the patriarchal narratives God had revealed Himself as in the character and nature (*beth essentiae*) of El Shaddai (the God of miracle-working power). But now in the exodus and wilderness experience, as the enlarged family prepared for nationhood, God would reveal Himself in the character and nature of Yahweh (the God who would be there; Ex. 6:3). Besides connecting the patriarchal and exodus periods together, the text of Exodus adds to the declaration of Genesis that God would be a personal deity to Abraham, Isaac, and Jacob, the fact that Israel would be His "son" (Ex. 4:22-23), His "people" and "[special] possession" (Ex. 19:5-6). To receive the entitlement of "my people" meant more than a mere ethnic social designation. They would be God's "[choice], treasured possession" (*segullah,* Ex. 19:5), that is, His moveable treasure as opposed to real estate, which could not be moved about.

This uniquely owned, treasured, and holy possession was destined to be a

royal priesthood composed of the entire congregation. While the whole
world belonged to the Lord, in the midst of these nations God had placed
Israel with the special responsibility of being His people with all the rights
and duties pertaining thereto.[5]

In spite of the fact that the term "people of God" referred predominantly
to the Israelites throughout the Old Testament, it was not limited to them.
In the messianic times, "Many nations will be joined with the Lord in that
day and will become my people" (Zeph. 2:11, author). Isaiah likewise looks
forward to the day when the Lord Himself will say not just of Israel, but
also of others, "Blessed be Egypt my people, Assyria my handiwork and
Israel my inheritance" (Isa. 19:24-25). Had not Solomon prayed at the dedication of his temple that "all the peoples of the earth may know your name
and fear you, as do your own people Israel" (1 Kings 8:43)? Thus, even
before New Testament times the concept of the people of God encompassed
both believing Israel and those believing outside of that nation.

In the New Testament the term *ekklesia,* "church," became the more
usual designation for the Christians. The term "people of God" still retained its importance, but it was mostly in connection with the Old Testament roots of the church. In fact, those who believed in Christ were called
"Abraham's seed" (Gal. 3:29), "like Isaac" (Gal. 4:28). Similar to Israel,
Christians were called "a chosen people, a royal priesthood, a holy nation, a
people belonging to God" (1 Pet. 2:9), "a people that are his very own"
(Titus 2:14).

It is clear from these New Testament citations of Old Testament texts
that in some very real way, believing Israel shared with the believing church
its unique status of peoplehood. Nevertheless, the Gentiles no more ceased
to be *ethne,* "Gentiles" when they were incorporated into the church than
did Israel cease to be Jewish. Even though the "middle wall of partition"
had been broken down in Christ (Eph. 2:14, KJV) and there was no longer
"Jew nor Greek, slave nor free, male nor female, for you are all one in Christ
Jesus" (Gal. 3:28), this did not mean that members of the church could no
longer determine if they were male or female or if they were Jewish or Gentile. The point was that these issues no longer mattered or were points in
contention.

A People from the Gentiles

Nowhere does this issue of Israel and the church reach a higher pitch
than at the Jerusalem Council in Acts 15. The dispute between the exclusi-
vistic forces, which wanted circumcision and key features of Mosaic customs to remain intact if a person were to experience salvation, and the inclu-
sivistic forces, which wanted to make room for the Gentiles without

requiring all these Jewish trappings of the Torah, was sharp and intense. It seemed as if no one would be able to harness this dispute. Peter tried to explain how his vision and meeting with Cornelius had changed his mind, but this was strictly relational theology and carried no normative weight as far as the combatants were concerned. Barnabas and Paul added what they had seen God do on their missionary journey among the Gentiles, but little was changed. Finally James spoke up and appealed to the Old Testament prophet Amos (9:11-12). That finally settled the debate abruptly and conclusively, for it carried the weight of Scripture and it had the prestige of authoritatively signaling what had been the plan of God all along.

Even the *Scofield Reference Bible* notes that "dispensationally, this [Acts 15:13-18] is the most important passage in the N.T."[6] This is because the final regathering of Israel is seen as the focus of the passage. There is no doubt in my mind that that is part of the truth taught here. But just as dramatic is the teaching about the *extent* of the kingdom in Amos 9:11-12. And that is how James introduced this quotation from Amos in Acts 15:14-15. "Simon has described to us how God at first showed his concern by taking from the Gentiles a people for himself. The words of the prophets are in agreement with this." Then follows the citation from Amos 9:11-12.

Amos had clearly argued in the eighth century B.C. that the reestablishment of the "House of David" (2 Sam. 7) from its dilapidated and crumbling present status as a tent, hut, or booth was not only to reunite the ruins of the ten Northern tribes with the two Southern tribes (note Amos's feminine plural suffix on "its ruins"), and to restore the new David, even Messiah to the throne (note Amos's masculine singular, "restore it") and build her (i.e., the tent, hut or booth), the fading replica of the ancient glorious house of David (a feminine singular suffix referring to the feminine word *sukkah,* "booth, hut, tent,"). It was done by the Lord Himself in order "that the remnant of men may seek the Lord, even all the Gentiles who bear my name."[7]

Whenever the Lord or man placed his name over anything, whether cities (2 Sam. 12:28; Jer. 25:29; Dan. 9:18-19), the temple (1 Kings 8:43; Jer. 7:10), or men or women (Isa. 4:1; Jer. 14:9; 2 Chron. 7:14), they were owned and became part of the respective person's treasure. In this case, James affirmed that it had been part of God's plan all along to make the Gentiles part of His holy possession in the grand design of His kingdom that had involved David, his seed, his throne, and his kingdom. There were just no two ways about it. God had meant for the remnant of all humanity to share in the same spiritual benefits that had been offered to Israel.

The "Charter for all humanity" (*torat ha'adam*) of 2 Samuel 7:19 was viewed by Amos and many other Old Testament writers as embracing "all peoples on earth" (Gen. 12:3). God had visited the Gentiles in order to take a people out of them for His name and to make them part of the seed of Abraham and the house of David. That is the grandest argument for continuity between Israel and the church to form the one "People of God."

Israel as the People of God

It is impossible to talk about the biblical concept of salvation without seriously involving the Jewish people at the very center of this doctrine.[8] All too frequently Romans 9—11 is treated as a parenthesis in the argument of Paul's great tractate on soteriology. But that point of view fails to account for the announcement of Paul's theme in Romans 1:16, "I am not ashamed of the gospel, because it is the power of God for the salvation of everyone who believes: first for the Jew, then for the Gentile." Paul interlaced Jew and Gentile all through his argument in Romans. But it is in Romans 9—11 that he focused on a number of puzzling questions about the concept of Israel as the people of God.

First, if the gospel is to the Jew first, then why is it that so few are receiving salvation from their sins? Paul's answer in Romans 9:1-5 is that he still had a great love and deep sorrow for his people Israel. The failure is not in the promises of God (vv. 6-13) for "God's gifts and his call are irrevocable" (11:29) and His covenant with the patriarchs and David was unconditional and solely dependent on God.[9] However, this was not the end. One day in the future there would be a great turning to the Lord from Israel.

Second, if God had not as yet fulfilled His promises to Israel, how did the Gentiles know they could trust Him? Well, the answer in part is that it was not God's fault. Furthermore, Israel's rejection of God was not total, for there always had been a remnant that accepted Jesus as Messiah. But again, the nation will one day receive Jesus as their Messiah.

Third, had not the offer of the gospel to the Gentiles nullified all God's national promises to Israel? It is in Romans 11:11 that Paul picked up the question originally introduced in Romans 9:30-33. Was God's purpose in permitting Israel's stumbling such that He might reject His national people and cast them off forever? Paul answered so decisively in the negative that it is clear we have judged badly and simultaneously hit on an open nerve.

The reason God allowed Israel's stumbling or fall was so that the riches of salvation might also be shared with the Gentile world. This, in turn, would once again provoke the Jew to jealousy (Rom. 11-14; cf. Deut. 32:21). So Israel did not fall into an irreversible tumble. In fact, marveled Paul, if the casting away of Israel for a time has meant the reconciliation of the Gentile world to Christ, how much more spectacular will be the result when Israel returns to the Lord?

Paul's point by now should be abundantly clear. It was decisively in accordance with the plan of God that Israel would reject the messiahship of Jesus while the gospel went out over the whole earth. But it is just as much in the plan of God that this salvation of God would so grip the hearts of the Gentiles that it would lead to a provoking of jealousy among God's ancient people Israel and that eventually all Israel would be saved.

The Theology of the Olive Tree

Few illustrations are as decisive as the olive tree in Romans 11 in demonstrating that there is a unity and oneness to the people of God, while both Israel and the church retain their identities. Verses 16-24 gives us this illustration of the olive tree. The connecting "for" in verse 21 provides us with the reason for believing in a future national restoration of the nation Israel.

The sap of the olive roots is the covenantal promise made to the forefathers, Abraham, Isaac, and Jacob. This nation was set aside and consecrated to God. The principle, based on Numbers 15:17-21, is that the holiness or consecration of the firstfruits and the root is passed on to the whole lump or branches, which in this case are the Israelites. Accordingly, just as the offering of the firstfruits consecrates the whole harvest, so the Abrahamic covenant consecrated Israel and anticipated a harvest that would come some day.

Amazingly, the natural branches of Israel were lopped off and the wild olive branches of the Gentiles were grafted in (even though in the real realm of botany the process is the reverse, but for the purposes of illustration, it is turned upside down). But it was just as unnatural for Gentiles to be put in the place of Israel. But out of this unnatural process God would bring a blessing upon both Gentiles and Jews.

Gentiles became partakers with the Jews of the blessing of Abraham and David (Eph. 3:1-6,11-16). But Gentiles must beware lest they think they earned their salvation or their place in the program of God. They should also resist vaunting themselves over the Jews and the natural branches. If these formerly wild branches should suddenly forget these facts, they would be removed from their place of blessing.

Paul pressed the argument for Israel's eventual restoration in Romans 11:23-36. God is able and will graft in the natural branches again. After all, it is Israel's own olive tree! This partial hardness of Israel would continue "until the full number of the Gentiles has come in" (v. 25). The "mystery" of verse 25 was not that the salvation of Israel or the Gentiles was not revealed in the Old Testament; rather, it was the partial and temporary hardening of Israel until the full number of the Gentile conversions was reached.

The "covenant" mentioned in verse 27 is none other than the New Covenant spoken of sixteen times in the prophets, but especially in Jeremiah 31:31-34. The quotation here is from Isaiah 59:20-21; 27:9. Paul's comments on these verses from Isaiah's prophecy are found in verses 28-29. Where the gospel is concerned, the Jews, for the most part, continue to be enemies of it so that the Gentiles might temporarily benefit. But where election is concerned, mark it down that Israel continues to be beloved for the sake of the fathers Abraham, Isaac, and Jacob. God, the real covenant-keeper will fulfill all that He has promised in His covenant promises.

If Gentiles have received mercy in part because Israel was disobedient, so too Israel will experience that same mercy of God (vv. 30-32). Paul concluded his olive-tree theology with a grand doxology in verses 33-36. It extols the wisdom and graciousness of the plan of God in dealing with Israel and the believing Gentiles.

Conclusion

How much more clearly could the biblical writer put the fact that there is only one people of God even though there are at least two aspects: Israel and the church. God's olive tree began with the roots God planted in the promises given to the patriarchs. From this root grew the Jewish people. Suddenly the wild branches of the believing Gentiles were grafted into the olive trunk while the natural branches were for a time "separated from Christ, alienated from the commonwealth of Israel, strangers to the covenants of promise, having no hope and without God in the world" (Eph. 2:12, RSV). But, thanks be to God, one day Israel will be provoked to jealousy and will be restored to the roots and the trunk from which she has been separated for these years.

The doctrine of the church must carefully set forth the unity and singularity of the people of God, but it must also be careful to note that the gifts and calling of God are irrevocable. As such, all reports of Israel's death and demise are, as Mark Twain quipped, premature.

Notes

1. Charles C. Ryrie, *Dispensationalism Today* (Chicago: Moody, 1965), 44-45.

2. William E. Cox, *Amillennialism Today* (Philadelphia: Presbyterian and Reformed, 1966), 34.

3. George Eldon Ladd, *The Gospel of the Kingdom* (Grand Rapids: Eerdmans, 1959), 117.

4. Walter C. Kaiser, Jr., "Promise," in *Holman Bible Dictionary*, gen. ed. Trent C. Butler (Nashville: Holman Bible Publishers, 1991). Also idem, *Toward an Old Testament Theology* (Grand Rapids: Zondervan, 1978), 32-35.

5. Kaiser, *Toward an Old Testament Theology*, 100-13.

6. *Scofield Reference Bible*, 1343.

7. For a more in-depth discussion of the grammatical and theological issues connected with this passage, see Walter C. Kaiser, Jr., *The Uses of the Old Testament in the New* (Chicago: Moody, 1986), 177-94.

8. See the superb discussion of this point by Bruce Corley, "The Jews, The Future and God: Romans 9-11," *Southwestern Journal of Theology* 19 (1976): 42-56.

9. Although the conditionality of the covenants have been vigorously defended, we have argued that the case will not stand. See Walter C. Kaiser, Jr., *Toward Rediscovering the Old Testament* (Grand Rapids: Zondervan, 1987), 50-54.

8
Images of the Church in the Synoptic Gospels

by James A. Brooks and Beverly C. Brooks

It is well known that the word *church* (Greek *ekklesia*) appears only three times in the Synoptic Gospels, in Matthew 16:18 (once) and 18:17 (twice). It is not so well known that some scholars question the authenticity of these references. With or without these passages it is obvious that Jesus Himself and the Synoptics which record His teaching say very little, explicitly at least, about the church. This chapter will attempt to examine carefully the church passages in Matthew and then to explore whether there is any implicit teaching about the church in the Synoptic Gospels.

Matthew 16:13-20; 18:15-20

The question of authenticity focuses upon 16:17-19. Prior to the rise of form and redaction criticism it was sometimes claimed that these verses were a scribal interpolation to support the claims of Rome. The decisive objection to this claim is that no extant manuscript or version of Matthew omits the passage, although no manuscript of this portion of Matthew is earlier than about 350. Even so, the time of false decretals such as "The Donation of Constantine" was still far in the future.

Today it is often claimed that many of the sayings which are attributed to Jesus in the Gospels were in fact composed by the primitive church (the view of form criticism) or the evangelists themselves (the view of redaction criticism) to meet various needs or to develop theological themes. The commentaries of Eduard Schweizer[1] and Francis W. Beare[2] are examples of those who argue that Matthew 16:17-19 was the product of the early Palestinian church, whereas Robert H. Gundry contends that Matthew himself composed the passage "in order to portray Peter as a representative disciple."[3]

Objections to Jesus having spoken the words in question include the following. First, the passage has no parallel in the other Gospels, nor does the word *church* appear in the other Gospels. Here use is being made of the criterion of multiple attestation which claims that a saying or an event is more likely to go back to Jesus if it is attested by two or more strands of the tradition such as Mark, Q, M, and L rather than one only. Few would question that multiple attestation makes authenticity more likely, but single attestation does not prove that saying is unauthentic. None would claim that Jesus spoke frequently about the church; therefore, the absence of the word in other traditions is simply an instance of accurate reporting. If form criticism is correct that the early church frequently placed its concerns on the lips of Jesus, we might expect many references to the church in the Gospels because they abound in Acts and the Epistles. The paucity of references to the church in the Gospels may actually favor a dominical origin of those in Matthew 16:18 and 18:17. If it were well known that Jesus did not speak about the church, is it likely that Matthew would have created some instances?

Second, it is claimed that the idea of building a church betrays a later ecclesiastical interest. It will be shown below that if verses 17-19 did not originate with Jesus they must have originated in the early Palestinian church (i.e., before the outbreak of the Jewish rebellion in A.D. 66, rather than in the Gentile church). It is very doubtful, however, that the Palestinian church ever had as much "ecclesiastical interest" as the claim presupposes. Furthermore Peter was not for long the leader of the Palestinian church but gave way to James the brother of Jesus in the early 40s (cf. Acts 9:32; 12:17; 15:13). Still further, the claim assumes that the word "church" is used here to refer to an organization or institution. In the Greek Old Testament, however, the word *ekklesia* is often used to translate the Hebrew *qahal* which usually refers to the congregation or community of Israel and thus to the people of God. Although there is some difficulty in Jesus speaking of an institution, there is none of Him envisioning a new congregation of the people of God who would adhere to His teaching. "A Messiah without a Messianic Community would have been unthinkable to any Jew."[4] The building metaphor is in fact quite appropriate in connection with the word "rock."

A third objection to the authenticity of Matthew 16:17-19 is that Peter never enjoyed the privileges set forth in the passage. If that is true, then why did the early church or Matthew invent the saying? The very difficulty of the statement favors the traditional view that Jesus did in fact speak the words but that they mean something other than what appears on the surface. What they do mean will be explored later.

Fourth, the passage assumes that Peter understood the implications of his confession in verse 15 and that Jesus accepted it at face value, whereas verse 22 indicates that neither of these assumptions is true. If however, there is a discrepancy between verses 17-19 and what precedes and follows, why did

Matthew or someone before him juxtapose incompatible items? Peter is not praised for possessing full understanding but for being the first to recognize that Jesus is, in fact, the Messiah.

There are some, however, who admit that Jesus spoke the words but who locate them during the institution of the Lord's Supper[5] or following the resurrection.[6] Such possibilities cannot be ruled out because none of the Gospels is strictly chronological, and topical arrangement is frequently used. Nevertheless the question must be asked why the pronouncement is more appropriate at the end of Jesus' life or after His resurrection than at the time He was confessed as Messiah. Even if it were more appropriate later, was it inappropriate at the time of Peter's confession? If Matthew were the only Gospel, it is doubtful that any questions would have been asked. The only problem is that Mark and Luke do not record it. Certainly in Mark's case an explanation is ready at hand. Mark minimizes the achievements of the disciples and Jesus' commendation of them in order to indicate to his own community that despite their failures Jesus could still use them.

A Palestinian origin of the passage is assured by the terms "Bar-Jona" (*bar* is an Aramaic word meaning "son of"), "flesh and blood" meaning "a human being" (cf. Wis. 12:5; Sir. 14:18; 17:31; 1 Cor. 15:50; Gal. 1:16), "gates of Hades" meaning the "powers of death" (Isa. 38:10), "bind" and "loose" (rabbinic terms meaning "prohibit" and "allow"), "keys of the kingdom of heaven" (Isa. 22:15-25 and especially v. 22), and the pun on the word "rock" (*petros* and *petra* in Greek but *kepha* in both instances in Aramaic where the pun is clearer).[7] If, however, the passage is certainly Semitic in character, there is a real possibility that it goes back to Jesus Himself. It is very difficult to determine with confidence that one thing comes from Jesus and another from the Palestinian church after Him. Whether or not Jesus actually spoke the words cannot be determined by rational evidence. Suffice it to say there is no decisive reason why He could not have done so. The burden of proof should be on those who claim that He did not, not vice versa. To say the least, authenticity has not been disproved, and the discussion will proceed on the basis that Matthew 16:17-19 probably goes back to Jesus Himself.

The main objection to Jesus having used the word "church," or rather the Aramaic equivalent, in 18:17 is that it is used in a different sense from 16:18. It has been claimed that in 16:18 the reference is to the universal church, whereas in 18:17 it is certainly to a local congregation. This is no more of a problem in Matthew than elsewhere in the New Testament where both meanings are found. By the nature of the case the church is both single and multiple. It is not so certain, however, that the universal idea is exclusive in 16:18. For the time being at least, Jesus was probably thinking of building a group of disciples who were analogous to a local synagogue. How much He saw beyond that depends upon one's view of His insight and prophetic ability within the context of limitations during His earthly life.

Another objection to attributing Matthew 18:17 to Jesus is the claim that He would never have spoken disparagingly of Gentiles and tax collectors. Certainly Jesus gave acceptance to such persons, but this consideration does not rule out the possibility that He would have used a common term without questioning its appropriateness. Compare His use of the word "dogs" to refer to Gentiles in Matthew 15:26 and Mark 7:27.

If then there are no decisive reasons for denying the word "church" to Jesus in Matthew 16:18 and 18:17, what did He reveal about it? First, He indicated that it was to be based upon confession of Him. This is true regardless of what one decides about the exact reference of the word *petra*. The occasion for Jesus' first statement about the church was Peter's confession at Caesarea Philippi. Without such confession there can be no church. A church by definition is a group of people committed to Jesus. Nor is it unthinkable that Jesus would have thought in terms of allegiance to Himself. Rabbis had disciples who were committed to their interpretation. Jesus did also. The difference between Him and the rabbis is that people committed themselves not only to His teaching but also to His person.

Second, Jesus taught that in some sense His church was to be founded upon Peter. This, of course, has always been the Roman Catholic position, but for that reason most Protestants have denied it and have claimed instead that Jesus intended to build the church on Himself (cf. 1 Pet. 2:5-8; 1 Cor. 3:11), or on His teaching (cf. 7:24), or on the particular truth He revealed to Peter here (note the word "revealed" in v. 17), or on Peter's faith or profession. No significance should be attached to the fact that two different words are used in the Greek text: "you are *Petros* and on this *petra* I will build my church." As already indicated, in the Aramaic in which Jesus no doubt spoke, the word in both instances was *kepha*. *Petra* is by far the better word to indicate a foundation, denoting as it does a large slab of rock, a shelf of rock, bedrock, whereas *petra* usually refers to a small, detached stone. The feminine *petra*, however, could hardly be used as the name of a man.

Just as Jesus is Christ in verse 16, Peter is the rock in verse 18. The nature of the pun requires this conclusion. The objection has been made that Peter was not rock-like in his character. This objection can be answered in two ways. One is that Peter's character later became much more firm and that Jesus was referring not to what he was at the time but to what he would become. A better explanation is that Jesus was referring not to Peter's character but to his function.[8] He was the foundation stone in the sense that he was the first to confess Jesus as the Messiah and the Son of God, in the sense that he was the first to proclaim Christ publicly after His death and resurrection (Acts 2), and in the sense that he was the first to offer the gospel to Gentiles (Acts 10). It was Peter's spiritual perception that was especially commendable. The identification of Peter as the foundation of the church is not out of line with Ephesians 2:20 and Revelation 21:14 where all of the apostles are identified as its foundation. Of course, it is impossible to separate Peter from his confession of faith, and Peter's confession was representative of many which would follow. To that limited extent the foundation upon which the church is built includes the confession and commitment of all who are a part of it, but Jesus was thinking primarily of Peter himself. It is crucial to observe that nothing whatsoever is said about any successors to Peter or their function. It is at this point that Catholic exegesis goes astray and not in claiming that Peter is the foundation stone.

Verse 19 describes further the function of Peter. He is to receive the keys to the kingdom of heaven and with those to bind and loose. As indicated above, the background of the keys metaphor is Isaiah 22:15-25 and verse 22 in particular. Shebna was the chief minister of Hezekiah who, contrary to Isaiah, advocated rebellion against Assyria and alliance with Egypt. Isaiah predicted that he would be removed and replaced by Eliakim who would then have "authority" to "open" and "shut" as symbolized by "the key of the house of David." The authority was not to give entrance to persons but to determine policy and practices. Similar is the background of the binding and loosing metaphor. These were technical terms used by scribes for their practice of pronouncing binding rules of conduct and providing exemptions from them. As applied to Peter, the keys were symbols of his role in determining when, where, and to whom the gospel would be preached and what would be required of those who accepted his message. Matthew 23:13 suggests that in Jesus' day the scribes claimed to have the keys to the kingdom of heaven; the present passage suggests that the keys will be taken from them and given to Peter as the first and representative Christian.

There is a serious problem with the tense of the verbs translated "shall be bound" and "shall be loosed" in most English versions. The form is a periphrastic future perfect which theoretically should be translated "shall have been bound" and "shall have been loosed." If, in fact, the meaning is that of the future perfect rather than the future, the idea is not that heaven (a Jewish substitute for God) will affirm what Peter binds and looses but that Peter may bind and loose only what has already been bound and loosed by God! Grammarians and commentators are much divided on the matter,[9] and it is not possible to deal with all the arguments here.[10] Certainly there are many instances of verbs which are perfect in form but do not have perfect meaning. And there are instances where a perfect in the fulfillment clause of a conditional sentence does not denote a prior action.[11] Nevertheless a significant reason for accepting the future perfect idea is that the simple future was readily available to Matthew if he had wanted to convey that idea.[12] Therefore he must have wanted to indicate the future perfect idea. The conventional future perfect form was probably not an option because it was rarely used during the first Christian century. Therefore Matthew had to use the periphrastic formation despite the possibility of ambiguity. Certainly Jesus did not give Peter or anybody else a blank check to do anything he wanted. Peter's decisions must be regulated by the prior decisions of God, but Matthew did not indicate such limitations.

The third thing which Jesus indicates about the church is that the "gates of Hades" (literal translation, NIV, NASB) or "powers of death" (RSV) or simply "death" (GNB) will not have power against it. Hades was the Greek place of the dead and is the equivalent of the Hebrew Sheol (cf. Isa. 38:9-10; Wis. 16:13; cf. also Ps. 9:13; 107:18 where a different word is used). Therefore, the idea is not that the forces of evil will never overcome the church or that they will not be able to withstand the assault of the church but that death, including martyrdom, will not obliterate the church (i.e., the new people of God). The church will never die!

Fourth—and at this point we move from 16:13-20 to 18:15-20—the people of God who constitute the church must maintain positive relationships with one another and discipline those who disrupt such relationships by their sin. In 16:15-17 the word "you" is singular. The last statement in verse 17, therefore, does not certainly refer to discipline by the whole church but to the withdrawal of fellowship of one Christian from another. In verses 18-20, however, the plural is used throughout. Therefore, whatever power of binding and loosing is given to Peter in 16:19 is in 18:18 given to all the original disciples of Jesus and presumably all later disciples as well—a most important consideration in evaluating any claim of the supremacy of Peter. Because of the use of the plural in verses 18-20, it is reasonable to conclude that the entire passage does, in fact, deal with collective discipline. The process of discipline will ordinarily begin with an individual. There is, of course, no reference to popes, bishops, councils, or even local pastors or boards of deacons and elders. There is, therefore, some slight intimation of the democratic nature of the church.

Fifth, the church is a local congregation (clearly in 18:17) as well as a universal body (the dominant but not exclusive emphasis in 16:18—see above). This fact anticipates the Epistles where the word is used much more often for a local assembly of believers than for all the people of God everywhere, even including those in heaven.

In addition to the relatively small amount of *explicit* teaching about the church, the Synoptic Gospels also contain a large amount of *implicit* teaching. The most important part of the implicit teaching is that which pertains to the kingdom of God.

The Kingdom of God

The term "kingdom of God" does not appear in the Old Testament, but ideally Israel was always a theocracy, and when she was a kingdom that kingdom theoretically belonged to God. The prophets often spoke of God as king.

According to the Synoptics the kingdom of God was the primary subject of Jesus' teaching. The term itself appears fifty times in the Synoptic Gospels. To this should be added the thirty-two appearances of the term "kingdom of heaven" in Matthew because the two refer to the same thing as a comparison of parallel passages will show.[13] Still further the term "kingdom" alone is used thirteen times in Matthew and seven in Luke when it refers to the kingdom of God or that of Jesus Himself. The total of all references in the Synoptics is 102. By way of contrast "kingdom of God" appears two times in John, six in Acts, eight in Paul, and once in Revelation. "Kingdom," referring to that of God and/or Christ, appears three times in John, once in Acts, six times in Paul, two times in Hebrews, two times in the General Epistles, and once (implied) in Revelation. The total of all references to God's kingdom outside the Synoptics is thirty-two.

The New Testament, including the Synoptic Gospels, describes the kingdom as both present and future, but the emphasis is on the present aspect. In its present form it is not a place. It is not a group of people. It is the rule of God in the lives of people. The background of the New Testament use of the Greek word *basileia* is not a Greek or Roman concept of a kingdom or empire but the Hebrew word *malkuth* which refers "to power rather than to locality."[14] Indeed Moffatt and Goodspeed often translate the term "Reign of God."[15]

What is the relationship of the church and the kingdom?[16] The concepts are closely related as can be seen from Matthew 16:18-19: "You are Peter, and on this rock I will build my church. . . . I will give to you the keys of the kingdom of heaven." A relationship may also be suggested by the relationship of frequency of references to the kingdom and the church in the Synoptics on the one hand and in Acts and the Epistles on the other. The kingdom is frequent in the Synoptics but rare in Acts and the Epistles (above); the church is rare in the Synoptics (three times) but frequent in Acts and the Epistles (106 times). It is almost as though references to the church in Acts and the Epistles have replaced those to the kingdom in the Synoptics.

Nevertheless the church and kingdom are not synonymous. The kingdom is primarily the sovereignty, the authority, and the rule of God. Only in a secondary and derived sense is it the people who are ruled. Only in Revelation 1:6 and 5:10 are Christians called a kingdom and there only because they rule as kings.[17] The church is the new people of God who submit to the lordship of Christ. The kingdom is invisible and internal. The church is mainly a visible and external society. The church results from the reign of God in individual lives.[18] It grows out of the kingdom and is a partial manifestation of the kingdom. "The Church is a form which the kingdom assumes in result of the new stage upon which the Messiahship of Jesus enters with his death and resurrection."[19] Jesus and, to a lesser extent, the apostles proclaimed the kingdom, but they never proclaimed the church. The New Testament speaks of building the church but never the kingdom and of entering the kingdom but not the church. The church has a democratic aspect, although it is certainly not a true democracy as is sometimes claimed; on the other hand the kingdom is an absolute monarchy. Perhaps the relationship of the church and the kingdom can best be illustrated by two circles which partially overlap.[20] The circles are not equal in size, however. The kingdom is much the larger of the two.

Therefore the kingdom of God, which is a dominant subject in the Synoptic Gospels, implies the church. The church is also suggested and anticipated in other ways.

The Disciples

Just as there is no question that the Old Testament prophets, the scribes, and John the Baptist had dedicated groups of followers, so there is no question that Jesus gathered around Him a group of disciples. There was a smaller, inner group whom Jesus Himself called to be with Him all the time and a larger, outer group who were sympathetic with Jesus and who heard Him and otherwise followed Him from time to time. There is no good reason for doubting that the inner core were twelve in number. The number "twelve" recalls the twelve patriarchs and the twelve tribes of Israel and is therefore symbolic of the true Israel. Whether Jesus Himself designated the twelve as apostles is much debated and cannot be pursued here because it is not crucial to the subject of this essay.[21] It is the claim of this essay that the twelve disciples constituted the nucleus of the church. Jesus was the Messiah, and the disciples were the messianic community. They were the remnant of Israel. If, in fact, Jesus saw anything unique about His theology and ethics, and if He sought people to commit themselves to His teaching and person, He must have at least hoped that they would continue to do so after His death. This, of course, actually happened. The same disciples who followed Jesus during His lifetime experienced a unique filling of the Spirit on the

Day of Pentecost and soon began to refer to themselves as the church. They already were the church in embryo form, however, when Jesus first called them. After having called the disciples Jesus taught them and sent them on a mission. The purpose of the mission was to make and teach other disciples. It remained only for the disciples to recognize their uniqueness, to add to their number, to call themselves the church, and to begin the process of structure and organization which continues until the present day.

The Church's Mission

The Synoptic Gospels do not indicate that either Jesus or His disciples baptized (cf. John 3:22; 4:1-2). Matthew 28:19 records a command of Jesus for His disciples to baptize.[22] Because of the improbability that the early church would have appropriated a rite associated with John the Baptist unless it had the example and/or command of Jesus, it is highly likely that Jesus or at least the disciples did baptize during His ministry and that He commanded His disciples to continue to baptize after His death. By establishing baptism as a rite to be practiced by His disciples, Jesus laid the foundation for a community which would later be known as the church.

The "Great Commission" of Matthew 28:19-20 is not the only mission charge, however. Another is in Luke 24:46-49.[23] Outside the Synoptics there are mission charges in John 20:21-22 and Acts 1:8. Both Matthew and Luke indicate that the mission was to be all nations. The mission charges were anticipated by a mission or missions on which the disciples were sent during the lifetime of Jesus. All three of the Synoptics record a mission of the twelve (Matt. 10:1-15; Mark 6:7-13; Luke 9:1-6). Luke alone also records a mission of the seventy (10:1-12). The latter is often regarded as a doublet of the former. Whether it is or not, in Luke's Gospel the mission of the twelve functions as a symbol of the mission to the Jews and the mission of the seventy as a preview of the mission to the Gentiles, the latter of which is a major theme in the companion volume, Acts. The same truth may be portrayed in Matthew and Mark by the feeding of the 5,000 on the one hand and the 4,000 on the other. The significant thing is that the mission charges and the early mission(s) indicate that Jesus expected that people would continue to give their allegiance to Him and form a distinct community. That community became the church.

The Promise of the Spirit

The promise of the Holy Spirit is admittedly much more prominent in the Fourth Gospel than the first three Gospels, but it is not absent from the Synoptics. In Matthew 10:20 and Mark 13:11 Jesus assured the disciples that when they were being persecuted and were called upon to defend themselves, the Spirit would give them words to speak. Likewise Luke 12:12 promises, "The Holy Spirit will teach you at that time what you should say"(NIV). Verse 13 states, "If then you who are evil know how to give good gifts to your children, how much more will your Heavenly Father give the Holy Spirit to those who ask him?" Acts 2 records the coming of the Spirit in the fullness of power at Pentecost, and Acts and the Epistles indicate that the dominant role of the Spirit is one of the most distinctive things about the church age. Jesus' promise of the Spirit therefore was, in effect, a promise of the church. The church would not be the church without the presence, leading, and empowerment of the Spirit.

The Parables

Several of the parables of Jesus imply that there would be a body of God's people such as the church. In the parable of the wheat and the weeds (Matt. 12:24-30) Jesus stated that the two would have to grow together until the harvest (i.e., until the judgment). The wheat, of course, represents the new people of God, and Jesus indicated that they would persist until the end of the age. Similar is the parable of the seed growing secretly (Mark 4:26-29). The kingdom is like seed which grows unobserved until the harvest. The parable of the fishing net (Matt. 13:47-50) also depicts the separation of the good and evil at the judgment. Perhaps the best example is the parable of the mustard seed (Matt. 13:31-32, Mark 4:30-32, Luke 13:18-19). The tiny seed would grow until it became a huge shrub or, according to Luke, even a tree. Inasmuch as the church is something which can be observed much better than the kingdom, it is easy to see the church in the tree. The point is this: none of these parables would make sense unless Jesus foresaw the continuation of the disciple band until the end of the age. What they would be called was not yet a consideration. That they would continue to exist was crucial.

Faith

The concept of faith, especially faith in Jesus Himself, is not as prominent in the Synoptics as in John and Paul. Nevertheless the verb "to believe" appears forty times and the noun "faith" twenty-four times in the first three Gospels. Jesus' initial proclamation of the gospel emphasized the central place of believing: "The kingdom of God is at hand; repent and believe the gospel" (Mark 1:14). A few more than half of the references to faith are in connection with the miracles. Healings took place as a result of faith (e.g., Matt. 8:10,13; 9:22,29; 15:28), and where faith was not present Jesus did not often heal (Matt. 13:58). Healing of the body, however, was a sign of the greater healing of the entire person including spiritual salvation and forgiveness of sins. Jesus connected faith with answer to prayer (Matt. 21:22) and accomplishing great things for God (Matt. 17:20; 21:21). There is one passage which seems to associate faith with salvation. Luke 8:12, which is a part of the explanation of the parable of sower, states: "Then the devil comes along and takes away the word from their hearts so that they may not believe and be saved."

In Acts and the Epistles, faith is set forth as a fundamental Christian attitude. Primarily it is trust in and commitment to Jesus Christ for salvation from sin. It pervades the entire relationship of the Christian and Jesus—so much so that Christians are often called "believers." Secondarily, faith involves acceptance of the truths of the Christian message. Faith therefore is indispensable for those who constitute the church. By putting so much emphasis on faith Jesus anticipated the church. It should be carefully noted that it was the believers' church—the subject of the present collection of essays—that Jesus anticipated.

A large part of the Synoptic Gospels is devoted to the ethical teaching of Jesus. His teaching was intended for His followers in all ages. It hardly seems likely that Jesus would have devoted so much of His teachings to ethical matters if they were intended only for the twelve and only for a few months or years. He must have foreseen a continuing group of disciples who would need guidance for the way they should live. Furthermore the ethical standards set by Jesus are so high that only a unique, empowered community—the church—could understand and practice them.

Synonyms

Jesus' teachings are filled with terms which might be looked upon as synonyms for the word *church.* The most common is the word *disciples* which has already been dealt with in another connection. Others include *sheep* in Matthew 25:33; 26:31, Mark 14:27; *flock* in Matthew 26:32; and *little flock* in Luke 12:32. Similarly, Jesus alluded to Himself as a shepherd in Matthew 25:32; 26:31; Mark 14:27. Compare also Matthew 18:12-13; Luke 15:3-6,19-10. A shepherd implies a flock. The church became the flock of Jesus. Yet another synonym is *family.* Note how Jesus identified His "family" not as His relatives but as those who did the will of His Father (Matt. 12:46-50; Mark 3:19-20; Luke 8:19-21). Therefore the word *church* does not have to be used in order to have the concept.

In conclusion it should be clear that the Synoptics abound in images of the church. Little is explicitly said about the church because it could not exist until after the death and resurrection of Jesus and the coming of the Spirit with the resulting transformation of Jesus' followers.

Notes

1. *The Good News According to Matthew*, trans. D. E. Green (Atlanta: John Knox Press, 1975), 336-39.

2. *The Gospel According to Matthew* (San Francisco: Harper & Row, 1981), 353-54.

3. *Matthew: A Commentary on His Literary and Theological Art* (Grand Rapids: Eerdmans, 1982), 331.

4. W. F. Albright and C. S. Mann, *Matthew* in the *Anchor Bible* (Garden City, N.Y.: Doubleday, 1971), 195.

5. Oscar Cullmann, *Peter: Disciple, Apostle, Martyr*, 2d ed., trans. F. V. Filson (Philadelphia: Westminster Press, 1962), 176-91.

6. Raymond E. Brown, Karl P. Donfried, and John Ruemann, eds., *Peter in the New Testament* (Minneapolis: Augsburg Press and New York: Paulist Press, 1973), 83-101.

7. Schweizer, 336.

8. R. T. France, *Matthew*, vol. 1 of *Tyndale New Testament Commentaries*, ed. Leon Morris (Grand Rapids: Eerdmans, 1985), 254.

9. Among those arguing for the future perfect idea are J. R. Mantey, "Mistranslation of the Perfect Tense in John 20:23, Matthew 16:19, and Matthew 18:18," *Journal of Biblical Literature* 58 (1939): 243-49; idem, "Evidence that the Perfect Tense in John 20:23 and Matthew 16:19 is Mistranslated," *Journal of the Evangelical Theological Society* 16 (1973): 129-38; idem, "Distorted Translations in John 20:23; Matthew 16:18 and 18:18," *Review and Expositor* 78 (1981): 409-16; and Nigel Turner, *Grammatical Insights into the New Testament* (Edinburgh: T. & T. Clark, 1965), 80-82. Among those against it are H. J. Cadbury, "Meaning of John 20:23, Matthew 16:19, and Matthew 18:18," *JBL* 58 (1939): 251-54; and most grammars and commentaries briefly.

10. A concise, objective treatment may be found in D. A. Carson, "Matthew," *Expositor's Bible Commentary*, 12 vols., ed. F. E. Gaebelein (Grand Rapids: Zondervan, 1976-   ), 8:370-72. His conclusion is: "Where questions dealing strictly with Greek syntax are asked, it seems impossible to reach a firm decision."

11. Matthew 16:19b could be construed as a conditional sentence: "If you bind anything on earth, it shall be bound in heaven. . . . "

12. Cf. Carson, 372.

13. Matthew no doubt uses 'kingdom of heaven' much more often than 'kingdom of God' (four times) because his Gospel was written to Christians of Jewish background and because Jews and presumably Jewish Christians also were reluctant to speak or write the divine name. Heaven was a typical Jewish substitute for God.

14. *New International Dictionary of New Testament Theology*, s. v. "King, Kingdom" by B. Klappert.

15. Moffatt also sometimes translates it "Realm of God." This is confusing if not inaccurate. The kingdom in its present aspect is not a realm but the exercise of divine rule. As Archibald M. Hunter, *The Message of the New Testament* (Philadelphia: Westminster, 1944), 55, puts it: "If we construe 'the saving Sovereignty of God' statically—conceiving the *Basileia* as a 'realm' rather than a 'rule'—we shall never properly understand the Gospels. For a Jew, God was the *living* and redeeming God, a God who was known by what he did."

16. One of the best treatments of the relationship of the church and kingdom is that of George Eldon Ladd in *Jesus and the Kingdom* (New York: Harper & Row, 1964), ch. 11; idem, *The Presence of the Future* (Grand Rapids: Eerdmans, 1974), ch. 11; and idem, *A Theology of the New Testament* (Grand Rapids: Eerdmans, 1974), ch. 8. Also very helpful are Raymond O. Zorn, *Church and Kingdom* (Philadelphia: Presbyterian and Reformed, 1962), 75-84; and Geerhardus Vos, *The Kingdom of God and the Church* (reprinted., Nutley, N.J.: Presbyterian and Reformed, 1972), ch. 10.

17. Ladd, *Theology*, 111.

18. His previous statement not withstanding, Hunter, *Message*, 55-56, says: "God's Rule

does not operate in the void. It demands a sphere of rule. It implies a people living under that Rule. It involves the formation of a community. Thus, the *ecclesia* or people of God is the inevitable correlative of the Rule of God."

19. Vos, *Kingdom and Church*, 85-86. Cf. Zorn, *Church and Kingdom*, 81: "The Church, in short, is a present manifestation of the Kingdom of God and in her the Kingdom's transforming power operates and from her its life and blessedness flows to form an oasis in the desert of this world's sin." In both statements the indefinite article *a* should be emphasized and not replaced by the definite article *the*. Vos in fact tends to go too far in identifying church and kingdom. "So far as extent of membership is concerned, Jesus plainly leads us to identify the invisible church and the kingdom" (86). With reference to the visible church he says, "Our Lord looked upon the visible church as a veritable embodiment of his kingdom" (87). Later he qualifies his position: "It does not necessarily follow, that the visible church is the only outward expression of the invisible kingdom. Undoubtedly the kingship of God, as his recognized and applied supremacy, is intended to pervade and control the whole of human life in all its forms of existence" (87).

20. *New Bible Dictionary*, 2d ed. s.v. "Kingdom of God" by H.N. Ridderbos, 658a.

21. Only Luke 6:13 affirms that Jesus Himself called the twelve apostles. In view of the strategic role apostles play in the theology of Luke-Acts, it is possible that the author has attributed to Jesus a term used by the early church. Nevertheless there is no reason why Jesus could not or should not have called His close disciples "apostles" in the nontechnical sense of "missionary" or "representative."

22. Actually the word "baptize" is a participle rather than an imperative as it appears in English translations. It could be interpreted as an imperatival participle which gets its force from the imperative "make disciples," or it could be a circumstantial participle which describes something which is to accompany the making of disciples.

23. The one in Mark 16:15 is part of the so-called long ending of Mark which has little claim to authenticity. It is not found in the two earliest and generally regarded best manuscripts of Mark. Some manuscripts which do contain it label it as suspect. Its language is quite different from the remainder of Mark.

9
Images of the Church in John

by Gerald L. Borchert

Introduction

The Gospel of John has been and continues today to be a powerful testimony for the church of what it means to be authentically Christian (John 20:31). Moreover, this testimony was confidently confirmed by the Johannine community of believers to be a genuine witness to the early church's thinking through a specific colophon or certification of trustworthiness at the end of the book (21:24). While the content of this Gospel is about Jesus Christ, the Son of God, the actual focus as indicated in the purpose statement, is upon the true followers of Christ who experience life as the result of authentic believing (20:30-31). Embedded into the stories of Jesus in this Gospel, therefore, is a message for the church, the family of God—a testimony that is far more powerful than any history report or mere newspaper story about Jesus. It is a magnificent theological document that reminds one of a brilliantly composed symphony which carries many themes to a striking climax without losing any of those themes in the intricacies of its movement.[1]

The Post-Resurrection Perspective and the Church

The entire Gospel is laced with a post-resurrection perspective (e.g., 2:22, etc).[2] Accordingly, the stories are not merely about a Jesus who walked the paths of ancient Palestine, but of equal importance these stories raise the issue of the implications that flow from the fact that the incarnate Jesus (1:14) is also the risen Lord of the church (20:28). The various confessions such as:

—the Lamb of God who takes away the sin of the world (1:29,36);
—the Savior of the world (4:42);
—the one speaking words of eternal life (6:68);
—the Christ, the Son of God, the coming one (11:27; 1:49);
—the one dying for the people (11:50);
—the king of Israel (1:49; 12:13; 18:33-39; 19:21; etc);
—Lord and God (20:28 and 21:7)

are absolutely meaningless if there were no resurrection of Jesus and no followers of Christ in the church proclaiming the power of God in Christ at the time when this gospel was set down in writing. The evangelist/disciple/ witness who wrote this Gospel and the community/church/family of God that authenticated this book (21:24) knew very well both that Jesus had been raised from the dead and that this Gospel was written to strengthen the church whenever it was to be read.

The stories in the Gospel, therefore, are written to build genuine faith within the church and to clarify authentic and inauthentic believing. They remind us that Jesus has always known what humanity is like. Indeed, it is pointedly stated that Jesus knew what true believing is (2:23-24) and what it means to confess Jesus and to follow Him (6:66-71; 12:42-43; 13:36-38).

The Nature of the Images in the Gospel

Typical of Jewish pictorial thinking which was represented in much of the Old Testament, the writing in this Gospel is filled with pictorial images. Many of these images are used to portray various aspects of the church. Most of these pictorial symbols have been discussed to a greater or lesser extent in Paul Minear's important catalog of nearly one hundred such word pictures appearing in the New Testament.[3] What should be pointed out here, however, is that the important images in the Gospel of John are dynamic, family or life-oriented symbols. These images involve such phenomena as growing or living things like a vine with its branches and a flock of sheep; family concerns like birthing and child-parent relations; human activities like dwelling, washing, eating, drinking, and fishing; to say nothing of concepts like living, dying, knowing, believing, and obeying. The clear impression one gains from studying such images and ideas in John is that the church from John's perspective should be viewed primarily as a dynamic organism which is called into being and is enlivened by God. It is not to be understood merely as an organization or institution constructed by human effort.

Moreover, when one reads this Gospel, one must be sensitive to the fact that the evangelist is not writing in a vacuum. He always has the church, the family of God, in mind when he is detailing the stories of Jesus. This fact makes the reading of John sometimes a little complicated since one can note several levels of discourse in the Gospel. But this fact also means that the stories and images can be very relevant. Although centuries of time and great differences of social custom separate the contemporary reader from the implied reader of John,[4] the Johannine writer was very sensitive to the task of communicating with his readers. Accordingly, he included in his Gospel many reader-oriented asides and interpretive notes (e.g., 1:38,41; 2:6,9,22; 3:23-24; 4:2; 5:13; 9:7,22; 10:35; 11:51-52; 12:4,6; etc.).

Because the evangelist constantly sought to maintain contact with the readers of his church, he contributed dynamically to making this Gospel a very engaging document for twentieth-century members of the church. It is definitely a reader/church-oriented Gospel, and its images of the church are intended to communicate to church members/readers what the Christian style of life ought to be like.

Is the Gospel Community Oriented?

Yet not all scholars have been convinced that John has in mind much of a concern for the church when writing this Gospel. Rudolf Bultmann, for example, relegated any ecclesiastical concerns to the role of a later ecclesiastical redactor.[5] Likewise Eduard Schweizer, while not following Bultmann, has been convinced that John's concern was focused not on the community but on the individual Christian. He emphasized this point by noting that in Johannine literature nothing is mentioned about ecclesiastical officials, organization, church order, or diversity of spiritual gifts.[6] A slightly different view is suggested in Gary Burge's recent work, *The Anointed Community,* although once again the emphasis is not on the institutional church.[7] Even when one reads the studies of scholars who emphasize the community aspects of the church such as Raymond Brown and Rudolf Schnackenburg an interesting pattern emerges.[8] Assuming that John has a community in mind, there is not a great deal about a specific organization or pattern of church life detailed in this Gospel. Indeed, the term "church" itself is not used here by the evangelist.[9]

But such a conclusion does not end the matter because most of our ideas about the church emerge from literature like the Pauline Epistles and Acts, certainly not from Gospel literature. Indeed, the specific use of the term "church" does not appear in the Gospels except at two places in Matthew (16:18 and 18:17). Yet it would be absolutely incorrect to suggest that because of a concern for individual relationship to Jesus in John there is no community relationship or activity implied in this Gospel (or in the Johannine Epistles). Gospel literature deals primarily with the life of Jesus, but the implied readers are living their Christian lives in the context of a Christian community or church. They are, in fact, a family birthed by God (born from above, 3:3) who live their lives as children of God (1:12). The message that is being delivered, therefore, must be read with that type of context in mind. Accordingly, the word pictures or images that appear in the Gospel are employed because they have meaning to that community or family context. The selection of materials (what is remembered and passed on about Jesus in the traditions of the church), therefore, provides us with an important witness not only about Jesus but also about the church!

The Farewell Discourses as a Model
for Understanding the Community

In our concern for the church, one particular section of John, I believe, offers some extremely significant insights. Having discussed the public ministry of Jesus in chapters 1—12 of his Gospel, frequently designated by scholars as the Book of Signs, the evangelist then turned his attention more particularly to matters of advice for the followers of Jesus. This section, embracing chapters 13 to 17, has been designated as the Farewell Discourses because they point our concern to the departure of Jesus and the implications which follow for the disciples and the church. Throughout these chapters the reader cannot help but sense that, while the discussion takes place in the context of the early disciples, the focus is on the Johannine community or family of God that is succeeding these early disciples. Attention therefore is directed to these chapters beginning with chapter 17 and moving back to 13. The point of using this method is hopefully to highlight for the reader the presuppositions upon which each of the chapters rests.

In the intercessory prayer of Jesus in John 17, there are at least four striking issues which Jesus mentioned concerning His disciples that would need attention as a result of His departure or hour of glorification (v. 1).[10] Jesus prayed first for their protection in the midst of a hateful world (vv. 11-15); then, for their purity or sanctification in a sinful, earthly context (vv. 17-19); thereafter, for their unity in the midst of a fragmented environment (vv. 20-23); and finally for their destiny in a world setting that lacked purpose and a failure of nerve (vv. 24-26).[11] But these concerns are not merely issues which affect individual Christians. They are absolutely critical issues which must receive attention if the church is to operate with a sense of direction and strength in the midst of a hostile world. It does not take much imagination, therefore, to envisage how these issues were on the front burner of concern for a persecuted Johannine community.[12] If the church lacked a sense of security, holiness, unity, and purpose, it would flounder in the first-century world of hostility and rejection.

The Paraclete or Spirit sayings of chapters 14—16 are therefore very instructive. In the first Paraclete saying, the presence of the Counselor is promised in response to those who love Jesus and keep His commands (14:15-16). The loneliness and fear that threatened the disciples by the departure of Jesus (vv. 1,18,27) would be relieved according to the second Paraclete saying by the sending of the Counselor who would act as teacher and consultant in place of Jesus (v. 26). In this context of the worry and concern of the disciples, it is interesting to note that Jesus delivered to them His words of "peace" (v. 27), words that were repeated after the resurrection (20:19)! These words of Jesus were the impetus for the familiar "giving of peace" in worship services of a number of churches, particularly in the liturgies of the Lord's Supper.[13] In the third Paraclete promise the focus is placed upon the role of the Spirit in bearing witness to Jesus (15:26-27). That role is expanded in the fourth saying, where the emphasis is upon the threefold role of the Spirit in relationship to the disobedient world, a world which must be brought to understand the nature of sin, the vindication of Jesus, and the condemnation of evil or the evil one. (16:7-11) By implication these statements also would mean that judgment applies to all those who are disobedient. In the fifth and final promise the stress is upon the Spirit as guide of truth and proclaimer of the way of Jesus (vv.13-15).

All of these sayings are addressed in the plural to the company of the disciples.[14] While one can legitimately argue that the perspectives here have application to individual Christians, the gift of the Holy Spirit is not to be understood in these texts merely as an individual matter. The giving of the Spirit (and with it the experiences of power) in this Gospel clearly is to be understood to have taken place in a corporate/family/community setting after the resurrection (20:22).

At this point it seems important to digress from the Farewell Discourses in order to emphasize the liturgical nature of the appearance stories in John 20. According to John the appearance of Jesus took place on the *first day of the week* when the disciples were *gathered together*. Within that context the "peace" is bestowed (v. 19) and the Holy Spirit is given (v. 22). In an effort to make this *corporate* liturgical emphasis clear, the Johannine writer not only details this first corporate appearance in the above context but he goes further to indicate that the *second* appearance of Jesus together with the second *giving of peace* occurred eight days later within the security of a house or home context (v. 26). According to this ancient pattern of reckoning, the first day in recounting an event is the very day on which the speaker starts the count instead of the next day as is our accustomed pattern. Thus eight days later is, in fact, from our perspective one week later.[15] The secure presence of Jesus is thus experienced in the corporate setting of the family of God.

The fact that the physical presence of the risen Lord was actually sensed in the corporate experience of the early church has given rise to a number of developments including the theory that the physical presence of Jesus could be made effective through the words of institution in the Lord's supper. Such a view of course is what we currently call transubstantiation. Yet the point of this resurrection text is not aimed at developing ways of assuring the physical presence of the risen Lord. Instead, it is aimed at asserting the need for the same type of assured sense of Christ's presence and its natural accompanying confession by the church even *without* that *physical presence* as a support to believing.

But it is time to return to Farewell Discourses and move from the prayer of Jesus (John 17) and the Paraclete sayings (John 14—16) to the mashal or parable of the vine and the branches together with the theological affirmations that flow from this well-known text (15:1-17). In the study of this passage it should be quickly noted that we have entered the arena of symbolism, an area in which John seems to have been particularly at home. For our twentieth-century scientific generation (and for much of Protestantism), however, the concern for symbolism is often relegated to categories of little interest. But symbols and images were apparently very important to the early Christians, particularly to the readers of Johannine literature (from the Gospel to the Apocalypse), to say nothing of the use of symbolism by Jesus in His parabolic teaching.

The parable of the vine and the branches in chapter 15, from my point of view, forms a central core to a chiasmatic pattern of argument in the Farewell Discourses of John. It provides a magnificent illustration of Jesus' relationship to the disciples and thus to the church. The vine is Jesus and believers are the branches (15:1, 6). The followers of Jesus must never get these categories confused and think that they can operate on their own. Confused identity resulting in disobedience was *the great sin of Adam and Eve* (Gen. 3:5-6). Instead, attachment to Christ is the only basis for being productive branches and avoiding the purging destruction of the vineyard keeper (15:4-6). But the purpose of the parable is not aimed primarily at threatening the disciples. The point is to call them to realize their goal of being true disciples (v. 8) so that they might experience the *joy* that comes from obedience and fruitful service (vv. 10-11).

In the comments that follow this mashal, an idea related to election (familiar in the Pauline Epistles) is mentioned. The followers of Jesus are reminded again (v. 16; cf. 6:70) that they did not choose Jesus but that He chose them. Such statements in the Bible related to the choosing power of God have caused great problems for many of those today who have drunk too heavily from the "self-made" philosophy of the nineteenth century. The idea that people are totally *free* and *not interdependent* is *not* an adequate picture of reality. We know much about predetermined factors today and about many who are subject to various types of bondage that result from economic, racial, and social factors in which they had no choice. Yet we often act as though the will is absolutely free. Jesus, however, knew that the bondage of evil was the overarching bondage so that even when He came to His own people and place, they did not receive their Creator and Savior (1:10-11). Instead, they served their father, the devil (8:34,44). Their actions thus made obvious both their status and their basic family or community orientation. Their functioning identified their primary parental relationship, a crucial factor in understanding the biblical notion of election.[16]

The coming of Jesus and the summons to follow Him was the final stage of God's great action to reverse this bondage of the world. That summons provided the opportunity for people to "receive" the invitation and believe in Jesus (1:12). But such reception was not a natural reaction which flowed from human bloodline or human determination. Sonship and daughterhood in the Johannine community resulted from the power of God (1:13). Christians must be constantly aware, therefore, that they are not their own but have been bought with a price, to use a Pauline expression (cf. 1 Cor. 6:20; 7:23). Their task, as John indicates in this mashal, is to bear authentic fruit which will endure.

To assist Christians in their fruit-bearing goal, Jesus told the disciples to ask God to supply their petitions (15:16). This idea of asking God and the supporting promise of God's response is repeated three more times in the Farewell Discourses of John (14:13; 15:7; 16:24). There is no question, therefore, that John challenges the Christian church to pray to God with expectancy. But these statements have often been misunderstood by well-meaning church members who have petitioned God with all kinds of personal requests. Accordingly, it is important to understand that behind all of these Johannine statements of Jesus there lies a singular presupposition which is stated in various ways. This presupposition is that the Christian church and its members (the family of God) must be firmly committed to *doing* the will (*thelema*) of God: namely, to seeking not their own ends but the purposes of God in sending Jesus. The whole of Jesus' life was directed to doing the will of God (e.g., 4:34; 5:30; 6:38-40) and He expected His followers to copy that model (e.g., 7:17; 9:31; 21:22). Such is the presupposition necessary when one asks in the name (or nature) of Jesus (14:14; 15:16; 16:24). Asking implies that one abides in Jesus (15:7) and one loves the family of God (v. 12). Asking in the name of Jesus is not simply a repetition of words; it is a life-confession of a commitment to think and to act like Jesus; to follow the model of Jesus! When humans follow this model they are no longer regarded by Jesus as mere servants, but they are actually called friends of the Lord (v. 14), a designation applied to Abraham, the father of the faithful (cf. Isa. 41:8; and Jas. 2:23).

This idea of the model of Jesus (cf. Phil. 2:1-11) reminds us that John identified two crucial aspects of that model in the two previous chapters of the Farewell Discourses. In chapter 14 Jesus is shown to be deeply concerned that the disciples might be able to grasp the correct instructions or model road map to God. In the previous chapter (13) Jesus Himself epitomizes the model of love in the powerful footwashing episode.

Chapter 14 is not merely to be understood as a text for a funeral service that calls us to a sense of hope during a traumatic experience in the loss of a loved one. Chapter 14 is even more a great word of hope for all Christians who fear alienation in a world that does not understand the meaning of Christian family life and pilgrimage. While the family of God does indeed have a face, Christians traverse this life without seeing and touching Jesus in the manner that the early disciples did (cf. 1 John 1:1-3). But even those disciples had to learn that they were not orphaned children (v. 18) because they and we have a Paraclete (a divine associate) in the Spirit (vv. 15-17) who reminds us of Jesus (15:26) and who, in turn, introduces us to our heavenly Father (14:6-7), thus assuring us of a genuine sense of "at homeness" with God (vv. 1-2).

The Christian sense of at homeness and the idea of pilgrimage are uniquely intertwined in this chapter so that the journey is not merely relegated to a time after death but is also rooted in the *presentness* of knowing that the one called the Lamb of God is also Himself the way (road), the truth, and the life (v. 6). There is no need then for the church to find a separate road map as Thomas requested. What becomes necessary for the family of God is that it adopts the authentic road and realizes that being related to Jesus actually means being related to "Father" God (vv. 10-11).

The foundation for understanding the nature of the family of God and the way of Jesus in the Farewell Discourses is set in the previous footwashing scene of John 13. The story begins with the crucial note that it was just before Passover and almost the hour of His departure, the time set by God (vv. 1-3).[17] Of all the events in the life of Jesus, this intriguing story (not found in the Synoptic Gospels) focused the thinking of John's readers on the church which would carry on the work of Jesus after His departure. It is a story filled with great pathos and moving contrasts. This chapter encapsulates both who Jesus is and what He expects of His church. At the same time it reminds the readers what kind of raw material Jesus faces in forming the church.

The towel and the washpot are the symbols of a slave's work. Indeed, only slaves touched people's feet. Students of great Jewish teachers were expected to honor the rabbi by doing for him almost every menial task done by a slave *except* the most degrading tasks of untying the rabbi's shoes or washing the rabbi's feet![18] John the Baptizer, however, proved that he would be an ideal follower of Jesus because he reckoned himself of less worth even than a slave in comparison to the Lord when he indicated he would not even be worthy to touch the thong of Jesus' sandals (1:27).[19]

What a shock it must have been for the disciples, therefore, when Jesus took the role of a slave! Peter, the pathetic spokesperson for the disciples (and coincidentally for any misguided segment of the church), voiced his strong disapproval of this pattern for Jesus (their religious leader) and stoutly asserted that he would have no part in such a degrading picture of Jesus (13:6-8). Fortunately for him, however, he was willing to reconsider his position when he learned that he was jeopardizing his entire state with God. But like an ignorant bull in a china shop, he supposed that the issue was water and not slavery. Accordingly, he was ready to jump in for a shower or a bath to prove his devotion to Jesus (v. 9). He is like many in the church today who enthusiastically want to follow Jesus but who are unable to perceive that it is, in fact, a difficult way of self-denial and slavery.

The basic motivation of the church, Jesus told us, is *love*. By evidencing love, Jesus indicated, the world would know those who are, in fact, His disciples (v. 35). Love is something that is easily talked about. It is easily preached from pulpits. But to practice love requires a transformed spirit in human beings and in churches. It is unfortunately a rather *rare commodity* in much of church life as it is among humanity in general. Thus, it should give us great cause to ponder whether everything that goes on in the name of the church is actually related to Jesus and the gospel.

The command of Jesus is for His followers to evidence love and not merely talk about it (v. 34). Talk about love is probably the devil's way of keeping Christians from actually loving one another, from being a true family of God. Moreover, we must not forget that according to John, Jesus designated the religious leaders of His day as being children of their father the devil. The reason Jesus said He categorized them with the devil is that they followed the desires of the devil (8:44). Their actions evidenced hatred as they sought to discredit and kill Jesus (6:41-65; 7:19-24; 8:39-44; etc.). It is clear then that the judgment of God is based not merely on what one says or thinks, but that it is equally important what one does (cf. for example Matt. 25:31-46; Rev. 20:12). Jesus has always known what is in human beings, and He has never been confused by words of believing (John 2:23-25).

Authentic believing is the goal of the Gospel of John (20:30-31). The idea appears with such regularity that the evangelist must have recognized a great deal of partial or pseudo-believing not only among the Jews of Jesus' time but also among Christians of his day. As a result, he was concerned to make the point absolutely clear (see, for example, 6:66-71; 12:42-43).

The issue of mixed or alien motives is brought to focus in chapter 13 through the figures of Judas and Peter. Judas is clearly one of the chosen ones (6:70), but his devil nature gives way as Satan (the father of lies, 8:44) enters him (13:27). The entire scene then becomes black as *night* (v. 30). Though he may have been in the company or family of the chosen, his actions proved otherwise. Peter, on the other hand, stoutly defended his faithfulness to Jesus not only in his enthusiastic reversal at the footwashing scene (v. 9) but also in his verbal insistence that he would lay down his life for Jesus (v. 37). Yet Jesus was not confused by Peter's good-intentioned verbosity. He knew what all humans are like. Today He likewise deals with people as they really are.

Even after the resurrection the situation did not change much, and the "believing" Peter proved he was not unlike many church members of today. He readily affirmed a threefold confession that he loved Jesus (21:15-17). When Jesus told him of his destiny to die for Him, however, Peter was concerned more about what would happen to someone else. God does not deal with everyone in the same way, but human beings—even church members—do not readily accept difficult situations in which they, rather than others, must take up their crosses. Like Peter (v. 18) they do not consider it to be fair if they are called to suffer when others seemed to prosper. Therefore, like Peter (v. 21) they usually begin to compare themselves with others. If they have to suffer for Jesus, then hopefully everybody else in the family will have to do the same! But such is not reality. Some of us are called to suffer for Jesus in one way, and some are given a different role. Christians are not made in the same mold. Yet all are called to authentic believing and living. Moreover, human notions of fairness need to be placed in the perspective of the life of Jesus. It is hard to conceive that it was "fair" for Jesus to die. Yet such is exactly what the Son of God willingly did as He became the Lamb of God that takes away the sin of the world (1:29).

Each person in the church has different tasks to perform. Each has the potential for failure like Peter. But each must also be conscious of the fact that within those numbered among the chosen family of the church there may indeed be lurking a Judas. Therefore, everyone should look deeply into his or her own motivations and pray to God that the spirit of Judas may not seize any of those who are part of the family fellowship. In writing to the early churches, John, in his First Epistle, knew all too well that the spirit of Judas was still present in the church, and he identified the evil spirit with the spirit of antichrist. That spirit of self-seeking ultimately denies the lordship of Christ (1 John 2:15-19).

Conclusion

The Farewell Discourses of John thus provide careful Christian readers with some important insights into the early church. By implication the images and word pictures have a great deal to say about the nature and mission of the church today. When one focuses on each of these pericopes, one soon discovers that these discourses are dealing with some vital issues for the church or family of God, including the nature of a Christian's relationship to other Christians (ch. 13); the implications of not being able to have the actual physical presence of Jesus in the church as leader and guide as well as the implications of separation through death (ch. 14); the nature and work of the Holy Spirit in the church and in the world (chs. 14—16); the nature and purpose of Christian life including the basis for, test of, and the joyful results of the church of living with Christ (ch. 15); and the fundamental concerns for the followers of Christ in living in a hostile, unholy, divided, and purposeless world (ch. 17).

Beyond the content of these chapters, the organization of these Farewell Discourses is nothing less than the work of a skillful artist. The Farewell texts begin with an act of Jesus that epitomizes His very nature and mission, and they conclude with a totally self-giving prayer. The whole point of this prayer for the glorification of Jesus is directed towards the church. The Lord's concern is not for His own suffering and death. His concern is for the church that would follow Him. Jesus' focus is on the protection, holiness, unity, and destiny of His people. What a model for contemporary prayers! Every pulsebeat of this prayer is directed toward the mission of Jesus in the world through the church. Most modern prayers and actions of Christians appear like empty shells of self-interest when compared to the prayer of Jesus and to His act of washing the disciples' feet.

In this context of act and prayer the promise that Jesus would not leave His church orphaned (14:18) but the coming Paraclete would be the Christian's constant companion (vv. 16,26-27), serving as the alter ego of Jesus (15:26; 16:12-14), catches the intimate heart-throb of the Lord. This beating of Christ's heart ought to grip the Christian family with a stirring challenge to aspire to the Lord's model for the fellowship of faith.

In this context of model act, promise, and prayer, therefore, the mashal of the vine and the branches takes on special significance as the focal image of Christ and the church. As the branches receive their life from the vine, the Christian church lives because of its relationship to Christ. Apart from the sustaining vitality of God the Christian and the church can do absolutely nothing (15:5). But if Christians abide in Christ (v. 4) and love one another (v. 12), their prayers (v. 7) and actions (v. 8) will count for eternity and the church will fulfill its destiny of glorifying God and bringing joy to the world (v. 11).

As the church fulfills its destiny, the world will truly see that in the church the Lord has come among human beings. That Lord—who became flesh and "tented" in the midst of humanity, full of grace and truth—has made known to the world the God whom no human being has ever seen (1:14-18). Jesus Christ, the only Son (v. 14), however, has been seen and actually touched by humans (cf. 1 John 1:1-2). It is He who has personally made God known (John 1:18). It is He who has provided for the church a genuine sense of familyness or fellowship (*koinonia*, 1 John 1:3). Moreover, it is He who continues to make God's love known to the world through the witness of the church by the powerful presence of the Holy Spirit. God's love and the church's task are intimately intertwined. Therefore, obedience to the Lord is the crucial mark of a faithful church (John 15:14). Accordingly, as the risen Lord summoned Peter with a cryptic command, so He calls the church with those same unforgettable words, "Follow me!" (21:22).

Notes

1. For the idea of the Johannine Gospel as a symphony see G. Borchert, "The Fourth Gospel and Its Theological Impact," *Review and Expositor* (1981): 249-58.

2. See G. Borchert, "The Resurrection Perspective in John: An Evangelical Summons," *Review and Expositor* 85 (1988): 501-13.

3. See Paul S. Minear, *Images of the Church in the New Testament* (Philadelphia: Westminster Press, 1960). Of the ninety-six images that Minear considers apply to the church in the New Testament approximately twenty (fish, wine, branches of vine, fig tree, bride, twelve tribes, flock, lambs, holy temple, son of man, God's glory, light, life, sanctified, followers and disciples, road, coming and going, friends, servants, sons of God) appear from my reading of his study to be related in some greater or lesser extent to the Gospel of John. Twenty-four appear to be related to the Apocalypse of John and seven to the Johannine Epistles. In this respect notice how few images Karl Ludwig Schmidt recognized that are present in Johannine materials as he discussed *ekklesia* in his article in TDNT, 3:501-36. He does mention the living images of flock and the use of the term "church" in 3 John and Revelation, however. *TDNT*, 3:501-36.

4. For an excellent discussion of the literary features of this Gospel see R. Alan Culpepper, *Anatomy of the Fourth Gospel: A Study in Literary Design* (Philadelphia: Fortress Press, 1983).

5. See Rudolf Bultmann, *Theology of the New Testament*, 2 vols. (New York: Charles Scribner's Sons, 1955), 1:7-10, 91-92 and 113.

6. Eduard Schweizer, "The Concept of the Church in the Gospel and Epistles of St. John," in *New Testament Essays in Memory of T. W. Manson*, ed. A. Higgins (Manchester: University Press, 1959), 230-45.

7. See Gary M. Burge, *The Anointed Community: The Holy Spirit in the Johannine Tradition* (Grand Rapids: Wm. B. Eerdmans, 1987).

8. See Raymond E. Brown, *The Community of the Beloved Disciple* (New York: Paulist Press, 1979); idem, *New Testament Essays* (New York: Paulist Press, 1965), 36-47, and idem, *The Gospel According to John (i-xii)*, Vol. 29, The Anchor Bible (Garden City: Doubleday and Co., 1966), cv-cxiv. See also Rudolf Schnackenburg, *The Church in the New Testament* (New York: Herder and Herder, 1965), 103-17; and *The Gospel According to John: Commentary on Chapters 13-21*, (New York: Crossroad, 1987), 3:203-17.

9. While the word *church* (*ekklesia*) does not appear in the Gospel of John, it appears twenty times in Revelation (thirteen of them in the plural) and three times in 3 John.

10. The idea of glorification in John is related to the fulfillment of Jesus' purpose in coming to earth to die and serve as the Lamb of God that takes away the sin of the world (John 1:29). It is linked directly with the idea of hour in John as is done in John 17:1. The hour is the hour of

Jesus' death which is encapsulated in His words from the cross "It is finished!" (19:30).

11. For a further discussion of these points please see G. Borchert, *Assurance and Warning* (Nashville: Broadman Press, 1987), 134-37.

12. For a discussion of the sociological setting behind the Fourth Gospel see Bruce Malina, *The Gospel of John in Sociolinguistic Perspective*, ed. H. Waetjen (Berkley: Center for Hermeneutical Studies in Hellenistic and Modern Culture, 1985). For a discussion of the social implications of Johannine mysticism see the remarks of Howard C. Kee, *Christian Origins in Sociological Perspective* (Philadelphia: Westminster Press, 1980), 157-65.

13. See for example the liturgy of the United Church of South India. For an interesting discussion of Eucharist and baptism in John see Brown, *New Testament Essays*, 77-95.

14. The plural "you" (*humas* and *humin*) is used throughout this text. It, of course, applies to the disciples in this story. But the Johannine stories usually have an application beyond the stories themselves and need to be understood in the early church context as well.

15. If one understands the pattern of counting at this time, it may help with the prophetic idea that Jesus was raised on the third day or after three days (as both are expressed by the Gospel writers), a notion that often confuses contemporary readers of the Gospels (cf. Matt. 16:21; 17:23; 20:19; Luke 9:31; 18:33; 24:7,21,46; Mark 8:31; 9:31; 10:34; Matt. 27:40,63; John 2:20. Cf. also Acts 10:40; 1 Cor. 15:4).

The three days are Friday, Saturday (the sabbath), and Sunday (the first day of the week which comes to be known as the Lord's Day or the day of the resurrection).

16. Election is a troubling idea for many contemporary Christians who have been brought up with nineteenth-century individualism and freedom as the presupposition of their thinking. But it is important to understand that whereas the Greek-Western mind ask questions like: What is it? What is it made of? (the question of composition and nature), the Semite-Eastern mind asks questions like: What does it do? What is it good for? (the question of use). For example in 1 Peter 1:2 note that Christians are chosen (elected) and destined . . . unto (for the purpose of) obedience to Jesus Christ.

17. Please see my forthcoming article "The Passover and the Narrative Cycles in John" (first presented to the Society of Biblical Literature meeting in Chicago, 1988) to be published in *Perspectives in John* by Mercer Press.

18. In the rabbinic tradition a disciple was expected to accept all forms of service for his teacher that a slave would do for the master except that of untying the shoes. Labor which involved touching the feet was regarded as too degrading (*Keth.* 96a. See Str-B I. 121).

19. In the Fourth Gospel John the Baptizer is always portrayed as an ideal follower. There is no hint of doubt by the Baptizer as in Luke 7:18-35 and Matthew 11:2-19.

10
Images of the Church in Acts

by Carey C. Newman

Introduction

It is fitting that an essay on the church in Acts should be included in this volume, for Acts records the first collective steps of Jesus' earliest followers. Chock-full of chronological and geographical textual markers, Acts can be read as the church's first "history."[1] Acts narrates how the church, through the tireless efforts of two apostles, Peter and Paul, made its way from Jerusalem to Rome in thirty years.

To construe Acts as merely sermons framed by travelogue is, however, to decline the true invitation of Acts. Acts is not just "history," but also a fine piece of theology: Acts records, reflects, and preaches theology. Indeed, Acts is considered by some to be so theological that the book sacrifices history at the altar of theology.[2] But to read Acts as only a piece of church (produced) theology poses a false dichotomy between history and theology, much like that suggested by more recent attempts to read Acts only in terms of its literary value (i.e., a dichotomy between history and literary architecture).[3]

Whatever one decides concerning the precise generic classification (a decision which may well be impossible to render with any certainty), generic properties are not mutually exclusive: why shouldn't an accurate history of the earliest followers of Jesus be theologically edifying and at the same time provide readers, both ancient and modern, with immense delight? By artistically and kerygmatically chronicling progress and expansion, Acts bids the reader to come join the sometimes chaotic, sometimes apocalyptic, but always marvelous world of Jesus' earliest followers. Whether Acts should be labeled an edifying historical theology or an entertaining theological history is in some ways a moot question. Acts is both.[4]

The rather fluid generic properties of Acts produce numerous interpretive problems; this is especially evident when it comes to the tableaux of the fledgling church. Acts does not set before the reader a comprehensive description of what the church was like: Acts does not narrate all of the church's history. Nor does Acts provide a systematic, prescriptive statement on what the church should be: Acts certainly does not present a doctrine of the church. Even in contrast with other New Testament documents, Acts does not employ the same connotative imagery to define the church.[5] Acts simply speaks of the "thatness" of the church without defining the essence.[6]

What Acts does accomplish is to chart the imprints and ripples of the church as it traversed the sands and seas of the Greco-Roman world. It is up to the modern investigator to collect, collate, and interpret the textual clues in order to reconstruct the image(s) of the church in Acts. To this investigator, the text of Acts suggests at least two dominant images: (1) the church as recipient of apocalyptic revelation, and (2) the church as bearer and proclaimer of a decidedly apocalyptic message. Though separated for the sake of discussion, the two images are but glimpses of the same entity: the church as an apocalyptic community.

That "apocalyptic" will be considered as a legitimate adjective to describe the church in Acts is especially surprising since Acts is so often charged with performing major, reconstructive surgery on early Christian eschatology. Though defending the thesis that "apocalyptic" was the mother of early Christian theology, Ernst Käsemann argues that Acts was something of an illegitimate stepchild of "apocalyptic."[7] Instead of presenting the early church as an apocalyptic community, Acts portrays the church as an "early catholic institution."[8] By "early catholic" it is meant that the church had become a highly organized and structured institution with official church officers and hierarchy. The static character of the church was a response to the delay of the Parousia: as a way of coping with delay, Acts programmatically replaced the belief in Jesus' imminent Parousia with the gift of the Spirit and thereby situated the church as the middle point in salvation-history.[9] The church of (Luke-) Acts, in effect, becomes the dispenser of salvation.

Acts' deliberate reshaping of pristine "apocalyptic" has, at least in some circles, become a mark of assured criticism. As James D. G. Dunn surmises:

> To present such a picture of first generation Christianity, so even tempera-
> tured from beginning to end, so remarkably *un*apocalyptic, could certainly
> constitute a qualification for the title "early Catholic."[10]

However, recent research into early Jewish "apocalyptic" may well render the picture of a decidedly *un*apocalyptic church in Acts questionable.[11] Following Paul Hanson, scholars now distinguish between apocalypses (a literary genre or subgenre), apocalypticism (a social movement) and apocalyptic eschatology (a religious perspective).[12] Today we are in a better position both to ask and answer questions concerning the relationship of early Jewish "apocalypses" and "apocalypticism" to Christian origins in general[13] and to the picture of the earliest community fossilized specifically within Acts.

The Church as Recipient of Apocalyptic Revelation

John J. Collins defines an "apocalypse" as

> . . .a genre of revelatory literature with a narrative framework, in which a revelation is mediated by an otherworldly being to a human recipient, disclosing a transcendent reality which is both temporal, insofar as it envisages eschatological salvation, and spatial, insofar as it involves another, spiritual world.[14]

Christopher Rowland, in his study of early Jewish and Christian apocalyptic expressions, also highlights the disclosure of information as a key motif in identifying the genre.

> What we are faced with in apocalyptic, therefore, is a type of religion whose distinguishing feature is a belief in a direct revelation of the things of God which was mediated through dream, vision or divine intermediary.[15]

Though these definitions by Collins and Rowland, which focus upon the communication of heavenly knowledge as a/the central feature of "apocalypses," certainly place in a completely new light the programmatic statements of Käsemann (and others) about the centrality of the (supposedly delayed) Parousia,[16] questions still remain. Can Acts be tolerably construed as an "apocalypse"? And what does this say about the character of the earliest community of Acts?

Acts presents the earliest followers of Jesus as possessing an almost unrestricted access to the heavens. Indeed, Acts records something of an invasion of earth, with Jesus' exaltation inaugurating the heavenly descent.[17] It is through these various invasions that heaven continues to communicate with earth (the exalted Jesus with His witnesses).

Acts 1:1-11 opens by analeptically resuming the plot of Luke: "In the first book, O Theophilus, I have dealt with all that Jesus *began* to do and teach," which could be completed with, "I will now tell you, O Theophilus, all that Jesus *continued* to do" author's italics).[18] But Acts 1:1-11 also proleptically sounds a shift in key: though still continuing the Jesus story of the Gospel, the plot to be narrated in Acts concerns an exalted Jesus.

Resonating with the language of the primal, archetypical theophany of God to Moses (Ex. 24 LXX),[19] Acts opens with the disciples watching the exaltation of Jesus to the right hand of God. Having repeatedly "presented Himself alive" (*parestesen heauton zonta*), "appearing" (*optanomenos,* 1:3) to His disciples over the period of forty days, Jesus was "taken up" (*ane-lemphthe*, vv. 2,11) into heaven. While gazing into the heavens (*atenizontes esan eis ton ouranon*, v. 10), the apostles were chided by two angelic beings who had also "become present" (*pareistekeisan)* beside them: why are you looking into the heavens? Do you not know that Jesus will "come" from heaven in the same way as you saw him exalted into heaven (v. 11)? In early Jewish and Christian literature, "to be present," "to appear," "to take up," "to gaze into the heavens," and "to come" all echo the technical language and forms of early Jewish apocalypses.[20]

This promised "coming" finds immediate expression in the theophanic arrival of the Spirit on Pentecost (Acts 2:1-42). The coming of the wind-like sounds of heaven (*ek tou ouranou*) and the "appearance" (*ophthesan*, v. 3) of tongues divinely legitimizes the preaching of the supposedly intoxicated disciples. Peter's sermon on Joel 2 intertextually situates the Spirit invasion of Pentecost in a long line of theophanic, visionary, and heavenly invasions. However, the "coming" not only bodes the extraordinary events of Pentecost but also augurs the many times the exalted Jesus will "come" to His followers within the confines of Acts. Indeed, as the Joel prophecy states (again echoing the language of early Jewish apocalypses), the invasion had just begun: "your young men shall see visions [*horaseis*], and your old men shall dream dreams" [*enupniois enupniasthesontai*] . . . before the day of the Lord comes [*elthein*], the great and manifest [*epiphane*] day" (vv. 17-20).

Acts has now set the pattern for the church: through the often-repeated "apocalypses" of the exalted Jesus, special, divinely inspired information will be mediated to the newly formed community. Though taking many forms—dreams/visions, angelophanies, throne visions, and even Christophanies—the miniapocalypses all disclose key information to key characters at key junctures in the narrative. The apocalypses guide, and even propel, the newly formed community of followers in an ever-outwardly spiraling adventure of progress and expansion, an adventure which ultimately stretches from Jerusalem to Rome.

For example, through a "vision" (*hormamati*, 9:10-12) the Lord spoke to Ananias, instructing him to go and lay hands on God's especially "chosen instrument"(v. 15), Saul, the apostle to the Gentiles. After falling into a trance (*egeneto ep auton ekstasis*, 10:10; 11:5), Peter was supernaturally confronted with a heavenly "vision" (*horamati*, 10:3,17,19; 11:5) and received its interpretation through a heavenly "voice" (*phone*, 10:13,15; 11:7,9).[21] The vision, divinely interpreted, led Peter to the radical decision to extend the good news of Jesus' death and resurrection to the Gentiles.[22] Paul, too, after experiencing a night vision (*horama dia nuktos to Paulo ophthe*), concluded that God had called him to extend the gospel to Europe (16:9-10).

The viability of Paul's eighteen-month Corinthian ministry was confirmed through a vision (*horamati,* 18:9). In making his defense to the people, Paul admits freely that he was something of a practicing mystic. The apostle states that while praying, he fell into a trance (*genesthai me en ekstasei,* 22:17) and heard God instruct him to leave Jerusalem.[23] In each case the visions and dreams disclosed crucial information critical to the expansion and progress of the church.

The various angelophanies recorded in Acts occur for the purposes of rescue, guidance, judgment, and encouragement. An angel of the Lord, after opening the prison doors, released the apostles and instructed them to continue preaching to the people (5:19-20). An angel of the Lord gave specific verbal, geographical directions which resulted in the evangelization of the Ethiopian eunuch (8:26). After baptizing the eunuch, Philip, like Elisha's heavenly journey of old, was supernaturally transported away by the Spirit (*pneuma kuriou herpasen Philippon,* v. 39; cf. 2 Kings 2:16, LXX).[24] Peter's release from prison was effected through the light-accompanied appearance and activity of an angel of the Lord (12:7)—though Peter initially confused the angel's appearance with a vision (*edokei de horama blepein,* v. 9).[25] An angel of the Lord was directly responsible for the death of the defiantly arrogant King Herod (v. 23). It was an angel of God which stood beside Paul (*pareste gar moi . . . aggelos),* reassuring him that he was, in turn, to stand before Caesar (27:23-24).

Stephen's experience of seeing the "heavens opened" (*theoro tous ouranous dienoigmenous,* 7:56; cf. 10:11; Rev. 4:1), recorded in Acts 7, should certainly be classified as a "throne vision"—akin to the "throne visions" of early Jewish and Christian apocalypses.[26] Most importantly, however, the "throne vision" identifies the once-crucified, but now-exalted Jesus as God's chief agent and supreme object of revelation. As two great salvation-historical poles, the Stephen narrative begins and ends with references to the theophany of God's *doxa* (vv. 2,55). The references to *doxa,* a unique, constitutive feature of early Jewish apocalyptic "throne visions," function to identify intertextually the exalted Jesus—"the prophet" whom God will "raise up" (37), the one who spoke with the angel in the congregation (*ekklesia*) of the wilderness (but who now speaks with the new *ekklesia,* v. 38), the "Righteous One" (v. 52), the "Son of man" (of Dan. 7 and Ezek. 1, v. 56)—as God's endtime *kabod/doxa.* The glory inclusions serve to highlight Jesus as God's chief agent of revelation in this "throne vision."

The Acts accounts of Paul's encounter with the risen Christ (Acts 9:1-9; 22:6-21; 26:12-18) echo the great prophetic call passages of the Hebrew Bible.[27] Often overlooked is the apocalyptic character of the reports in Acts. The revelation of Jesus to Paul on the Damascus road also possesses strong form-critical and tradition-historical ties with "throne visions" of early Jewish apocalypses.[28]

Acts reports that as Paul traveled to Damascus, a great "light out of heaven" (*phos ek tou ouranou,* 9:3; 22:6; 26:13) flashed about him. Paul fell to the ground and heard a "voice" (*phonen,* 9:4; 22:7; 26:14) which spoke with him directly. In the course of the Christophany, Paul discovers the identity of the "voice": it is the once-crucified messianic pretender, Jesus, the now-risen and thus-vindicated Messiah—it is He who appeared (*ho ophtheis,* 9:17) to Paul. Through the Christophany, Paul discovers that he has been appointed by God "to know his will, to see the Just One, and to hear a voice from his mouth" (22:14). Paul is to be a witness of all that he has seen and heard (*hon heorakas kai ekousas,* v. 15; *eis touto gar ophthen soi,* v. 16) and of what the risen Christ will yet show to him (*hon te ophthesomai soi,* v. 16). Transformed by this heavenly [throne] vision (*ouranio optasia,* v. 19), Paul obediently preaches Jesus as the apocalyptic "Son of God" (9:20, 26:19-20).

Through the gaping hole in the sky, ripped open wide by the exaltation of Jesus, Acts portrays heaven as consistently communicating with earth. While one should be reticent to construe the whole of Acts as an "apocalypse"—though one privately wonders what sort of case could be made—the presence of visions/dreams, angelophanies, throne visions, and Christophanies demonstrates that the earliest community in Acts is portrayed as apocalyptic in character. That heaven "invaded" earth on a continual basis, granting to the earliest followers of Jesus special knowledge and insight, does argue for a highly apocalyptic picture of the earliest church. Acts is a major New Testament source for dream-visions, and it is these miniapocalypses which serve to direct the narrative.[29]

The Church as Bearer and Proclaimer
of an Apocalyptic Message

As opposed to the literary phenomenon of apocalypses, Paul Hanson defines apocalypticism as a visionary system of thought, a symbolic universe, espoused by a specific, marginalized community. In response to historical and social conditions, the apocalyptic community generates an alternative symbolic message to protest and/or oppose the ideology of those in power. As a codified system, apocalypticism establishes group identity vis-à-vis other segments of society and eases the contradictions between hope and alienation.[30] Such notions compel us to inquire whether Acts depicts the earliest community as an expression of apocalypticism?

The text of Acts suggests that the early church possessed self-awareness as a "sect" (*hairesin,* 24:14,5; 28:22), with a definite "beginning" (11:15) distinct from other Jewish "sects" (5:17; 15:5; 26:5). Acts employs various social signifiers to demarcate the group of Jesus' earliest followers—for example: disciples (*mathetes*), church (*ekklesia*), Way *(odos)*, flock (*poimne*), Christians (*christianos*), faithful *(piste)*, saints *(hagioi)*, and witnesses (*martures*).[31] In contrast, the "established" Jewish (and Greek) groups are identified as the people (*laos*), Greeks (*Hellen*), synagogue (*sunagoge*), sons/house/people of Israel (*huioi/oikos/laos Israel*), Pharisees (*Pharisaios*), Sadducees (*Saddoukaios*) or the multitudes (*plethos*).[32]

Recent sociological readings reinforce Acts' linguistic distinctions. Pentecost transformed the small introversionist band of followers into a "strong" conversionist sect.[33] Though never formally articulated, the group had something of a localized structure and extended varying degrees of acceptance to wandering charismatic preachers.[34] Based upon their expectations for an imminent return of Jesus, the early community assembled for daily worship, shared common meals, and instituted the apocalyptically significant practice of sharing goods (2:43-47; 4:32-37).[35] Constantly harassed by traditional authorities, the church was oppressed and suffered persecution (8:1; 13:50). The conclusion: the earliest followers of Jesus organized themselves into a distinct group in contrast to other "established" groups, Jewish and/or Greek, and suffered the effects of social marginalization.[36]

The self-aware, distinct, and marginalized community also expressed an alternative symbolic world centering in the descent and ascent of an apocalyptic, divine mediator. Further, though sharing a common heritage, the early Christian construal of the Hebrew Bible narrative, based as it was upon the apocalyptic events surrounding the figure of Jesus, stood in sharp conflict with readings generated by the established Jewish communities.[37] The early Christian message not only defined the group as distinct from the more established ways of interpreting Jewish tradition, but also significantly contributed to the process of social marginalization.

Among many scholars, there is a growing sense of awareness that Jesus as the resurrected and exalted Lord should be read against the horizon of early Jewish apocalyptic, divine agents.[38] Personified powers and attributes, exalted patriarchs and principal angels were the linguistic vehicles for expressing divine agency in early Jewish apocalypticism. Acts pictures Jesus by means of such apocalyptically charged language. Acts employs the attributes "righteousness" ("Righteous One," 3:14; 7:52; 22:14), "holiness" ("Holy One," 2:27; 3:14,18,20; 4:27; 13:35) and "glory" (7:55-56) to define Jesus. To be compared favorably with the patriarchal figure of Moses (3:22; 7:37) and the "servant" of Isaiah (3:13,22-24,26; 4:25,27-30), Jesus is repeatedly named as *the* Anointed One, the Christ (2:31,36; 4:26-27; 5:42; 9:22; 17:3; 18:5; 26:23). Acts also depicts Jesus as the angelic being of Daniel's vision, the Son of man (7:56).[39] But in Acts, Jesus is more than just

God's chief agent; Jesus is the Lord God Himself. That the church considered Jesus on a par with God Himself can be seen in the startling, and particularly Christian, innovation of worship. Through prayer (1:24; 7:59-60) and formal confessional pronouncements (2:38; 3:6; 5:42; 9:22; 10:36; 11:27; 21:10-11; 22:16) Jesus is given worship as a second power in heaven, God Himself.[40] The worshiping of Jesus as God functioned sociologically to reinforce internal and external group boundaries and, no doubt, led to further theological reflection.[41]

In early Jewish apocalypticism, the divine agent's mission was oftentimes transferred to the elect.[42] Within the confines of Acts, the mission of the exalted Jesus is so executed through His earthly followers. The chief means of portraying the democratization is through the activity of the "Spirit" and the various deeds performed "in the name" of Jesus.[43] The Holy Spirit is the divine empowerment for the earliest followers of Jesus, while the "name" is the means by which miracles, preaching, and baptism are effected.

Though acting through His "Spirit" and in His "name," the church wrestled with the implications of fully identifying with the risen Lord. Just what did it mean to continue the mission of Jesus? In the drama of salvation, the casting of the Gentiles in a key role did not occur without reflection and, particularly, without some divine prodding. The narratives concerning Peter and Cornelius (Acts 10) and the apostolic council (Acts 15) show how slowly the church came to recognize the universal implications involved in their shared mission with the risen Lord. Once accepted, however, the universal scope of missionary expansion was quite consistent with the Hebrew Scriptures: the promise is for all people (e.g., 2:39; 28:28). The church's mission to the Gentiles grew out of its own sense as an apocalyptic community who identified with the mission and message of an exalted mediator.

Identifying Jesus as God's chief servant, the crucified Messiah who has been exalted to the right hand on high, signaled a rereading of traditional Jewish texts.[44] The bold, charismatic, interpretive moves taken by the preachers in Acts engendered a series of powerful sociological consequences. From the start, the church's exegesis and application of the Scriptures landed them on the wrong side of traditional Jewish belief. In particular, the attempt to "prove" the identification of Jesus as the crucified and exalted Messiah and to ground the legitimacy of the Gentile mission in the Scriptures caused persecution, charges of religious apostasy and political sedition. In some cases, such interpretive moves could even result in martyrdom (Acts 7).

Though sharing a rather common structural pattern with many Hellenistic religions (both Jewish and Greek), early Christian reflection upon Jesus demonstrates a highly significant innovation.[45] As seen in the sermons of

Acts, the descent/ascent pattern was fleshed out with historical specificity. The church of Acts possessed a very particular story about their apocalyptic divine agent: in the coming of Jesus, the promises of God made in the Scriptures have been fulfilled; Jesus of Nazareth went about doing good, performing signs and wonders by the power of God; this Jesus was crucified, raised from the dead, and is thus the exalted Lord at God's right hand; this same Jesus will come again to judge the world and restore the kingdom.[46] The sermons demonstrate that the church of Acts possessed a historically nuanced story about their apocalyptic divine agent.

The apocalyptic kerygma of Acts compares favorably with primitive, pre-formed traditions (creeds, hymns, confessions) within the New Testament and with traditional material within second-century Christian authors.[47] Thus, a well-established trajectory of an apocalyptic message, centering in the life, death, and resurrection of a Jewish Messiah, can be plotted from the earliest days of the church to the fixed confessional forms of the second- and third-century church. In concert with the evidence of other early Christian sources, the church of Acts reflects a particularly unique symbolic construal of the apocalyptic divine agency tradition, differing significantly from traditional Jewish and proto-Gnostic construals.[48]

Conclusion

Despite the claims of some, the church of Acts should be viewed as an apocalyptic community. Acts portrays the church as a continual recipient of divine information—information which is transmitted through the apocalyptic forms of dreams/visions, angelophanies, throne visions, and Christophanies. Acts also depicts the church as an expression of apocalypticism. As an identifiable and marginalized group within traditional Judaism, the church was the bearer and proclaimer of an apocalyptic message, a message centering in the universal significance of the death and resurrection of Jesus, the Messiah. That Acts is read here as a witness to the first steps of the church may well fly in the face of traditional criticism. However unpopular and unfashionable it may be, this author considers Luke to be an able and accurate historical-theologian (or, theological-historian). That the categories of "history" and "theology" could and should go together was a lesson first learned at the feet of my teacher, James Leo Garrett, Jr.

Notes

1. W. M. Ramsay, *St. Paul the Traveller and Roman Citizen* (London: Hodder and Stoughton, 1895); W. W. Gasque, *A History of Criticism of Acts of the Apostles* (BGBE 17; Tubingen: Mohr-Siebeck, 1975); F. F. Bruce, *Commentary on the Book of Acts* (NICNT; Grand Rapids: Eerdmans, 1954); Martin Hengel, *Acts and the History of Earliest Christianity* (Philadelphia: Fortress, 1979) 1-68; Colin J. Hemer, *The Book of Acts in the Setting of Hellenistic History*, ed.

Conrad H. Gempf (WUNT 1/49; Tubingen: Mohr-Siebeck, 1989).

2. On the theological *Tendenz* of Acts, see Ernst Haenchen, *The Acts of the Apostles: A Commentary* (Philadelphia: Westminster, 1971) or Hans Conzelmann, *Acts of the Apostles* (Hermeneia; Philadelphia: Fortress, 1987).

3. Richard I. Pervo, *Profit with Delight: The Literary Genre of the Acts of the Apostles* (Philadelphia: Fortress, 1987). Pervo pushes the argument of Haenchen to its logical conclusion. If Acts was intended for "edification," then Acts should be read in light of ancient "popular" literature. Acts thus sacrifices history (and theological integrity) for the purpose of entertainment. For a more positive use of literary categories to read Acts, see Leland Ryken, *Words of Life: A Literary Introduction to the New Testament* (Grand Rapids: Baker, 1987), 77-88.

4. Howard Marshall, *Luke: Historian and Theologian* (Grand Rapids: Eerdmans, 1970); Hengel, *Acts,* 59-68.

5. For discussions of New Testament church imagery see Paul S. Minear, *Images of the Church in the New Testament* (Philadelphia: Westminster, 1960); and Hans Küng, *The Church* (Garden City, N.Y.: Image Books, 1967), 35-46, 113-24.

6. Though *ekklesia* appears often in Acts (5:19; 8:1,3; 9:31; 11:22,26; 12:1,5; 13:1; 14:23,27; 15:3-4,22,41; 16:5; 18:22; 20:17,28), little information about the community can be obtained from the references—outside the facts that the church suffered and grew, met for worship and preaching, was comprised of individual members, possessed some form of leadership, and was established in various locations from Jerusalem to Corinth. See K. L. Schmidt, *"Ekklesia,"* *TDNT* 3:504-5; F. F. Bruce, "The Church of Jerusalem in the Acts of the Apostles," *BJRL* 67 (1985): 641-61; and, more generally, Küng, *Church,* 117-23.

7. Ernst Käsemann, "The Beginnings of Christian Theology," in *New Testament Questions of Today* (Philadelphia: Fortress, 1969): 82-107; idem, "On the Subject of Primitive Christian Apocalyptic," *Questions,* 108-37; Philipp Vielhauer, "On the 'Paulinism' of Acts," in *Studies in Luke-Acts,* eds. L. E. Keck and J. L. Martyn (London: SPCK, 1966), 33-50; and Hans Conzelmann, *The Theology of St. Luke* (Philadelphia: Fortress, 1961).

8. Ernst Käsemann, "New Testament Questions of Today," in *Questions,* 26; Vielhauer, "Paulinism," 49; cf. I. Howard Marshall, " 'Early Catholicism' in the New Testament," in *New Dimensions in New Testament Study,* eds. R. N. Longenecker and M. C. Tenney (Grand Rapids: Zondervan, 1974), 217-31.

9. Conzelmann, *Theology,* 207-34.

10. James D. G. Dunn, *Unity and Diversity in the New Testament: An Inquiry into the Character of Earliest Christianity* (Philadelphia: Westminster, 1977), 384.

11. In addition to the literature cited in the notes below, see the older studies of early Jewish "apocalyptic" by H. H. Rowley, *The Relevance of Apocalyptic: A Study of Jewish and Christian Apocalypses from Daniel to Revelation,* 3d ed., new and rev. (New York: Association Press, 1963); D. S. Russell, *The Method and Message of Jewish Apocalyptic 200 BC-100 AD* (OTL; Philadelphia: Westminster, 1964); and Klaus Koch, *The Rediscovery of Apocalyptic* (SBT 2/22; London: SCM, 1972).

12. Paul D. Hanson, *The Dawn of Apocalyptic* (Philadelphia: Fortress, 1975); idem, "Apocalypse, genre," in *IDBSup,* 27-28; idem, "Apocalypticism, *IDBSup,* 28-34.

13. James Charlesworth, *The Old Testament Pseudepigrapha and the New Testament: Prolegomena for the Study of Christian Origins* (SNTSMS 54; Cambridge: Cambridge University Press, 1985); Niel S. Fujita, *A Crack in the Jar: What Ancient Jewish Documents Tell Us about the New Testament* (New York and Mahwah, N.J.: Paulist Press, 1986); John J. Collins, *The Apocalyptic Imagination: An Introduction to the Jewish Matrix of Christianity* (New York: Crossroad, 1987); James H. Charlesworth, *Jesus within Judaism: New Light from Exciting Archaeological Discoveries* (ABRL; New York: Doubleday, 1988).

14. John J. Collins, "Introduction: Towards the Morphology of a Genre," *Semeia* 14 (1979): 1-20; idem, "The Jewish Apcalypses," *Semeia* 14 (1979): 21-59. Subsequently, Collins updated his work, critically interacting with the ongoing debate, in *Daniel, with an Introduction to Apocalyptic Literature* (FOTL 22; Grand Rapids: Eerdmans, 1984), 2-24, where he

follows his earlier definition of apocalypse. Though a postexilic literary phenomenon, apocalypses share many typical features and motifs with the writings of the prophets. The historical trajectory of early Jewish apocalypses can be traced back to the visionary material of Zechariah, Ezekiel, Jeremiah, Isaiah, Amos, Micaiah ben Imlah (in 1 Kings 22), and even into Canaanite religion—though none of this earlier material can really be classified as an apocalypse. Both Guy Couturier ("La Vision du Counseil divin: etude d'une forme commune au prophetisme et a l'apocalyptique," *ScEs* 36 [1984] 5-43) and Alan J. McNicol ("The Heavenly Sanctuary in Judaism: A Model for Tracing the Origin of an Apocalypse," *JRelS* 13 [1987]: 66-94) explain the *form* of apocalypses as a literary development of "council"/"call" scenes contained within the Hebrew Bible (e.g., 1 Kings 22; Isa. 6; Ezek. 1).

15. Christopher Rowland, *The Open Heaven: A Study of Apocalyptic in Judaism and Early Christianity* (New York: Crossroad, 1982), 21. On the hotly deabated question of genre in general, see Lars Hartman, "Survey of the Problem of Apocalyptic Genre," in *Apocalypticism in the Mediterranean World and the Near East*, ed. D. Hellholm (Tubingen: Mohr-Siebeck, 1983), 329-41; and E. P. Sanders, "The Genre of Palestinian Jewish Apocalypses," in *Apocalypticism*, 447-60.

16. Howard Marshall, "Is Apocalyptic the Mother of Christian Theology?," in *Tradition and Interpretation in the New Testament: Essays in Honor of E. Earle Ellis for His 60th Birthday*, eds. G. F. Hawthorne and O. Betz (Grand Rapids/Tubingen: Eerdmans/Mohr-Siebeck, 1987), 33-42.

17. On the different structural forms that apocalypses (heavenly ascensions/invasions) can take, see Alan F. Segal, "Heavenly Ascent in Hellenistic Judaism, Early Christianity and their Environment," *ANRW* II 23.2 (1980): 1333-94; Martha Himmelfarb, *Tours of Hell: An Apocalyptic Form in Jewish Christian Literature* (Philadelphia: University of Pennsylvania, 1983); Mary Dean-Otting, *Heavenly Journeys: A Study of the Motif in Hellenistic Jewish Literature* (Judentum und Umwelt 8; Frankfurt am Main: Peter Lang, 1984); and David J. Halperin, "Ascension or Invasion: Implications of the Heavenly Journey in Ancient Judaism," *Religion* 18 (1988): 47-67.

18. Howard Marshall, *The Acts of the Apostles* (Tyndale New Testament Commentaries; Grand Rapids: Eerdmans, 1980), 55-6.

19. Intertextual echos can be discerned in the references to giving of "commandment" (1:3; cf. Ex.. 24:12, LXX), the time of "forty days" (1:3; cf. Ex. 24:18, LXX), the being covered by a "cloud" (1:9, cf. Ex. 24:16), and the location on a "mountain" (1:12; Ex. 24:16). By means of such imagery, Acts not only links Jesus with Moses, but parallels the resurrection/ascension with the great Sinai theophany.

20. Segal, "Heavenly Ascent," 1371-72. *Paristemi,* "to be present," is commonly associated with angelophanies (Zech 4:14, 6:5, LXX; 1 Enoch 14:22; T. Abr. 7:11, 20:10; Sib. Or. 3:429; Luke 1:19; Acts 27:23) and appearances after death to life transformations (Acts 9:41). *Optanomai,* "to appear," which is relatively rare, is used here because a present participle was demanded and is thus equivalent with the technical *ophthe* language of the great theophanies of the Hebrew Bible (see Wilhelm Michaelis *"Horao,"* *TDNT* 5:317, n.12; 344, 372-73; cf. T. Lev. 18:2B27). *Optanomia* denotes the resurrection appearance of Jesus. "Taking up" (*analempseos; analambano; anabaino; hupolambano*) can refer to temporary travels into the heavens (2 Kings 2:9-11, LXX; Sir. 48:9; 49:14; 1 Macc. 2:58), confrontations with God (Ex. 24:12, LXX) or special forms of Spirit possession (Ezek 2:2; 3:12, 14; 8:3; 11:1, 24; 43:5, LXX). With regards to Jesus, "taking up" refers to His exaltation to the right hand of God. This exaltation is the necessary predicate for His subsequent invasions via Spirit. See Acts 1:2, 9, 11, 22; 2:34; 10:4, 9). That "taken up" appears in the creedal formulation of 1 Timothy 3:16 demonstrates that the phrase had become an eschatological technical term for Jesus' exaltation in early Christian tradition outside of Luke-Acts. See further, Gerhard Delling, *"lambano,"* *TDNT* 4:7-9. *Atenizo,* "to gaze," is used specifically of throne visions (Adam and Eve 33:2, T. Abr. [Recension B] 8:4; 12:6; Acts 7:55 [!]. For an excellent discussion of *erchomai* as a technical term for the theophanic arrival of God in the Hebrew Bible and early Jewish apocalypses, see G. R. Beas-

ley-Murray, *Jesus and the Kingdom of God* (Grand Rapids/Exeter: Eerdmans/Paternoster, 1986), 3-51.

21. On the apocalyptic function of the "voice," see James H. Charlesworth, "The Jewish Roots of Christology: The Discovery of the Hypostatic Voice," *SJT* 39 (1986): 19-41.

22. Rowland, *Open Heaven,* 373.

23. See especially, Otto Betz, "Die Vision des Paulus im Tempel von Jerusalem: Apg 22, 17-21 als Beitrag zur Deutung des Damakserlebnisses," in O. Bocher and K. Haacker, eds., *Verborum Veritas: Festschrift fur Gustav Stahlin zum 70. Geburtstaq* (Wuppertal: Theologischer Verlag, 1970), 113-23.

24. Heanchen, *Acts,* 313, n.2; Segal, "Heavenly Ascent," 1352.

25. On *dokein* as an introductory formula for dreams/visions in Hellenistic religion, see John S. Hanson, "Dreams and Visions in the Graeco-Roman World and Early Christianity," *ANRW* II.23.2 (1980): 1409.

26. Rowland, *Open Heaven,* 369-71.

27. For example, Jer. 1; Ezek. 1; Isa. 6, 40, 49; see Krister Stendahl, *Paul among Jews and Gentiles* (Philadelphia: Fortress, 1976), 7-23.

28. Seyoon Kim, *The Origin of Paul's Gospel,* 2d ed. (WUNT 2/4; Tubingen: Mohr-Siebeck, 1984): 28-31, 205-52; Alan F. Segal, *Paul the Convert: The Apostolate and Apostasy of Saul the Pharisee* (New Haven: Yale University Press, forthcoming), 22-27, 30-39.

29. Hanson, "Dreams and Visions," 1413, 1422. It is now appropriate to question the relationship of the literary expression of apocalypses (visions/dreams, angelophaines, throne visions, Christophanies) to an actual, historical religious experience. Recent research into early Jewish and Christian apocalypses has argued for a positive relationship between many early Jewish and Christian texts and mystic praxis. No longer can one rule out of hand that authentic mystical experiences, be they exoteric or esoteric, do not lie behind the ancient texts. It seems to me that the aversion in believing that texts could arise out of profound religious experience is more a commentary on the world view of modern interpreters than it is an accurate historical reading. See Ithamar Grunewald, *Apocalyptic and Merkavah Mysticism* (AGJU 14; Leiden/Kolin: Brill, 1980); Rowland, *Open Heaven;* Carol Newsom, *Songs of the Sabbath Sacrifice: A Critical Edition* (HSS 27; Atlanta: Scholars Press, 1985); Fujita, *A Crack in the Jar,* 158-200; and Segal, *Paul.*

30. Hanson, "Apocalypticism," 28-34.

31. In some places, the signfiers are equated; see 11:26 (church = multitude = disciples = Christians); 16:1 (disciple = believer); 18:27 (brethern = disciples); 19:9 (Way = disciples); 20:28,32 (flock = church = disciples = those who are sanctified); 24:14 (Way = sect). See further, Adolf Harnack, *The Mission and Expansion of Christianity in the First Three Centuries* (New York: Harper & Brothers, 1961), 399-421.

32. For a fairly comprehensive listing of the paradigmatic field signifiers employed for socio-religious groups, consult *Greek-English Lexicon of the New Testament Based on Semantic Domains,* 2 vols., eds. J. P. Louw and E. A. Nida; New York: United Bible Societies, 1987), 1:123-30.

33. Derek Tidball, *The Social Context of the New Testament: A Sociological Analysis* (Grand Rapids: Zondervan, 1984), 51-55.

34. Gerd Theissen, *The Sociology of Early Palestinian Christianity* (Philadelphia: Fortress, 1977), 8-9, 12, 15.

35. Martin Hengel, *Property and Riches in the Early Church* (Philadelphia: Fortress, 1974), 31-34, who, following the lead of Ernst Bloch, reads the "sharing of goods" in the early community as an expression of apocalyticism.

36. John C. Gager, *Kingdom and Community: The Social World of Early Christianity* (Englewood Cliffs, N.J.: Prentice-Hall, 1975), 20-37, especially 25.

37. Wayne Meeks, *The First Urban Christians: The Social World of the Apostle Paul* (New Haven: Yale, 1983), 164-92. The way in which Meeks relates the sociological phenomenon of a Pauline church with an apocalyptic "pattern of belief" would be comparable to the way in

which the Acts depicts the church and its pattern of belief.

38. Larry W. Hurtado, *One God, One Lord: Early Christian Devotion and Ancient Jewish Monotheism* (Philadelphia: Fortress, 1988); Ragnar Leivestad, *Jesus in His Own Perspective: An Examination of His Sayings, Actions, and Eschatological Titles* (Minneapolis: Augsburg, 1987), 41-83; A. E. Harvey, "Christ as Agent," in *The Glory of Christ in the New Testament: Studies in Christology in Memory of George Bradford Caird*, eds. L. D. Hurst and N. T. Wright (Oxford: Clarendon, 1987), 239-50; Larry W. Hurtado, "The Binitarian Shape of Early Christian Devotion and Ancient Jewish Monotheism," *SBLSP* 24 (1985): 377-91; Alan F. Segal, *Two Powers in Heaven: Early Rabbinic Reports about Christianity and Gnosticism* (SJLA 25; Leiden: Brill, 1977).

39. See further, C. F. D. Moule, "The Christology of Acts," in *Studies in Luke-Acts,* 159-85; Richard N. Longenecker, *The Christology of Early Jewish Christianity* (SBT 2/17; London: SCM, 1070); Joseph A. Fitzmyer, *The Gospel According to Luke (I-IX)* (AB 28; Garden City, N.Y.: Doubleday, 1981), 192-227.

40. Hurtado, *One God, One Lord,* 93-124.

41. Martin Hengel, "Hymns and Christology," in *Between Jesus and Paul: Studies in the History of Earliest Christianity* (Philadelphia: Fortress, 1983), 79-96.

42. Helmut Koester, *Introduction to the New Testament: History, Culture and Religion of the Hellenistic Age,* 2 vols. (Berlin: de Gruyter, 1980), 1:230-34.

43. References to the "Spirit" occur some fifty-seven times in the Book of Acts. See further, Fitzmyer, *Luke,* 227-31, 266-67, and the literature cited there. "Name" is used some thirty-four times to demonstrate the continued activity of Jesus through His witnesses. See Longenecker, *Christology,* 41-46; Marshall, *Luke,* 170, 192; and, on the apocalyptic implications inherent in "name," Jarl Fossum, *The Name of God and the Angel of the Lord: Samaritan and Jewish Concepts of Intermediation and the Origin of Gnosticism* (WUNT 1/36; Tubingen: Mohr-Siebeck, 1985).

44. Donald Juel, *Messianic Exegesis: Christological Interpretation of the Old Testament in Early Christianity* (Philadelphia: Fortress Press, 1988), especially 82-85, 109, 146-47, 151-52.

45. Acts' employment of "divine agency" language broadly conforms to a descent/ascent *(katabasis/anabasis)* pattern, a pattern common to many religions of the Hellenistic era; see Segal, "Heavenly Ascent," 1334-42, 1385-88.

46. Acts 2:14-26; 3:12-26; 4:9-12; 5:30-33; 7; 16:40; 14:15-18; 17:22-31; 20:18-35; 22:1-21; 26:2-23; 28:25-29; C. H. Dodd, *The Apostolic Preaching and Its Developments* (London: Hodder and Stoughton, 1936), 7-35.

47. Romans 1:3-4; 4:24; 8:34; 10:8-10; 1 Corinthians 8:6; 15:3-11; Galatians 4:4-5; Ephesians 4:4-6; Philippians 2:5-11; Colossians 1:15-20; 1 Timothy 2:5; 3:16; 6:13; 2 Timothy 2:8-13; 4:1; Hebrews 1:3; 3:18 (See also 1 Clem. 27.4; 34.2; 36.2; 46.6; 49.6; 59.2; Barn. 1.6; 5.61 7.2; 12.7, Did. 9-10; Ign. Eph. 7.2; 18.2; 20.2; Ign. Magn. 11b; 13.1; Ign. Trall. 9.1; Ign. Smyrn. 1.1-2; Ign. Pol. 3.2; Pol. Phil. 1.1; 2.1; 7.1). See further, J. N. D. Kelly, *Early Christian Creeds,* 3d ed. (London: Longman, 1972).

48. Compare Walter Bauer, *Orthodoxy and Heresy in Earliest Christianity,* eds. R. A. Kraft and G. Krodel (Philadelphia: Fortress, 1971), and James M. Robinson and Helmut Koester, *Trajectories Through Early Christianity* (Philadelphia: Fortress, 1971).

11
Images of the Church in Paul

by Robert B. Sloan

The doctrine of the church is making something of a comeback in Pauline studies. Whereas earlier models for understanding Pauline theology would have conjured up the image of the frustrated individual (say, a Martin Luther) agonizing over the way to peace with God, more recent studies in the theology of Paul have focused upon the relationship of Jew and Gentile as a more historically appropriate matrix for understanding the mind of Paul, as reflected in his letters. Indeed, one recent New Testament scholar has gone so far as to assert that

> [w]hat Paul finds in Scripture, above all else, is a prefiguration of the *church* as the people of God. . . . Paul uses Scripture primarily to shape his understanding of the community of faith; conversely, Paul's experience of the Christian community—composed of Jews and Gentiles together—shapes his reading of Scripture. In short, Paul operates with *ecclesiocentric* hermeneutic.[1]

On the face of it, this assertion is startling to those of us who would have more readily referred to Paul's reading of Scripture (the Old Testament) as *Christocentric*, but closer analysis confirms the fact that it is the church, even more so than Christ, that occupied Paul's attention when he was motivated to search the Scriptures. Of course, it must be recalled that what Paul *argued* in his letters was not necessarily the same thing that he *preached* in typical evangelistic settings. Indeed, we should expect that Paul's letters—because they were written to communities of faith whose members had already confessed faith in the risen Lord—would be less likely to rehearse the evangelistic basics of a Christocentric reading of the Scriptures than would his preaching to the unconverted in a synagogue setting. Put another way, given what we know of the Jewish and/or Judaizing pressures placed upon Paul throughout his missionary/pastoral career, it should not surprise us that Paul's letters, which reflect more his argumentative reactions to various polemical situations, especially situations involving the relationship of Jew and Gentile, should contain more with respect to the doctrine of the church than to Christology. On the other hand, Paul's Christocentric hermeneutic, employed more in evangelistic settings, probably does stand as the basis and presupposition of his ecclesiocentric plumbing of the scriptural depths. However that may be, it is still impressive to realize that, as far as the letters of Paul go, the life of the church does indeed seem to receive more attention than what we would traditionally call "Christology."

Sources of Pauline Ecclesiology

The correspondence materials of the New Testament are frequently referred to as "occasional literature." By the term "occasional," we mean to highlight the fact that none, for example, of the Pauline letters may claim to be an abstraction of Pauline theology. That is, Paul nowhere in any one of the extant letters—including Romans—gives us a systematic accounting of his central convictions. The letters represent Paul's responses to various "occasions." Still, Paul was no doubt a systematic thinker, and although he did not in written form lay out for us a systematic theology, we may assume that Paul's letters are a literary application of his own central convictions in response to the problems and issues of a given situation. The churches of Galatia, for example, were under siege by various Judaizing influences. Paul felt his own apostleship and the nature of the gospel to be threatened by these Jewish Christian attempts to enforce Mosaic law-keeping upon Gentile converts. In response, Paul wrote to the churches of Galatia a pastoral letter which speaks to the issues of circumcision, the Mosaic law, and, in short, the freedom that belongs to those who are in Christ. Similarly, 1 Corinthians represents Paul's applied pastoral reflections, based no doubt upon his central theological convictions, relevant to a whole host of problems in the church at Corinth. Division, a matter of church discipline, lawsuits between Christians, immorality with pagan prostitutes, questions related to marriage and celibacy, the issue of meat offered to idols, wives praying and prophesying without their heads covered, disorder at the Lord's table, disruptions in worship, theological disavowals of the resurrection of the dead, and an offering for the church in Jerusalem were all "occasional" issues requiring some response from the apostle, a response which he gave out of the resources of his theology as applied to the given needs.

A primary question, therefore, for Pauline studies in general, relates to the "central convictions" which Paul applied and adapted to the various occasional needs of his congregations. Granted that Paul had certain central convictions, where did he get them? For the purposes of this study, however, we will ask, what were the sources of Pauline ecclesiology?

We may be sure that Paul's theology of the church had its roots in his own *Jewish experience*, a fact evidenced by Paul's use of a very traditional term for Israel in reference to the church. The word *ekklesia* is the most common word for the church in the Greek New Testament, and of some 114 instances of *ekklesia*, 62 are in the traditional Pauline corpus. The term itself comes from the Septuagint (the Greek Old Testament, which was apparently the primary source for Paul's Old Testament citations and allusions) and was a translation of the Hebrew word *qahal*. The *ekklesia* of God referred to in the Septuagint was none other than the congregation of Israel, particularly Israel assembled before the Lord (at Mount Sinai, Ex. 19:1ff.; or Mount Horeb, Deut. 1:6) to hear the word of the Lord. The use of such a term in reference to the community of those who confess the crucified and risen Lord tells us (as we shall see) a great deal about Paul's understanding of the nature of that community. Of course, to speak of Paul's religious heritage as a source of his ecclesiology is to speak primarily of the Jewish Scriptures. The Scriptures, more than any other theological source, served as the privileged intellectual and literary predecessor for Pauline theology.

In this connection, we should not underestimate the importance of Paul's Pharisaic training with respect to the sources of his theology. The Scriptures, to be sure, stand as the great literary and theological ancestor to Paul's thought, but we should not assume that these Scriptures were uninterpreted for Paul. He was trained, according to Acts 22:3 (cf. 5:34), in Jerusalem, at the feet of Gamaliel, a great Pharisaic teacher who was probably the grandson of the great Hillel.[2] The Pharisaic devotion to purity, the Pharisaic attempt to teach and make applicable for Israel the laws of God, the Pharisaic focus upon oral tradition, and the Pharisaic belief in the resurrection of the dead no doubt gave interpretive focus to Paul's reading of Scripture. Even at the end of his itinerant career, Paul could still refer to himself, in the present tense, as "a Pharisee, a son of Pharisees!" (Acts 23:6). It was certainly *not* with a highly individualized self-understanding that Paul, who was "of the nation of Israel, of the tribe of Benjamin, a Hebrew of Hebrews; as to the law, a Pharisee" (Phil. 3:5), conceived questions and issues related to the nature of the church of Jesus Christ. As an influence upon one who had been zealous for the purity of Israel and the application of God's laws to everyday experience, Paul's Pharisaic experience certainly affected his later Christian conceptions of the church.

With these influences, however, one must not fail to mention the overwhelming significance of the Damascus Road experience on all of Pauline thought. It was an event that proved to be more than a conversion experience,[3] for as Galatians 1:11 and following makes clear, it was a Christophany, "a revelation of Jesus Christ" (v. 12) which constituted the precipitating origin of Paul's Christian *theology*: "For I would have you know, brethren, that the gospel which was preached by me is not according to man. For I neither received it from man, nor was I taught it, but I received it through a revelation of Jesus Christ" (vv. 11-12). Though we must, of course, allow for continuing thought and reflection by Paul regarding the implications of his Damascus Road vision, and must assume as well that further missiological experience served to provoke an ongoing development and unpacking of his theology, we must nonetheless reckon with the critical and formative role of the Christophany as a significant source for the theology of Paul.[4]

Certainly the Damascus Road encounter had a profound impact upon Paul's Christology, and, if that is true, we must assume as well that it exerted considerable influence upon Paul's ecclesiology, given the connection between those two doctrines in the Pauline letters. For example, surely Paul's vision of Christ the resurrecting Spirit[5] and Christ the Image and Glory of God[6] had, respectively, a significant impact upon his view of the church as the community of the Spirit (cf. 2 Cor. 3:1-3), his understanding of the church as the "new man" (Eph. 2:14), and his description of the community of faith as those who "bear the image of the heavenly [man]" (1 Cor. 15:49).

At least as suggestive as these expressions, however—expressions which reflect the visual impact of the Christophany upon Paul's theology—is the dialogue between the risen Christ and Saul on the road to Damascus: "Saul, Saul why do you *persecute me?*" "Who are you [Sir]?" "I am *Jesus*, whom you *persecute*" (Acts 9:4-5, GNB, author's italics). Saul the Pharisee, according to Luke, discovered on the road to Damascus several startling things, but among them was (1) the fact that the crucified Nazarene, who was the object of Christian preaching, was—as the Christians had maintained—alive and therefore was indeed the Messiah of God; (2) in persecuting Messiah's people, Paul found—as twice emphasized in that traumatic dialogue—that he was persecuting *Jesus* (the Messiah) Himself. It is this striking solidarity between Messiah Jesus and His people, as reflected in Christ's haunting words to Saul, "Why do you persecute *me?* . . . I am Jesus, *whom you persecute*," which crystallized for later Pauline theology the inextricable link, forged especially in the fires of suffering, between Christ and His people. Pauline references to being "in Christ," Paul's view of the church as "the body of Christ," Paul's references to his own and/or the church's suffering with Christ, Paul's frequent application of Christological terminology to the church and/or the individual behavior, and Paul's attribution to the church of experiences consonant with the history of Jesus ("you died with Him," "were buried with Him," "were raised with Him," "are seated with Him in the heavenlies") all reflect the profound solidarity between Christ and the church essential to Pauline theology.[7]

Ecclesiological Imagery

It is typical in studies of this sort to focus upon the Pauline images of the church as reflected in his letters. Indeed, such a point of entry into the subject of Pauline ecclesiology can prove fruitful.[8] A survey, for example, of 1 Thessalonians evidences a great variety of imagery employed in Paul's reflections upon the church. The Thessalonians are called "beloved" and "chosen" in 1:4, thus implying some level of allusion to Israel. In 2:7,11, Paul's references to himself as "mother" and "father" place the Thessalonians in the status of "children" in a family. In verses 14,17 the family imagery is continued, but this time the Thessalonians are "brethren." In verse 19 Paul likened himself to an athlete and/or a combatant for whom the Thessalonians are his trophy, his "crown" of rejoicing. In 3:5 Paul feared that Satan might have drawn the Thessalonians away from their initial commitments of faith, thus rendering his "labor" in vain, an expression which may well imply the Thessalonians as Paul's "workmanship" or "product." In 5:2,4, references to the Lord coming as a "thief in the night" convey to the Thessalonians the metaphorical status of "property owners" (i.e., those who, if they are well prepared, will not experience loss from the appearance of the "thief"). In verse 5 family terminology is continued with references to the Thessalonians as "sons of light and sons of day." If "the day" of verse 5 refers to the "Day of the Lord," then this sonship is also a divine sonship, since they live under the dominion of the Lord of that "day." In verse 8 the exhortations to sobriety and alertness evoke the images of soldiers who are called to be alert and watchful. The command in verse 11 to "build up one another" calls to mind various references in the Pauline corpus to the church as a "building" or a "temple."[9] In verse 12 the Thessalonians are charged to "[respect] those who diligently labor among you, and have charge over you in the Lord," which implies at the least that the Thessalonian Christians are conceived of by Paul as a band of people under some level of charge or order. Finally, the benediction of verse 23, whereby Paul prays, "the God of peace Himself sanctify you entirely, and may *your* spirit and soul and body be preserved complete, without blame at the coming of our Lord Jesus Christ" (author's italics), suggests that the entire company of the Thessalonians (note the plural "your") may be described with the terminology of the individual human, as though the collective company possessed (the following terms are expressed in the singular), a "spirit," "soul," and "body."

This kind of exercise could certainly be multiplied to great benefit. Images and metaphors abound, for example, in 1 Corinthians, where the church is, within the space of but a few sentences, a "plant," a "field," a "building," and the "temple of God" (3:6-17). The dominant images studied, when this particular approach to Pauline ecclesiology is taken, are typically "body," "temple," and "bride."[10] Looking briefly at the term "body," it is both a commonplace and necessary observation to note the differences between Paul's use of "body" in Romans and 1 Corinthians, on the one hand, and Colossians and Ephesians, on the other. In the former, "body" seems to be a more self-conscious metaphor emphasizing the variety and unity of the church (Rom. 12:4-5; 1 Cor. 12:12-26), with no special focus upon the "head" of the body as being in any way different from any other bodily parts (see 1 Cor. 12:21). In Colossians and Ephesians, however (Eph. 1:22-23; 2:15-16; 3:6; 4:4,12-16; 5:22-33; Col. 1:18,24-25; 2:18-19), the body imagery seems less consciously metaphorical and points to Christ as the "head" of the church, suggesting both His lordship over His people and His role as the origin of the ongoing nourishment and life of the church. Considering the church as the "temple" (1 Cor. 3:16-17; 2 Cor. 6:16; Eph. 2:19-22; cf. 1 Cor. 6:19; Col. 2:7), we see that such expressions imply the fellowship of Christians as the spiritual environment where God is rightly worshiped (cf. Phil. 3:3) and, furthermore, as the place of presence for the risen Lord— both notions together suggesting the company of the believers as a place of purity and separation from the world. References to the church as the "bride" (Eph. 5:22-33; 2 Cor. 11:2; cf. Rom. 7:1-6) tend to occur in contexts that demand purity and fidelity on the part of the church with respect to her devotion to Christ and also emphasize the unity that exists between Christ and the church (though even this unity, as the husband-wife analogy of Ephesians 5:22-33 suggests, is not one whereby the covenant partners lose their distinctives).

Such approaches to Pauline ecclesiology make a valuable contribution to our understanding of the various nuances in Pauline ecclesiology, but the massive amounts of detail may cause us to lose sight of the larger theological unities which not only pervade Pauline ecclesiology, but in fact underlie the various terminological patterns. With that in mind, we now proceed to summarize the theological substructure of Pauline ecclesiology, a substructure which both permits and sends forth into his letters this great variety of images.

The Theological Substructure of Paul's Ecclesiological Imagery

The Church as an Eschatological Sign

Paul's training as a Pharisee brought with it his commitment to the Jewish doctrine of the two ages.[11] That is, as a Pharisee, Paul believed that this present evil age would be brought to a catastrophic end and that, with the appearance of Messiah and the resurrection of the dead, God would usher in a glorious new age (cf. Gal. 1:4). Given Paul's commitment to Jesus as Messiah, the long-awaited Son of David who appeared in fulfillment of the ancient Scriptures (Rom. 1:4; 1 Cor. 15:3), it is not surprising to note that Pauline theology is irrepressibly eschatological. Paul believed that the ends of the ages had come (1 Cor. 10:11; cf. 1 Cor. 2:6; 3:18). In and through Christ, the resurrection of the dead had begun (1 Cor. 15:21), and the gift of God's Spirit upon all those who believe in the crucified and risen Jesus (1 Cor. 12:3-13; Rom. 8:9-11; Eph. 1:13-14; cf. Acts 1:17-18,33) was an eschatological sign whereby all those in the Spirit have *already* begun to participate in the glorious age to come (note the use of "pledge" and "firstfruits" as central Pauline terms for the gift of the Spirit to God's people; Rom. 8:23; 2 Cor. 1:22; 5:5; Eph. 1:13-14; cf. also Rom. 14:17; 8:15; Gal. 4:6) and indeed have God's promise of participation in the eschatological kingdom. The church then, as the company of the Spirit, the fellowship in which the powers of the age to come are manifested in various gifts and ministries (Rom. 12:3-8; 1 Cor. 12-14; Eph. 4:7-13) is itself a sign of and witness to the coming manifestation of God's kingdom. Thus, the church is an eschatological community, a fellowship of those who participate already in the future blessings of resurrection life (Rom. 6:3; 2 Cor. 5:17). All that can be said about Pauline ecclesiology must keep in mind the pervasively eschatological aura which has been cast over all that the church is and does in Pauline theology. With that in mind, we now proceed to discuss several central Pauline convictions regarding the nature of the church as an eschatological community.

The Church in Union with Christ

Pauline ecclesiology, as with every other feature of Pauline theology, cannot be separated from Christology. Because the crucified and risen Jesus is the long-awaited Messiah (and therefore the "ends of the ages" have dawned; 1 Cor. 10:11) and now the exalted Lord, the church, which is in union with Christ, also shares in the eschatological character of the work of Christ. While it is certainly true that the subject of much of the polemic in the Pauline corpus has to do with ecclesiocentric matters—fellowship, the relationship of Jew and Gentile, the relationship of the given churches to Paul and/or his gospel—it is nonetheless true that Christology is the substructure of Pauline thought. While the situations in the Pauline churches force him to *argue* with an ecclesiocentric strategy, his underlying central convictions are predominantly Christocentric in shape (i.e., the story of Christ provides the theological wherewithal to inform the nature of mission and discipleship in the church). Put another way, the story of Christ becomes the story of the church and/or the individual believer.

Examples of this Pauline phenomenon abound. The traditional gospel (1 Cor. 15:3-8), which focuses on the story of Jesus at certain central points— especially His death, burial, resurrection, and appearances—is also the story of the one who is "in Christ." The one who has heard and believed the gospel is identified with Christ at precisely these points of gospel focus. Those who are baptized in the name of Christ are baptized *into* Christ, into union with Him in His death, His burial, and His resurrection (Rom. 6:3-5; Col. 2:11-13). A short but powerful example of this sort of "story incorporation," whereby the story of Christ becomes the story of the believer, is seen in Paul's brief rehearsal of a traditional kerygma in 2 Corinthians 5:21, when he states, "He made Him who knew no sin to be sin on our behalf, , *that we might become the righteousness of God* in Him" (author's italics, see also 1 Cor. 1:30-31). Such an identity with the story of Jesus is also clearly exemplified in Paul's description of his apostolic experience in such passages as 2 Corinthians 4:7-18, where a certain "cross-resurrection pattern" characterizes the life of apostolic suffering: "Always [bearing] about in the body the dying of Jesus, that the life of Jesus may be manifested in our body." The "participation in the sufferings of Christ" that characterizes the apostolic story (2 Cor. 1:3-6) is also, in other situations, applied more broadly to the experience of Christians in general, as when Paul declares, "if indeed we suffer with Him . . . we may be glorified with Him, " (Rom. 8:17). The same theological assumption of solidarity between Christ and the believer is reflected in 1 Corinthians 1:26-31 where—having argued in verses 18-25 that it is not the preacher who saves, but salvation is rather a product of the preaching of "the word of the cross"—Paul points to the Corinthian social status as an illustration of God's use of "the foolish things of the world . . . the weak things . . . the base things" (vv. 27-28) to accomplish His work. In this way, their lowly social status is comparable to the cross, which likewise is the "foolishness" and "weakness" of God (v. 25). Their lowly social standing and the cross are both manifestations of the saving power of God whereby He has used "the things that are not, [in order to] nullify the things that are" (v. 28). Again, the fact that Christ's story has become for Paul the defining characteristic of the church's story is also evidenced in the well-known Ephesian prayer passage, in which Paul longs for the church to know the same resurrection power of God whereby He raised and exalted *Christ* to His right hand (1:19-23). Similarly, but a few sentences later, Paul refers to himself and his readers as those whom God has already "raised . . . up with Him and seated . . . with Him in the [heavenlies]" (Eph. 2:6). In the same vein, the fact that Christ's story has now become the church's story is also reflected in the enigmatic reference in 1:3-4 to the readers' being "blessed with every spiritual blessing in the [heavenlies] in Christ"—a blessed participation in Him that extends even to union with Him in His preexistent, precreation chosenness—"just as He chose us in Him before the foundation of the world." Finally, we may note two other (implied) examples of the church's solidarity with Christ in resurrection. Since He is now, by virtue of His resurrection from the grave, the "first-born" of God (Col. 1:18; Rom. 8:29), the final resurrection of the dead, which means that He will then be the firstborn "among *many* brethren" (Rom. 8:29, author's italics), has actually begun in Him.

What was for Paul a particular story, about a particular man—the everlasting Son of God who came to earth for our salvation—has become more than a Christology; it has become—by virtue of our hearing and believing the gospel and our consequent incorporation into Him and receipt of His Spirit—an ecclesiocentric revelation of the purposes of God. Though we never reach a "sonship" of precisely the same kind as His, we become nonetheless sons/children of God through Him, heirs of God, and fellow-heirs with Christ our brother (Rom. 8:14-17). This participation in Christ, this identification with Him whereby His story becomes the believer's story, is accomplished by virtue of the *telling* of His story (the preaching of the gospel), a message which is accompanied by the power of God (1 Cor. 2:4-5; see also Rom. 1:16-17). This powerful new word of creation (cf. 2 Cor. 5:17) joins the believer to Christ and makes the history and future of Christ the history and future of the one who calls upon His name. Not only as individuals do Christians participate in the suffering and resurrection of Jesus, but the church (note well: it is the *church* in Eph. 2:15 that is called the "new man") is collectively identified with Him. It is this latter, corporate identity with Christ that no doubt best explains those several unusual expressions (1 Cor. 1:12; 12:12; Col. 1:24) in which the terms "Christ" and "church" seem synonymous. Paul senses such a solidarity and union between Christ and His people that he may ask rhetorically (expecting a "no" answer), when confronted with division within the Corinthian congregation, "Has *Christ* been divided?"(1 Cor 1:3, author's italics) Or, when in 12:12 he uses the analogy of the human body to describe the "variety within unity" of the church, he declares "so also is *Christ*" (when we should have expected the expression, "so also is the *church*, "author's italics). And the strange expression in Colossians 1:24 regarding Paul's "filling up that which is lacking in *Christ's* afflictions"(author's italics) is best understood as Paul's own suffering as one who is representatively completing the sufferings which the *church* must endure—and thus in turn the sufferings which *Christ* endures with and in His people.

Certainly the source of such a theological commitment to the unity between Christ and His people could be found, for example, in the representative solidarity between the king and Israel in Old Testament theology. The king and/or the priest often represented the people before God and God before the people. Therefore, that Christ the Messiah and Lord should represent His people is not surprising; but the extent to which Paul presses the union seems to go beyond that of monarchical representation in the Old Testament. There is no better place to search for the source of Paul's committed conviction regarding identity between Christ and His people than that haunting question posed to Him on the Damascus Road, "Saul, Saul, why do you persecute *me?*" (Acts 9:4; 22:7, GNB, author's italics, see also 26:14).

It is this kind of theological commitment that should be understood as the substructure for the various Pauline references and images which reflect identity between Christ and His people. The "in Christ" terminology, references to the church as the "body," the "bride," and/or the "temple" of God, all have their roots, at least in some measure, in the fundamental Pauline conviction of a sense of intimacy, union, and solidarity between Christ and His people.

The Israel of God

The notion of the church in solidarity with Christ immediately brings to mind the notion of the church as Israel, for to be in solidarity with *Messiah/Christ* is to suggest that those with whom Messiah is in union must, since Messiah is the deliverer of Israel, be identified with Israel, the Old Testament people of God. To raise this issue engrosses us immediately in some rather thorny theological underbrush. Is the Gentile church a *substitute* for Israel, so that we could say that the church has *superseded* Israel? Is the church something *completely other* than Israel, so that one could argue[12] that what God has done in saving the Gentile church is not in fulfillment of His promises to Israel, and that those promises await a completely future fulfillment? Or should we say that the church is *identified* with Israel, but say it in such a way that we mean organic continuity with Israel, but not the supersession of Israel?[13] We have not the space, nor is it ultimately the purpose of this present study to elaborate fully the issues involved in deciding which of the three models above should be followed. The best that can be done here is to state a conclusion and thereby, in the process of elaborating and/or substantiating that conclusion from the Pauline materials, hope to prove persuasive. In short, we shall opt for the third of the possibilities mentioned above, which asserts that Gentiles who believe in Christ, indeed all who believe in Christ, Jew or Gentile, stand in continuity with Israel, but not in such a way as to deny the faithfulness of God to unbelieving Israel and/or to foreclose God's future dealings with them in Christ. As will be seen from the following discussion, we certainly maintain (with Paul, we believe) that there is no salvation outside of participation in Christ, even for unbelieving Israel ("they also, *if* they do not continue in their unbelief, will be grafted in, for God is able to graft them in again," Rom. 11:23, author's italics), but we are also convinced that God's faithfulness to "Israel" (a name which refers in Rom. 9—11 to Paul's "kinsmen according to the flesh," but does not necessarily refer to a geopolitical entity) as revealed in the gospel, has not been transferred *in toto* (as in the supersessionist view) to Gentiles who now believe in Jesus. In the first place, we would maintain that both Jews and Gentiles who believe in the crucified and risen Lord partici-pate even now in what Paul would call "the Israel of God" (Gal. 6:16). Second, it is evident from the presence and tone of Romans 9—11 that Paul was grieved at Israel's unbelief for reasons related to the faithfulness (read: integrity) of God (9:6; 11:1-2,11,25-29), and that, for the same reasons, Paul prophesied that currently disobedient Israel will be saved (see 9:4-5; 11:2,25-29; also note the repeated references to God's mercy—a covenant term—in 11:30-32).

The simplest place to begin in these matters is perhaps with Ephesians 2:11-3:21 and Romans 9—11, where Paul flatly asserts, among other similar expressions, that the Gentiles have been incorporated into "the common-wealth of Israel" (Eph. 2:12), are now "fellow-citizens with the saints" (v. 19), are "grafted in among them, and have become partakers with them of the rich root of the olive tree" (Rom. 11:17). Thus, the Gentiles are "fellow-heirs and fellow members of the body, and fellow partakers of the promise in Christ Jesus through the gospel" (Eph. 3:6)—a fact which Paul declares to be a "mystery" now "revealed" to God's "holy apostles and prophets in the Spirit" (v. 5). Therefore, whether Jew or Gentile (cf. Gal. 3:28), the prom-ises of God to Abraham have been fulfilled in Abraham's "seed," that is, Christ, the son of promise who is also a true descendant of Abraham. All who believe in Christ are incorporated into Him and thus, by virtue of par-ticipation in Christ—for example, sharing in His history—themselves be-come the "seed" and offspring of Abraham (Gal. 3:15-29). For Paul, there-fore, "Israel" is constituted not merely by those who are the physical descendants of Abraham (Rom. 9:6), though physical descendancy certain-ly does not exclude one from participation in Abraham, but by those who, *ek pisteos* ("by faith" in Christ and/or "through the faithfulness of" Christ), are "in Christ." In this way, the inheritance of salvation is "in accordance with grace, in order that the promise may be certain to all the descendants, not only to those who are of the law, but also to those who are of the faith of Abraham, who is the father of us all" (4:16).

Gentile believers, thus, are in continuity with the promises of God made to Israel. This theological fact for Paul may be evidenced not only by his explicit statements, but—in some ways even more convincingly, given its nature as an almost unconscious assumption—in his theologically reinterpreted use of the Scriptures with reference to Gentiles. Of course, there are explicit citations employed by Paul which in their original contexts point to the inclusion of the Gentiles, as, for example, the use in Romans 15:10 of Deuteronomy 32:43, "Rejoice, O Gentiles, with His people." Or, we may note Paul's explicit reference to Isaiah 11:10, cited in Romans 15:12, where Israel's Messiah, who comes from "the root of Jesse" would be one who will "rule over the Gentiles" and one in whom "the Gentiles shall hope." But along with such explicit citations of Gentile incorporation into the congregation of Israel are those texts in which Paul—based upon prior theological commitments (the truth of the gospel) and experience (such as his own witnessing of Gentile conversion), or perhaps extrapolating from his reading of other scriptural texts—appropriates Old Testament passages which, in their original contexts clearly refer to Israel, as references to the Gentiles. Given his assumption that Gentiles too, by virtue of their possession of the Spirit and their incorporation into Christ, have received the promised blessings of Abraham, and are now legitimately called "the Israel of God," we may well understand (and agree with) Paul's creative appropriation of Israel's Scriptures on behalf of the Gentiles, but we should not overlook the rather daring nature of his hermeneutical movements. For example,[14] Paul's use in Romans 9:25-26 of Hosea 2:23 and 1:10 (LXX 2:25 and 2:1, respectively) is a quite innovative (if not shocking) reapplication of these texts, which in their original context referred to Hosea's application of God's restoration of sinful *Israel*, as a reference to the divine intention to call out His people "from among *Gentiles*" (Rom. 9:24, author's italics). Similarly, Paul's citation of Exodus 16:8, "He who gathered much did not have too much, and he who gathered little had no lack," in 2 Corinthians 8:15 is, on the face of it, rather awkward, since the Old Testament text refers to God's provision for His people in the wilderness (Israel) and the 2 Corinthians text places the *Gentile congregation at Corinth* in the position of those who, being amply supplied by God, now have an abundance for sharing with others. First Corinthians 10 likewise contributes to this gathering impression of Gentile Christians as participants in the Israel of God inasmuch as Paul refers to the Jewish forefathers in the wilderness as *"our* fathers" (v. 1, author's italics), and in so doing almost subconsciously reflects his theological intuition that the Gentile Christians at Corinth are in the lineage of Israel. Of course, what Paul subconsciously reflected in verse 1 is explicitly stated in verse 6, when he refers to Israel's experiences in the wilderness as things that "happened as examples for us," where "us" surely includes not only Paul, the Jewish Christians, but also the Gentile Christian Corinthians. First Corinthians 12:2 continues Paul's association of the Corinthian Gentiles with Israel as Paul refers to their former life outside of Christ as the time "when ye were *Gentiles*"(KJV, author's italics), a status which apparently Paul no longer predicates of those Gentiles at Corinth who are now "in Christ."

These kinds of expressions in Paul make sense only when Paul's assumption for reading Scripture (i.e., the preunderstanding that Gentiles are now in the role of Israel, the people of God), is granted. But, as Romans 9—11 makes clear, Paul's insertion of Gentiles into the history of Israel, that is, his way of reading Scripture—even texts that refer exclusively to Israel—as finding its fulfillment in the story of the church, is not simply a supersessionist view of the Gentile church as a substitute for Israel. Romans 9—11 pointedly maintains that the called of God include both Jews and Gentiles (9:23-29; 11:1-6). Moreover, not only did the Pauline church include both Jews and Gentiles, a fact sufficient to temper any radically supersessionist views of a putatively Gentile church's role over Israel, but for Paul even unbelieving Israel was still the object of the faithfulness of God (9:11-32). Paul believed that, in His mysterious purposes, God had used the unbelief of his "kinsmen according to the flesh" to bring salvation to the Gentiles; and, furthermore, that God would also use Israel's unbelief—via the historical agency of Gentile acceptance of the gospel and Israel's subsequent jealousy for her husband/God who is now also the God of the Gentiles—to bring mercy and salvation to Israel (11:11-12,25-32). Paul saw a kind of historical, sequential interplay of God's faithfulness, a faithfulness revealed in the gospel and experienced through the divine purposes—as manifested in apparently historical contingencies—of Jewish rejection, Gentile acceptance, Jewish jealousy, and finally Israel's being "regrafted" (vv. 16-24) into her own covenant history.

Again, this is no simple taking over of Israel by the Gentiles; rather, it is a recasting of the constitutive character of Israel (9:6) so that Israel is all those—Jew or Gentile—who participate in Christ. Jesus and/or the gospel becomes the expression of God's faithfulness and thus bridges the gap from Israel to the church, inasmuch as the church (again, both Jew and Gentile) is constituted of those who *believe* in Jesus the *Jew*. In this way, Paul never finally broke the dialectic, a dialectic which is subsumed in Jesus, between *ethnic* Judaism (Jesus is after all a son of David and a son of Abraham) and the Abrahamic covenant of *promise*. Paul's "kinsmen according to the flesh" (v. 3), who are the "Israelites" referred to throughout 9—11, reflect the ethnic discussion of this salvation-historical dialectic. Paul's kinsmen are still "beloved for the sake of the fathers" (11:28-29) and will, Paul prophesied, be saved (v. 26). But this salvation of Israel is not outside of Christ. Just as Gentile salvation is not outside of *Israel* (belief in Jesus is after all belief in Jesus, the Jewish Messiah who is the descendant of Abraham and David), so also Jewish salvation is not outside the *gospel*, for the ultimate child/"seed" of the *promise* to Abraham is Jesus. Israel will be saved, Paul predicted, but not apart from Christ, for what Paul stipulated as a condition of salvation (namely, faith: "If they do not continue in their *unbelief*, they will be grafted in; for God is able to graft them in again," v. 23), he surely also presupposes in his prophecy of salvation. That is, unbelieving Israel *will* one day be saved (v. 26), and that will, by the faithfulness of God, take place through faith in the crucified and risen Lord.

The Church as a Missionary People

Paul's own status as apostle and, as such, a (preeminently) gifted member of the church (1 Cor. 12:28-29; Eph. 4:11-12), is itself sufficient to establish his understanding of the church as involving a missionary task. That Paul, though occupying a unique role in salvation history, clearly perceived himself as a participant in the Spirit-empowered functions of the church, is also a fact that needs little substantiation.[15] Conversely, Paul also regarded his churches as having a participation (*koinonia*) in his apostolic preaching of the gospel (Phil. 1:5; 2:1; 4:14-20; 2 Cor. 1:7-11; cf. Rom. 1:11-12; 2 Cor. 10:15-16). While it is certainly true that the gift and role of apostle is now no longer in effect (since the term was inextricably linked to those who were eyewitnesses of the resurrected Lord[16]), and, furthermore, that the other ministries, roles, and gifts of the Spirit in the church (including "evangelist") are not experienced by all in the church (1 Cor. 12:28-30; cf. Eph. 4:11-12), it is nonetheless clear that the missionary mandate, though not falling equally, in terms of giftedness, upon all members, nonetheless devolves upon the church corporately.

The commonplace Pauline references to the various churches and their members as "lights" and "children of light" (1 Thess. 5:4-5; Rom. 13:11-14; Eph. 5:8-14; Phil. 2:12-15) suggest very strongly the witness and revelatory function of the church in the world. Just as the gospel is the word of God spoken in human history, bearing witness to the saving faithfulness of God revealed in the Person of the crucified and risen Jesus, so also the life of Christian obedience stands as a gospel witness. It is no mere coincidence that many of the ethical exhortations in the Pauline corpus are best described as "baptismal" and/or "gospel" ethics, for such exhortations are specifically linked theologically to the believer's participation in the death and resurrection of Jesus. In both Ephesians and Colossians, for example, the recipients are encouraged to "put off" and "put on" (Eph. 4:22-25; Col.

3:5-17) various kinds of behavior and attitudes, expressions which clearly refer to the believer's baptism and participation in the death ("putting off") and resurrection ("putting on") of Jesus (Col. 2:11 to 3:4).[17] Paul's summary of the Christian life as a "[walking] in newness of life" (Rom. 6:4) itself reflects the believer's kerygmatic participation in the death and resurrection of Jesus (see also 13:11-14). The cross and resurrection become the constitutive pattern of the behavior of the Christian (8:17; cf. 2 Cor. 4:7-18; Gal. 5:24). Therefore, just as participation in the Lord's Supper is a spiritual reenactment of the death of the Lord (1 Cor. 11:16), so the life of obedience to Christ is a living participation in Christ and as such a witness to the decisive events of His saving death and resurrection. Indeed, the new humanity created by the death of Jesus is none other than the life of love expressed in the church by those who were formerly enemies and alienated from one another (Eph. 2:11-22). This mystery of God which has now been revealed in Christ Jesus and especially accomplished in His reconciling of Jew and Gentile into "one new man, thus establishing peace" (v.15), is the manifold wisdom of God that is now being "made known through the *church* to the rulers and the authorities in the heavenly places" (3:10, author's italics). The church, therefore, stands as the ensign and token of the new humanity created by God through Jesus Christ and as such is a witness to the coming Day of the Lord, when all things will be fully "[summed] up in Christ" (1:10). As those who are children of light, and therefore anticipate the *Day* of the Lord, His followers are to live "as in the *day*" (Paul's pun is intentional, author's italics), with behavior which is morally proper, characterized by love, and may be ultimately described as "put[ting] on the Lord Jesus Christ" (Rom. 13:8-14).

The witness of the church involves not only an active and gifted proclamation of the gospel (no small task itself), but also a conformity to a new standard of values, a standard which is not according to the values of this evil aeon (Rom. 12:1-2; Gal. 1:4; Eph. 2:1-3). In this latter regard, the church's behavior in the world is not to be thought of as simply moral conformity to certain abstract values, but, again, is rather a participation in Jesus Christ. The fruit of the Spirit (Gal. 5:22-23) is a life that is in the sphere of Christ and thereby gives expression in the world to His lordship. This expressed lordship, however, is not to be understood as triumphalism, for, in the final analysis, it is likely to be more akin in this life to what Paul called a "fellowship of His sufferings" (Phil. 3:10). It is this latter type of witness that is instinctively anathema to human experience and (while probably the most essential—remember the dominical exhortation to "take up [the] cross and follow me," Matt. 16:24) is often the first mandate jettisoned in modern Christian experience. The call to suffer is not an empty call to revolutionary heroism, however; it is rather the call to moral perseverance and courage (Eph. 5:3-14) in this present evil age, a call which (we must note with fear and trembling) seems to represent a necessary feature of salvation history and thus the purposes of God.

In this latter connection, we may recall that much Jewish literature anticipated, prior to the end of the age, a period of time that could be described as the days of "the messianic woes."[18] The coming of Christ seems to have retained something of this notion of the appearance of messianic woes, but also seems to have altered the anticipated sequence, to say nothing of introducing the notion that Messiah Himself should bear these curses. The messianic woes, or judgments, according to the typical Jewish apocalyptic timetable, were to have preceded the days of resurrection from the dead. In the case of the particular history of Jesus, it could be said that the days of woe, that is the accursed suffering of Jesus, did indeed precede the days of resurrection blessing. But in the resultant Christian apocalyptic eschatology, it was certainly noted (no doubt rather acutely) that the resurrection of Jesus did not immediately precipitate a general resurrection of the dead. Pauline eschatology (and indeed Paul shared this view with other New Testament writers) seems to have understood the resurrection of Jesus as a "firstfruits" resurrection (1 Cor. 15:23; cf. Rom. 8:29; Col. 1:18), and, therefore, though it *initiated* the resurrection of the dead (1 Cor. 15:21) and thus the dawning of the new age, it did not bring to an end this present evil age. The age of suffering is thus not yet done. We often refer to this duality in the Christian apocalyptic timetable as living "between the ages." But such a characterization, though true, does not do justice to one other crucial point. Namely, that the ongoing (present) life of the church in the world is a life "in Christ," and that present life in Christ is predominantly characterized by Paul as *a participation in His suffering* (Rom. 8:17; cf. 2 Cor. 1:5; 4:7-18). Or, to put it another way, the suffering of Christ is, in some sense, not yet finished (see Col. 1:24). The "messianic woes" thus continue in the ongoing suffering of Messiah's people, and, ironically (but not surprisingly, given what we now know of our suffering Lord), in the ongoing suffering of Messiah Himself *in the suffering of His people*. Therefore, the suffering which the people of God now endure in this present evil age, a suffering which includes not only persecution for the cause of Christ, but also all the untoward experiences of this present evil age (cf. Rom. 8:17-18 with vv. 35-39), is a suffering that comes under the canopy of Christ, which means both that it is a "suffering with Christ," and also that it is an ongoing aspect of the messianic woes. This fact explains why it is uncommon for New Testament authors to describe the persecution and affliction of Christians as a subset, though having a different purpose and outcome, of the larger experiences of divine judgment upon the earth (read Rom. 2:9 with 8:17-18,35-39, esp. v. 35; see also 5:3-5; 2 Thess. 1:4-10; 2:13-15; cf. 1 Pet. 4:12-19; Rev. 6:1 to 19:10, especially the judgments of the seals, the trumpets, and the cups, judgments *specifically poured out by the exalted Lord*). Thus, the suffering of the church, a suffering which takes place "in Christ," is a suffering whereby the eschatological, salvation-historical purposes of God are being accomplished. Indeed, if we may appropriate for the church generally the apostolic testimony of Paul with regard to his own missionary experience (and Paul himself did tie his own sufferings to the necessary sufferings of the church, Col. 1:24), the experience of the church, especially its participation in Christ's suffering, is a most significant sharing in God's redemptive purposes, for "[we] always carry about in the body the dying of Jesus; *so that the life of Jesus also may be manifested in our body*; for we who live are constantly being delivered over to death for Jesus' sake, *that the life of Jesus also may be manifested in our mortal flesh*" (2 Cor. 4:10-11, author's italics). Thus, what the church endures by way of suffering in this present evil age is both an evangelistic witness (v. 15) and a witness to the world of the coming, righteous judgment of God (2 Thess. 1:4-10). Such judgment is, in the case of God's people, a redemptive judgment of purging and transformation (Rom. 5:3-5; 8:17), but will, in the case of those outside of Christ, prove to be an "everlasting destruction away from the presence of the Lord and from the glory of his power" (2 Thess. 1:9).

While the apostolic office has passed from the scene, surely the apostolic witness is still a responsibility of the church. Those who have believed in the crucified and risen Jesus are truly a missionary people who must take seriously their charge both to proclaim Christ and to live, in this present evil age, in courageous solidarity with the crucified and risen Jesus. Just as Christ "did not regard [his] equality with God [as consisting in clutching], but emptied Himself, taking the form of a bond-servant, and being made in the likeness of men. And being found in appearance as a man, He humbled Himself by becoming obedient to the point of death, even death on a cross," so we too, as His servants, must "work out [our] salvation with fear and trembling, for it is God who is at work in [us] both to will and to work for His good pleasure." The serious nature of such eschatological undertakings "[through] us" means that "[we must thus] Do all things without grumbling or disputing," so that we may "prove [ourselves] to be blameless and innocent, children of [light] above reproach in the midst of a crooked and perverse generation," among whom we are called upon to "[shine] as lights in the world" (Phil. 2:5-15, author).

Notes

1. Richard B. Hays, *Echoes of Scripture in the Letters of Paul* (New Haven: Yale University Press, 1989), 86.

2. John Drane, *Introducing the New Testament* (San Francisco: Harper & Row, 1986), 248.

3. Krister Stendahl, *Paul Among Jews and Gentiles* (Philadelphia: Fortress, 1976), 7-23, and others who do not think of Paul's Damascus Road experience as a "conversion"; but even if one discounts the evidence of Acts, certainly the evidence of, for example, Galatians 1:11-23 implies rather strongly something akin to a dramatic change of direction for one who had begun to preach "the faith which once he tried to destroy" (v. 1:23). Of course, if "conversion" means the worship of a different god, then Paul the Christian was not "converted," for he continued to worship the God of Abraham, Isaac, and Jacob. But this is too great a stricture upon the normal meaning of the word "conversion." (Cf. also 2 Cor. 3:16, where Paul, apparently likening his own experience to that of Moses, refers—in what seems to be an allusion to the Damascus Road experience—to a "turning" to the Lord.

4. See Seyoon Kim, *The Origin of Paul's Gospel* (Tubingen: J. C. B. Mohr, 1981; reprint, Grand Rapids: Eerdmans, 1982), who argues persuasively for the centrality of this experience for the formation of Paul's theology.

5. 1 Corinthians 15:45.

6. 2 Corinthians 3:18; 4:5-6; Colossians 1:15 (cf. 3:10).

7. The discussion that follows will provide specific textual citations relevant to the Pauline terms, phrases, and ideas alluded to in this sentence.

8. Paul S. Minear, *Images of the Church in the New Testament* (Philadelphia: Westminster Press, 1960).

9. See the following discussion for references.

10. P. T. O'Brien, "The Church as a Heavenly and Eschatological Entity," in *The Church in the Bible and the World*, ed. D. A. Carson (Grand Rapids: Baker Book House, 1987), 88-119.

11. Cf. James D. G. Dunn, *Unity and Diversity in the New Testament* (Philadelphia: Westminster, 1977), 312.

12. As "dispensationalism" has traditionally done. See John F. Walvoord, *The Blessed Hope and the Tribulation* (Grand Rapids: Zondervan, 1976), 64-68.

13. See the excellent discussion of the issue of "supersession" versus "continuity" in Hays, *Echoes*, 95-121, 177.

14. See Hays, *Echoes*, for detailed treatments of the following examples of Paul's readings of the Jewish Scriptures and, as read by Paul, their references to Israel as finding contemporary expression in the Pauline/Gentile churches.

15. In addition to the "gift" passages cited above, see also 2 Corinthians 1:21 and Galatians 2:15-21.

16. See the forthcoming article on "Apostles, Disciples" by Robert B. Sloan, in *Layman's Bible Dictionary* (Nashville: Holman Bible Publishers, 1991).

17. F. F. Bruce, "The Epistles to the Colossians, to Philemon, and to the Ephesians," *The International Commentary on the New Testament*, (Grand Rapids: Eerdmans, 1984), 123-60, 353-65.

18. R. H. Charles, "A Critical and Exegetical Commentary on The Revelation of St. John," 2 vols. in *International Critical Commentary* (Edinburgh: T. & T. Clark, 1920; reprint, 1971), 1:153; G. R. Beasley-Murray, "Revelation" in *New Century Bible Commentary*, (Grand Rapids: Eerdmans, 1981), 27, 122-30; Dunn, 313.

12
Images of the Church in the General Epistles

by Marty L. Reid

This inquiry examines images of the church which are found in the General Epistles. Two historical factors which shaped the rubrics of "the people of God" within these writings deserve mention: the problem of suffering and persecution within the Christian communities, and the continued escalation of theological heresy[1] during the post-apostolic period.[2] These historical patterns represent two common strands that run throughout the General Epistles, and, for this reason, primarily influenced the authors' portrayals of the church. With this in view, the investigation surveys these images in the context of each writing.

The Wandering People of God and the Book of Hebrews

The structure of Hebrews represents a dynamic interplay between paraenetic and Christological material.[3] The principal motif of this structure is "the wandering of the People of God."[4] After the introduction (1:1-4), which poetically encapsulates the major doctrines of the body, the presentation of a Christological theme begins, depicting Christ as the eternal Son and ultimate High Priest (1:5 to 2:18). The next major section (3:1 to 4:13) continues a development of the book's Christological theme.

Of particular importance for this study is 3:1-6, where the author makes a comparison between the old order of Moses with the new of Christ. Verse 5 explains how Moses was "faithful" *(pistos)* in all God's house as a "servant" *(therapon).* Verse 6 indicates that Christ was faithful over God's house "as a son." With the notion of sonship, believers are described as "God's house" *(oikos tou theou),* but with a condition: "if we hold fast our confidence and pride in our hope." This admonition was directed to a church which was confronted with persecution to the point of neglecting their own fellowship.[5] The church was reminded that they were "God's house."[6] In the new covenant, the house of God finds its fruition in the faithfulness of Christ as God's son and representative. In short, the household of God has a Christological basis. Thus, verse 6 presents a functional Christology, in that the author focuses upon the work of Christ in contradistinction to His person.[7]

In addition, verse 6 provides a second assertion in a conditional state-ment: "we are his house if we hold fast our confidence and pride in our hope." Participation, then, in the house of God involves a faith proposition with an eschatological orientation. "Confidence" *(parresian)* and "pride" *(kauchema)* were necessary ingredients for the readers who found them-selves in a situation which provoked an unbelieving heart and the notion that God was no longer active in their lives (v. 12). The eschatological as-pect of membership is found in the language of hope, in the latter part of verse 6.[8] Thus, the imagery depicts the church as an eschatological commu-nity in that its existence is both present and future. This view of the church was important for an audience who had perceived that the *parousia* was imminent.[9]

The investigation at this point[10] resumes in 4:1, in which the theme of the promised rest is developed: "Therefore, while the promise of entering his rest remains, let us fear lest any of you be judged to have failed to reach it." The summons to enter this rest continues, with a poignant summary given in verses 9-10: "So then, there remains a sabbath rest *(sabbatismos)* for the people of God *(to lao tou theou)*." Here, the author presented the church as a corporate entity. The description also stresses the intimate relation be-tween God and His people.[11]

Within 5:11 to 6:20, the third major section of the body, a number of important images of the church are found. Hebrews 6:9-12 admonishes its readers to consider the eschatological aspects of their salvation. He desires that they not become sluggish, but imitate "those who through faith and [endurance] inherit the promises."[12] Two important aspects of the church are mentioned in verse 12. First, the church is a community which involves participation by way of faith and endurance.[13] Second, with the themes of "inheritance" and "promise," the writer underscored that the church has an eschatological orientation. Such encouragement to participate and refocus one's perspective—"in realizing the full assurance of hope until the end" (v. 11)—provided a significant admonition for a church which was becoming sluggish.

Verses 13-20 explain, by way of the example of Abraham, how the readers had a surety of hope based upon God's sure promises, which was demon-strated by the priesthood of Christ. In a historical context of persecution and imprisonment,[14] the author envisioned his readers as refugees who needed "strong encouragement to take hold of the hope set before them" (v. 18).

Hebrews 8:1 to 10:18 provides "an exegetical homily on Christ's sacrifi-cial act."[15] Introducing this section, 8:1-6 presents a comparison between the earthly and heavenly sanctuaries. In the description of the heavenly sanctuary, verse 2 describes Christ as "a minister of the sanctuary and the true tent, which [the Lord but not persons has built]." In short, the author depicts this heavenly sanctuary as "the tent which the Lord has built." The church, then, as a heavenly temple, exists in light of Christ's exaltation.[16]

The church, as the heavenly sanctuary, was foreshadowed by the earthly tent which Moses erected (v. 5); but through Christ the new covenant, by which the heavenly sanctuary exists, includes a greater promise (vv.7-8). "The first covenant had regulations for worship and an earthly sanctuary, for a tent was prepared" (9:1-2). "But when Christ appeared as a high priest of the good things which have come,"[17] a greater and more perfect tent was provided (v. 11).[18]

Since Christ is the mediator of the new covenant, the church receives the promise of the eternal inheritance (v. 15). The author portrayed the church as "those who [have been] called."[19] This phrase recalls the readers' spiritual pilgrimage. Their existence was rooted in the divine and dynamic activity of God. Their calling into the community of the faith had been consummated, but at the same time entailed participation,[20] lived out through faith, endurance, and eschatological hope.[21] Hebrews 11:13 reminded its readers how the patriarchs acknowledged their estrangement and exile on earth. The Book of Hebrews thus presents the church as a "wandering" (*planomenoi*) people (v. 38). To summarize, the church, during a period of early formation and development, was faced with a paradox. On the one hand, its members should recognize that their existence of faith was one of a stranger living in an alien society, a society which had scorned the Christian church for its religion.[22] On the other hand, the people of God were admonished to endure a secular society and to view their own suffering as having a teleological end.[23]

This latter theme of "faith and endurance in the realm of suffering" is presented in homiletic form in chapter 12.[24] Within this chapter, the author portrays the church with the imagery of "sonship." Verse 5 gives a primary statement: "Have you [altogether] forgotten the exhortation which addresses you as sons?" Believers are portrayed as sons who are disciplined by their father. Such discipline demonstrates the love of the father for his children (vv. 6-7) and legitimizes their relation with him (v. 8). Verses 10-12 indicates that suffering has an eschatological purpose: "that we may share [in] his holiness;"[25] and by discipline's training, the children may yield "the peaceful fruit of righteousness." This admonition was predicated upon their relation to the Heavenly Father as His children.[26]

In the concluding section (12:14 to 13:25),[27] the author employs two images to portray the church: a heavenly Zion (12:18-24) and an unshakable kingdom (vv. 25-30). The former provides one of the most graphic portrayals found in Hebrews:

> But you have come to Mount Zion and the city of the living God, the heavenly Jerusalem, and a myriad of angels in a festal assembly and to the assembly of the firstborn who have been enrolled in heaven, and to the judge of all, who is God, and to the spirits of the righteous ones who have been made perfect, and to Jesus, the mediator of the new covenant, and to the sprinkled blood of Jesus, which speaks better than that of Abel (vv. 22-24, author's translation).

Here, the church (*ekklesia*)[28] is distinguished as "the city of the living God" and as "the heavenly Jerusalem." Its heavenly existence forces the audience to consider the eschatological dimensions. The church, in all its glory, is not imposed by spatial limitations. Hebrews 13:14 reflects a similar perspective: "For here, we have no [abiding] city [*menousan polin*], but we continue to seek the city which is to come [*mellousan*]." As this text stresses, the Book of Hebrews presents the Christian assembly as "the wandering [people of God]" on a pilgrimage in search of the eternal city, where God dwells and where they will no longer be sojourners and exiles as they were on this earth. In the meantime, they were to live joyfully and obediently with the guarantee that the Lord Jesus would watch over them as "the great shepherd of the sheep" (vv. 17-20). The Book of Hebrews closes aptly with a Christological formula, reflecting the exalted Christology whereby Christ's sufficiency was demonstrated to its readers. At the same time, the imagery of "the sheep" for the people of God (v. 13:21) reminded the readers not only of the sole sufficiency of Christ for their time and situation but also of their complete and total dependence upon the Author and Perfecter of their faith.

The Exiles and Sojourners of 1 Peter

Much like Hebrews, one can characterize 1 Peter as a book of "exhortation" and "instruction."[29] The investigation begins in the prescript of the letter (1:1-2), where the audience is addressed as "chosen exiles" *(eklektois parepidemois)*. The author considered his Christian readers as sojourners, resident aliens who were not at home in this world. This designation also emphasizes that believers are elected by God.[30] The prescript reveals that the imagery of "chosen exiles" predominates throughout 1 Peter.

First Peter 1:3 to 2:10 includes a paraenetic section, providing admonitions for the Christian life. First Peter 1:17 introduces the major theme of the letter—how to function as exiles and Christians in the Roman society—with the following statement: "Conduct yourselves with fear throughout the time of your exile."

The significance of this notion can be seen by considering the historical context of the letter. First Peter 2:13-14 colors the setting as a period when the Roman emperor was supreme. In fact, governors were sent by the emperor to punish the innocent—who presumably were the Christians—and to praise those who practiced evil. This milieu illustrates the appropriateness of the motif of "sojourners" and "exiles," one which had application in Rome ever since the Neronian persecution.[31]

In such a context, Christians were to conduct themselves as "servants of God" (v. 16). This description, much like the phrase "people of God" found in Hebrews, denotes God's ownership of His people, or perhaps, from the standpoint of the believer, indicates the Christian's allegiance toward God.[32] Verse 16 thus presents an interesting paradox for the church, both then and now. Christians are free, but they are only free as "servants of God." The ethical implications of this admonition were far-reaching. Four are mentioned in verse 17: Honor all people, love the brotherhood, fear God, and honor the emperor.[33]

Verses 1-10 include encouragement for the believer's growth within salvation. The author presents Christ as "the living stone though rejected by humankind, chosen and precious to God" (v. 4, author). Then follows an exhortation: "You, as living stones, build up yourselves as a spiritual house for the purpose of being a holy priesthood to offer spiritual sacrifices which are acceptable to God through Jesus Christ" (v. 5, author). From this statement one can make the following observations about the church. First, the text emphasized that the church involved active and dynamic participation by its members. This notion is brought out by the paradoxical phrase of "living stones" *(lithoi zontes)* and the verb, "build yourselves up."[34] Second, the Godward and community aspect of the church is reinforced by the imagery of "a spiritual house."[35] The purpose for which the church was being built is given in verse 5: "to be a holy priesthood [which entails offering] spiritual sacrifices which are acceptable to God through Jesus Christ."[36]

With the conclusion of an argument in verses 4-8, the description of the church continues:

> But you are a chosen race, a royal priesthood, a holy nation, a people for his possession in order that you might proclaim the virtues of the one who has called you from darkness into his marvelous light. You once were not a people, but now are the people of God, those who were not shown mercy but now have been shown mercy (vv. 9-11, author).

The church is described as "a chosen race" *(genos eklekton)*. That the notion of "election" is a major theme of 1 Peter is obvious. In 1:1 the author approached his readers as "chosen exiles". Furthermore, Christ, portrayed as "the living stone" (2:4), is also spoken of as being "chosen." The question, however, remains: What does it mean to be "a chosen race?" At the outset one can certainly conclude that the community and corporate aspect is an important element of this imagery. The employment of the racial term *(genos)* points out that the church has no ethnic barriers. But the text does not stop here. Verse 9 includes a string of phrases which help clarify the above mentioned question.[37] Beginning with the phrase, "a royal priesthood," this description, along with those that follow, define the meaning of "a chosen race."[38] If this interpretation is correct, three emphases can be noted: the royalty of the church, the holiness of the church, and God's possession of the church.

According to verse 9, the purpose for which the people of God were chosen was declaration and proclamation: "that you might proclaim the wonderful virtues of the one who has called you out of darkness and into his wonderful light"(author).[39] Because of God's calling and election, they became God's people. They had found God's mercy (v. 10).[40] In short, the church was predicated upon the demonstration of God's mercy.

In the overall structure of the body, a slight transition occurs in verse 11. The remainder of the epistle concerns warnings for the Christian in a secular world. Verses 11-12 provides advice about conduct toward outsiders. The theme of believers as "aliens and exiles" resumes in verse 11.[41] The author's admonitions focus upon ethical issues. The readers' "good deeds" opposed the physical lusts that pervaded their society, to such a degree that their manner of life could result in the glorification of God (v. 12). In certain respects, then, the ethical behavior of the Christian community was of such importance that even their manner of life carried eschatological implications. By way of this introduction, 1 Peter reminded its audience of the church's ethical responsibility.

The latter part of the epistle (3:13 to 5:11) develops the theme of Christian suffering. In the readers' circumstances, the nurturing of the church was most important.[42] Consequently, this context describes the church as "the flock of God" (5:2). The charge is given to the elders to "Tend the flock of God which is among you, not by compulsion but willingly according to God, neither in fondest of dishonest gain but eagerly"[43] (author). The imagery of "the flock" pictures the church as a nurturing community. This notion also implies the church's dependence upon its leaders as shepherds. Those in charge were to be examples to the flock (5:3). Verses 2-3 indicate that perhaps some were abusing their places of leadership. Verse 2 provides a pointed reminder in this regard. The flock was not the possession of its leader, but ultimately belonged to God.[44] Verse 4 reinforces this point by referring to God as "the chief Shepherd." The epistle closes, reminding the readers of the church's calling, suffering, and eschatological nature (vv. 8-11). The time would come when the church would receive her "unfading crown of glory" (v. 4).[45]

Jewish Christianity and the Book of James

James 1:1 introduces the recipients as "the twelve tribes in the Dispersion." Whether or not this phrase should be interpreted in a racial or theological sense,[46] this Jewish terminology legitimizes the church within the scheme of salvation history. As God revealed Himself to the twelve tribes of Israel in the old covenant, so has a fuller revelation been given to the church as the new Israel.

If "the twelve tribes" refer to the church as the eschatological Israel, it then follows that the reference, "in the Dispersion" (v. 1), speaks of scattered Christians on a wandering journey, a theme found in both Hebrews and 1 Peter. The audience of James struggled for theological balance. They were confronted with an illegitimate form of the Pauline gospel[47] that had lost sight of the church's ethical obligations, both within and without.[48]

Though this investigation has not focused upon the earliest development and structure of the church, one notices that James uses the Jewish term, "synagogue" (*synagoge*), to refer to the Christian assembly (2:2, author). The book also speaks of the "teachers" (3:1) and "elders" (5:14) of the church. To what degree these positions represented a formal office is not clear. However, one can say that the church had established Christian pastoral duties[49] and that teachers played an important role in its ministry.

The survey concludes, mentioning two remaining imageries of the church. First, 1:18 states: "He [God] brought us forth by the word of truth that we should be a kind of first fruits of his creatures."[50] The passage depicts the church as the primal mover of all redemption, an event for which even creation groans.[51] Second, in a pericope which warns against partiality (2:1-13),[52] verse 5 makes a statement about the church's existence in the world: "Listen, my beloved [people]. Has not God chosen those who are poor in the world to be the rich in faith and heirs of the kingdom which he has promised to those who love him?" From this text one can elicit notable themes about the church. First, God's providence has overseen the church. Second, the church, or those who make up the church, live a paradoxical existence. Those who respond to God through love, though poor in the present world, become rich in His kingdom. Third, the theme of promise emphasizes that the church is an eschatological community in that it awaits the Day of the Lord.[53]

The Elect Lady and the Johannine Epistles

The language of the Johannine Epistles reflects the development of the church in Asia Minor during the latter decades of the first century.[54] The church was faced with correcting a Gnostic movement which advocated a docetic Christology. In a theological climate which resulted in ethical short-comings, the church needed instruction.[55]

The recurring imagery by which the church is portrayed in the Johannine Letters is "children." Some passages describe the relationship between the author and his readers.[56] Others refer to the relationship between God and believers, and thus to the church.[57] The Johannine circle viewed the church as a community where the fatherhood of God is experienced. Thus, the church operates out of her parental relationship with the father through Jesus Christ. Ultimately, the church, especially from the standpoint of 1 John, is a place of fellowship.[58]

In addition to the Johannine notion of the church as "the offspring of God," one discovers a second image. Second John 1 refers to the church as "the elect lady and her children" *(eklekte kyria kai tois teknois autes)*. First, the phrase should be understood as a corporate reference. This interpreta-tion is supported by the plural address of "children" as well as the observa-tion that 2 John addresses a community and its problems. Second, the image recalls "the biblical personification of Israel as a woman, or Jerusalem as the 'mother' of Israel,[59] and the New Testament picture of the church as the 'bride' of Christ.[60] Third, verse 1 alludes to the church in its local expres-sions as an "elect" congregation, an expression also found in 1 Peter 5:13. In the Johannine church, members were viewed as the elect lady's offspring. As in 1 John, the term describes the fellowship of all Christians. Thus, the church is viewed as a family of believers.[61]

Early Catholicism: 2 Peter and Jude

Second Peter and Jude represent a period in which the earliest expecta-tions of the *Parousia* had weakened and the church had become institution-alized through an organized ministry. To what degree "early Catholicism" *(Fruhkatholizimus)* can be found in the New Testament is a question that scholars continue to debate.[62] They do agree, however, that these two let-ters reflect a mutual dependence. Thus, 2 Peter and Jude present a picture of the church just before the emergence of the Catholic Church in the mid-second century.

Conclusion

At a time when the church was attempting to determine its orthodoxy, the images of the church were varied and diverse. When the earliest Chris-tians made a distinctive break from Judaism, their own assembly *(ekklesia)* was born. The church became a community which was not accepted by the prevalent Greco-Roman societies. For this reason, Hebrews and 1 Peter described the church as a "wandering" people and as "exiles" and "sojourners." The church, however, experienced the mercy and grace of God. It was a community which was God's possession and a place for human transformation. The church, as the elect, survived under God's providence; and its future was predicated on God's promises and on the living hope which Christ had provided.

The Book of James instructed the church about its obligations, both to itself and to those outside. The Johannine Epistles emphasized that the church is composed of God's offspring. Consequently, her members had the ethical responsibility to act accordingly. By the end of the first century, Jude and 2 Peter portrayed the church in a more organized form, battling issues of dogma and discipline.

Perhaps the unity and diversity of images of the church in the General Epistles provide a hermeneutic for understanding the church today. The possibility exists for a diversity of ecclesiastical traditions, but the modern church must not lose sight of the apostolic kerygma which shaped the image of the early Christian communities.

Notes

1. Consult Walter Bauer, *Orthodoxy and Heresy in Earliest Christianity*, 2d ed., trans. the Philadelphia Seminar on Christian Origins, ed. Robert Kraft and Gerhard Krodel (Philadelphia: Fortress, 1971); James D. G. Dunn, *Unity and Diversity in the New Testament: An Inquiry into the Character of Earliest Christianity* (Philadelphia: Westminster Press, 1977); and Daniel Harrington, "The Reception of Walter Bauer's *Orthodoxy and Heresy in Earliest Christianity* During the Last Decade," in *Light of All Nations: Essays on the Church in New Testament Research*, Good News Studies 3 (Wilmington, Del: Michael Glazier, 1982), 162-73.

2. Though an exact dating of the General Letters remains difficult, one can assume a rough estimate of A.D. 60-100. See Bo Reicke, *The Epistles of James, Peter, and Jude* AB (Garden City, N.Y.: Doubleday & Company, 1964), xv-xxix; Harold Attridge, *The Epistle to the Hebrews* (Hermeneia: A Critical and Historical Commentary on the Bible, ed. Helmut Koester (Philadelphia: Fortress, 1989), 6-9. For a consideration of the entire corpus of the General Epistles, consult Werner George Kümmel, *Introduction to the New Testament*, rev. ed. (Nashville: Abingdon, 1975), 387-451; and Donald Guthrie, *New Testament Introduction*, 3d ed. (Downers Grove, Ill: Inter-Varsity, 1970), 685-930. For a critical assessment of the assumptions taken in reconstructing the chronology of the New Testament writings, compare John A. T. Robinson, *Redating the New Testament* (Philadelphia: Westminster Press, 1976).

3. Since Hebrews lacks the structure of the ancient epistle, most scholars classify the book as a sermon or homily (cf. Heb. 13:22). In addition Hebrews parallels ancient Hellenistic-Jewish and early Christian texts that seem to be based upon homilies. For discussion see Lawerence Wills, "The Form of the Sermon in Hellenistic Judaism and Early Christianity," *HTR* 77 (1984): 277-99; Hartwig Thyen, *Der Stil der judisch-hellenistischen Homilie* (FRLANT 47; Gottingen: Vandenhoeck & Ruprecht, 1955); James Swetnam, "On the Literary Genre of the Epistle to the Hebrews," *NovT* 11 (1969): 261-69; and Attridge, 13-14.

4. Ernst Käsemann has suggested this thesis in *The Wandering People of God: An Investigation of the Letter to the Hebrews*, 2d ed., trans. Roy Harrisville and Irving Sandberg (Minneapolis: Augsburg, 1984). On a larger scale, Paul Hanson (*The People Called: The Growth of Community in the Bible* [San Francisco: Harper & Row, 1986]) has attempted to present a

unified biblical theology around the theme of "community."

5. Hebrews 10:25 indicates that one of the purposes for which Hebrews was written was to bring the Christian community back into the mainstream of Christian fellowship. This text reveals that the problem was so severe that the neglect of regular meetings had become a habit. Such observations also disclose the degree of the persecution of the Christian community.

6. Compare Hebrews 11:7,10. The term, *oikos*, was employed to designate communal groups or households, including the people of Israel (cf. Jer. 12:7; 31:13 cited in Heb. 8:8), the Davidic dynasty, and various Jewish and Christian communities (cf. 1 Pet. 2:5; 4:17). For discussion see Otto Michael, *"oikos,"* *TDNT* 5 (1967): 119-31; Bertil Gartner, *The Temple and the Community and the New Testament*, SNTSMS 1 (Cambridge: Cambridge University Press, 1965); and Attridge, 108-9.

7. A similar notion is found in Hebrews 10:19-25. Verse 21 describes Christ as "a great priest over the house of God." As elsewhere in this epistle, verse 23 also emphasizes the place of hope in the church's experience and existence coupled with a promising God who is faithful. (Cf. the following statement made by Käsemann, 156: "The community of the redeemed as *oikos* of the Son is the fruit of his activity as apostle and the sum of believers called to the heavenly city.") See Hebrews 3:1 where the author designates Jesus as an "apostle" (*apostolos*, literally, "one who is sent") and high priest (*archierea*).

8. The objective genetive, *tes elpidos*, indicates that the object of their boldness and pride was their hope in Christ. A similar notion is found in 1 Thessalonians 1:3, where the setting is much like the historical setting of Hebrews, though 1 Thessalonians reflects a more apocalyptic viewpoint, which by the time Hebrews was written required modification in light of the delay of the *Parousia*. Compare Hebrews 6:11,18; 7:19; 10:23; 11:1; 1 Peter 1:3.

9. During the A.D. 60s, a problem for the second generation was the practical delay of the *Parousia*. Leonhard Goppelt (*Theology of the New Testament: The Variety and Unity of the Apostolic Witness to Christ* [2 vols., trans. John E. Alsup, ed. Jurgen Roloff; Grand Rapids: William B. Eerdmans, 1981-82], 2:157-59) explains that "what resulted was a sharp tension between the calling into the new existence of eschatological freedom and the abiding link to the structures of historical life. . . . The Epistle to the Hebrews, e.g., countered a relaxed standard in the community of faith with nothing other than a renewed proclamation of the eschatological message of salvation."

10. In continuing the discussion, one should keep the structure of Hebrews in mind. Hebrews 3:1-5:10 presents Christ as the faithful and merciful one, with 3:1-4:13 providing a homily on faith and 4:14-5:10 including a discussion of Christ, the merciful high priest. This analysis by and large follows the suggestions of Attridge, 19. Albert Vanhoye (*La structure litteraire de l'epitre aux Hebreux*, 2d ed. [Rome: Desclee de Brouwer, 1962], 11-59), detects a similar structure.

11. *[T]ou theou* occurs in the genitive case, which in the Greek language is the case of description. In this text the possessive genitive is the preferred interpretation. This exegesis suggests that the genitive also denotes "a certain intimate relation." For discussion see Maximilian Zerwick, *Biblical Greek*, Eng. ed. Joseph Smith (Rome: Scripta Pontificii Instituti Biblici, 1963), 14-16; *BDF*, 89-90; and *BAG*, 467.

12. The *hina* clause of Hebrews 6:12b is taken as a result clause.

13. The adversative conjunction, *de*, in verse 12 makes a comparison between those who are "sluggish" and "those who receive the promises through faith and endurance." The latter represents those whom the readers should mimic. The genitive substantive article, *ton*, following a noun of action (*mimetai*) is taken as an objective gentive. For discussion of the objective gentive, see *BDF*, 90.

14. See Hebrews 12:3; 13:3; 13:22.

15. Attridge, 19.

16. Notice Hebrews 8:1: "Now the point in the things being said is this: we have such a high priest, who has been seated at the right hand of the throne of the majesty in heaven" (author's translation). A detailed exegesis of the temple imagery goes beyond the boundaries of this

inquiry. Consult Attridge, 222-24, esp. 224: "The interior reality that the heavenly temple symbolizes is not a principle or virtue generally available to humankind, but a relationship made possible by Christ. The earthly-heavenly dichotomy of the temple imagery intersects with, interprets, and is at the same time transformed by another dichotomy, that of new and old."

17. In Hebrews 9:11, the genitive absolute, *Christos de paragenomenos archiereus ton genomenon agathon*, has temporal force.

18. See also Hebrews 9:11c: "(not made by hands, that is, not by this creation.)" For recent discussion, see Attridge, 244-48; and Harald Hegermann, *Der Brief an die Hebraer*, THKNT 16 (Berlin: Evangelische Verlagsanstalt, 1988), 177-78.

19. Hebrews 9:15 states: "And for this reason, Christ is the mediator of the new covenant, so that [*hopos*] those who have been called might receive the promise of the eternal inheritance, since death has come about for the redemption of the transgressions under the first covenant" (author's translation). In the larger context, *dia touto* refers back to 9:11-14. The genitive absolute, *thanatou genomenou*, is taken as adverbial with causal force. Finally, *hopos* introduces a subordinate result clause.

20. The "consummative perfect" of the participle, *hoi keklemenoi*, includes both of these aspects. Since there is no English equivalent for the Greek perfect tense, it is difficult to convey these notions in translation. For discussion of the consummative perfect, see *BDF*, 1975-77; and Ernest D. Burton, *Syntax of the Moods and Tenses in New Testament Greek*, 3d ed. (Chicago; University of Chicago, 1900; reprint Grand Rapids: Kregel, 1976), 37-44. For the idea of continual participation, compare Hebrews 10:14, where the author describes the church as "those who are continually being sanctified" (*tous hagiazomenous*). This present passive participle includes the notion of continuance with the present tense, and also the idea of divine agency with the passive voice.

21. These three notions seem to be motifs that run throughout Hebrews as well as other General Epistles.

22. Compare Käsemann, 44: "Viewed from the world, the church must appear as a band of deserters when it forsakes encampment in an existence where all else is intent on solidarity and total union."

23. This theme is also taken up in 1 Peter 2:11-12. (Also cf. 1 Peter 2:13-4:19.) For discussion see Hanson, 3.

24. For a structual analysis, see Vanhoye, 196-204.

25. The articular infinitival clause, *eis to metalabein*, is an adverbial infinitive denoting purpose. For discussion of the purpose infinitive consult *BDF*, 197.

26. Hebrews 12:9 draws a distinctive between "our earthly fathers" and "the Father of [the] spirits." This unusual designation of God as "Father of [the] spirits" probably originates from traditional Jewish formulations. (Cf. Num. 16:22; 27:16; and 1 Clem. 59.3; 64.1.) For discussion see Attridge, 362-63.

27. This structural analysis follows Attridge's suggestion (*Hebrews*, 19); compare Vanhoye, 205.

28. The only place where *ekklesia* occurs with reference to the heavenly Jerusalem is Hebrews 12:23. Since *panegyris* follows, the imagery brings to mind a festal gathering in heaven as there are festal gatherings on earth. For the other occurrences of *ekklesia* in the General Epistles see Hebrews 2:12; James 5:14; and 3 John 6,9-10. For discussion see *BAG*, 240-41; and K. L. Schmidt, *"ekklesia,"* *TDNT* 3 (1965): 501-36.

29. The words, *parakalon* and *epimartyron*, are taken from 1 Peter 5:12 which indicate the epistle's nature and purpose; compare Hebrews 13:22 which characterizes the book as "a word of exhortation" (*tou logou tes parakleseos*).

30. The verbal adjective, *eklektos*, has a passive force which emphasizes divine agency. Compare 1 Chronicles 16:13; Psalms 88:4; 104:6; Isaiah 65:9,15,23. For discussion see *BAG*, 242.

31. Tacitus' account (*Ann.* 15.44.2-8) of Nero's actions provides the earliest record of offi-

cial persecution against the Christians. The underlying problem was one of hostility, and even though Tacitus reflects an aristocratic point of view, similar feelings may have been shared by the common people. By the decade of the 60s, Christians were considered to be a distinct group from the Jews. First Peter 4:16 could indicate that one who associated with the name *Christianos*, the name given to the followers of Christ by outsiders (Acts 11:26), provided sufficient evidence for punishment. Although Nero's persecution applied only to Rome (cf. 1 Pet. 5:13), his actions did set a precedent. The Christians, as with the Jews, were eventually charged with being enemies of all people because of their withdrawal from pagan society. Suetonius (*Life of Nero* 16.2) wrote: "Punishment was inflicted on the Christians, a class of [people] given to a new and wicked superstition." In short, a time came when the traditional pagan society viewed Christianity as a threat to its way of life. Compare Tacitus, *Hist.* 5.5; 1 Peter 1:6; 4:1; 5:1,9-10. For discussion, see W. H. C. Frend, "The Persecutions: Some Links Between Judaism and the Early Church," *JEH* (1958): 141-58; and Everett Ferguson, *Backgrounds of Early Christianity* (Grand Rapids: William B. Eerdmans, 1987), 472-81.

32. Both of these ideas could be indicated by the genitive possessive *theou* in verse 16.

33. Leonhard Goppelt develops this point in *Der erste Petrusbrief* (Gottingen: Vandenhoeck & Ruprecht, 1978), 186-89.

34. The verb, *oikodomeisthe*, can be interpreted to be in the indicative or imperative mode. In light of the imperative verbs in 1 Peter 2:1 (*apothemenoi*); 2:2 (*epipothesate*); and 2:4 (*proserchomenoi*), it seems best to interpret *oikodomeisthe* as an imperative denoting command. Also worthy of notice is the middle voice of this verb, which can be taken as an indirect middle. The indirect middle represents the subject as acting for oneself or by oneself. This interpretation emphasizes the place of active participation, as suggested in the above exegesis. For discussion of the middle voice, see Curtis Vaughan and Virtus E. Gideon, *A Greek Grammar of the New Testament* (Nashville: Broadman, 1979), 90-93; *BDF*, 165-66; and Zerwick, 75-76.

35. It is interesting to notice the play on words by use of the cognates *oikodomeisthe* and *oikos*. (Cf. 1 Pet. 4:17).

36. This translation brings out the adverbial accusative (*eis hierateuma*) denoting purpose. The infinitival clause (*anenegkai pneumatikas thysias*) provides a descriptive meaning of what is involved in being a holy priesthood. Taking the infinitive in this sense seems more likely than purpose, since purpose has already been indicated by the adverbial accusative, *eis hierateuma*. For discussion see Goppelt, *Petrusbrief*, 143-47.

37. A word about the context and structure of the verse is in order. Previously, 1 Peter 2:4-8 explained how Christ, as the living stone, provided a basis for the readers' existence. In light of this Christology, the author provides an interpretation of their position as the community of believers in 1 Peter 2:9-10. A contrast is made between those who did not receive the word and those who did. One should therefore notice the transition between verses 8 and 9, which is reinforced by the adversative conjunction, *de*. Finally, the discussion in 1 Peter 2:4-11 provides a theological basis for the paraenetic material that follows in 1 Peter 2:11-3:7.

38. This interpretation suggests that *genos* functions as a predicate nominative of *hymeis*, and that the following nominatives serve as appositional phrases to the main predicate of *genos*. (Cf. Goppelt, *Petrusbrief*, 151-59.)

39. *Hopos* with the subjunctive is taken as a purpose clause.

40. *BAG*, 249, translates 1 Peter 2:10b as follows: "who once had not found mercy, but now have found it." *[E]leeo* in the passive can be translated either as "find" or "be shown mercy." The suggested translation centers upon the readers' participation of finding mercy. By becoming a part of God's people, they had experienced God's mercy.

41. Cf. the wandering motif in 1 Peter 2:15: "For you were straying like sheep, but have now returned to the Shepherd and Guardian of your souls."

42. When suffering did occur, the church had as its model the example of Christ. Notice especially the motif of the sufferings of Christ on behalf of believers and the motif of sojourning ("that you should follow in his [Christ's] steps") in 1 Peter 2:21; compare also 1:6; 3:14; 4:1; 5:1,9-10.

43. The translation does not include the textual variant, *episkountes*. Since the shorter reading is preferred, one can explain its inclusion as an exegetical expansion, in light of 1 Peter 2:25. The textual evidence of *kata theon*, though found in a variety of witnesses representing several text types, is also uncertain. For the textual evidence and discussion, see *UBSGNT* 802; and Bruce Metzger, *A Textual Commentary on the Greek New Testament*, corrected ed. (London, New York: United Bible Societies, 1975), 695-96.

44. This notion is found in the possessive genitive. See *BDF*, 89-100; and Zerwick, 12-19.

45. See 1 Peter 5:2.

46. Ralph P. Martin, *James* (WBC; Waco, Tex.: Word Books, 1988), 8 attempts to combine these two interpretations and suggests the (tentative) view that James' address is "directed to the worldwide community of believing Jews of the messianic faith." Though Martin provides a good presentation of the evidence, his argument is not persuasive. Because of the lack of particularities regarding the situation of the recipients and due to the paraenetic form, James should be viewed as a document of instruction written to the church as the new people of the twelve tribes. See Leonhard Goppelt, *Theology*, 2:200. For a discussion of the genre of paraenesis, see Martin Dibelius, *James*, rev. by Heinrich Greeven, trans. Michael Williams; Hermeneia: A Critical and Historical Commentary on the Bible, ed. Helmut Koester; Philadelphia: Fortress Press, 1976), 1-7.

47. See especially James 2:14-26.

48. See, for example, James 1:19-2:17.

49. James 1:27 mentions the care of orphans and widows. James 5:14-15 refers to the praying and anointing of the sick by the elders.

50. The articular infinitive, *eis to einai*, denotes purpose and should be related to *apekyesen*.

51. It is helpful to compare Paul's discussion of salvific and eschatological hope of the children of God in Romans 8:18-25, especially verse 23 where he speaks of them "who have the first fruits of the Spirit." Compare also 1 Peter 1:23.

52. One of the primary problems which James addresses is the mistreatment of the poor by the rich (cf. Jas. 1:9-11; 5:1-6).

53. The delay of the *Parousia* does not seem to be as much a problem as in some of the other General Epistles in that the event still seems to be imminent. See James 5:7-11,20. For the role of eschatology in James, cf. George Ladd, *Theology of the New Testament* (Grand Rapids: William B. Eerdmans, 1974), 589-91; and Rudolf Bultmann, *Theology of the New Testament*, trans. Kendrick Grobel, 2 vols. (New York: Charles Scribner's Sons, 1951-55) 2:162-63.

54. For discussion of background see Kummel, 434-51; Guthrie, 864-904; and Stephen S. Smalley, *1, 2, 3, John* (WBC; Waco, Tex.: Word Books, 1984), xxi-xxxiv.

55. For the purpose and problems of the Johannine setting see 1 John 1:4; 2:22,26; 4:2-3. Cf. Smalley, xxviii: "Belief and behavior, Christology [sic] and ethics, are together a consistent concern of the writer; and his insistence . . . flows directly from the evident stresses and divisions within the Johannine circle."

56. See 1 John 2:1,12,18,28; 3:7,18; 5:21; 3 John 1:4.

57. See 1 John 3:1,2,10; 4:4; 5:2,19; 2 John 1,4,13.

58. On the basis of 1 John 3-4, one can argue that this exegesis ties in with the major thrust of the letter. The author states that proclamation was given for the purpose of fellowship: "we proclaim to you, in order that (*hina* purpose clause) you might have fellowship with us (*koinonian meth' hemon*)," a fellowship "with the father and with his son, Jesus Christ. And we write these things that (*hina* final purpose clause) our joy may be complete."

59. Cf. Isa. 54:1-8; Gal. 4:25; Rev. 12:17; 21:2.

60. Smalley, 318. Cf. 2 Cor. 11:2; Eph. 5:22-32.

61. Cf. 2 John 1:5,10,13.

62. See Harrington, "The 'Early Catholic' Writings of the New Testament: The Church Adjusting to World History," 61-78.

Part 3
Historical Developments

Christian history reflects diverse viewpoints of what the church is and how it lives out its mission. The locus of authority supporting these often competing viewpoints is equally diverse. Scripture, apostolic authority, tradition, reason, experience, the leadership of pastors or bishops, and various other sources have been offered, with plausible and vigorous defenses, as the basis of authority in the church. Many movements in church history have been dominated by attempts to bypass all forms of authority and tradition in order to recapture the "normative" patterns for church life. Sometimes these renewal and reform movements have been breaths of fresh air for the people of God. On other occasions attempts at restoration have resulted in near revolution. The essayists in this section recognize that the Believers' Church movement has developed from renewal efforts, yet they seek to capture the unity and variety of expressions in God's redemptive program.

E. Glenn Hinson focuses on the unity in diversity in the second century in his essay on "Patristic Views of the Church." The movements within the medieval period are outlined by Glenn O. Hilburn. C. Penrose St. Amant brilliantly analyzes the "Reformation Views of the Church." The radical wing of the Reformation provided one of the best-known examples of a renewal/restoration movement. The Believers' Church tradition owes much to this movement capably summarized by John J. Kiwiet in his chapter "Anabaptist Views of the Church."

Often Believers' Church movements have resulted in a form of separationism or primitivism that secluded them from the larger body of Christ. William L. Pitts examines these obstacles in his essay on "The Relation of Baptists to Other Churches." It has not been uncommon for the Believers' Church tradition to define itself in distinction to the Roman Catholic Church, yet renewal movements in the Roman Catholic Church since Vatican II have resembled many of the characteristics of the Believers' Church. Doyle L. Young offers his perspective on these issues in the concluding chapter of this section, "Modern Roman Catholic Views of the Church."

Although Christian bodies in these different time periods in the history of

179

the church have manifested various traits and emphases and have provided specific heritages for those who have followed, they all nevertheless have shared a common adherence to the lordship of Jesus Christ as head of the church. As individuals and as churches, these diverse movements have attempted to be faithful witnesses to the gospel of Jesus Christ and thus have left behind their testimony to the larger Christian community. The variety of expression has provided a healthy balance for the church as it seeks to embody a common and unified commitment to Jesus Christ. An examination of the variety of expressions enables us to understand better the meaningful contribution of the Believers' Church tradition.

13
Patristic Views of the Church: Unity and Diversity in the Second Century

by E. Glenn Hinson

Modern scholarship and ecumenism owe a considerable debt to Walter Bauer[1] for smashing the illusion that Christianity has ever glided through a phase of perfect unity. Thanks to the debate which *Orthodoxy and Heresy in Earliest Christianity* occasioned once the initial shock of it passed, we can now recognize that unity and diversity existed alongside one another or, perhaps more accurately stated, unity existed in diversity.[2] It is important to note here that the half-century debate has taken a substantive turn from the question of "orthodoxy" and "heresy" to that of unity and diversity as a consequence of factors difficult to pinpoint precisely, but including a growing ecumenical sensitivity embracing all of church history as the history of us all. The key question historians are asking is: How did Christianity establish and maintain its identity as it emerged from a Jewish matrix and grew up in a predominately non-Jewish (Greco-Roman, Syrian, Mesopotamian, Egyptian, African, etc.) environment?

The contextual issue will be the chief concern of this chapter, for I think ecumenical progress of recent years demands a more serious reply to another facet of Bauer's thesis than historians have given up to now, namely, that Rome created orthodoxy. Only in the case of Rome, Bauer argued, can we state confidently that orthodoxy possessed the upper hand. And the distinctive character that marked Rome from the outset passed over to Corinth around the year 100, where it remained.[3]

As Bauer sketched the rise of orthodoxy, Rome pulled off a mighty feat in extending the sway of orthodoxy to all the other parts of the Empire, where "the heretics considerably outnumbered the orthodox."[4] Rome's "tactics which 1 Clement rather more conceals from us than reveals"[5] included: appeal to the apostles (Peter and Paul) for justification, exercise of a teaching influence upon Christians elsewhere, donation of money which Rome had in abundance due to subscriptions like those of Marcion, and calling suitable leaders to its helm. In sum,

> Essentially unanimous in the faith and in the standards of Christian living, tightly organized and methodically governed by the monarchical bishop, the Roman church toward the close of the second century feels inclined and able to extend further the boundaries of her influence. In Asia, Syria, and Egypt we saw her aiming at conquests and replacing by a more resolute procedure the earlier, more cautious attempts to work her will at Corinth.[6]

Bauer's argument has plenty of holes in it, but none gapes as wide as his assumption that the Roman Church was "essentially unanimous in the faith and in the standards of Christian living" and "tightly organized and methodically governed by the monarchical bishop" toward the end of the second century. Bauer's judgment regarding the pressure toward conformity which the Roman Church exerted during the second century fails to take seriously the intense struggle for unity in diversity that characterized the church there throughout the century. More than Marcion and Valentinus presented a challenge to Roman "orthodoxy" or unity.[7] The struggle of the Roman Church throughout the second century entailed more than the creation of an "orthodoxy" which the departure of Marcion and Valentinus could effect. It had to do, rather, with a search of diverse groups for common ground in a highly diversified and pluralistic setting not unlike the one the churches face today in metropolis.

Jewish/Christian Roots

To appreciate fully the complexity of Rome's problem we must recognize not only the crazy-quilt character of the city (of about one million) itself but the likely diversity of Jewish life in Rome before Christianity appeared on the scene. Unlike cities such as Antioch and Alexandria, Rome had no Jewish "quarter," although there would have been some concentrations in communities, presumably known to Christian missionaries.[8] Outside Palestine, and to some extent even inside, as the lifetime researches of E. R. Goodenough[9] have demonstrated, rabbinic Judaism never established itself as "normative." Of eleven known Jewish communities in Rome the most ancient and largest was probably the one in Trastevere (near the Vatican), which has furnished the oldest and most abundant epigraphic material. However, Jews lived in at least four other urban areas.[10] The majority would have been of modest social station and education, initially brought to Rome largely as slaves, though a few may have been more prominent. Catacomb inscriptions indicate considerable accommodation of Jewish ideas to pagan even in such basic matters as the names used to address God.[11]

One of the intriguing diversities in Jewish communities which may have affected Christian communities in Rome from the beginning was Essenism. Although direct evidences for Essene communities exist only for Palestine, we cannot dismiss the possibility that Essene "camp-communities" existed in cities outside of Palestine as well as in it. The *Damascus Document* provided for "such camp-communities as may come into existence throughout the Era of Wickedness . . . ."[12] Philo,[13] Josephus,[14] and Hippolytus,[15] moreover, all attested the dispersion of the Essenes to "every city." Although we probably cannot suppose any *voluntary* settlements of Essenes in Rome, it is likely that considerable numbers were brought there as prisoners after the Jewish war of 66-70 C.E. A community composed largely of Essenes in Rome would explain extensive evidence of Essene impact on Christian thinking in Hebrews,[16] 1 Clement,[17] and Hermas.[18]

From the beginning, then, I think we should say, the Jewish/Gentile Christianity which found its way to Rome came to expression in diverse Jewish communities diversely affected by the Roman context. Quite likely, it came itself in different packages. Raymond E. Brown[19] has posited four types in early Christian literature: (1) Jewish Christians and Gentile converts who practiced the Mosaic law fully and thought that observance necessary to attain fullness of salvation; (2) Jewish Christians and Gentile converts who did not consider the entire Mosaic law salvific but required observance of some Jewish purity laws; (3) Jewish Christians and Gentile converts who did not consider circumcision salvific for Gentile Christians and did not require observance of food laws; and (4) Jewish Christians and Gentile converts who did not insist on circumcision and observance of Jewish food laws and saw no abiding significance in the temple cultus in Jerusalem. Although Brown thinks one of the more conservative types (the second) came first, thus necessitating Paul's Letter to the Romans,[20] the other types soon put in an appearance and generated some tension. Some Romans evidently accepted the more moderately stated views of Paul found in Romans, for 1 Peter and 1 Clement reflect some of the same motifs: a frequent use of Jewish cultic language, insistence on obedience to civil authority, and increasing articulation of church structure.[21] The author of Hebrews, however, belongs in category four, among those who did not insist on circumcision and observance of Jewish food laws and saw no abiding significance in the temple cultus in Jerusalem, alongside "Hellenists" such as Stephen (Acts 6).[22] First Clement, knowing Romans, 1 Peter, and Hebrews, reformulated the Jewish cultic heritage and related it to church order in a manner that would help to shape Christianity for centuries.[23]

Rome's counsel to Corinth about effecting unity was doubtless shaped by the Roman situation itself. "We send these not only to instruct you, beloved," Clement wrote, "but also to remind ourselves, for we are in the same arena and the same struggle lies before us" (7.1). He did not elaborate, but the thrust of his argument makes struggle for unity more likely than an assumption that Clement alluded to persecution.[24] As a solution to frag-mentation, Clement predictably counseled humility and obedience. More broadly, he rejected the position of the group who would weaken ties with the Jewish heritage, citing only the Old Testament authoritatively in sup-port of liturgy and church order, and pitched his tent in a broad field cir-cumscribed by Romans and 1 Peter. Most basic of all, he laid claim to the two great apostles as those "most righteous pillars of the Church" put to death on account of jealousy and envy (5.1-7). From thence he laid out a scheme for apostolic succession which would identify the true church in its manifold locations and expressions: Christ, who is "from God" (42.2), taught the apostles and commissioned them after His resurrection; the apos-tles, "preaching region by region and city by city, appointed their first con-verts as bishops and deacons of those about to believe, testing them by the Spirit" (42.4). Undergirding this would be attention to rank and place. Each should please God according to proper rank, as in the Old Testament cul-tus, wherein "to the highest priest have been given his own services and to the priests has been arranged their own place, and to the Levites have been set their own ministries. The layperson is bound by the ordinances for the laity" (40.5). Yet, Clement warned, varied "sacrifices" "are not offered everywhere but only in Jerusalem" (41.2). Translated into the Roman or Corinthian setting, this would mean that worship is not to be conducted in private assemblies without authorization of the appropriate clergy.[25] Diver-sity but not unauthorized diversity!

Struggle for Unity Amidst Exploding Diversity

Compared with what they would become by about midcentury, Roman waters were rather calm in Clement's day. Incorporation of an increasing number of Gentiles into Jewish/Gentile Christian communities raised more urgently still questions of identity and adaptability. By this time some com-munities had probably grown large enough to necessitate accommodation of houses to liturgical usage.[26] Each undoubtedly experienced a heightening of tensions as it incorporated converts in an era when the catechumenate had not yet reached maturity.[27] Serious conflict surfaced regarding the question of repentance for serious sins (presumably of apostasy, adultery, or murder) after baptism. A rigoristic group within or among the Roman communities held that repentance and forgiveness of sins are unique and therefore not repeatable (Hermas, *Mand.* 4.3.1). They discouraged repentance (*Sim.* 8.6.5). Although some have theorized that these were sectarians, it seems more likely that they belonged to the mainstream, where Hebrews (cf. 6:4ff.) exerted considerable influence.[28] In his reaction against this position Hermas did not propose leniency. He saw no hope for certain apostates who betrayed and blasphemed the church; "these then have been destroyed forever by God" (*Sim.* 8.6.4), for they have not repented. For others, however, Hermas projected hope in one exceptional second repentance after baptism (*Mand.* 4.3.6). This position commended itself not only at Rome but elsewhere.

Changing constituencies within these communities doubtless stirred up a potful of arguments about all sorts of doctrinal and moral issues, thus necessitating the shaping of more definite catechetical and disciplinary procedures such as those attested by Hippolytus and Tertullian for the early third century. Threats and challenges to Christian unity, however, were not as serious there as those posed by certain satellite groups who vied with the mainliners as definers of Christian identity, somewhat as the electronic church and other parachurch groups do in our day.

Parachurch groups that heightened the struggle for unity included evangelistic philosophical schools operated by Justin and by Valentinus and his successor Ptolemaeus. Justin's school stood in quite close proximity to at least one of the Roman communities. According to the early account of his martyrdom along with several of his converts and "their community (*synodia*), " Christians in Rome at that time (163/165) met "where each chose and could" meet, since all could not meet in a single place. Justin lived, and probably conducted his school, "above the baths of Martinus" during the entire time of his two stays in Rome (*Martyrdom of S. Justin and others,* 3; Musurillo, 44- 45). The community may have assembled there as well. In his *1 Apology,* moreover, he wrote in the first person plural with obvious familiarity with the sacraments and the Sunday worship as if a serious participant (65-67). His writings show that he considered himself responsible not just to attract students to his school but to present and defend Christianity as "the true philosophy." He composed not only the three apologetic works which have survived but also some kind of treatise *Against Marcion* and another *Against All Heresies.*[29] In the *Dialogue with Trypho* (35), composed around 160, he condemned Valentinians, Basilidians, and Saturnilians as well as Marcionites.

The relationship of the school of Valentinus and Ptolemaeus to the Roman communities is somewhat fuzzier.[30] It has usually been assumed that Valentinus never belonged to a Christian community such as that depicted earlier on the basis of Justin's denunciation of Valentinus in *Dialogue with Trypho* (35) and subsequent classification of Valentinus as a heretic by Irenaeus, Tertullian, Epiphanius, and others. Gerd Lüdemann, however, has argued persuasively that the *Dialogue,* in which Justin first mentioned Valentinus, was a late writing, composed not long before Justin was martyred, and that Justin did not regard Valentinus as a heretic when he wrote the *1*

Apology around 150-55. This would mean that Valentinus had good standing in Roman communities for as much as twenty years.[31] Undergirding this hypothesis is the fact that the Valentinian Ptolemaeus, who suffered martyrdom around 152 under the Roman Prefect Urbicus, thought of himself, just as Justin did, as standing in continuity with Roman Christianity. Evidently both Valentinus and Ptolemaeus operated their school in at least a loose relationship with a Roman community. As evidence of that, Ptolemaeus, Lüdemann argues, wrote his *Letter to Flora* against Marcion and his followers, siding in it with the larger Roman community in affirming God as the lawgiver. Certainly, Ptolemaeus' view of the Old Testament stands closer to Justin's than to Marcion's. In his *Dialogue* Justin also distinguished between different parts of the Old Testament. At the end of the second century, Victor suppressed the writings of a presbyter named Florinus because he was a Valentinian, a further sign that the status of the Valentinians had not become completely clarified even then (Irenaeus, *Fragmentary Letter in Syriac*.)[32]

If we accept Lüdemann's hypothesis, we need to envision a still fluid situation in Rome which the withdrawal or expulsion of Marcion and his followers probably solidified in a hurry. The case of Marcion's predecessor, Cerdo, underlines the fluidity of things prior to Marcion himself. According to Irenaeus (perhaps following Justin's lost treatise *Against All Heresies* cited in *1 Apology* 26), Cerdo, arriving in Rome at the time of Hyginus, maintained a tenuous fellowship with a Roman community from which he probably withdrew voluntarily.

> Coming often into the church and making confession, he thus remained, at one time teaching secretly, at another again making confession, and at another being reproached because he taught badly and withdrawing from the assembly of brethren (and sisters).[33]

I would conclude on careful study of the Greek text that Cerdo bounced in and out of the fellowship on his own and not as a consequence of action taken by the Roman Church. Indeed, it does not sound as if he withdrew definitely. This would explain why Marcion could associate with him for a time and remain in fellowship with a Roman community.

What raised the level of concern about Marcion was that he founded a competing church which attracted substantial numbers. Aberrant congregations and schools did not pose the kind of problem a powerful and aggressive schism did. It took some time, however, for Marcion to stir Rome to action. According to Irenaeus (3.4.3; Harvey, II, 18), succeeding Cerdo, he "grew powerful (*invaluit*) under Anicetus," which would probably explain the latter's anxiety about the Quartodecimans in Rome and Justin's vigorous repudiation in his *1 Apology*. A wealthy shipowner from Sinope in Pontus, according to Hippolytus (*Syntagma* in Epiphanius, *Baer.* 42), Marcion came to Rome around 140 after having been excommunicated by his father for "defiling a virgin" (42.1.4). Presumably without knowing his status in his father's church, a Roman community accepted him into their fellowship, welcoming his generous gift of 200,000 sesterces (Tertullian, *Adv. Marc.* 4.4). Making love and forgiveness the centerpiece of his "gospel," he evidently joined Cerdo in organizing his followers into a separate community. It is this that led to his formal excommunication, the date of which is uncertain, after which he devoted himself to the propagation of his gospel of love and to the organization of communities throughout the Empire. The degree of his success is clearly attested by the geographical spread of his critics: Dionysius at Corinth, Irenaeus at Lyons, Theophilus at Antioch, Philip at Gortyna, Tertullian at Carthage, and Bardesanes at Edessa, as well as Justin, Hippolytus, and Rhodo at Rome.[34]

The firing up of Marcion's movement at the beginning of Anicetus's term as head of the Roman Presbytery (155-66) probably occasioned a visit to Rome by the venerable Polycarp, Bishop of Smyrna, who, at the advanced age of eighty-six, surely would not have undertaken the arduous and lengthy journey except by invitation of Anicetus himself. Anicetus needed the strongest voice and best counsel he could summon. Although Irenaeus does not mention an invitation, he leaves no doubt that refutation of heretics, especially Marcion, was the main purpose of the visit. Polycarp, he boasted, "turned many away from the aforementioned heresies to the Church of God, proclaiming that he had received the one and only truth from the Apostles, namely, what had been handed down by the Church" (A.H. 3.3.4; Harvey, II, 13). He delivered a special rebuke to Marcion as "the first-born of Satan" when the latter, on meeting him, asked if Polycarp knew who he was. Polycarp's visit to Rome, probably attended by the then youthful Irenaeus,[35] established in the latter's mind the Roman pattern of achieving unity in diversity which he conveyed to Victor toward the end of the century and which he reflected in his own writings.

Rome moved slowly and hesitantly here, perhaps to avoid widening the rift, and welcomed help wherever it could secure that. Roman leaders did not act to excommunicate Cerdo and Marcion until the two of them cut themselves off.[36] By the time of Anicetus, Marcion had gained sufficient following to rouse the bishop to more definite action. Marcion's gospel of no-fault love must have proved popular enough for him to unite the diverse Roman communities and perhaps many of the clergy behind himself. Roman leaders employed several means to shore up their own leadership and to unite the communities behind them. (1) They probably tightened up the catechumenate, incorporating some anti-Marcionite slant into the old Roman symbol.[37] (2) They welcomed the support of apologists such as Justin who recognized the danger of Marcion's movement. (3) More important still, they enlisted collegial assistance from Asia Minor in the person of Polycarp, who could claim firsthand contact with John the disciple of the Lord (Irenaeus, A.H., 3.3.4) and whose credentials thus could not be questioned. Polycarp would have exerted his strongest sway over Asians, whose numbers must have been substantial. At this point Anicetus could not afford to alienate them and thus let the predominately Asian communities continue to observe the Asian custom concerning Easter (Eusebius, H.E. 5.24.16-17). Anicetus's successors up to Victor continued the same policy.

More of the Same

Contrary to Bauer's impressions, then, I cannot find in Rome during the second century the homogeneity of faith and practice which he assumed would allow Rome to impose orthodoxy on the churches in other areas. Almost the opposite is true. Roman Christians were themselves caught up in a struggle to attain unity in a highly controverted situation which required them to cry out for help from others. And matters got worse before they got better. As George La Piana observed in a brilliant study of "The Roman Church at the End of the Second Century," published in the *Harvard Theological Review* in 1925,

> About the end of the second century the Christian community of Rome was far from presenting the appearance of a strong organization destined to survive; on the contrary it seemed in process of complete disintegration. The main problem with which the Church of Rome was then confronted—a problem of the greatest importance on account of its far-reaching implications— was whether Christianity was to be a conglomeration of churches, schools, and sects, widely differing in doctrinal tenets and in liturgical practices but all coming under the general denomination of "the Christian Church," or whether it was to form a compact body of believers governed by the strict law of doctrinal unity and of practical uniformity. In other words the great problem of Christian unity came to be formulated in a striking way and to demand an immediate solution within the Christian community of Rome, which its narrow boundaries did not make less truly representative of the whole of Christianity.[38]

Space, unfortunately, will not permit me to review La Piana's detailed argument. It will have to suffice to note that Victor, an African, employed a far more authoritarian style than his predecessors. La Piana has summarized the main features as follows:

> 1. The monarchical form of the Roman episcopate overcame the last resistance of the local opposition, and at the same time a vigorous attempt was

made to enforce within the Roman Christian community the principle of unity of faith and of doctrine and of uniformity in discipline and liturgical practices.

2. For the first time clear evidence appears that the Church of Rome did not hesitate to impose on other churches its own traditions, assuming thus the right to represent the genuine and authoritative tradition of Christianity.

3. The Church of Rome, in its determined effort to achieve internal unity and to gain cohesion, tried to overcome all kinds of divisive doctrinal and practical divergences by recourse not so much to theological debate and philosophical speculation as to disciplinary measures, which increased the power of its hierarchical organization and led gradually to the elimination of all groups and tendencies that could not be conquered or assimilated.

4. A general reconstruction of the system of ecclesiastical administration of the Roman Church took place in that period. Through favorable circumstances the Christian community as such acquired even the possession of cemeteries and meeting places for the cult.

5. And finally, in this period the Church of Rome, which up to that time had the aspect of a community of Greek speech and traditions, gradually began to assume the character of a Latin church, different in many ways from the churches which had been established in the countries of the eastern Mediterranean basin.[39]

One can assert with qualification, however, that Rome stood in a better position to influence the shape of Christianity in other parts of the Roman Empire at the end of Victor's episcopate than it did at the beginning. We must not forget that, besides the diversities already noted, Monarchianism reared its head in Rome at this time. The adoptionistic or dynamistic Monarchian Theodotus the Cobbler or Leather-seller came to Rome from Byzantium. He gathered followers, notably Asclepiodotus and Theodotus the moneychanger, who persuaded the confessor Natalius to be their bishop. Theodotus the Cobbler was the first person excommunicated by Victor, but Natalius did not realize the error of his ways until the time of Zephyrinus (199-217), who barely accepted him back into communion (Eusebius, H.E. 5.28.8-13). According to Tertullian, Praxeas imported the modalism of Noetus from Asia Minor when Victor "was on the point of recognizing the prophecies of Montanus, Prisca, and Maximilla, and as a result of that recognition was offering peace to the churches of Asia and Phrygia."[40] Sabellius joined Praxeas during the episcopate of Zephyrinus. Modalists evidently had good standing in Roman churches until the time of Callistus (217-22), who, Hippolytus charged (*Ref.* 2.6), led Sabellius into the modalist heresy and then excommunicated him because of apprehension of Hippolytus himself (*Ref.* 9.7), who had already begun his schism in 217.

Rome's difficulties here, however, did not stem solely from the pluralism of the Roman community. Rome moved in the direction of the monepiscopate more slowly than cities in the East—Antioch, Ephesus, Smyrna—and North Africa. In consequence, it displayed much more ambivalence and greater hesitancy in dealing with diversities and divisions. Anicetus, a Syrian, and Victor, an African, both of whom would have known a structure far more decisive than the Roman, were the two bishops who prodded Rome toward a more centralized government. Although they gained something by that, they also, particularly Victor, paid a high price. Irenaeus, himself a Romanophile, had to remind Victor that Romans did not do things the way he was handling the Quartodeciman question. Roman-style unity left more room for diversity and made fewer demands for conformity, and thus made room for a broader constituency. Perhaps it was the willingness of Rome in the second century to take the great risk such an approach required which will give us the most insight into the struggle the churches face today.

Notes

1. *Orthodoxy and Heresy in Earliest Christianity,* 2d German edition, trans. by a team from the Philadelphia Seminar on Christian Origins and ed. Robert A. Kraft and Gerhard Krodel (Philadelphia: Fortress Press, 1971; original edition 1934).

2. Bauer, of course reversed the traditional sequence of orthodoxy and then, as a deviation, heresy. Indeed, he contended (194) that, judged on the basis of amount of literature, except for Rome, "the heretics considerably outnumbered the orthodox." For a more extended assessment of Bauer's thesis, see Jerry Rees Flora, "A Critical Analysis of Walter Bauer's Theory of Early Christian Orthodoxy and Heresy" (Ph.D. diss. Southern Baptist Theological Seminary, 1972).

3. Bauer, 193.

4. Ibid., 194.

5. Ibid., 111.

6. Ibid., 129.

7. Bauer, 128, may have been right in concluding that "Marcion presented the greatest danger to which Roman orthodoxy was opposed," but he erred gravely in judging Roman Christianity nearly homogeneous, as the rest of this chapter will show.

8. Romano Pena, "Les juifs a Rome au temps de l'Apotre Paul," NTS, 28 (1982): 326.

9. See *By Light, Light. The Mystic Gospel of Hellenistic Judaism* (New Haven: Yale University Press, 1935); *Jewish Symbols in the Graeco-Roman Period,* 13 vols. (Princeton, N.J.: Princeton University Press, 1953-68); and *An Introduction to Philo Judaeus,* 2d ed. (Oxford: Basil Blackwell, 1962).

10. Ibid., 331-32.

11. Ibid., 333-36.

12. *Dam. Doc.* xii.22; trans. from *The Dead Sea Scriptures,* trans. Theodor H. Gaster (Garden City, N.Y.: Doubleday Anchor Books, 1956).

13. *Quod omnis probus liber sit,* 75, 76, 85.

14. *Bell. Jud.* II, viii, 4.

15. *Philos.* IX, xxi.

16. On Essene ideas in Hebrews see Jean Danielou, *The Dead Sea Scrolls and Primitive Christianity,* trans. S. Attanasio (Baltimore: Helicon Press, 1958), 111-14.

17. On possible impact of the Essene pattern on church order see E. Glenn Hinson, "Evidence of Essene Influence in Roman Christianity: An Inquiry," *Studia Patristica,* XVIII: 697-701.

18. Jean-Paul Audet, O.P., "Affinites literaire et doctrinales du Manuel de discipline," *Revue biblique,* 60 (1953): 41-82, has noted Essene influence on Hermas' understanding of the Holy Spirit, emphasis on good and evil spirits, concept of the Son of God, and doctrine of the Church. Hermas, it should be noted, was brought up as a slave, perhaps as a child of Essenes brought to Rome around 70 C.E.

19. "Not Jewish Christianity and Gentile Christianity by Types of Jewish/Gentile Christianity," *Catholic Biblical Quarterly,* 45 (January 1983): 74-79.

20. Raymond E. Brown and John P. Meier, *Antioch and Rome: New Testament Cradles of Catholic Christianity* (New York: Paulist Press, 1982), 110, concluded that "Paul appealed for Rome's help because *the dominant Christianity at Rome had been shaped by the Jerusalem Christianity associated with James and Peter, and hence was a Christianity appreciative of Judaism and loyal to its customs.* "This necessitates the recognition that Paul changed his emphases-between his writing of Galatians and his writing of Romans (114, 120).

21. Brown, *Antioch and Rome,* 136ff.

22. Ibid., 141. Brown, however, views Hebrews as a letter addressed *to* Rome and thus known there early, by the time of 1 Clement, but never accorded apostolic status (147-49). He thinks it was "directed to a Christianity that had attitudes toward a cult similar to those of the Qumran Essenes" (153, n. 325). Whether written *in* Rome or addressed *to* Rome, however, it confirms the point I am making about the diversity of Roman Christianity.

23. Barbara Bowe, *Church in Crisis: Ecclesiology and Paraenesis in Clement of Rome* (Minneapolis: Fortress Press, 1988), has challenged the thesis of Bauer that the primary objective of 1 Clement was to establish Roman authority. She has argued, effectively I think, that the letter appealed rather for interdependence, solidarity, and harmony against the background of an ecclesiology rooted in such biblical images as "the Elect of God," the city-state, the brotherhood, etc. Clement's concern for peace and harmony accounts for the strong emphasis on submission and humility. The letter "claims no superior authority but comes from church to church and conveys the advice of partners in a common struggle (1 Clement 7.1)" (121). Here I agree with Brown, *Antioch and Rome,* 159, about Clement's view of Jewish cultic practices but would see an impact of considerable force from the Essene/Christian community.

24. See Robert M. Grant and Holt H. Graham, *The Apostolic Fathers* (New York: Thomas Nelson & Sons, 1965), 28.

25. See ibid., 70.

26. One of these *tituli* which may date to the second century is that under San Clemente, which belonged to T. Flavius Clemens, nephew of the Emperor Vespasian and husband of Flavia Domitilla, appointed consul in 95 C.E. and probably martyred. It is believed that the large house built in 128 under the site of Santa Pudenziana was converted to liturgical usage in the third century. For a more detailed treatment see Joan M. Petersen, "Some Titular Churches at Rome with Traditional New Testament Connexions," *Expository Times* 84 (June 1973): 277-79.

27. Justin, *1 Apol.* 61, hinted at instruction of some kind prior to baptism, but, as Benoit has noted, it is difficult to see in what he said "an allusion to an already organized catechumenate" (A. Benoit, *Le bapteme chretien au second siecle* (Paris: University of France Press, 1953), 145. W. Bornemann, "Das Taufsymbol Justins des Martyrers," ZKG, 3 (1879): 1-27, thought that "as many as are persuaded and believe that what we teach and say is true" referred to a precise catechesis with doctrinal symbol, which is likely. G. Bardy, *La conversion au Christianisme durant les premiers siecles* (Paris: 1949), 171, construed the confession as similar to the one outlined by Hippolytus in *The Apostolic Tradition,* but this assumes further development. See further E. Glenn Hinson, *The Evangelization of the Roman Empire* (Macon, Ga.: Mercer University Press, 1981), 73ff.

28. See Graydon F. Snyder, *The Apostolic Fathers,* 6:123.

29. For the latter compare *1 Apol.* 26; Eusebius, H.E. 4.11.8-10. Both Irenaeus, A.H. 4.6, and Eusebius, H.E. 4.118, quoted the work *Against Marcion.*

30. According to Irenaeus (A.H. 3.4.3; Eusebius, H.E. 4.11.1), Valentinus came to Rome

during the episcopate of Hyginus (136-40), flourished under Pius (140-55), and remained until the time of Anicetus (155-66).

31. Gerd Lüdemann, "Zur Geschichte des ältesten Christentums in Rom. Valentin und Marcion: Ptolemaeus und Justin," ZNW, 70 (1979): 86-97.

32. Lüdemann, 97-114.

33. Irenaeus, A. H. 3.4.2; Harvey, II, 17. The middle voice almost certainly was intended to emphasize a voluntary dissociation rather than excommunication.

34. Cf. *The Oxford Dictionary of the Christian Church,* 2d ed., ed. F.L. Cross and E.A. Livingstone (London: Oxford University Press, 1974), 870f.

35. See on this F. R. Montgomery Hitchcock, *Irenaeus of Lugdunum* (Cambridge University Press, 1914), 3, who thought it "not unlikely that he had opportunity of witnessing that impressive scene in the church between Polycarp and Anicetus, Bishop of Rome, which he describes so vividly in his letter to Victor."

36. This is clearest in the case of Cerdo. Whether Marcion withdrew before he was excommunicated is debated, but that appears probable. Irenaeus's report that Polycarp converted many from the heresies would indicate that he *sought* contacts with them, otherwise he could not have won them over. Moreover, it says nothing about an excommunication. Indeed, it would appear that Marcion tried to win Polycarp over to *his* side. See Hans von Campenhausen, *Ecclesiastical Authority and Spiritual Power in the First Three Centuries,* trans. J. A. Baker (London: Adam & Charles Black, 1969), 144f. Lüdemann, 76, concluded that Irenaeus, A.H. 3.4.3, does not permit any definite judgment about the status of Cerdo and Marcion and that it is highly doubtful whether Cerdo or Marcion had been excluded from the Roman Church.

37. This has long been debated. A. C. McGiffert, *The Apostles Creed: Its Origin, Its Purpose, and Its Historical Interpretation* (New York: Charles Scribner's Sons, 1902), 107-8, contended that the word "Almighty" and the phrase "his Son" responded to Marcion's differentiation between the God of the Old Testament and the God presented by Jesus, that the phrase "to judge both living and dead" repudiated Marcion's view that the good God will judge no one, and that the phrases "born of the Virgin Mary, was crucified under Pontius Pilate and was buried," and those about resurrection replied to Marcion's docetism. Numerous others have regarded all phrases of the symbol sufficiently biblical to have been in place before Marcion. See C. A. Briggs, *The Fundamental Christian Faith* (New York: Charles Scribner's Sons, 1913), 19-21, who followed Kattenbusch and Harnack, but J. N. D. Kelly, *Early Christian Creeds,* 3d ed. (London: Longman, 1972), 53, 63, 65, 97, 156f., while favoring this view, leaves the question somewhat open.

38. George La Piana, "The Roman Church at the End of the Second Century," HTR, 18 (July 1925): 207.

39. Ibid., 204.

40. *Adv. Prax.* 1.5; CC, II: 1159, trans. Ernest Evans, 130. Tertullian does not name Victor, but he would have been the one who restored communion with the Asians.

14

Medieval Views of the Church

by Glenn O. Hilburn

The content of Western theology at the end of the old Roman imperial era was essentially that of Augustine of Hippo. When he died in 430, the Gothic invasions had already begun, and the form which he gave to Latin theology was, in general outline, the form in which it was passed on to the medieval church. This was particularly true in regard to ecclesiology. It is interesting to note that in medieval theological systems prior to the fourteenth century "no special place is given for the doctrine of the church."[1] None of the early scholastics considered it an essential topic for extensive discussion. This suggests, among other things, that the church was self-evident and foundational for medieval life and therefore not a matter requiring doctrinal elaboration. To study the doctrine of the church between the fifth and fourteenth century requires an examination of discussions about the hierarchy, the sacraments, church-state relations, and canon law. In such discussions a doctrine of the church was indeed implicitly developed.

By the end of the fifth century the old Roman order in the West, battered by successive Teutonic and Scythian conquerors, had finally been broken. In the course of a century and a half the face of the Western world was changed almost beyond recognition. Social, political, economic, and educational systems were in a state of decline with grim hope for survival.

The towering figure who appeared toward the end of the sixth century to stand against the steady decline of civilized life in the West was Pope Gregory the Great. He had been a Roman courtier, a distinguished diplomat, and a devotee of Benedictine monasticism. His talents were not primarily intellectual for he was neither a scholar nor systematic thinker. He had steeped himself in the writings of Augustine and counted himself a humble follower of the Augustinian tradition. His primary talents were those of an administrator and a preacher.

For fourteen years (590-604) Gregory headed the Roman Church. His greatest achievement was in making the Roman Church the guardian of what remained of the old culture and the focal point for the construction or foundation work for the new culture—the medieval, European culture, which was yet to come. Borrowing from the Nicene Creed, Gregory identified the four distinctive marks of the church by which it is to be distinguished from all other human institutions; the church is "one, holy, catholic, and apostolic." The first mark is unity. Its unity is guaranteed by its relation to Christ as its head and is dependent upon faith and love. The unity of the church "comprehends all true believers of the past, the present, and the future, from Abel to the last just man [person] who shall be born into the world." The "Church of the elect before and after Christ is one."[2] The second mark is holiness. In line with his Roman predecessors Gregory conceived the holiness of the church primarily in sacramental rather than moral terms. Again, "through its union with Christ and through the operation of the Holy Spirit the Church possesses an ideal identity, which is not impaired by the fact of its actual members, the majority of which are reprobate."[3]

The third mark is catholicity. Here, he followed Augustine's reasoning in referring to the church's geographical and social inclusiveness. The church has members in all parts of the world, and it is an all-inclusive fellowship.[4] The fourth mark is apostolicity. The church is apostolic in regard to both doctrine and succession. It still preaches and teaches the teachings of the apostles. This doctrine had been transmitted from generation to generation from the New Testament era through the apostles to their episcopal successors. Following the interpretation of Leo I, Gregory endorsed the position of Petrine and Roman bishop primacy. He believed that the pope "had authority over the whole church, both in West and East."[5]

With regard to the relationship of the church to the empire or state, Gregory maintained that secular officials should guard the church's secular interests and assist in compelling the church's enemies to submit to its authority. Under no circumstance, however, should the state interfere in things ecclesiastical. In like manner, he disapproved of ecclesiastical officials meddling in secular affairs. In general, he agreed with Gelasius I and his doctrine of two swords and dual powers.

Gregory spoke of the church as the custodian of the means of grace, the sacraments. He used the term only in reference to baptism and the Eucharist. He apparently accepted Augustine's definition of the sacraments as symbols and occasions of the working of the Holy Spirit. His understanding of baptism and the Eucharist was consistent with that of his admired predecessor.

Although earlier Roman bishops, notably Innocent I, Leo I, and Gelasius I, had set forth much of the content of the doctrine of Roman papal primacy and authority, it was Gregory who by teaching and practice provided the significant turning point for the papacy, both theologically and jurisdictionally.[6] According to R. W. Southern, by the year 700 "no one in the West denied that the pope possessed all the authority of St. Peter over the Church."[7]

In the six centuries following Gregory's pontificate, papal primacy slowly but certainly moved in the direction of a papal monarchy with the pope becoming not only the supreme head of the church but also the supreme head of the state and all temporal affairs. Walter Ullmann dates the beginning of the trend toward papal monarchy as 692 when Pope Sergius I (687-701) openly and successfully defied the Eastern emperor Justinian II. The emperor had ordered Sergius to cosign the decrees of the imperially convened Trullan Synod. The pope refused, thus demonstrating a measure of authority greater than the emperor. Ullmann observed, "In this we might well see the heralding of a new age."[8]

The new age was a time of consolidation and of fresh beginning rather than a time of important new construction. The problems of the period were primarily practical. What the church encountered was a medley of new peoples, most with little or no understanding of the old Roman culture and with little experience upon which the officers of the church could build a competent understanding of membership in the Christian community. The conception of the church and pope as authoritative was antithetic to that represented by the loose conglomeration of tribal societies settling within the borders of the historically Roman territory. They viewed religion as a function of secular society and therefore dependent on secular authority for approval and existence.

Those who recognized the acute need to win over the new peoples to accept the authority of the Roman church often resorted to strange and questionable devices to consolidate the influence they were seeking to exert. Primary devices were the so-called "forged" decretals (so named because of their spurious claim of authorship and date). The most influential of these were the *Donation of Constantine* and the *Decretals of Isidore.*

The *Donation of Constantine* claimed to be the last will and testament of Constantine I. In gratitude for his Christian conversion and miraculous healing from leprosy, he stated his intent to transfer to the pope his Roman imperial palace and his imperial authority over all "provinces, places, and *civitates* of the Western regions."[9] It was also his wish to confer on Bishop Sylvester (314-35) and all his successors primacy over all patriarchal sees and all other churches throughout the empire.

The *Decretals of Isidore*, purported to have been compiled by Isidore of Seville (d. 636), came into prominence in the last half of the ninth century when Pope Nicholas I (858-67) first used them to document his authority for certain pronouncements. It contained forged canons from councils and letters from popes to the time of Gregory II (d. 731), collectively intended to accomplish four purposes: (1) to unify the church by centralizing authority in Rome; (2) to free bishops from the tyranny of metropolitans; (3) to remove ecclesiastical cases from secular tribunals; and (4) to guarantee the independence of bishops from temporal powers.[10]

After Nicholas I the forged documents were not used extensively until the pontificate of Leo IX (1049-54). The summary effect of the documents was to give legal sanction to the steps which Gregory I had found necessary to the accomplishment of his administrative and spiritual goals. The church was well on its way to establishing itself as the only institution capable of accomplishing the political and economic reorganization of the West. Symbolic affirmation of this fact was the crowning of Charlemagne as emperor of the Holy Roman Empire on Christmas Day 800 in the basilica of Saint Peter by Pope Leo III. As Cannon has observed, "What Leo has done neither Charlemagne nor any of his successors could undo. Leo convinced the people of the Middle Ages that the imperial crown was the gift of the church."[11]

The period following Nicholas I to the mid-tenth century could best be described as a time of anarchy and confusion. Between 896 and 904 there were ten popes. From 904 to 962 the papacy was in the control of the Italian nobility. The period is often described as the era of pornocracy, connoting lewdness and gross immorality in the papal office which was controlled by unscrupulous and wicked men and women. From 962 to about 1050, popes were named and controlled by Germanic emperors. The Papacy and the Roman Church had declined to their lowest point in prestige and power. With the ascension of Leo IX (1049) and Gregory VII (1073) to the papal office, a new day was dawning for the beginning of the move toward victory for papal monarchy. In less than two centuries the victory would become an accomplished fact.

Agreement with the emerging doctrine of papal monarchy was not universal. There was, in general, common agreement on Roman Church primacy and on the special place of preeminence of the Roman bishop. A number of scholars insisted on collegial episcopacy. Among these were the Venerable Bede (d. 735), Paul the Deacon (d. 800), Haymo of Halberstadt (d. 853), Rabanus Maurus (d. 856), Rathier of Verona (d. 974), and Gerbert of Aurrilac (d. 1003). They interpreted Matthew 16:18 in conjunction with Matthew 18:18 and John 20:22-23 and concluded in favor of church authority residing in bishop collegiality rather than in the pope only.[12] Hincmar, archbishop of Reims (d. 882), was by far the most vocal of the proponents of collegial episcopacy. He was a vigorous defender of the administrative autonomy of metropolitan bishops. He also insisted that papal decisions must be harmonized with the Scriptures, orthodox tradition, and canon law. For him, canon law was particularly important, since it represented the will of the church through the decisions of ecumenical councils. In this regard he anticipated the position of the conciliarists of the fifteenth century.[13]

The final struggle for papal monarchy which would end in victory began with the elevation of Leo IX to the papal office in 1049. Immediately after being elected, he began to reform the church from its decadence of a century and a half. By personal example he did much to foster a wholly new ideal of the papacy. Celibacy was enforced on all clergy from the rank of subdeacon upward, and decrees were promulgated against simony and other ecclesiastical abuses. He cultivated cooperative relationships with secular rulers and did much to prepare the way for the advancement of papal monarchy. He stood firm in defense of Roman Church primacy over all churches, even those in the Greek East. It was in the context of the power struggle between Leo IX and Patriarch Michael Cerularius that the "Great Schism" resulted in the apparent separation of the Latin West from the Greek East in 1054.[14]

Archdeacon Hildebrand, one of Leo IX's most capable advisers, was unanimously elected pope in 1073. Choosing the papal name Gregory VII, he immediately took up the reform agenda of his predecessors. He conceived his life mission to be the establishment of the "kingdom of God on earth" under the active guidance of the pope, to whom Christ had given power over everybody and everything pertaining to salvation. A major portion of his program was the reduction of royal-monarchic power and the increasing of papal-monarchic power. His scheme "presupposed a strict hierarchial ordering of society, at the apex of which stood the pope as monarchic Ruler."[15] Rigid application of papal monarchy was perceived to be the only means by which the chief defects of contemporary society could be eradicated. The defects were simony and concubinage; the investiture of ecclesiastical officers by lay lords; and the power of bishops, metropolitans, and provincial synods as legislative entities. Each of these obstructed the efficient exercise of monarchic government by the papacy.

In an extant remnant of the official Register of Gregory's pontificate there is a collection of Roman church prerogatives called *Dictates of the Pope*.[16] Gregory's doctrine of the church as a papal monarchy was clearly and succinctly summarized in this work. Papal monarchy was rooted in the affirmation that the Roman Church alone was founded by Christ and that it was infallible. It has never erred and never will. The pope is the universal bishop, empowered to intervene throughout Christendom in all matters deemed by him as detrimental to the Church. The pope can judge all but can be judged by no person or council. He can depose, translate, and restore bishops. He alone can issue laws valid for the whole Church. He can divide or unite dioceses and erect new abbacies. The pope is entitled to preside over synods through his legates and to summon ecumenical councils. No decrees of a council or synod can become universally binding until approved by the pope. All important ecclesiastical disputes must be referred to him for adjudication.

The *Dictates* further declared that the pope is entitled to depose emperors. He can release the subjects of a ruler from oaths of allegiance and fidelity. He alone can demand that princes kiss his feet at imperial coronation ceremonies. As a true monarch the pope alone is entitled to wear the imperial insignia, a practice consistent with the *Donation of Constantine.*

Gregory demonstrated the supreme authority of pope over crown when in 1076 he excommunicated and deposed Henry IV of Germany. Henry's excommunication was lifted only after obtaining papal absolution a year later at Canossa in the castle of Margravine Matilda in the Apennines.[17] The significance of this, and all events leading to the occasion, was that a king who had been excommunicated, not for any aberration from the faith but for defiance of papal law and disobedience to papal orders, had sought and obtained absolution from a pope. This was the first time that the Papacy was able to display such authority toward a powerful European king. The doctrine of papal monarchy had been defended and demonstrated. Indeed a new era had dawned for the medieval church.

Protestations were quick in coming from both ecclesiastics and secular officials. These, however, accomplished little of lasting effect. The new ecclesiastical policy formulated by Gregory VII became more fixed during the next century and a half. Learned canonists and eminent popes, such as Alexander III (1159-81), Innocent III (1198-1216), Gregory IX (1227-41), and Boniface VIII (1294-1303), adopted in theory and practice the hierocratic program of Gregory VII.

The high point of Gregorian agenda for a papal monarchy was reached during the pontificate of Innocent III. He vigorously employed the power and opportunities that came to him through the favorableness of historical circumstances. Convinced of his position and power, he acted as head of Christendom and arbiter over peoples and nations, emperors and kings, and exercised a sort of ideal world rule. In a letter to the patriarch of Constantinople (1199) he "expressly declared that Christ had committed to St. Peter and his successors not only the primacy over the Church, but over the kingdoms of the world."[18] He was the first pope to employ the title "Vicar of Christ."[19]

The crowning event of Innocent III's pontificate was the convening of the Fourth Lateran Council (1215), the first genuinely ecumenical council in the medieval West. No item of relevance or importance to the church was omitted in the council's decrees. The first major dogma since the Second

Synod of Orange (529) was promulgated in the council's definition of the dogma of transubstantiation.

Ullmann concluded his assessment of the Innocentian pontificate by boldly stating that it is an "incontrovertible fact that the prestige of the papacy as an institution of government and as the final arbiter in all matters affecting the essential fabric of contemporary Christian society was never higher than when Innocent III closed his eyes on 16 July 1216."[20] That which was done symbolically on Christmas Day in 800 when Leo III crowned Charlemagne emperor of the Holy Roman Empire was now consummated as a factual reality. The evolution of the doctrine of papal monarchy was complete, but there was no guarantee of perpetuity. In less than one century the institution based on the doctrine would begin to crumble and fall.

Innocent III's successors, although hindered by the defiance of Emperor Frederick II until his death in 1250, further secured the authoritative claims of the papal office in realms both spiritual and temporal. Gregory IX (1227-41), in particular, accepted as his mission the upholding of the papal supremacy ideals of Innocent III. The thirteen pontiffs between Gregory IX and Boniface VIII (1294-1303) were content to prosecute their tasks by the momentum generated by their predecessors, Innocent III and Gregory IX.

The last pope of the thirteenth century, Boniface VIII, was as committed to the ideals of papal monarchy as Gregory VII or Innocent III. Unfortunately, for him the temper of the times had changed, and when he attempted to exercise his authority in temporal affairs, he met with determined opposition. Early in his pontificate he came into conflict with France, the most powerful state of the day. Two papal bulls in particular resulted in strong reaction from King Philip IV (the Fair). In 1298 Boniface issued the bull *Clericis laicos* forbidding clerics to give up ecclesiastical revenues or property to laymen without papal approval and forbidding princes or their officials to exact or receive taxes from the clergy.[21] Philip was infuriated. Four years later in 1302 Boniface issued his most famous bull *Unam Sanctum*, a classical statement of the doctrine of papal monarchy. Philip's anger was intensified, and he began to work diligently for Boniface's deposition. Boniface responded with a bull of excommunication of Philip, but it was never promulgated, since the pope was captured by French mercenaries, tortured, released, and shortly thereafter died as the result of maltreatment and humiliation. Six years later, the papal headquarters was moved to Avignon, which became the ecclesiastical capital of the West for the next sixty-nine years. This period is usually designated the Babylonian Captivity of the Papacy. The death knell for papal monarchy had been sounded and the question of authority once again became a central concern for both church and state.

Unam Sanctum was based on accepted canonical principles and quoted lengthy passages from the writings of Innocent III, Bernard of Clairvaux, Hugh of St. Victor, Thomas Aquinas, and Giles of Rome. According to the document, there is one holy, catholic, and apostolic church, outside of which there is no salvation. She has one body and one head, Christ and His representative, the Roman pontiff. In the keeping of the church there are two swords, the spiritual and the temporal, the first borne by the church, the second used for the church; the first by the hand of the priest, the second by the hand of the king, but under the direction of the priest. No one may judge the pope, but the pope has the right to establish and guide the secular power and also to judge it when it does not act rightly. This relationship of the two powers is ordained by God, and whoever opposes this power ordained by God, opposes the law of God and is like a Manichaean, who accepts two principles.[22] The concluding sentence reads: "We therefore declare, say, and affirm that submission on the part of every man to the bishop of Rome is altogether necessary for his salvation."[23]

Within the church and in view of the collapse of the Papacy in the face of rising nationalism, *Unam Sanctam* provoked a new and deeper interest in the doctrine of the church. This, however, is not to suggest that the theological discussions and treatises of the era had been devoid of ecclesiological considerations, nor is it to suggest that there was unanimous support for papal monarchy. Implicit in the writings of most of the scholastics, a doctrine of the church may be found, especially in their writings on Christology and sacraments. In general, the theologians of the twelfth and thirteenth centuries relied upon the Augustinian understanding of the church. Some, however, varied from Augustine in making a distinction between the church and the mystical body of Christ.

Bernard of Clairvaux (1090-1153), the father of medieval mysticism, described the church as both the mystical body of Christ and the spouse of Christ. In his sermons on the Song of Solomon he spoke of "the union of the soul and the Bridegroom" as the fulfillment of the incarnation and "the realization of the union of Christ and the Church." The church is one with Christ; "the Church is not one soul; it is the unity or, better yet, the unanimity of many souls," each indebted to all others.[24]

Hugh of St. Victor (c. 1096-1141), director of the monastic school of St. Victor in Paris, identified the birth of the church with the flowing of water and blood from the side of Christ on the cross rather than at Pentecost. The church is the mystical body of Christ through whom the Holy Spirit comes, and sacramental grace flows to Christians who have become incorporated by baptism into Christ. Hugh also made a major shift in the definition of a sacrament. Augustine had conceived of sacraments as symbols and occasions of the working of the Holy Spirit. Hugh defined a sacrament as "a material or physical element clearly and publicly presented, which by similitude represents, by institution signifies, by consecration contains an invisible spiritual power."[25] Sacraments, therefore, became containers and conveyors of grace through the acts of priestly consecration and priestly administration. Actually, what Hugh did was to articulate more precisely what had been taught and practiced since the ninth century with reference to the Eucharist. His definition anticipated the decision of the Fourth Lateran Council (1215) in its dogmatic declaration on transubstantiation.

Alexander of Hales (c. 1170-1245), an Englishman by birth and a renowned teacher at Paris, distinguished between membership in the mystical body of Christ and in the church. Faith of divine formation or charity was essential for incorporation into the body of Christ whereas faith of assent to the teachings of the Roman Church was sufficient for institutional church membership. Baptism made one a member of the church in point of number; faith of divine formation or charity made one a member of Christ in point of merit. The "faith of divine formation" concept was derived from Paul's "faith working through love"(RSV) in Galatians 5:6.[26]

Bonaventure (1221-74), a student of Alexander of Hales and also a teacher at Paris, followed his mentor in distinguishing between membership in the mystical body of Christ and membership in the church. He further distinguished between the status of repentant and unrepentant sinners in the church. Unrepentant sinners may be considered members of the church but not members of the mystical body of Christ. Without genuine repentance and union with Christ by charity and living fellowship, one cannot be a member of the body of Christ. The church was conceived as the institution through which salvation occurred and sacramental grace flowed to make possible membership in the mystical body by merit. Bonaventure approximated the doctrine of papal infallibility when he declared that "to assert anything in a matter of faith or morals which is contrary to what he [the pope] has defined is an evil in no way to be tolerated."[27] This plenitude of power was conferred by Christ on the church through Peter and his Roman successors.

Albertus Magnus (1206-80), a Dominican teacher at Paris and Cologne, adopted the same distinctions between membership in the nuptial body of Christ and in the church as had his scholastic predecessors. His interpretation was thoroughly sacramental. Incorporation into the mystical body results from sacramental participation in the Eucharistic incarnational body of Christ. Effecting the union with the body of Christ was viewed as the work of the Holy Spirit, the principle of unity and sanctification of the church.[28]

Thomas Aquinas (c. 1225-74), learned Dominican teacher at Paris and student of Albertus Magnus, followed generally his teacher in speaking of the church. He, like his immediate scholastic predecessors, was thoroughly Augustinian in ecclesiology. Apparently he was sufficiently satisfied with Augustine and Gregory I's expositions that he saw no need for further elaboration in his theological *magnum opus*, the three-volume *Summa Theologica*. As Yves Congar observed, "I am forced to ask myself if it be not a deliberate act on St. Thomas' part that he refused to write a *separate* treatise *De Ecclesia*, seeing that the Church pervaded his theology in all its parts."[29]

In describing the church metaphorically as the mystical body of Christ, Thomas used the Pauline analogy of the human body performing varying functions with different organs under the direction of the head (1 Cor. 12). The head of the body is the center of order, because it is the top; the center of perfection, because it is the center of all senses; and the center of power, because it is the origination point for all force, control, and human quality. In similar manner Christ is the head of the church, His mystical body. He cautioned, however, that the human body-mystical body analogy should not be labored, since the analogy was at best one of resemblance and not identity.[30] One obvious difference between the two is that "the members of an organism are all together at one given period of time, whereas the members of the mystical body are dispersed throughout the ages . . . from the beginning of the world until its end."[31]

The church on earth, the institutional church, derives its existence not only from Christ's passion but from the Holy Spirit. "As in one single human begin there is one soul and one body but many members, so the Catholic Church has one body but many members. The soul animating this body is the Holy Ghost. Hence the Creed [Apostles' Creed] after bidding us believe in the Holy Ghost, adds 'the Holy Catholic Church'."[32] The Holy Spirit also anoints the church in the same manner as he anoints faithful believers to accomplish their sanctification. The Holy Spirit, therefore, is the ultimate principle of the church's unity.[33]

Thomas saw the institutional church as "a society of saints" and as "the congregation of believers of which each Christian is a member."[34] The society of saints is not a perfect society, since it is composed of the unrepentant as well as the sacramentally forgiven.[35] Nevertheless, perfection is the goal to be achieved "in heaven and not on earth." This is an assured consequence of Christ's passion, for the church is ultimately and eternally to be "a glorious church, not having a spot or wrinkle" (Eph. 5:27).[36]

In his *Exposition on the Apostles' Creed* Thomas repeated the four distinguishing attributes of the church (one, holy, catholic, and apostolic) and gave a succinct commentary on each.[37] Quoting The Song of Solomon 6:9, "My dove, my perfect one, is only one," he defended the unity of the church which is likened to Noah's ark, "outside of which nobody can be saved." Ideal oneness of the church resides in a shared agreement of faith, hope, and charity: of faith, because all share the same truths; of hope, because all share the same assurance of eternal life; of charity, because all are united in a shared love of God and each other.

Thomas appropriated the temple imagery of 1 Corinthians 3:16 to describe the church's holiness. Members of the church have been consecrated by the cleansing of the blood of Christ and by the sanctifying of the Holy Spirit, even as a sacred edifice has been consecrated by washing and anointing. The church is uniquely "holy by the indwelling of the Blessed Trinity."

Apostolicity was defended on the traditional grounds of Petrine-Pauline-Roman primacy. Thomas granted the pope plenitude of power in the spiritual realm and declared that he alone is the final authority in matters of faith and practice. Furthermore, the pope only is empowered to summon, convene, prorogue, and close general councils. His authority is greater than that of a council. Thomas denied the pope authority in the secular realm, except in the sense of the spiritual dimensions of secular activity.

As noted earlier, the fourteenth and fifteenth centuries witnessed a renewed interest in the doctrine of the church. While the church remained the foremost and strongest cultural force in the European world in that period, many were no longer able to see an intimate connection between church and state or church and culture. Ecclesiastical life was in a state of ferment and faced a serious crisis. At the beginning of the period the papal claims to world rule received a severe blow from France; and during the Avignon exile the Papacy became servilely subject to French control. The empire, stripped of its universal character and overshadowed by emerging national states was no longer able to render assistance to the church. General indignation at the long extant and increasing abuses among the clergy, in monasticism, and among the laity found expression in the cry: "Reform of the Church in head and members," a cry echoed until an Augustinian monk named Martin Luther posted his ninety-five theses of protest on the Wittenberg church doors and initiated the Protestant Reformation. The cries for reform precipitated a number of treatises and councils concerned with, among other issues, the doctrine of the church.

Within the same year of the promulgation of *Unam Sanctam* (1302), two Augustinian monastics released treatises on the church. Giles of Rome (c. 1247-1316), archbishop of Bourges, published *Power of the Church*, while James of Viterbo, who has been credited with "the first treatise on the church" (because it was devoted exclusively to the doctrine of the church), confined his discussion to three topics: the church's "distinctive marks, its organization in the form of a kingdom, and the authority which rules it."[38] His work was entitled *Church Government.*

Both Giles and James insisted on the extension of the plenipotentiary authority of the pope to all spiritual and temporal matters, specifically in support of Boniface VIII. During the next three decades this same position was taken by other scholars, such as the Italian Augustinian, Augustinus Triumphus of Ancona and the Spanish Franciscan, John Alvarus Pelagius. They attributed power to the Papacy that even the popes themselves had never claimed.[39]

Other writers vehemently opposed the doctrine of papal monarchy represented by Giles of Rome and James of Viterbo. Among these the most perceptive and persuasive were John of Paris (1240-1306), Dante Alighieri (1265-1321), Marsilius of Padua (c. 1275-1342), William of Ockham (c. 1290-1349), John Wycliffe (c. 1328-84), and John Hus (c. 1369-1415). The first of these, a Dominican antipapalist, argued in *Royal and Papal Power* (1303) that a secular ruler could proceed against a pope in cases where the papacy was involved in fomenting rebellion against a king.[40] This provided a rationale for the actions of Philip IV against Boniface VIII. John also anticipated later conciliarists when he declared that authority in the church is derived from God and resides in the whole church. The head of the church is Christ, not the pope. Faith and morals can only be defined by a general council since it is the only true representative of the church.[41]

Dante Alighieri, the great Italian poet, followed John of Paris in assailing the papacy and popes. In *On Monarchy* (1313) he argued that neither the Papacy nor heads of states should meddle in the affairs of the other. He insisted, however, that both popes and kings should work for the mutual well-being of their subjects.[42]

Marsilius of Padua, at one time rector of the University of Paris, published in 1324 a work entitled *The Defender of the Peace.* In the writer's opinion it was the Papacy that disturbed the peace of the world; therefore, peace could only be restored to the world by eliminating the offending institution as a governing authority.[43] For Marsilius the church was comprised of the totality of the faithful who believed in and had called upon the name of Christ. Bishops and priests were viewed as essentially equal with distinctions determined by appointment of temporal rulers. The state was held to be the great unifying power of society to which the church must be completely subordinated. The church derives its authority from the people, who retain the right to censure and depose kings. The church, on the other hand, has no inherent jurisdiction, whether spiritual or temporal. The church's only rights are those given by the state. The church may own no property; it can use only what the state provides. Marsilius rejected the Petrine-Roman church primacy tradition and denied that the Papacy had any prerogatives whatsoever. The principal authority in all ecclesiastical matters was to reside in ecumenical councils composed of both clergy and laity.[44] Marsilius' work sounded the prelude to the sixteenth-century Reformation.

William of Ockham, nominalist philosopher and teacher at Oxford, advocated a radical separation of the church from the world, denied to the pope all temporal authority, and conceded significant powers to the laity and their representatives through general councils. His major work in criticism of the Papacy was entitled *On the Authority of Emperors and Popes.* He defined the church as the community or congregation of the faithful "living at the same time in this mortal life." His emphasis was upon the liberty of individuals to become "true and real persons" by professing faith in Christ and becoming constituent members in the mystical body of Christ.[45] Like Marsilius he prepared the way for the conciliarists of the next century.

The days of the Babylonian captivity of the Papacy ended in 1377 with the return of Gregory XI (1370-78) to Rome. The following year an even worse calamity than the captivity of the Papacy befell the church. Latin Christendom divided into two ecclesiastical allegiances, one with headquarters at Rome, the other at Avignon. A schism (the Western Schism) began which lasted until its resolution by a general council, the Council of Constance (1414-17), thirty-nine years later. From 1378 to the Council of Pisa in 1409 there were two competing popes; from 1409 to 1417 there were three. The schism plunged the church into a sea of doubt and distress and did immeasurable harm to the Papacy and ecclesiastical life. It was within the context of the closing years of the Babylonian captivity of the Papacy and the beginning of the Western Schism that two powerful voices for reform began to be heard: one in England, John Wycliffe (c. 1328-84); the other in Bohemia, John Hus (c. 1369-1415). Both were extremely critical of the papal conception of the church, and both advocated basically the same ecclesiology.

John Wycliffe, pioneer English reformer and sponsor of the first translation of the Bible into English, began his career as a political agitator against particular ecclesiastical abuses which he felt adversely affected England. Everything he wrote and did was rooted in Scripture, which he declared boldly to be the sole criterion for faith and practice.[46] He also leaned heavily upon Augustine, and his ecclesiology was quite reminiscent of the Augustinian understanding of the church.

Wycliffe defined the church in *De Ecclesia* as "the universality of the predestinate."[47] The true church of Christ consists of the whole body of those elected by God to salvation. Wycliffe did, however, distinguish between the true church and the visible institutional church of Rome. The former was discussed in terms of a threefold division, "part triumphant in heaven, part sleeping in purgatory and part militant on earth."[48] In other words, it is composed of the predestined or the elect only. He said that the elect were the church, "and their membership could not be jeopardized even by mortal sin" nor by lapsing from membership in the visible church. In contrast, he stated that the institutional church with its center in Rome included both "the sheep and goats." Both elect and nonelect could kneel side by side at the same Mass, neither knowing with certainty which was which. Only God would know. Wycliffe argued that membership in the Roman Church was no guarantee of membership in the true church. Central to his ecclesiology was the doctrine of the dominion or lordship of Christ over the individual convert who had been admitted into true church membership. He did not suggest doing away with prelates and priests, but he would insist that the clergy recognize their office as ministry and not as justification for lordship.[49] Adapting the Chalcedonian doctrine of the two natures of Christ, he identified Christ as the dual head over the church; head of the invisible or mystical church and also head of the incarnate or human visible church on earth. Yet, in view of the unity of the two natures of Christ, there is but one head of the church which is the body of Christ.[50]

Wycliffe's teachings found fertile soil in Bohemia where John Hus, a teacher at the University of Prague, appropriated his reform ideas and shared them in the classroom, from the pulpit, and in writing. His ecclesiology was essentially the same as that of Wycliffe and therefore there is no need in this presentation for additional elaboration. Both Wycliffe and Hus' teachings were condemned at the Council of Constance. Tragically for Hus, he was burned as a heretic at the stake and his ashes were thrown into the Rhine. But this could not stop what Wycliffe and Hus had begun, for in the case of both, disciples arose and carried the torch of reform forward.

To complete the study of the doctrine of the church in the Middle Ages, brief note should be made relative to conciliarism. Several writers referred to earlier in this essay were staunch defenders of the authority of general councils over the Papacy. The Council of Constance brought the issue to the forefront, and the ideas of men like Pierre d'Ailly and Jean Gerson, staunch conciliarists, prevailed. The council decreed that the supreme authority of the church resides in ecumenical councils which represent the whole body of the faithful.[51]

Notes

1. Paul Tillich, *A History of Christian Thought* (New York: Harper & Row, 1968), 149.

2. F. Homes Dudden, *Gregory the Great: His Place in History and Thought* (London: Longmans, Green, and Co., 1905), 2: 406-7. Compare Reinhold Seeberg, *Textbook of the History of Doctrines* (Grand Rapids: Baker Book House, 1956), 2:25.

3. Ibid., 409-10.

4. Ibid., 411.

5 Ibid.

6. Jaroslav Pelikan, *The Christian Tradition: A History of the Development of Doctrine*, vol. 1, *The Emergence of the Catholic Tradition (100-600)* (Chicago: University of Chicago Press, 1971), 352.

7. R. W. Southern, *Western Society and the Church in the Middle Ages* (Grand Rapids: Wm. B. Eerdmans, 1970), 94.

8. Walter Ullmann, *The Growth of Papal Government in the Middle Ages*, 3d ed. (London: Methuen & Co., 1970), 43-44.

9. *The Oxford Dictionary of the Christian Church*, s.v. "Donation of Constantine." (Henceforth cited as *O.D.C.C.*).

10. William R. Cannon, *History of Christianity in the Middle Ages: From the Fall of Rome to the Fall of Constantinople* (Nashville: Abingdon Press, 1960), 96.

11. Ibid., 81.

12. Eric G. Gay, *The Church: Its Changing Image Through Twenty Centuries* (Atlanta: John Knox Press, 1980), 103.

13. Jaroslav Pelikan, *The Christian Tradition: A History of the Development of Doctrine*, vol. 2, *The Growth of Medieval Theology: 600-1300* (Chicago: University of Chicago Press, 1978), 48.

14. Cannon, 153.

15. Walter Ullmann, *A Short History of the Papacy in the Middle Ages* (London: Methuen & Co., 1974), 148.

16. Ibid., 152-53.

17. Oliver J. Thatcher and Edgar H. McNeal, *A Source Book for Mediaeval History: Selected Documents Illustrating the History of Europe in the Middle Ages* (New York: Charles Scribner's Sons, 1907), 155-60.

18. Karl Bihlmeyer and Herman Tüchle, *Church History*, vol. 2, *The Middle Ages* (Paderborn: Ferdinand Schoningh, 1963), 256.

19. *O.D.C.C.*, s.v. "Innocent III."

20. Ullmann, *Short History*, 226.

21. Thatcher and McNeal, 311-13.

22. Ibid., 314-17.

23. Ibid., 317.

24. Jean Leclercq, "Introduction," *Bernard of Clairvaux: Selected Works*, trans. G. R. Evans (Mahwah, N.J.: Paulist Press, 1987), 51.

25. Robert L. Calhoun, *Lectures on the History of Christian Doctrine* (New Haven: Yale Divinity School, 1948), 297.

26. Gay, 115, 422.

27. Ibid., 116.

28. Ibid., 116-17.

29. Yves Congar, *The Mystery of the Church* (Baltimore: Helicon Press, 1960), 117.

30. Thomas Gilby, *St. Thomas Aquinas: Theological Texts* (London: Oxford University Press, 1955), 337-38.

31. Gilby, 338.

32. Ibid., 340.

33. Gay, 118.

34. Gilby, 340.

35. Gay, 118-19.

36. Ibid.

37. Gilby, 340-41.

38. Bihlmeyer and Tüchle, 365-66.

39. Congar, 97.

40. M. J. Wilkes, *The Problem of Sovereignty in the Later Middle Ages: The Papal Monarchy with Augustus Triumphus and the Publicists* (Cambridge: Cambridge University Press, 1963).

41. Ullmann, *Growth of Papal Government,* 385, n. 5.

42. Gay, 127-28.

43. *O.D.C.C.,* s.v. "Dante."

44. Ullmann, *Short History,* 285.

45. Thatcher and McNeal, 317-24.

46. Gay, 130-32.

47. John Stacey, *John Wyclif and Reform* (Philadelphia: Westminster Press, 1964), 73-89.

48. Matthew Spinka, *John Hus at the Council of Constance* (New York: Columbia University Press, 1965), 28.

49. Stacey, 99.

50. Ibid., 101.

51. Gay, 134.

15
Reformation Views of the Church

by C. Penrose St. Amant

This topic requires a focus on the major ecclesiologies that emerged in the sixteenth century: Lutheran, Reformed, Anabaptist, and Anglican. The spectrum suggested by this theme exhibits a wide ecclesiological range, from the congregationalism of the early Luther to the territorial church supervised by the prince, from the Holy Commonwealth of Zwingli in Zurich and Calvin in Geneva to Presbyterianism, from the basic congregationalism of the Anabaptists in Zurich to a variety of later ecclesiologies, and from Roman Catholic papal supremacy in England through its rupture by Henry VIII into Protestant (Edward VI) and Roman Catholic reactions (Mary Tudor) to Elizabethan episcopacy. In a single chapter, it is, of course, possible to deal only with selected aspects of this spectrum.

Lutheran

Martin Luther's view of the church, Roland Bainton believed, was "derived from his theory of the sacraments."[1] His understanding of the Lord's Supper pointed in one direction and his view of baptism in another. As a result his early ecclesiology was congregational and his late view of the church was territorial.

It seems strange to say that Luther's conception of the efficacy of the Lord's Supper and baptism is close to that of the Anabaptists, whom he mistakenly identified with the *Schwärmer* (fanatics). This is the case because he believed the efficacy of the sacraments depended upon the faith of the person who received them. For Luther, as for the Anabaptists, faith was individual and personal. "As to the need for faith in the sacraments," he said, "I will die before I recant."[2] This view implies that the church should be made up of those who have personal faith and thus should be a gathered community. "[There is] no priestly class," he said, "for all of us who have been baptized are priests. Ordination can be nothing other than a certain rite of choosing a preacher in the Church."[3] A congregational view of the church, suggested by his conception of ordination, was alluded to, though not worked out, in his early lectures. But he did not follow that road. He might have done so had he embraced the doctrine of believers' baptism. He, of course, did not do so in spite of his insistence upon personal faith as a prerequisite for the efficacy of the sacraments. His reluctance to follow the logic of his view of faith was rooted in his Roman Catholic heritage and in his fear of radical change growing out of his rigorous doctrine of original sin, by which he meant an inordinate self-love. Accordingly he preferred social and political order to the risk of change. This is one reason he tended to justify ecclesiological order at the expense of freedom in the church. His fear of anarchy made him skeptical of congregationalism and opened the door to the authority of the prince in the church.

He sought to sustain the medieval idea that the same people constituted the state and the church. The alternative seemed to him to be anarchy. He could not bring himself to reject the alliance between church and state, which he believed was the basis not only of Christian society but also of social concord. Deep in the European mind the idea persisted into the Reformation and beyond that a state church was essential for harmony and justice in society. Except for a brief period when he leaned toward congregationalism, Luther, along with most of his contemporaries, accepted this view.

Infant baptism and the state church are corollaries. One implies the other.[4] All children become members of the church by baptism. The idea of a single and stable society, rooted in the state church concept, symbolized by infant baptism, was more powerful in Luther's mind than his belief that the efficacy of a sacrament depended upon the personal faith of the recipient. Justification of infant baptism was required by his basic presupposition of the essentiality of the state church, of which every person was a member. He insisted that infant baptism had "been practiced since the days of the apostles,"[5] but did not cite sources to justify his claim. He talked about the implicit faith of an infant comparable to the faith of a person in the state of sleep. He sometimes spoke of "infantile faith." Later he shifted from the alleged implicit faith of a child to the faith of a child's sponsor at baptism, as if one person could have faith for another, which stands opposed to his belief that personal faith is needed in the sacraments. He wrote: "The sacraments do what they do not by their own power but by the power of faith, without which they do nothing at all."[6] Again, he said, "To seek the efficacy of the sacrament apart . . . from faith is to labor in vain."[7]

Luther's ambivalence was rooted in his inability to give up the profound individualism of the Lord's Supper, whose efficacy depended upon personal faith, and the corporateness of his view of baptism, which linked the church to society. Bainton speaks of it as a "sociological sacrament" derived from the Middle Ages, where state and church were tied together to form the

basis of a Christian society. Luther found it impossible to surrender "either
the individualism of the Eucharistic cup or the corporateness of the baptismal font."[8]

The church for the early Luther was basically the community of the redeemed living and dead known only to God and exhibited on earth in conclaves of "earnest Christians" (*Ernst Christen*) bound together by the Holy
Spirit. He did not believe it could be actualized but he was not satisfied with
the idea of a disembodied church. In 1522 he considered the idea of forming
an association of those who wished to receive the Eucharist in both kinds,
bread *and* wine, apart from others. Two years earlier, in 1520, he spoke of
the baptism of the believer by immersion in water. "This," he said, "is
doubtless the way it was instituted by Christ. The sinner does not so much
need to be washed as he needs to die in order to be fully renewed and made
another creature, and to be conformed to the death and resurrection of
Christ." He continued, "It is far more forceful to say that baptism signifies
that we die in every way and rise to eternal life than to say that it signifies
merely that we are washed clean of sins." This comment about baptism by
immersion of the "sinner" who "needs to die in order to be fully renewed"
seems to presuppose personal faith for, he says, "It is not baptism that justi-
fies . . . but it is faith, [which] is the submersion of the old man and the
emerging of the new (Eph. 4:22-24; Col. 3:9-10)."[9] When he spoke of the
"sinner" and the *"old man"* he surely was not thinking of *infant* baptism.

Luther's hope of gathering "true believers" into a group within the larger
group was shattered on the altar of a church that comprised the entire community, which came out of medieval society. His dream died to be realized
by the Anabaptists, who rejected the territorial church. Luther's dilemma,
which he never really resolved, was that he wanted a confessional church
made up of people who exercised personal faith and a territorial church
consisting of everyone, including infants, in a given area.[10]

The early Luther was inclined toward congregationalism, suggested by
his opposition to the removal of Zwilling from Zwickau by a powerful person against the desires of the people.[11] However, problems of doctrinal diversity, chaos in liturgical forms, and the difficulty of managing ecclesiastical properties no longer in Catholic hands posed grave problems he felt
could not be solved by congregational government. In 1525 Luther said,
"Everywhere the congregations are in very poor condition. No one contributes anything, no one pays for anything."[12] These problems would have
been dealt with by bishops, but bishops were no more since Luther believed
bishops in the New Testament were simply pastors. As a result, he moved
away from congregationalism to what became a territorial church. He created the office of superintendent to implement his plan. He turned to the

prince to function as an "emergency bishop" who took charge of church property. Visitors were appointed by Elector John of Saxony, including Luther and his theological colleagues, to survey liturgical practices and doctrine. Jurists were selected to deal with financial matters. Though the plan was provisional, it opened the door that led to the territorial church (*Landeskirche*). The line of demarcation between church and state set forth in his tract *On Civil Government* in 1523 was breached and the territorial church emerged.[13]

Reformed—Ulrich Zwingli

There is a similarity between Zwingli's early view that the final ecclesiastical authority rested in the local community of believers (*Gemeinde*) under Christ's lordship and the inspired Scriptures that point to Him and the Anabaptist view, which was largely the same. However, there are sharp differences. The sharpest difference is that Zwingli came quickly to believe this authority was exercised by the civil government allegedly acting in line with the teachings of Scripture. Anabaptists found the locus of authority completely in the congregation and repudiated any exercise of authority by the state over the church and rejected the notion that the total community belonged to the church through the rite of infant baptism (*Volkskirche*). Conrad Grebel, an Anabaptist leader in Zurich, said, "The Christian Church is the congregation of the few who believe and live right."[14] Zwingli and the Anabaptists disagreed basically concerning the nature of the church.

Zwingli's stress upon personal faith as the test of the elect and, therefore, of those who made up the church created an anomaly because he also identified the church with the total community, except for a few Catholics. He disdained the logic of personal faith that would have led to a believers' church, a group separated from the community as a whole. He leaned briefly toward believers' baptism and, therefore, toward a believers' church in 1523, the year the town council in Zurich, due to Zwingli's influence, decreed the break with the Roman Catholic Church. At this time Zwingli opposed infant baptism. Evidence for this tendency, which he quickly reversed, is a letter he wrote to Balthasar Hubmaier in which he conceded on the basis of the New Testament "that normally baptism ought to be preceded by instruction."[15]

But his nationalism, humanism, and Roman Catholic background quickly converged to counteract belief in believers' baptism and the believers' church, held by some of his followers who became Anabaptists (Felix Manz, Conrad Grebel), and caused him to retain his inherited belief in infant baptism and a state church. His deep devotion to Swiss life and culture could have led him to identify the church with a Swiss city. His humanism probably weakened the connection between the sacraments and faith so that baptism was largely a symbol of entrance into a new community, "an initiatory sign" analogous to the rite of circumcision in the Old Testament. He equated circumcision in the Old Covenant with baptism in the New. "Water baptism," he wrote, "is nothing but an *external ceremony*, that is an *outward sign* that we are incorporated and engrafted into Jesus Christ and *pledged* to live for him and to follow him."[16] Instead of allegedly objective marks of the "visible" church, Zwingli thought in terms of communities where Christ was openly confessed, rigorous Bible study pursued, and the pledge "to live for him and to follow him" became concrete realities. The early Zwingli attributed the authority to excommunicate to the congregation. The "invisible" church was made up of the whole company of the elect.

The Lord's Supper, instituted in the context of the Passover, was a symbol of entrance into the new Israel. For Zwingli baptism and the Lord's Supper were not really channels of grace but primarily symbols of entrance into a new community.[17] He compared the sacraments to a wedding ring that signifies a marriage. Zurich became the New Israel, in which church and state were profoundly intermingled. Zwingli believed the state church was the cement that held society together. Separation of church and state was, therefore, a dangerous innovation that he thought would lead to anarchy, a view also held by Luther and Calvin.

Reformed—John Calvin

Calvin was certain as to the marks of the church, a view that has persisted more or less in the Reformed tradition: correct faith, participation in the sacraments, and an upright Christian life. He accepted Zwingli's test of "faith," and the Anabaptists' test of "life," and added a sharing in the sacraments.[18] The Lutheran view, set forth in the *Augsburg Confession*, is similar: "The Church is the congregation of the saints, in which the Gospel is rightly taught [purely preached] and the sacraments rightly administered [according to the Gospel]."[19] The difference lies at the point of discipline, an area where Luther exhibited considerable flexibility. He was much less concerned than Calvin with respect to a specific structure of the Christian life and warned against "scruples [that] torture poor consciences to death." He was not averse to overeating and oversleeping to counter the arrogance of self-righteousness! Calvin was much more the legalist, who sought to implement a specific and a rather ascetic view of the norms of Christian conduct. No wonder somewhat oversimplified generalizations developed that Calvinists "took a certain pride in their pale faces" and that "every Calvinist was a monk."[20]

For Calvin, the tests of what constituted the church were relatively tangible, an explicit and precisely defined life-style was demanded of church members, deviation from which was treated harshly. Profession of faith was less subjective and personal. It was more a matter of doctrine, monitored by the Genevan authorities. The sacraments were much more than signs of initiation into a new community, Zwingli's view, since for Calvin they were clearly defined channels of communion with Christ and within the Christian community.

During Calvin's early years in Geneva, church and state were parallel, involving mutual support and collaboration. The goal was reciprocal aid between the two powers. The later Calvin tended to blur the distinction between the two realms. Church and state became two aspects of a single reality. He believed rulers should "advance the kingdom of Christ and maintain purity of doctrine."[21] Thus came about the curious fusion of the church embracing the entire community, symbolized by baptism of all newborns, and the church as a "sect" made up only of the elect, symbolized by rigorous moral standards. Only those who met the theological and ethical criteria of the church belonged to it. Those who did not meet the standards either left town voluntarily or were banished. "Thus Calvin," said Bainton, "succeeded in uniting the idea of a Church coterminous with the community and of a Church as a voluntary society of visible saints."[22] Citizenship in Geneva was contingent upon a Christian profession. Geneva resembled an Anabaptist conclave except, of course, for the persistence of infant baptism, a state church, and the use of the sword. Churches in Geneva were "believers' " churches except for infants and, of course, without believer's baptism and church-state separation.

For Calvin, the church was the community of the saints "from the beginning of the world," the totality of the elect. It was also the visible community, Christians who lived and worked together in the same parish. "The Church," said Calvin, "is wherever we see the Word of God purely preached and listened to, and the sacraments administered according to the institution of Christ." He manifested considerable latitude concerning the institutional structures and worship of the Church, about which he said, "God has prescribed nothing specific."[23]

He was absolutely sure that there could be no true church "where [he believed] lying and falsehood have gained ascendancy." "Members of the Church," he said "[are] those who by confession of faith, by example of life, and by partaking of the sacraments profess the same God and Christ."[24] Ecclesiastical discipline must be added to preaching of the Word and administration of the sacraments as a means of preserving the purity of the Church, though strangely enough Francois Wendel in his excellent study of Calvin's thought questions discipline as a criterion of Calvin's church. He says, "To Calvin . . . discipline was . . . not of the very essence of the notion of a Church."[25] Nevertheless, Wendel also says that "discipline is indispensable if a Church has any desire to preserve its character as the Church of Christ."[26] If "discipline is indispensable" to preserve the character of the church, it follows that it is one of the marks of the church for Calvin. To say, as Wendel does, that discipline belongs "to the organization and not to the definition of the Church"[27] in Geneva offers an ingenious but unconvincing distinction between the "organization" and the "essence" of the church. As early as 1536 Calvin sketched the aims of discipline as follows: "Heretics, schismatics, [and] dissolute members must be expelled" so that "the good should not be corrupted by the conduct of the bad," and the expelled "overcome by shame may repent."[28] In the final edition of the *Institutes,* he remarked, "If the true Church is the pillar and foundation of truth [1 Tim. 3:15], it is certain that no Church can exist where lying and falsehood have gained sway."[29]

Calvin devoted a chapter in his *Institutes* to the issue of discipline,[30] which he held to be "necessary in the Church" for it serves as "the sinews through which the members of the body hold together, each in its own place." Discipline "is like a bridle to restrain and tame those who rage against the doctrine of Christ."[31] Contrary to Wendel, it seems evident that the church set up by Calvin possessed the power by alleged "divine appointment . . . to frame laws and procedures for its own orderly life" and "to exercise censures and to restore the penitent to communion."[32] Discipline was without doubt an essential attribute of the Genevan church.

There is a curious similarity between the moral rigor Calvin required in the church and the rigorous requirements of the Anabaptists. In Calvin's case the effort was to create as "pure" a church as possible within the context of a state church system and the practice of infant baptism. A "believers' " church was sought through careful surveillance of its members and the excommunication of those who did not measure up morally or theologically. The Anabaptists sought a similar goal, a "pure" church, by restricting membership to baptized believers and the use of the "ban" to remove the unfaithful.

Calvin stressed faith as essential to the efficacy of the sacraments. He said, "We are not made partakers in Jesus Christ and his spiritual gifts by the bread, wine, and water, but . . . we are brought to him by the promise, so that he gives himself to us, and, dwelling in us by faith, he fulfills what is promised and offered to us by the signs."[33] He also asserted, "He who would have the sign with the thing, and not void of its truth, must apprehend by faith the word which is there enclosed."[34] His point is that Christ grants His gifts in the sacraments "by faith," against the Roman Catholic view of *ex opere operato*—that is, by the act duly performed. A personal response by the believer is required. The believer alone can have communion with Christ. But, like Luther, he did not follow through the implications of his view. His understanding of the Lord's Supper pointed in the one direction and his view of baptism in another. As a result, his view of the sacraments is ambiguous. If the believer alone can enter into communion with Christ, such union in the Supper and baptism is the effect of faith. Nevertheless, in 1536 Calvin spoke of the "faith of children [infants in whom] God acts secretly . . . without our knowing how." Later he abandoned that view and replied to those who believed that baptism is a sacrament of faith, of which infants are not capable, by saying, "That objection is resolved in one word [*sic*], if we say that they are baptized for their future faith and penitence, whereof, although we see none in appearance, nevertheless the seed is here implanted by the hidden working of the Holy Spirit."[35]

Calvin clung to the practice of infant baptism despite his inability to find a basis for it in Scripture. He sought to demonstrate its validity by implications and analogies derived from the alleged parallel between circumcision in the Old Covenant and baptism in the New Covenant (Col. 2:11-12) and the blessing of children by Jesus (Matt. 19:13-15). In addition, he relied on alleged patristic evidences "right back to the primitive church" without citing his sources.[36] The usually rigorous exegetical method Calvin commonly employed is notably absent in his effort to defend infant baptism on the grounds of analogy with circumcision, the blessing of children, the "faith" of infants, and their "future faith." It is likely that the major factor in Calvin's insistence upon infant baptism is rooted in his ecclesiology, which required that all members of the community must be members of the church. Church and state owed collaboration and aid to each other. The magistracy was bound to protect the church, made up of all persons in the community, and to ensure its theological and ethical purity.

Anabaptist (Radical)

For the Anabaptists only believers should be baptized, and these alone made up the church. The church could not coincide with the total community unless it was constituted only of baptized believers, as was the case in several Anabaptist communitarian conclaves, such as those organized by the Hutterites, who renounced private property. The Anabaptists were "regenerated believers" who sought to restore primitive Christianity. They believed not so much in reformation of the church as in its restitution on the basis of their reading of the New Testament.

The purity of the church, theologically and ethically, was protected by the "ban," a form of excommunication of "brethren and sisters . . . who slip sometimes and fall into error and sin," based on Matthew 18:15-17. That was the only penalty enforced entirely by the church, for church and state should be separate. Civil government was necessary in a sinful word but Christians should not share in it, should not engage in military activities, and should not take any form of an oath. They were not anarchists; they simply left government to others. Most Anabaptists preached withdrawal not only from the folk church but also from participation in the life of the state.

Balthasar Hübmaier was an exception. He believed the Christian must support the state; he countenanced a just war and capital punishment. There were other differences within the ranks of those known as Anabaptists. Nevertheless, Anabaptism exhibited a certain ecclesiological continuity, especially in the beginning.

The Anabaptists took the Sermon on the Mount literally and applied it to all members of the church, an aspect of their effort to restore primitive Christianity. Roman Catholics also took it literally but its rigoristic features were confined to the monks. Since the Anabaptists applied the absolute moral demands of the Sermon on the Mount to all church members, they were, in a sense, monks. Anabaptist baptism, says Robert Friedmann, "might . . . be compared with a monastic vow."[37] What differentiated this Anabaptist "vow" from the Roman Catholic view was that Anabaptists did not reject marriage.[38] Luther regarded the Sermon on the Mount as a disposition, not a code. He rejected the monastic vow because he believed baptism was the only Christian vow.

There are interesting similarities at certain points between the Anabaptists and others, even Roman Catholics, in the Reformation period. But, of course, the differences, especially in ecclesiology, are wide and profound. That is the reason George Williams has spoken of *The Radical Reformation,*[39] which includes the Anabaptists as the most significant group. The term "radical" means "going to the root." They believed deeply that the magisterial reformers had stopped short of the "root," which was the Anabaptist understanding of the Bible, especially the New Testament, and, therefore, perpetuated much that was to them merely traditional in the medieval Church. They were also "radical" in a contextual sense for they stood out with sharp clarity in their opposition to what seemed self-evident to the religious and political establishment—state church, infant baptism, elaborate creeds, taking oaths, participation in war, and sharing in civil government. They questioned the basic convictions of more than a millennium of European history.

Anabaptist radicalism threatened the seemingly self-evident validity of the prevailing ecclesiastical, social, and political structures. As a consequence, the Anabaptists were frequently mistaken for anarchists. They held that the church was not made up of the community as a whole into which infants were baptized but was a conventicle one entered through personal faith and believer's baptism. They looked upon baptism not as a saving rite or an initiation but as a visible sign of an inward change that had already occurred. It was a symbol of death, which they faced daily, but also of glorious resurrection. To them infant baptism was not a baptism at all but only a Roman Catholic custom without biblical warrant. They, therefore, regarded themselves as baptizers, not as rebaptizers or Anabaptists or *Wiedertäufer*. Most of them desired to be designated only as *Brüder* (Brethren). The name "Anabaptists" was pinned on them to make them subject to the severe penalties exacted by the Justinian Code against the Donatists. In 1529 Roman Catholics and Lutherans concurred at Speyer in Germany that Anabaptists should be subject to the death penalty. The decree declared that "every Anabaptist . . . should be put to death by fire, sword, or some other way."[40] They were slaughtered unmercifully. An Anabaptist chronicler recorded the deaths of 2,173 of the brethren and continued: "They have borne all torture and agony without fear. The things of this world they counted only as shadows. They were thus drawn unto God [so] that they knew nothing, sought nothing, desired nothing, loved nothing but God alone. Therefore they had more patience in their suffering than their enemies in tormenting them."[41] It was their ecclesiology above all that made them targets of persecution and was likewise their most important contribution to Christian life and thought.

The Lord's Supper symbolized their communion within the community (1 Cor.10:17) and with their living Lord (v. 16). The corn and the grapes that went through a process of kneading and crushing suggested the kneading and crushing of "a martyr people by the hand of God . . . according to his purpose for them." Christ was present not in the elements but in the community of baptized believers, disciplined and purified by the "ban." All who were "unworthy" were excluded from the Supper.[42]

Anglican

The policy of Henry VIII, who became "head" of the Church of England in 1532, was "schism without heresy." In 1534 Parliament put the seal of legality on the breach with Rome. This meant a clean break with the Roman Catholic Church ("schism") but did not involve doctrinal deviation from Rome ("without heresy"). Henry still considered himself "defender of the faith," a title granted him by Leo X in 1521 for his efforts to refute Luther. He was determined to show the world that he was an orthodox Catholic except for papal authority, which he rejected. Accordingly, in 1539 Parliament approved *The Six Articles*,[43] which affirmed transubstantiation, vows of chastity, private Masses, auricular confession, and repudiated priestly marriage and communion in bread *and* wine. Called "the bloody whip with six strings," the *Articles* stifled any doctrinal reform in Henry's reign. But the ecclesiological change was drastic. Henry became "the only supreme head in earth of the Church of England called *Anglicana Ecclesia.*"[44] But, of course, he was not even a priest much less a bishop. The new national church headed by the king needed episcopal leadership. Thomas Cranmer, Archbishop of Canterbury, whom Henry had appointed with the concurrence of and confirmation by Clement VII in 1533, also became primate of the emerging Church of England. Thus the church had two heads—the English sovereign and the Archbishop of Canterbury. The Church of England continued its episcopal ecclesiology, which was sustained in the reign of Edward VI (1547-53), the son of Henry and Jane Seymour with an evident Protestant character, suggested by the repeal by parliament of *The Six Articles*. Since the new king was a frail child of nine years of age, power passed into the hands of the Duke of Somerset (1547-49), a convinced Reformer along Lutheran lines, and the Duke of Northumberland (1549-53), who favored Reformed tendencies. The influx of Protestants from the Continent reinforced the English reform but did not alter the episcopal ecclesiology. John Knox, who made his way to England in 1549 by way of Scotland and France, became a royal chaplain. He declined the bishopric of Rochester, perhaps because of his reservations about episcopacy.

Two Books of Common Prayer (1549 and 1552) were produced by Cranmer. The second version altered significantly not only the Roman Catholic theological outlook of the reign of Henry VIII, including transubstantiation, but the Lutheran perspective of the first Prayer Book, in which the prayer was that the elements in the Lord's Supper did not *become* (Roman Catholic) but might *be* Christ's body and blood, suggesting Luther's doctrine of concomitance (consubstantiation?), the view that Christ's "real presence" could come *with* the elements, "as heat is in an iron." The second Prayer Book removed everything that suggested "real presence" and stressed "remembrance" as the central theme of the Supper. The elements were offered with the words: "Take and eat *this* [the word *this* was not further defined] in remembrance that Christ died for thee [which sounds Zwinglian] and feed on him in thy heart by faith with thanksgiving [which sounds Calvinistic]. Drink this in remembrance that Christ's blood was shed for thee and be thankful [which again implies only the Zwinglian rite of commemoration]." That Christ's "real presence" in the Supper was rejected is suggested further by the fact that the *Agnus Dei* (Lamb of God), sung by Catholics and Lutherans, was removed.[45] "The priest became a minister,"

commented Bainton, "the altar a table, and the eucharist a com-
memoration."[46]

Mary Tudor (1553-58), the daughter of Henry and Catherine of Aragon,
sought to undo the revolution started by her father and brought to fruition
by her half-brother. Cardinal Reginald Pole was brought back from the
Continent, to which he had fled in the reign of Edward VI, to lead the Roman Catholic resurgence. Many Protestant Reformers fled to the Continent. Some of them, like Knox, went to Calvin's Geneva. The Edwardian
bishops were sent to martyrdom in the fires of Smithfield. The bishops who
leaned toward Romanism in the reign of Edward VI were granted high
posts. However, the process that began in the 1530s proved irreversible, and
at Mary's death in 1558, Elizabeth I (1558-1603), the daughter of Henry
and Ann Boleyn, came to the throne with an open agenda. She, nevertheless, proceeded with caution. The Supremacy Act of 1559, with Elizabeth's
concurrence, declared that she was only "Supreme Governor," rather than
"Supreme Head" of the Church of England. Nevertheless, she was excommunicated by the Pope in 1570.

What emerged in the religious settlement of Elizabeth was a policy of
theological and ecclesiological comprehension, set forth in the Act of Uniformity. An example of this is suggested by the question of Christ's "presence" in the Lord's Supper, which was intentionally left unresolved by com-
bining the formulas of the two Edwardian prayer books in the revised
edition of *The Book of Common Prayer* (1559) so that the minister says,
"The body of our Lord Jesus Christ which was given for thee preserve thy
body and soul into everlasting life. Take and eat this in remembrance that
Christ died for thee and feed on him in thy heart by faith and
thanksgiving."[47]

The *Thirty-Nine Articles* (1563),[48] a modification of Cranmer's *Forty-
Two Articles* (1553), were Protestant in tone but not theologically precise.
Bainton speaks of the "studied ambiguities" of the Elizabethan settlement
but adds, "Were they less satisfactory than the blinding clarity of the fires of
Smithfield?"[49] The Anglican Reformation occurred not primarily in the
field of theology but in ecclesiology and worship. The episcopal ecclesiological form, including the state church and infant baptism, derived from Roman Catholicism, was perpetuated but with a certain ambiguity as to its
history and authority. Confessional issues were not paramount. No theologian of the stature of Luther or Calvin emerged. No systematic theology of
significance appeared. The theological moderation of "the middle way" prevailed. Richard Hooker's *Laws of Ecclesiastical Polity* (1594) was concerned
not with theology but ecclesiology. He thought episcopacy was grounded in
Scripture but backed away from Archbishop Richard Bancroft's explicit

contention that only episcopacy was *jure divino* (divine law).[50] Hooker's "chief argument" in its defense was its "essential reasonableness."[51] According to a recent historian it was also "a constitutional necessity in the magisterial reformation of a national kingdom."[52]

Concluding Comment

This study points to the conclusion that the Reformation was about the "nature of the Church more than it was about justification or grace" and, therefore, that the "theological issues at stake were at root ecclesiological."[53] In addition, it seems clear that the ecclesiologies of Luther, Zwingli, Calvin, and Cranmer were shaped more by political than theological considerations.[54] Franklin H. Littell supports this contention in the following comment: "In its essence the pattern of establishment [the state church system] comprehended the entire population of a parish or of a territory, implied infant baptism and coordination with the state system, and tended either toward a rigid absolutism of doctrine and authority [Lutheran and Reformed] . . . or toward a latitudinarian dilution [Anglican]."[55]

This conclusion should not be surprising in the light of recent scholarship that stresses not so much the originality of the Reformation as its "imbeddedness in the spirituality of the later Middle Ages."[56] The state church system is an obvious example of the persistence of medievalism in magisterial Protestantism. Renaissance humanism had an impact upon both the magisterial and radical reformers due to its emphasis upon languages, which stimulated biblical studies. To this linguistic interest must be added the invention of the printing press with movable type by Johann Gutenberg about 1450. As a consequence, the Bible was made available to the magisterial and radical Reformers alike and engendered a variety of ecclesiologies, all of which sought more or less the support of Scripture. It became a weapon used by Protestants against Catholics, by Protestants against each other, and especially by the radical reformers against the claims of magisterial Protestants, who continued the principle of established churches tied to the practice of infant baptism.

The Anabaptists and later the Baptists were equidistant from magisterial Protestantism[57] (Lutheran, Reformed, Anglican) and Roman Catholicism. The Reformers thought in terms of *Reformatio* (Reformation); the Anabaptists carried on under the "more radical slogan of *Restitutito* (Restitution)." The Anabaptists espoused the direct authority of Scripture, believer's baptism, separation of church and state, religious liberty, a concern for the Great Commission, and the conviction that the church transcended national boundaries and local cultures. The unique "religious style" of the Anabaptists, which was largely an expression of their ecclesiology, offered an alternative in the Reformation period that differed sharply from the "old Christendom,"[58] the *Corpus Christianum,* the idea that church and state form a single "Christian Body." They tried desperately and pathetically to replace the *Corpus Christianum,* a coercive sociopolitical synthesis, with the *Corpus Christi,* "the Body of Christ," a voluntary nonpolitical community of discipleship.[59] The Lutheran, Reformed, and Anglican churches sought strenuously to perpetuate the *Corpus Christianum* within their respective spheres of dominance. Reformation views of the church can be understood only in the context of the relationships between church and state in that period against the background of the *Corpus Christianum,* in which the church and a completely baptized society coincided numerically. The magisterial Reformers did not question this arrangement and regarded those who did question it as desperate and deluded revolutionaries, whom they uncritically identified with the Peasants' War (1524-25) and the Münster Revolt (1534-35). Actually the Peasants' War was over (June 1525) at a time when Anabaptism was just emerging (January 1525) in Zurich. The Münster Revolt represents an Anabaptist aberration because most of them were opposed to violence in any form.

The Anabaptists and those who shared their view understood that the church was not simply a subdivision of society, for which it furnished stability and ethical sanctions, but a disciplined community made up of baptized believers unrestricted in their missionary concerns by territorial limitations. Thus the church, whatever else it might be, became again for them what it had been before the time of Constantine, a community of missionaries.[60]

Notes

1. Roland Bainton, *Here I Stand* (New York: Abingdon-Cokesbury Press, 1950), 140.

2. Martin Luther, cited by Bainton, *Here I Stand,* 139. See Walter Köhler, "Zu Luthers Kirchenbegriff," *Christliche Welt,* April 8, 1907, 371-77.

3. Luther, cited by Bainton, *Here I Stand,* 138.

4. See John Baillie, *What Is Christian Civilization?* (New York: Scribner's Sons, 1945), 13-15, 34-35.

5. Luther, *Luther's Works,* (Philadelphia: Muhlenberg Press, 1959), 40:254.

6. Ibid, 36:74

7. Ibid., 36:67.

8. Bainton, 142.

9. *Luther's Works,* 36:66-68. See Luther, *Deutsche Messe, Works of Martin Luther,* ed. C.M. Jacobs *et al.* (Philadelphia, 1932), 6:172-73.

10. Bainton, *Here I Stand,* 311.

11. Ibid., 312.

12. Luther, cited by Heinrich Bornkamm, *Luther in Mid-Career,* trans. E. Theodore Bachmann (Philadelphia: Fortress Press, 1979), 488.

13. Ibid., 312-15. See Luther, *Werke: Kritisch Gesamtausgabe.* Wiemar, Briefwechsel 3:595, 36. See Bornkamm, *Luther in Mid-Career,* chapter 18.

14. *Quellen zur Geschichte der Täufer in der Schweiz,* vol. 1 (16,15), cited by Fritz Blanke,

Brothers in Christ, trans. Joseph Nordenhaug (Scottdale, Pa: Herald Press, 1961), 13.

15. Ulrich Zwingli, "Of Baptism," *Zwingli and Bullinger* (Philadelphia: Westminster Press, 1950), 24:119. See "Drei Zeugenaussagen Zwinglis im Tauferprozess," *Huldreich Zwinglis Samtlichte Werke* (Leipzig, 1927), 4:169. See also J. M. Usteri, "Darstelling Der Tauflehre Zwinglis," and "Zwinglis Correspondenz Mit Den Berner Reformatorem Uber Die Tauffrance," *Theoligische Studien und Kritiken* 55 (1882): 205ff., 616ff. Leo Jud, Zwingli's assistant in Zurich, frequently questioned both infant baptism and the union of church and state. Cited by Franklin H. Littell, *The Anabaptist View of the Church* (Boston: King Starr Press, 1958), 13, 166.

16. Zwingli, "Of Baptism," 156. Italics mine.

17. Bainton, *The Reformation of the Sixteenth Century* (Boston: Beacon Press, 1952), 89.

18. Bainton, *The Reformation,* 115-16.

19. *The Augsburg Confession,* I, VII, Philip Schaff, ed., *The Creeds of Christendom* (New York: Harper and Brothers, 1882), 11-12.

20. Bainton, *The Reformation,* 116. Luther understood that conscience could engender pathological guilt and anticipated some aspects of modern psychiatry. See *Luther's Works,* 36:89.

21. John Calvin, *Commentary,* Isaiah 49:23. See William J. Bouwsma, *John Calvin: A Sixteenth Century Portrait* (New York: Oxford University Press, 1988), chapter 13, especially 210-13.

22. Bainton, *The Horizon History of Christianity* (New York: Avon Books, 1966), 285. See L. B. Schenck, *The Presbyterian Doctrine of Children in the Covenant* (Oxford: Oxford University Press, 1940), 13.

23. John Calvin, *Institutes of the Christian Religion,* ed. John T. McNeil (Philadelphia: The Westminster Press, 1960), IV, 1, 12.

24. Ibid., IV, I, 8. *Commentary,* 1 Corinthians 11:2.

25. Francois Wendel, *Calvin: The Origins and Development of His Religious Thought,* trans. Philip Mairet (New York: Harper and Row, 1963), 301.

26. Ibid., 299.

27. Ibid., 301.

28. Calvin, *Institutes,* IV, 12, 5. See Wendel, 299.

29. Calvin, *Institutes,* IV, 2, 1.

30. Calvin, *Institutes* IV, 22.

31. Ibid., IV, 12, 1. See John T. McNeill, "The Church in Sixteenth Century Reformed Theology," *The Journal of Religion* 22 (July 1942): especially 263.

32. McNeill, 269.

33. Calvin, cited by Wendel, 337.

34. Calvin, *Institutes,* IV, 14, 15.

35. Ibid., IV, 16,20. See Wendel, 327.

36. Calvin, *Institutes,* IV, 16, 8.

37. Robert Friedmann, "Recent Interpretations of Anabaptism," *Church History* 24 (June 1955): 147. See Michael Sattler, *The Schleitheim Confession,* paragraphs 1, 3, 4.

38. Bainton, *The Reformation,* 100.

39. George Williams, *The Radical Reformation* (Philadelphia: Westminster Press, 1962).

40. Cited by Bender, "The Anabaptist Vision," 32.

41. Cited by Bainton, *The Reformation,* 102.

42. Littell, *Anabaptist View of the Church,* 101.

43. *The Six Articles,* cited by Henry Bettenson, ed., *Documents of the Christian Church* (New York: Oxford Press, 1946), 233-34.

44. Cited by Bainton, *The Reformation,* 191.

45. Ibid., 201-2. See Peter Brooks, *Thomas Cranmer's Doctrine of the Euchrist* (New York: Seabury Press, 1965), 93, 104. Cranmer spoke of Christ's presence in the Eucharist as "true presence," which he called a "spiritual presence." What other kind of presence could there be?

46. Bainton, *The Reformation,* 202.

47. Cited in ibid., 209.

48. Cited by Schaff, *Creeds of Christendom,* 3:486-516.

49. Bainton, *The Reformation,* 209.

50. Schaff, *Creeds of Christendom,* 1:608, 708.

51. Williston Walker, *A History of the Christian Church,* 4th ed. (New York: Charles Scribner's Sons, 1985), 547.

52. Williams, *Radical Reformation,* xxvii.

53. Peter Hodgson and Robert H. King, *Christian Theology: An Introduction to Its Traditions and Tasks* (Philadelphia: Fortress Press, 1985), 256.

54. See W. P. Stephens, *The Theology of Huldrych Zwingli* (Oxford: Clarendon Press, 1986), 261. Stephens expresses a contrary view of Zwingli, whose "defense of infant baptism," he said, "was not, as it has been alleged, a matter of Church politics."

55. Littell, *The Free Church* (Boston: Starr King Press, 1957), 4.

56. Bouwsma, *John Calvin,* 3, 237. See Hekio Oberman, *The Harvest of Medieval Theology: Gabriel Biel and Late Medieval Nominalism* (Cambridge, Mass.: Harvard University Press, 1963.) See also Hans Baron, "Calvinist Republicanism and Its Historial Roots," *Church History* 8 (1939): 30-41.

57. The expression "Magisterial Protestantism" was coined by George H. Williams "to cover the various forms of legal establishment and control in the formative decades of Protestant Reformation: Magistrate = *Obrigkeit.*" See Franklin H. Littell, "The Anabaptist Concept of the Church," in Hershberger, ed., *Recovery of the Anabaptist Vision,* 123, n. 16.

58. Williams, *Radical Reformation,* xxvi, xxxi, 863-64, and Littell, "The Importance of Anabaptist Studies," *Archiv Fur Reformationsgeschichte,* 58 (1967): 17.

59. See Fritz Blanke, "Anabaptism and the Reformation," 67-68, and J. Lawrence Burkholder, "The Anabaptist Vision of Discipleship," 136-37 in Hersheberger, ed., *The Recovery of the Anabaptist Vision.* See also A. G. Dickens and John Tonkin, "Rediscovered Dimensions: The Reformation Radicals." *The Reformation in Historical Thought* (Cambridge, Mass.: Harvard University Press, 1985), 221-27.

60. See John H. Yoder, "The Prophetic Dissent of the Anabaptists," 97, and J. D. Graber, "Anabaptism Expressed in Missions and Social Service," 154, in Hershberger, ed., *Recovery of the Anabaptist Vision.* Littell in *The Anabaptist View of the Church,* 32, wrote: "The gathering of small congregations by believers' baptism went on apace, and Anabaptism spread in many areas closed to the state Churches by their acceptance of the principle of territorialism. The Anabaptists represent thereby an early Protestant vision of a world mission unrestricted by territorial limitations, and in a unique fashion foreshadow the later concept of the Church as a community of missionary people."

16
Anabaptist Views of the Church

by John J. Kiwiet

The twentieth century may well become known as the golden age of movements for emancipation and freedom. Such movements have been characteristic for the "First World" as well as for the "Second" and the "Third." In the First World we witnessed the civil-rights movement followed by the women's liberation movement and by a series of smaller emancipation movements. The Second World's search for freedom brought about such events as the Chinese student protest in Tiananmen Square and the removal by Germans of the Berlin Wall on November 9, 1989. The Third World in Africa and Latin America is still in its agonizing birth pangs searching for some form of economic-political coexistence of races and levels of society.

Rediscovery

This same century witnessed the discovery of the Anabaptist freedom movement. Its discovery in the 1880s happened somewhat accidentally by a romantic archivist in Berlin, Ludwig Keller.[1] He was of the opinion that the genuine Christian movement had been a semisecret society from its very beginning. A German sociologist followed up on this discovery by creating a sociological scheme in Hegelian fashion calling for a sectarian church in continuous tension with the established church. The synthesis of such a polarity was for him the mature individualist movements practicing a spiritualist or mystic religion. This sociologist, Ernst Troeltsch, published his best-known book in 1923 under the title: *The Social Teachings of the Christian Church.*[2] The rediscovery of the widespread Anabaptist movement fits appropriately the pattern of the twentieth century. It was a genuine civil-rights movement claiming freedom of expression and a life-style whose only fault was, according to Fritz Blanke, that it came too early.[3] Its claims upset political as well as religious authorities of the day. It suggested a social structure which in its nonconformist approach could not adjust to traditional agricultural or urban life-styles. Yet, thousands of men and women felt attracted to this movement, attempting to escape from the bondage of the medieval feudal society. These men and women chose to be burned or drowned than surrender their right to freedom. About 1200 persons are listed by name in the *Martyrs Mirror*, and a good number of their moving testimonies have been recorded for us in that same collection.[4] One of those martyrs was Weynken of Monickendam, who courageously refused a priest as her confessor in the moment of execution. "I have Christ, to whom I confess; nevertheless if I have offended any, I would willingly ask them to forgive me."[5]

Today these martyr stories are still recounted by Amish and Hutterite communities. The American Mennonites feel part of the same freedom movement of the sixteenth century. One of their scholars, Harold S. Bender, used the opportunity provided by Keller and Troeltsch to start Anabaptist research and to publish its results in the *Mennonite Quarterly Review.* Bender's doctoral thesis of 1925 was published in 1950 under the title: *Conrad Grebel, Founder of the Swiss Brethren.*[6] Soon a host of non-Mennonite scholars joined the campaign for the reestablishment of the Anabaptist movement. One of the pioneers was the Methodist scholar Franklin H. Littell, who introduced the term "Free Church" as a term of rehabilitation of this once-rejected and despised movement.[7] Harry Emerson Fosdick had already claimed that the demand for freedom was the essential characteristic of the Anabaptist men and women, who wanted "a voluntary, purified church of believers only . . . and complete freedom of worship."[8]

Context

This search for freedom had been unleashed by Luther when in the late summer of 1520 he waged his frontal attack on the power of Rome. During this crucial period Luther published his three "Reformation Treatises," as they became known.[9] Each of these treatises claimed the freedom to which a Christian is justly entitled. In the first treatise, "To the Christian Nobility," Luther enunciates the concept of the priesthood of all believers. In the second document on "The Babylonian Captivity of the Church" all seven sacraments are described as chains keeping the Christian in bondage to the clergy and ultimately to the Pope. Then finally in his concluding treatise, "On the Freedom of a Christian," Luther proclaims: "A Christian is a perfectly free Lord of all, subject to none." To this he added, however: "A Christian is a perfectly dutiful servant of all, subject to all." Thus the word *freedom* and its opposite *captivity* were the predominating axioms of the era.[10]

The sixteenth century was deeply influenced by the Dutch Reformer, Desiderius Erasmus. His *Praise of Folly* (1509) became the first best-seller since the discovery of the art of printing. In his equally popular book, *The Hand-*

book of a Christian Soldier, Erasmus asserts that the emancipation of humankind is based on personal knowledge of the Scriptures rather than giving lip service to the interpretation of priests and theologians. He argues from the Scriptures "that we should always be armed by prayer and with knowledge. . . . Prayer, indeed, makes intercession, but knowledge suggests what ought to be prayed for."[11]

The availability of the printed word created an atmosphere in which sixteenth-century men and women had the opportunity for emancipation from medieval oppression. They no longer needed the troubadours, the priests, and the traveling preachers as their intermediaries. They could read and express their aspirations and joy in their own hymns of faith. Moreover, the society had shifted from a feudal to an urban society where thrifty citizens lived a better life than many a nobleman in the past. The emerging Dutch art of the following generations reveals the emancipated person. There are no serfs and no kings in the paintings, neither are there angels or demons. The focus of attention is the common man and woman claiming the right of knowledge, initiative, recreation, and wit.

It is significant to see this wide backdrop of the stage on which the Anabaptist movement played its role. It explains the enormous variety of ideals and methods leading to that great number of Anabaptist groups, all wanting to reestablish the New Testament church. Several of these were therefore mutually exclusive in their teachings and attitude. The first Anabaptist document, written by the Swiss Brethren gathered in Schleitheim, was directed against the "Free Brethren" of Southern Germany.[12] The followers of Balthasar Hübmaier rejected the eschatological movements of Hans Hut as well as the communitarian movement of Jacob Hutter. The Mennonites attempted to undo the bad consequences of the Hofmannite apocalyptic interpretation of the Scriptures. All this speaks of the application of the principle of free expression in religious and social aspects of life. It is for this reason that the Harvard church historian, George H. Williams, saw the Anabaptist movement as one strand of the widespread "Radical Reformation."[13]

The common denominator for all these groups, including the Anabaptists, was the restitution of the New Testament church. The emancipation of the common person was seen as a corollary of the advent of the kingdom of God. For the most radical groups this advent was experienced in chiliastic dimensions, when the sword would be given to the common man and the rulers would be defeated forever. The moderate groups strongly resisted such ramifications of the restitution of the church as is evidenced by Grebel's letter to Thomas Müntzer.[14] Both radicals and moderates, however, believed in the restitution of the kingdom at large and of the congregation on a local level.

The symbol for participating in this restitution was believer's baptism. The earliest group performing this ordinance was the group in Zurich. The Hutterian Chronicles attempt to render the atmosphere of fear and trepidation:

> One day when they were meeting, fear came over them and struck their hearts. They fell on their knees before the almighty God in heaven and called upon him who knows all hearts. They prayed that God grant it to them to do his divine will and that he might have mercy on them. Neither flesh and blood nor human wisdom compelled them. They were well aware of what they would have to suffer for this.[15]

If this represents the first manifestation of the exercise of freedom we can qualify it as purely an act of religious freedom. The Swiss Brethren wanted to reestablish the ordinances without recourse to the established church and its leaders. If the priesthood of believers had any meaning at all, it would mean that purely religious acts could be enacted without recourse to outside religious or secular authorities. Bender points to the initial discussion in the fall of 1523 concerning the right to reform the ordinance of communion. He describes how Hübmaier and Grebel argued for an autonomous reform by the Christian community while Zwingli expected the city council to take the initiative.[16] It is clear that the Swiss Brethren claimed religious freedom, or the autonomy of the local church, as it was called later on.

The Swiss Brethren drew up their first confessional statement in 1527. They emphatically affirmed that they were free from the "popisch and repopisch works." Every believer was considered to be "freed from the servitude of the flesh and to be fitted for the service of God." All baptized believers belonged to "the perfection of Christ." No longer was the distinction between clergy and laity valid.[17] It was for this religious freedom that one of their first leaders, Felix Mantz, was drowned on January 5, 1527. He died uttering the words of so many martyrs before him: "Lord, in Thy hands I commit my spirit!"[18]

Implications

According to Bender the Anabaptist movement concluded at this point. The search for freedom was merely a quest for religious emancipation; there was no social or political dissatisfaction; they merely wanted to reestablish a New Testament church.[19] Very soon, however, other aspects of freedom made themselves felt. The peasants had proclaimed the equality of all citizens under God. One of their leaders, Hans Hut, had recanted the chiliastic foundation for such a freedom.[20] He gave up the use of force in introducing the eschatological kingdom of David coming down for the truly reborn believers. Hut did not give up, however, the genuine desire for economic

equality and the freedom to achieve this. It is for this reason that he established the community of goods in 1528, challenging each of the believers to
share all private belongings with the group.

When this first deed of sharing developed into a commune under the leadership of Jacob Hutter and later of Peter Riedeman and Peter Walpot, new
theological crystallization followed. The distinction between the old and the
new covenant was especially relevant for the economic implications of the
gospel. The eschatological dimension had become a sort of realized eschatology. The Hutterite leaders were stewards rather than bishops, and the
membership was daily involved in the realm of the kingdom rather than
merely on Sundays.

Thus the essence of the Anabaptist concept of the church had been extended from a purely religious exercise of freedom to include the socioeco-
nomic dimension as well. Few other Anabaptist groups became communal,
but all were characterized by a sober and thrifty life-style. By far the most of
them were involved in manual or agricultural labor, which meant a rural
life-style rather than an urban way of life. This sociological development
was based on the principle of the two kingdoms as it already had been expressed in the Schleitheim Articles. In the fourth article we read:

> For truly, all creatures are in but two classes, good and bad, believing and
> unbelieving, darkness and light, the world and those who have come out of the
> world, God's temple and idols, Christ and Belial, and none can have part with
> the other.[21]

Robert Friedmann observes that such a kingdom theology requires "a
close brotherhood of committed disciples as the citizens of the expected
kingdom."[22] There is an eschatological dualism between the children of this
world and the children of light. The sociological result of this dualism is that
the Anabaptists have mostly led a life of separation. This is in contrast to
Luther, who also had a two-kingdom theory. For him, however, each citizen participates in both kingdoms. There are two modes of divine rule. The
government rules through the God-given natural law, while the church
gives leadership to society through the divine law of the gospel. For Luther
there was an order of protection as well as an order of redemption in the
Christian society.[23]

Thus the Anabaptist concept of the church automatically led to a sociological withdrawal which evidenced itself in the Hutterite communes as well
as in the Amish communities. Also the more urban Mennonites basically
lived in small towns, thereby avoiding a deep involvement in modern indus-
trial society. The principles of nonconformity and nonresistance are a natural consequence of this sociological dualism. This outlook on life was also

one of the reasons that Thomas Helwys, one of the leaders of the later General Baptists, could not cooperate with the Mennonites in Amsterdam.[24]

The Baptists were closer to Luther's view of a mutual interaction between church and state, even though they did maintain a strict separation between the two realms. John Smyth maintained, "[t]hat the magistrate is not by virtue of his office to meddle with religion, or matters of conscience but . . . to handle only civil transgressions (Rom. XIII), injuries and wrongs of man against man, in murder, adultery, theft, etc. . . . "[25]

The different sociological stance between Baptists and Mennonites can also be observed in the early beginnings of the Anabaptist movement. Initially Balthasar Hübmaier worked closely with the Zurich Brethren. They agreed on issues of the reform of the Mass and baptism by the church rather than by the government. Yet when the Brethren were expelled from Zurich in January 1525, their relation with Hübmaier became strained. While they became exiles worshiping in secret, Hübmaier remained in charge of the town's church in Waldshut. The different role in society caused a different theological viewpoint. While the Swiss Brethren moved into the direction of a Separatist way of life, Hübmaier increasingly aimed for a reformationist stance. In the terms of Richard Niebuhr, the Swiss Brethren experienced a "Christ against culture," while Hübmaier attempted to introduce a "Christ transforming culture."[26]

Torsten Bergsten has described clearly Hübmaier's positive attitude toward civil authority, military service, and participation in public life.[27] Also the concept of baptism carried an additional implication, namely the willingness to be subjected to church discipline.[28] Finally Hübmaier's emphasis on the priority of the proclamation of the Word enhanced the role of the pastor in church and community.[29] While both the Swiss Brethren and Hübmaier rejected the civil stance of Zwingli, their different social situation propelled them in opposite directions. This attitude was shared to a certain degree by Hans Denck and Pilgram Marbeck.[30] While martyrdom was a virtue for the separatists in their tension with culture, Hübmaier, Denck, and Marbeck were no heroic martyrs and never mention it as a form of Christian discipleship.

One aspect of Hübmaier's conversionist approach was his desire for harmony with the civil authorities as well as with his fellow Reformers. He attempted to be reconciled to Zwingli after his escape from Waldshut. Only when he realized he could not come to an agreement with Zwingli did he break relations with him. Hübmaier's desire for order is also reflected in his attempt to involve the local leaders. He sought the support of Leonhard of Leichtenstein in Nikolsburg not because he wanted to create a state church, but because he aimed for order and peace.

Freedom

The Reformation era held forth the promise of freedom for nations and cities as well as for church leaders, citizens, and peasants. This promise emerged from the gospel promise, "The truth will set you free."[31] The application of this truth turned out to be widely divergent, however. Among the magisterial reformers there was just as much difference as among the radical reformers. Even within the narrower scope of the Anabaptists, the reach for freedom caused friction and misunderstanding. The group which made freedom and love the hallmark of its fellowship was most vehemently assailed by the Swiss Brethren. It was against this group, the Southern Germans, that the Schleitheim Articles were formulated.[32] The articles state that these "false brethren" have created a great offense with destructive consequences:

> It is also apparent with what cunning the devil has turned us aside, so that he might destroy and bring to an end the work of God which in mercy and grace has been partly begun in us . . . . But such have missed the truth, and to their condemnation are given over to the lasciviousness and self-indulgence of the flesh. They think faith and love may do and permit everything, and nothing will harm them nor condemn them, since they are believers.[33]

The two most influential leaders among the Southern Germans were Hans Denck and Pilgram Marbeck.[34] Both men were committed to a theology of freedom. They tried to keep a balance between the literalism of the Swiss Brethren and the libertinism of certain spiritualist groups. They were consistently involved in applying the tension between letter and spirit, between external and internal realities, to each aspect of the Christian life. Not only the letter of the Scriptures but also baptism, the Lord's Supper, preaching, and discipline have validity only when exercised and received in the power of the Spirit.

Marbeck related this dialectic of letter and spirit to the incarnate reality of the divine Christ. The reality of the new covenant is therefore both visible in its congregational order and invisible in its convenantal fellowship. Marbeck loved to quote Romans 10:9 in connection with the profession of faith of a genuine Christian.[35] The apostle Paul stresses both the audible confession with our lips as well as the intangible believing in our heart. This coordination of external and internal reality was for Denck as well as Marbeck the "order of God."[36]

With this incarnational criterion the Southern Germans or the Covenantal Brethren could first of all reject the sacramentalism of Rome as well as its lingering traces among the Lutherans. On the other hand they found here a platform against a variety of mystic and Spiritualist groups which did not seriously practice the external ordinances of our Lord. The Covenanters would agree with the Spiritualists that mere church membership has no value but at the same time they would reject their mere spiritual fellowship.

A crucial text for Zwingli, Hübmaier, and Marbeck was 1 Peter 3:21 as Luther translated it. Baptism as the *epiklesis* upon God for a clear conscience was rendered by Luther as "the covenant with God for a clear conscience."[37] Baptism testified for Marbeck to the reciprocal or bilateral covenant between God and humans. The covenant was not a decree about our eternal destiny; it rather makes for a free response to the offer of an omnipotent God. This Almighty God descended to our order of existence in the incarnate Christ. It is for this reason that humankind is really free.

This bipolar or contractual covenantal theory was adopted also by William Tyndale who lived in exile in the Rhineland area during the late 1520s.[38] Through his translation of the New Testament and its accompanying apparatus, he strongly recommended the covenantal hermeneutic as the key to understanding God's revelation in Christ. "The right way, yea, and the only way, to understand the scripture unto salvation," declared Tyndale, is to seek in it, "chiefly and above all, the covenants made between God and us."[39] Similar to Marbeck, he affirmed that any time the Scripture refers to a promise it also implies one of its covenants.[40]

Tyndale's tracts and Bible translation had a great impact upon the early stirrings of a Reformation in England.[41] However, soon he was overshadowed by John Hooper, who had lived in exile in Zurich under the tutelage of Heinrich Bullinger, the successor of Zwingli.[42] Along two lines Bullinger tried to complete the work of his predecessor: first by establishing a strong unilateral covenantal theology, and second by writing a tendentious history of the Anabaptist movement.[43]

Both efforts were rather damaging. The Anabaptist movement was, since Bullinger's work on its origins, indeed, considered as a mere fanatic eruption of the lower classes. Bullinger's theological contention of a unilateral covenant, an eternal decree by the Almighty, led to ruinous debates on predestination and limited atonement. Since Calvin and Beza joined him in this effort, the hopeful search for freedom ended up in a new establishment. It took two world wars to demonstrate that the time for the established church was finally over and that the time had come for a gathered church, a free church, depending only on the commitment of its members rather than on the power of the state.

Conclusion

The twentieth century may be the age of freedom movements, but we have yet to demonstrate that we have gained deeper insight than our forbears into the nature and structure of the church. Thus far the strongest movements among the evangelical churches have been fundamentalism and the charismatic movement. While the former has focused on the letter, the latter has opened itself up to the Spirit. If the Southern Germans are allowed to be our guide, we would welcome both the letter of the Bible and the Spirit of Christ in a constant interaction. The freedom of the Spirit needs the discipline of the Word.

During the Reformation the church became a redemptive agency in spite of all its oppression and failures. All Western nations received a Bible translation in their own tongue; each government has become more or less democratic; most citizens are receiving a basic education enabling them to be socially mobile; a great variety of denominations are free to spread the gospel not only in this hemisphere but all over the world. The list of redemptive events in the widest sense of the word could be extended much further. The challenge presented to us by our forbears is, however, simply to make one aspect of the Lord's Prayer our own again:

OUR FATHER . . . THY KINGDOM COME . . . ON EARTH AS IT IS IN HEAVEN.

Notes

1. Ludwig Keller, *Die Reformation und die älteren Reformparteien* (Leipzig: 1885).

2. Ernst Troeltsch, *The Social Teaching of the Christian Churches*, 2 vols. (New York: Harper, 1931; German ed. 1923).

3. Fritz Blanke, *Brothers in Christ* (Scottdale, Pa.: Herald Press, 1961, 71; German ed. 1955).

4. Thieleman J. van Braght, *The Bloody Theater or Martyrs Mirror*, 5th ed. (Scottdale, Pa.: Herald Press, 1950), 1145-49; original Dutch ed. 1660.

5. Van Braght, 422.

6. Harold S. Bender, *Conrad Grebel, Founder of the Swiss Brethren* (Goshen, Ind.: Mennonite Historical Society, 1950).

7. Franklin Littell, *The Free Church* (Boston: Star King Press, 1954); Donald F. Durnbaugh discusses the ambivalence of this term quoting at least five definitions; so also Winthrop S. Hudson; see Donald F. Durnbaugh, *The Believers' Church* (New York: Macmillian, 1968).

8. Harry E. Fosdick, ed., *Great Voices of the Reformation* (New York: Random House, 1952), 281.

9. For a current translation of these writings see: Martin Luther, *Three Treatises* (Philadelphia: Fortress Press, 1970).

10. Ibid., 277.

11. Raymond Himelick, transl., *The Enchiridion of Erasmus* (Bloomington, Ind.: Indiana University Press, 1939); quotes from 85 and 47.

12. For a translation of this text, see William L. Lumpkin, ed., *Baptist Confessions of Faith* (Philadelphia: Judson Press, 1959), 22-31.

13. George Williams, *The Radical Reformation* (Philadelphia: Westminster Press), 1962.

14. Published in Leonhard von Muralt, *Quellen zur Geschichte der Täufer in der Schweiz* (Zurich: Hirzel Verlag, 1952), 13-21.

15. *The Chronicle of the Hutterian Brethren,* trans. and ed. the Hutterian Brethren (Rifton, N.Y.: Plough Publishing House, 1987), 1:45.

16. Bender, 92.

17. John H. Yoder, *The Legacy of Michael Sattler* (Scottdale, Pa.: Herald Press, 1973), 38.

18. Felix Mantz, *Leben und Sterben des Zürcher Täuferführers* (Kassel: J. G. Oncken Verlag, 1957), 148.

19. Stayer argues for a stronger awareness of socio-eonomic issues in the Zurich area as well as in Southern Germany. The issue of the church tax occurs as a major grievance among the radical followers of Zwingli as well as in the "Twelve Articles" formulated by the peasants. See James M. Stayer, "Die Anfänge des schweizerischen Täufertums," in Hans-Jürgen Goertz, *Umstrittenes Täufertum* (Gottingen: Vandenhoeck & Ruprecht, 1975), 27-28.

20. John J. Kiwiet, *Pilgram Marbeck* (Kassel: Oncken Verlag, 1955), 43.

21. Lumpkin, 26.

22. Robert Friedmann, *The Theology of Anabaptism* (Scottdale, Pa.: Herald Press, 1973), 41.

23. For a discussion see Clarence Bauman, "The Theology of 'The Two Kingdoms' " in the *Mennonite Quarterly Review* (1964): 37-49.

24. Joh. Bakker, *John Smyth* (Wageningen: Veenman, 1964), 84-85.

25. Lumpkin, 170.

26. H. Richard Neibuhr, *Christ and Culture* (New York: Harper, 1951).

27. Torsten Bergsten, *Balthasar Hubmaier* (Valley Forge, Pa.: Judson Press, 1978), 371.

28. Christof Windhorst, *Täuferisches Taufverständnis* (Leiden: E. J. Brill, 1976), 75.

29. Ibid., 58, 70, 88.

30. Kiwiet, 117-18.

31. John 8:32.

32. Kiwiet, 44-45.

33. Lumpkin, 24.

34. John J. Kiwiet, "The Life of Hans Denck" and "The Theology of Hans Denck," in *Mennonite Quarterly Review,* vols. XXXI and XXXII.

35. Kiwiet, *Marbeck,* 112-14.

36. Kiwiet, *Marbeck,* 84-87.

37. Roland Armour, *Anabaptist Baptism* (Scottdale, Pa.: Herald Press, 1966), 31-33, 118-20.

38. William R. Estep, *Renaissance and Reformation* (Grand Rapids, Mich.: Wm. B. Eerdmans, 1986), 251.

39. Michael McGiffert, "William Tyndale's Conception of Covenant," *Journal of Ecclesiastical History,* vol. 32, 167.

40. Jens G. Moller, "The Beginnings of Puritan Covenant Theology," *Journal of Ecclesiastical History,* vol. 14, 52-53. Armour, 113-15.

41. L. J. Trinterud, "The Origins of Puritanism," *Church History,* Vol. 20, 43-44.

42. W. M. West, "John Hooper and the Origins of Puritanism," *Baptist Quarterly,* Vol. 15, 347.

43. J. W. Baker, *Heinrich Bullinger and the Covenant* (Athens, Ohio: University Press, 1980), 300. Heinrich Bullinger, *Der Widertöufferen Ursprung, fürgang, sekten* (Zurich: Froschauer, 1561).

17

The Relation of Baptists to Other Churches

by William L. Pitts

Introduction

One of the most significant developments in twentieth-century Christianity has been the emergence of a quest to overcome church division and to effect Christian unity. This movement is commonly termed the ecumenical movement. It has many meanings and takes many forms including cooperation at the personal and local level (community relief, joint worship, etc.), formal dialogues, cooperation through councils of churches, and mergers.

The focus of this study is institutional. How have Baptists as denominational groups related to other Christians? Many Baptists are involved in practical cooperation with other Christians. Few have experienced actual mergers with other denominations. For Baptists in the 1980s cooperation has focused especially on bilateral dialogues with other Christians, on discussions of infant baptism/believer's baptism, and on continuing cooperation through councils of churches.

Baptists have engaged in formal dialogue with other denominations moreactively in the 1980s than at any other time in their history. Both the Baptist World Alliance (BWA) and individual denominations have sponsored discussions. Attention has been focused especially on Lutheran and Roman Catholic dialogues.

One of the most significant developments in the ecumenical discussion of the 1980s is the enormous interest generated by the document "Baptism, Eucharist and Ministry" (BEM). It has pushed ecumenical discussion to a new level. Because it addresses baptism directly and because it has sought seriously to engage Baptist discussion, this document has received much attention by Baptists as well as by others. Baptism, Eucharist, and ministry are core doctrines and historic sources of division rather than of unity. Hence the Commission on Faith and Order of the World Council of Churches produced position documents (1982) which were to be sent to members of the World Council of Churches and to others for their candid response. Already the responses of six Baptist groups have been published.[1]

The issue of baptism was addressed by a significant consultation on believer's baptism held at Southern Seminary in 1979, sponsored by the Faith and Order Commission of the World Council of Churches. It was the first time paedo-Baptists and believer-Baptists gathered to examine the two traditions. Stephen Crawford noted that the acts of infant and believer's baptism are dramatically different and so are the understandings behind them.[2] In seeking agreement on the issue of baptism, Faith and Order recognized that the most difficult problems rested with the Baptists. Hence the consultation and the choice of site.

Among Southern Baptists few people have devoted more effort to Baptist relations with other Christians than has James Leo Garrett, Jr. Because of the vast scope of the topic of ecumenism, the contents of this paper must be selective. This essay is organized around three principal interests: (1) Baptists and the Believers' Church, (2) Baptists around the world relating to others, (3) Baptists and Catholics. To provide further focus emphasis falls on the past ten years—the decade of the 1980s.

Baptists and the Believers' Church

One major area of Garrett's ecumenical concern has been the relationship of Baptists to other members of the Believers' Church or Free Church. The phrase "Free Church" began to be used in England in the nineteenth century as a new and more positive term for Dissenters or Nonconformists. "Free Churchmen" began to be widely used as early as the 1850s, and in 1896 the Baptists, Congregationalists, Methodists, and Presbyterians formed the National Free Church Council.[3] In the United States Franklin Littell popularized the term in *The Free Church* (1957) and linked it closely to his Continental Anabaptist studies. He stressed traditions of laity, voluntarism, ethical concern, and missionary zeal.[4]

Max Weber coined the phrase "Believers' Church," but the terminology was popularized by a conference held at The Southern Baptist Theological Seminary in 1967 and by the publication of its proceedings.[5] Donald Durnbaugh has done much to make the concept intelligible.[6] Key ideas of the Free Church/Believers' Church include voluntary commitment, church discipline, authority of the Bible rather than of hierarchy or creed, missions, religious liberty guaranteed by separation of church and state, and the idea of the fall of the church and need for restitution.

Groups commonly placed in this ecclesiastical family include Mennonites, Baptists, Church of the Brethren, Quakers, Methodists, Moravians, and Disciples of Christ. There are clearly differences among these denominations, and their identities remain intact. Yet there are sufficient similarities for these groups to see themselves collectively as an alternative to more clearly identified traditions such as Reformed, Lutheran, Anglican, Catholic, and Orthodox.

If these groups comprise an ecclesiastical family, the Believers' Church becomes a natural forum for ecumenical dialogue. Participants can discuss common interests and make their combined contribution to the larger world church. John Briggs wrote that Baptists would be more effective in the ecumenical movement if they worked in closer harmony with "our closest cousins . . . the Believers' Church."[7]

Garrett rightly noted that "the use of the term Believers' Church is an effort to fashion an instrument of identification."[8] In the first conference, participants affirmed a common heritage and explored issues in terms of their history, theology, and contemporary relevance. So began the establishment of a very significant tradition for Baptist relations with others in the last third of the twentieth century. The conferences have continued to be held at approximately three-year intervals. The most recent was held in 1989 in Fort Worth, Texas, to celebrate the English translation of the works of Balthasar Hübmaier.

Baptist Relations with Other Christians: Models of Major Baptist Groups

Garrett was appointed by Josef Nordenburg in 1968 to chair the Baptist World Alliance Commission on Cooperative Christianity. The product of their work was an informative collection of essays called *Baptist Relations with Other Christians*.[9] Garrett edited the volume and provided a preface and an epilogue. Here he contributes to a second circle of ecumenical interest. His world vision of Baptists is clear. The perspective is extremely useful. It shows how important are context and tradition in the shaping of the thought and practice of different Baptist groups.

There is not space here for a comprehensive survey, but brief examination illustrates a variety of levels of contact with other Christians by Baptists in the United States (American Baptists, three Afro-American Baptist denominations, Southern Baptists), Brazil, the USSR, and India. These four nations and eight denominations are chosen because they represent the largest Baptist groups in the world, each having at least one-half million members.

The "Policy Statement on Christian Unity" is the key document in understanding the position of the American Baptist Convention, U.S.A., regarding relationships with other denominations. The document was adopted in 1967, prompted by the 450th anniversary of the Protestant Reformation, and reaffirmed in 1978.[10] The document comments on the fact of greater openness of Christians toward one another and affirms the value of learning from one another. On the one hand, Baptists can share their heritage of religious freedom, priesthood of the believer, and believer's baptism. On the other hand, "we recognize and are grateful for the particular witness of these other Christians who have had profound influence on our understanding of the Gospel."[11] Thus there is a clear understanding of a wider Christian community and the value of exchange of ideas from various traditions.

The statement affirms the importance of relating to other Baptists and to members of the free church tradition. However, these cooperative ventures are not as significant as relationships with the wider world church.

> Any position which we take on unity involving other Baptist groups must not compromise our position concerning the whole church and our determination to be a part of the trend toward Christian unity which is the "great new fact of this century."[12]

The document concludes that the mission of the church is to convey God's redemptive love in the world. The quest for unity among Christians is not an end in itself, but a means for the mission of God's redemption.[13] The convention's posture on unity was reaffirmed in the "Statement of Purpose of the American Baptist Churches in the U.S.A.," adopted in May, 1969.[14] Unity is a prominent issue in this major denominantional policy document.

American Baptists are eager to point out their affiliation with and support of conciliar ecumenism. They were charter members of both the National Council of Churches (1950) and the World Council of Churches (1948). They were well represented at the meeting of the World Council of Churches in Vancouver in 1983, and will be actively involved again in 1991. In short, the American Baptist Convention's commitment to conciliar ecumenism has remained strong. The denomination also decided to become an official observer in the National Association of Evangelicals, the major umbrella group of some eight conservative denominations.[15]

Baptist historian Robert Torbet called the Council on Church Union (COCU) the "boldest attempt" at church union in the course of the ecumenical movement.[16] The effort generated tremendous enthusiasm in the 1960s, but faltered. (New strategies—which leave denominational identities intact—have given COCU new life in the 1980s.) American Baptists were about evenly divided over COCU. In order to avoid dissension within the denomination, the Committee on Church Unity led the denomination to decline full participation and to adopt observer status.[17] The American Baptist Convention, U.S.A., was prepared for conciliar but not unitive Protestantism. Prompted by the BEM document, Mark Heim finds a deep reluctance on the part of the American Baptist Convention to respond to significant new appeals for unity.[18] The 1985 American Baptist Convention response to BEM is, in fact, cautiously worded. The General Board expressed gratitude that traditional Baptist emphases were more fully acknowledged in these documents than in previous proposals, but it also offered criticism for positions traditionally divergent from its own.[19]

In summary, the American Baptist Convention continues to live with the dilemma thoughtfully articulated by Robert Torbet in 1968: the ecumenical movement has called for greater unity with other Christians, but it has made them more self-conscious of their own distinctive doctrines.[20] This tension remains and is evident in the literature of the American Baptist Convention as the denomination enters the 1990s.

The three major Afro-American Baptist denominations in the U.S.A. are the National Baptist Convention, U.S.A., Inc., the National Baptist Convention of America, and the Progressive National Baptist Convention, Inc. Combined they represent about eleven million people. All three are members of the National Council of Churches in the U.S.A. and the World Council of Churches.

Deotis Roberts suggests that the major reason for their involvement in the World Council of Churches is their overriding quest for social justice. This is the most significant issue facing these denominations.[21] All three Afro-American conventions were drawn to the Council's stand on humanitarism and its effort to work for freedom and justice for all. They are also interested in cooperative educational efforts and mission, but issues of faith and order are secondary to their quest for human freedom.[22] The message of this 30 percent of Baptists in the world to fellow Christians is the message of Amos—a call for justice.

The Richmond Consultation (1984) produced an important document representing Afro-American concerns. It is organized around the traditional marks of the true church: unity, holiness, catholicity, and apostolicity. The document cries out against injustice perpetrated by white churches, and affirms that the church can never be one and holy apart from justice and liberation.[23] Specifically, racism, sexism, classism, and economic injustice must be addressed by those within the church who possess power to bring about change.[24]

Four of the thirty-two member denominations of the NCCC are Baptist; of the forty-two million Christians represented, over twelve million are Baptist. Current Baptist participation in conciliar Christianity is substantial.

Southern Baptists have generally been viewed as antiecumenical. They have rejected membership in both the World Council of Churches and the National Association of Evangelicals, and have opted instead for denominationalism. A central issue raised is why Southern Baptists have chosen not to become involved in conciliar work. Landmark teaching suggests that Baptists alone form true churches. Even where that notion has not persisted, the idea that the church is primarily local works against support of councils.[25] In addition, Southern Baptists have argued that the Baptist witness is distinctive, that the Convention cannot speak for local churches, that they should not join an organization over which they have no control, and that they should be fully free to organize their own missions and evangelism.[26] The isolation was perhaps enhanced by Southern regionalism. The irenic initiative of T. T. Eaton in the first two decades of the century was defeated by the isolationist position of J. B. Gambrell who thought energy should be confined to local churches and in denominational channels.[27] This position has prevailed throughout most of the twentieth century and is reflected in the two confessions adopted by Southern Baptists, which recognize other Christians but speak in terms of a "spiritual harmony"with them.

In the mid-1960s Southern Baptists began new ecumenical initiatives. Wayne Dehoney's 1965 presidential address, while affirming Baptist distinctives, urged the Convention to seek broader channels of communication and cooperation.[28] The Believers' Conference was the first ecumenical conference sponsored by an agency of the Southern Baptist Convention.[29]

Moreover, serious scholarship turned to the issue of Baptists and unity.[30] The Department of Interfaith Witness of the Home Mission Board took the initiative in relating Southern Baptists to other denominations. In the 1970s it arranged dialogues with other denominations—including regional conferences with Roman Catholic, Orthodox, and Lutheran bodies.[31] These dialogues continued in the 1980s through discussions with all three denominations. N. M. Vaporis, reporting on the second meeting with the Greek Orthodox (1981), mentioned "an atmosphere of extreme friendliness and goodwill."[32] He noted that each learned from the other and that the greatest value was the great "surprise" in learning how much both have in common. Instead of the usual emphasis on differences, he urged the desirability of shifting the focus to the "common faith" which is the foundation of abiding friendship and cooperation for all Christians.[33]

"A Plan for Lutheran-Baptist Conversations" was created in 1977, and was subsequently accepted by the Lutheran Council in the U.S.A. (representing three denominations) and the North American Baptist Fellowship (the Regional Baptist World Alliance organization representing nine denominations). It was chaired by Lutheran Lawrence Folkemer and Southern Baptist Glen Igleheart. The purpose was to increase understanding through genuine dialogue. The meetings were held in 1979-81, and reported in 1982, anticipating celebration of the five-hundredth anniversary of Luther's birth.[34]

The study of baptism has a long history in the WCC.[35] The Faith and Order Commission urged in the late-1970s that it was time to consult with Baptists to explore the infant/adult baptism issue. The two positions were to be explored on equal terms. The purpose was to seek mutual recognition, not merely lay out differences once again.[36]

The Louisville statement summarizing the baptism discussions noted important signs of bridge-building between paedo-Baptist churches and Baptists. The summary indicated the following: (1) Baptism in the New Testament was adult baptism, but the value of infant baptism has long been recognized in Christian tradition; (2) Personal faith is nurtured by believing communities in both types of communion; (3) Both require responsible attitudes and concepts of the catechumenate; (4) The pressures of contextuality affect the form and reason for baptism; (5) Indiscriminate baptism and "rebaptism" should be rejected.[37]

The challenge, the report concluded, is for us to accept each other. To do this we must accept each other's baptism.[38] This conference provoked much dialogue, especially in Britain. Most of Christendom recognizes baptism of infants. Baptists do not. This is distinctive of the character of Baptists and a central reason for their separation from other Christians. It is important that the issue be discussed. The 1979 Louisville Conference was a significant landmark for Baptist/non-Baptist discussions.

Thus at the beginning of the 1980s, Southern Baptists moved to a new level of relationship with other Christians. They engaged in formal dialogues aimed at better mutual understanding of major denominations in the U. S., and they seriously examined with others one of the most difficult theological issues separating Baptists from others. Orthodox and Lutheran conversations were productive, but even more energy was poured into a remarkable ten-year dialogue with Roman Catholics.[39]

Baptists in Brazil have been reluctant to join conciliar bodies. In 1965 the ecumenical movement was represented by the Evangelical Confederation of Brazil, and in that year they invited Brazilian Baptists to join, but the Baptists declined the invitation and articulated their reasons for not joining.[40] They have been willing to cooperate on practical levels, but have shown little interest in conciliar ecumenism. The long experience of Catholic dominance has made Protestants in South America wary of cooperation with Catholics. Baptist success has been remarkable, and there is little need felt for uniting with others. Reports from Brazil in the 1980s publicized the growth of large churches, successful evangelism, and foreign mission work by Brazilians. Southern Baptists have done much to foster the Brazilian Baptist Convention—and to shape its posture toward other Christians.

Baptists in the USSR have been a tiny minority in a predominantly Russian Orthodox society. After the October Revolution all Christians were faced with the overwhelming issue of their relationship to the hostile state. In 1944 Baptists united with other evangelicals to form the All-Union Council of Evangelical Christians-Baptists (AUCECB); it was expanded by the addition of Pentecostals in 1945 and the Mennonite Brethren in 1963.

On the eve of the 1980s, Denton Lotz reported on the vitality of the AU-CECB—its intense worship, lay preachers, and 10,000 baptisms per year.[41] In the mid-1980s the AUCECB asserted, "We have been living and working within a united multinational and multiconfessional fellowship for forty years . . . but we have found out that unity of witness to Christ is possible."[42] They cited biblical imagery of branches of the vine and members of the body to illustrate their notion of Christian unity. The AUCECB is a member of the World Council of Churches, the Conference of European Churches, and the Christian Peace Conference movement. When asked to respond to the baptism, Eucharist, and ministry document the AUCECB offered little hope for visible unity and reported that the ecumenics which concerned them was not essentially doctrinal, but rather common practical tasks: Bible translation, peace-making, aid to the suffering, education in the spirit of religious toleration, and respect among all confessions.[43] The AUCECB has repeatedly restated its concern for basic human problems in the world: peace, justice, and disarmament.[44] The response to the BEM text demonstrated a sense of being part of a great family of Christians willing to "extend hospitality to people who believe in another way . . . for the sake of their witness to Christianity."[45]

Mikhail Gorbachev's political initiatives have had a profound impact on the world in the 1980s—most dramatically in Eastern Europe in 1989. Likewise his willingness to meet with John Paul II in December 1989 has tremendously important implications for the practice of religion in the USSR. New freedoms are already being exercised by dissidents without official approval. Roman Catholics have begun to worship according to their own rite. Baptists began publishing their own newspaper in six regional editions in 1989.[46] An era of diminished political pressure against organized religion places the AUCECB in a new position with many options: among them, to use its new freedoms to become more isolationist in order to give a "distinctive" witness; or to imitate Baptists in the West; or to continue its traditional witness of practical ecumenism.

The most notable effort at union among Baptists is to be found in the Church of North India (1970), where many Baptists have joined other denominations in a remarkable experiment.[47] Stephen Neill cites several reasons for the uniting tendency in Indian Christianity: nationalism, the emergence of able national leadership, financial problems, and need for unity in the midst of a vast Hindu population.[48]

As heirs of British Christianity, Indian Christians had two major obstacles to overcome in achieving unity: Anglican teaching concerning the ministry and Baptist teaching concerning baptism. The Church of South India was a major breakthrough in church union efforts because for the first time nonepiscopal and episcopal traditions combined in the formation of a new church. The Church of North India overcame the baptism obstacle, another first in the church union, and worldwide attention was drawn to Indian ecumenism.[49] Serious unity discussions for the Church of North India began in the 1920s; Baptists related to the British were more open than those which were products of American and Canadian mission efforts.[50] Although many Baptists went into the Church of North India, a larger number did not join the new church.[51] Some of the non-uniting Baptists have joined the World Council of Churches; others have refrained. Thus the situation regarding relations with other Christians is mixed for Baptists in India.

When the Church of North India was created, Baptists took the unprecedented step of uniting with other Protestants. The major significance of the merger for Baptists is that these Christians found a way to accommodate infant and believer's baptism. Both forms had to be recognized as a condition to genuine intercommunion. The will of these Indian Baptists to be one in Christ was even more powerful than the cherished notion of baptism of believers only. The bold union movements in India have had "an enormous effect on ecumenical thinking."[52] This union, now twenty years old, stands as a reminder and an example to Christians elsewhere of the possibility of actual union by Baptists with other Christians.

Garrett's 1974 summary of Baptist relations with other Christians identified three major patterns. His systematic classification is extremely useful.[53] Review of major Baptist denominations in relating to other Christians in the 1980s suggests patterns of (1) conciliar cooperation (2) nonconciliar relations, marked by increased dialogue, and rarely, (3) union with other denominations. This area of Garrett's work suggests the value of the Baptist World Alliance which Garrett has served so well: the Alliance is able to provide a transdenominational perspective and thereby broaden the understanding and vision of all Baptists.

Baptists and Roman Catholicism

Pre-Vatican Council II ecumenical literature written by Baptists is divided in its sentiment. Wendell Holmes Rone, in his 1952 study of Catholicism, says he writes "in no unkind spirit." But his disclaimer is canceled in his next sentence which declares that the book has been written "to expose the falsities of a vicious religious system."[54] In that same decade Garrett was already seeking to combat misunderstanding by explaining Catholic doctrine to a lay Baptist audience.[55] The John F. Kennedy Presidential campaign of 1960 generated terrific debate, but its result, and Will Herberg's *Protestant, Catholic, Jew*, demonstrated that pluralism in American religion was well on its way to recognition.[56]

The Second Vatican Council (1962-65) must be reckoned one of the major events in twentieth-century church history. It declared a new openness to other Christians (now called "separated brethren"), invited non-Catholic observers, and elicited positive responses from many quarters. Ecumenical reflection increased among Baptists in the 1960s; moreover, the tone of many publications was now positive.

In the mid-1960s Garrett produced a massive study of Protestant attitudes toward Catholics (1966). He thought that the study was important because "the Protestant-Roman Catholic confrontation" which has been important "for Christianity and for civilization during the past four and a half centuries [has the] prospect of being significantly altered in the present."[57] He defined the change as shift from "anti-Popery" to "dialogue."[58] In concluding his study of Protestant-Catholic relations Garrett described (1) issues removed or greatly ameliorated, (2) issues reassessed in a new orientation, and (3) issues unaltered and persisting major differences.[59] The paper provided useful analysis and basis for further dialogue between Protestants and Roman Catholics.

In the course of his work, Garrett published *Baptists and Roman Catholicism*, a booklet which classifies the literary exchanges between the two denominations under the major categories of polemic, evangelization, and dialogue.[60] Garrett also investigated changing attitudes abroad. He sent questionnaires to missionaries who indicated in response a noticeable increase in religious liberty between 1960 and 1966 in Catholic-dominated countries.[61] In the decade of the 1960s, Garrett averaged reviewing more than three books per year on Catholicism for Baptist readers. In 1972 he published studies of two leading Protestant theologians—Reinhold Niebuhr and John Mackay—and found a significant shift in both: Niebuhr calling for an end to scandalous Protestant-Catholic hatreds and Mackay addressing the need for renewal in both branches of the church.[62] Thus, Garrett's Catholic scholarship was intense and prolific during the decade following the opening of Vatican Council II.

Among Southern Baptist institutional structures the Home Mission Board has been the denominational agency most responsible for relations with other Christians. In 1965 the board established a Department of Work Related to Nonevangelicals. The name was changed to the Department of

Interfaith Witness in 1970. Hugo Culpepper said that the new task was to relate to leaders of other faiths in fellowship and dialogue, and to educate Southern Baptist leaders and people.[63] To that end many state and regional conferences for Baptist-Roman Catholic dialogue were organized in the 1970s.[64]

But perhaps the most hopeful and important event of the 1980s was the decade-long sustained series of dialogues between Southern Baptists and Roman Catholics. Sponsored by the Bishop's Committee for Ecumenism and Interreligious Affairs and the Interfaith Witness Department of the Home Mission Board, organizers planned for three series of dialogues to run roughly three years each. The idea for the conferences grew naturally out of the regional meetings.

The dialogue was designed as a starting point in conversation between the country's two largest denominations. They learned from each other and about each other. They wrote about "how important Jesus has been for us personally" and "the desire to join with one another as Jesus' disciples in prayer, in service to the world and in mission."[65] The dialogue proceeded by exploring significant doctrinal positions from the standpoint of each tradition. Dialogue in the context of a desire to learn from each other resulted in recognizing many specific points of agreement as well as articulating disagreements. This represents diligent work in relating to other Christians.

The first series of dialogues met April 1978 to November 1980. Organizers determined to publish the papers in order to reach a wider audience. They appeared in a 1982 issue of *Review and Expositor* and consist of seven pairs of articles, some followed by epilogues. Participants examined the history of each tradition and the following doctrines: Scripture; salvation; spirituality; church and ministry; evangelization, mission and social action; and eschatology.[66]

The second round of talks (April 1982 to December 1984) focused on the subject of grace: (1) Grace in General: definition, nature, reception, and mediation of grace, (2) Beginnings in Grace: becoming a Christian and the issue of baptism, (3) Growth in Grace: discipleship, the Lord's Supper/Eucharist and the Communion of Saints, and (4) Grace Outside the Church. These papers were published in the spring 1986 issue of the *Southwestern Journal of Theology*. Garrett provided the editorial introduction and the Southern Baptist article on baptism which he approached from a historical perspective.[67]

The third triennium of work was reported in *The Theological Educator*.[68] This volume, subtitled "To Understand Each Other: Roman Catholics and Southern Baptists," focuses especially on missions. In the third round of discussions Garrett contributed the article, "Understanding the Church: A

Southern Baptist Perspective."[69] He contrasted Roman Catholic emphasis on the universal church with Baptist emphasis on the local church, compared doctrines of the Holy Spirit, showed that both traditions used similar metaphors of the church (body, people of God), and concluded that both Roman Catholics and Baptists recognize the same basic functions of the church: worship, teaching, fellowship, service, and evangelization. Garrett identified two major differences: Catholic doctrine of the Petrine office affirms that authority is vested in the Pope. Baptists reject the notion, relying on a differing interpretation of Matthew 16:18. They also disagree on baptism. Baptists teach a sequence of preaching, hearing, profession of faith, and then baptism of those who declare their faith whereas Catholics accept infant baptism. Garrett's conclusion is, "Differences concerning the church? Yes, but there are significant and increasing agreements."[70]

Garrett and John Donahue wrote the first draft of agreements and differences on the major issues to summarize the ten years of conversations.[71] The draft was "reviewed and amended in plenary session;" participants acknowledged that real differences are apparent but reported having expressed "mutual understanding and respect along with love and friendship."[72] Issues summarized included Scripture, salvation, spirituality (spiritual life, Bible, differences regarding Mary and the saints, approaches to worship), and church and ministry (people of God, body of Christ, differences in ministers, the laity). Grace was discussed at length. Both agree on salvation by grace, but Roman Catholics emphasize the ecclesiastical dimension—grace mediated through the sacraments—while Southern Baptists emphasize the personal dimension—grace mediated through experience of repentance and faith. Baptism and Eucharist were addressed as was the issue of whether one may fall from grace through serious sin. Missions—proclaiming the gospel and making disciples—is understood as a central task of the church in both communions. Finally, they set forth their respective positions on eschatology.

The conferences were characterized by a high level of scholarly competence, candor in stating respective positions, and a great desire to accept one another as Christians. The dialogues produced three major publications in the course of the decade, comprising a substantial body of theological reflection. The conferences were scholar's dialogues. The range of their influence on the denomination was probably limited. Still, the dialogues are an important event—and precedent. Such dialogues were virtually inconceivable before Vatican Council II. Should conversations continue and should relations between the two move to other levels of cooperation, the impetus may well be traced in part to the understanding fostered by these conversations. At any rate the participants were optimistic: the editorial introduction to the first series suggests that the dialogue reflects "the spirit of this new era in ecumenical relations."[73]

A high percentage of Baptists are affiliated with the Baptist World Alliance. This organization has been actively engaged in promoting better relations with other denominations—particularly at the level of formal dialogues. It is especially well organized to engage in work at the international level. In recent years it has provided a forum for important discussions with major traditions such as the Reformed, Lutheran, and Roman Catholic Churches.[74]

The Roman Catholic-Baptist Colloquium moved to the international level for the first time in 1984.[75] The agenda was familiar: the principal object of the discussion was reciprocal knowledge of resemblances and differences between Baptists and Catholics. But the symbolic significance was apparent. Baptists were engaged in dialogue with others at a higher level than ever before. The conference continued to hold meetings to the end of the decade.

In November-December 1985 David Russell represented the Baptist World Alliance as an observer at the Extraordinary Synod of the Roman Catholic Church, held to commemorate the twentieth anniversary of the closing of Vatican Council II, to examine how the Council had been implemented, and to facilitate better application of its guidelines.[76] Russell, former general secretary of the Baptist Union of Great Britain and Ireland, concluded his report to fellow Baptists by saying that there are obviously great doctrinal and practical differences between Baptists and Catholics which must not be passed over, "but to engage in discussions of this kind in an irenic spirit . . . does not involve a betrayal of divine truth and faith."[77]

Conclusion

The relationship expressed by Baptists toward others may be positive, negative, or indifferent, but some sort of relationship with other Christians is inevitable. The issue is what the relationship should be and how it should be expressed. Heated debate characterized American Baptist Convention, U.S.A. participation in the NCCC and WCC. Approximately one fourth of the British Baptist Union opposed joining the new process in 1989, largely because Roman Catholics would be full participants, and the BWA statements deriving from dialogues with Roman Catholicism were sharply challenged in 1989. Nonetheless, Baptists have recently engaged in numerous serious attempts to create good relations with other Christians. Despite criticism many Baptist denominations have continued to work with other Christians through conciliar organizations. Conversation and dialogue are absolutely essential in promoting good will—whether between friends, family members, nations, or churches. Baptists intentionally organized theological exchange with other Protestants, with the Orthodox, and with Roman Catholics. Both conciliar activity and new levels of dialogue have been important features in the history of Baptist relations with other Christians during the past decade. Baptists are a long way from being one with other Christians, but they have made significant new steps in openness and dialogue in the 1980s.

Notes

1. Max Thurian, ed., *Churches Respond to BEM*, vols. 1 and 3 (Geneva: World Council of Churches, 1986 and 1987).

2. Stephen Cranford, "Preface" *Review and Expositor* 77 (Winter 1980): 5.

3. Donald F. Durnbaugh, "Free Church, Baptists, and Ecumenism: Origins and Implications," in *Baptists and Ecumenism*, ed. William Jerry Boney and Glenn A. Igleheart (Valley Forge, Pa.: Judson, 1974), 4.

4. Ibid., 5.

5. James Leo Garrett, Jr., Preface to *The Concept of the Believers' Church*, ed. James Leo Garrett, Jr. (Scottdale, Pa.: Herald Press, 1969).

6. Donald Durnbaugh, *The Believers' Church* (New York: Macmillan, 1968, 2d ed., Scottdale, Pa.: Herald Press, 1985).

7. John Briggs, "Editorial: The Believers' Church," *Baptist Quarterly* 32 (January 1988): 207.

8. Garrett, Preface to *Believers' Church*, 5.

9. James Leo Garrett, Jr., ed., *Baptist Relations with Other Christians* (Valley Forge, Pa.: Judson Press, 1974). Since the writing of this chapter, Russian Baptists have announced that their numbers are far fewer than they regularly reported to the public in recent decades. *The Dallas Morning News,* March 17, 1990.

10. Martha M. Barr, ed. *Oneness in Christ: American Baptists are Ecumenical* (Valley Forge, Pa.: American Baptist Churches, n.d.), 39-41.

11. Ibid., 40.

12. Ibid.

13. Ibid., 40-41.

14. W. Hubert Porter, compiler, *The American Baptist Churches in the U.S.A.,* rev. ed. (Valley Forge, Pa.: American Baptist Churches, 1986), 6.

15. Frank Reeves, "Baptists Build Faith on Rich Heritage," The Philadelphia Inquirer, Neighbors sec., Sunday, December 3, 1989, 4-M.

16. Robert Torbet, "Consensus and Divergence on Visible Unity Among Baptists," *American Baptist Quarterly* 4 (June 1985): 227.

17. Ibid., 229.

18. Mark Heim, "Challenged to Confess: Can Baptists Cope with Ecumenical Progress?" *American Baptist Quarterly* 4 (December 1985): 339.

19. Thurian, 3:257-63.

20. Robert Torbet, *Ecumenism . . . A Free Church Dilemma* (Philadelphia: Judson Press, 1968).

21. Deotis Roberts, "Ecumenical Concerns Among National Baptists," in *Baptists and Ecumenism*, 43-44.

22. Ibid., 47-48.

23. "Towards a Common Expression of Faith: A Black North American Perspective," *American Baptist Quarterly* 4 (December 1985): 390, 393.

24. Ibid., 394.

25. Glenn A. Igleheart, "Ecumenical Concerns Among Southern Baptists," in *Baptists and Ecumenism*, 50.

26. Raymond O. Ryland, "Southern Baptist Convention (U.S.A.)," in *Baptist Relations with Other Christians*, 75-79.

27. Ibid., 67-79.

28. See Wayne Dehoney, "Southern Baptists and Ecumenical Concerns," *Christianity Today*, January 29, 1965, 435-36.

Ryland, 80.

30. See William R. Estep, Jr., *Baptists and Christian Unity* (Nashville: Broadman, 1966), and Jerry M. Stubblefield, "The Attitude and Relationship of the Southern Baptist Convention to Certain Other Baptist and Interdenominational Bodies" (Ph.D. diss., Southern Baptist Theological Seminary, 1967).

31. Igleheart, 59-60.

32. N. M. Vaporis, "Editor's Note," *The Greek Orthodox Theological Review* 27 (Spring 1982): 1.

33. Ibid.

34. "Editorial: Lutheran-Baptist Conversations," *American Baptist Quarterly* 1 (December 1982): 99.

35. See W. M. S. West,"Towards Consensus on Baptism? Louisville, 1979," *Baptist Quarterly* (January 1980): 225-32.

36. Ibid., 226.

37. "Report of the Consultation," *Review and Expositor* 77 (Winter 1980): 101-2.

38. Ibid., 102.

39. This topic will be treated in the final section of the chapter.

40. William R. Estep, Jr., "Latin America," in *Baptist Relations with Other Christians*, 142-43.

41. Denton Lotz, "Baptists in Eastern Europe," *Baptist Quarterly* (April 1979): 75.

42. Janis Tervits, "All Union Council of Evangelical Christians-Baptists in the USSR," in *Churches Respond to BEM*, ed. Max Thurian (Geneva: World Council of Churches, 1987), 3:227-29.

43. Ibid., 229.

44. "Union of Evangelical Christian Baptists of USSR," in *Handbook: Member Churches, World Council of Churches*, ed. Ans. J. van der Bent (Geneva: World Council of Churches, 1985), 183.

45. Tervits, 229.

46. Kenneth L. Woodward and Rod Nordland, "The Pope and the Pol," *Newsweek*, December 4, 1989, 90; also Fred Coleman, "From Underground a Church Blooms," *Newsweek*, December 4, 1989, 92, 94.

47. Vinjamuri Devadutt noted that it would become "the most comprehensive union in the Protestant world." See Vinjamuri Devadutt, "Baptists and Church Union in North India," *Foundations* 1 (1958): 24.

48. Stephen C. Neill, *The Story of the Christian Church in India and Pakistan* (Grand Rapids: Eerdmans, 1970), 128-69.

49. John W. Sadiq, "An Assessment of Church Unions in India," *Indian Journal of Theology* 25 (July-December 1976): 165.

50. The British Baptist Union continues to be strongly ecumenical, voting in October 1989, to join the new Inter-Church Process (to become effective in September 1990). See Brian Cooper, "Churches Say Yes to the Next Phase of the Process," *Baptist Times*, October 5, 1989, 13.

51. David B. Barrett, ed., *World Christian Encyclopedia* (Oxford: Oxford University Press, 1982), s.v. "India."

52. Louise Pirouet, *Christianity Worldwide* (London: SPCK, 1989), 72.

53. James Leo Garrett, Jr., Epilogue to *Baptist Relations with Other Christians*, 193-200.

54. Wendell Holmes Rone, *The Baptist Faith and Roman Catholicism* (Kingsport, Tenn.: Kingsport Press, 1952), vi.

55. James Leo Garrett, Jr., "Outside the Church No Salvation," *Baptist Standard*, September 1, 1958, 6-7.

56. Will Herberg, *Protestant, Catholic, Jew* (New York: Doubleday, 1955).

57. James Leo Garrett, Jr., "Protestant Writings on Roman Catholicism in the United States Between Vatican Council I and Vatican Council II: An Analysis and Critique in View of the Contemporary Protestant-Roman Catholic Confrontation" (Ph.D. diss., Harvard University, 1967), iv.

58. Ibid., x.

59. Ibid., 589-607.

60. James Leo Garrett, Jr., *Baptists and Roman Catholicism* (Nashville: Broadman, 1965). One of the many strengths of Garrett's scholarship is his thoroughness—evident in the dissertation; another is his systematic arrangement of materials—evident in his useful little study.

61. James Leo Garrett, Jr., "Roman Catholicism and Baptist Missions" (Address to Conference of Furloughing Missionaries, Foreign Mission Board of the Southern Baptist Convention, Detroit, Michigan, May 21, 1966. Mimeographed, Richmond, Va., 1966).

62. James Leo Garrett, Jr., *Reinhold Niebuhr on Roman Catholicism* (Louisville: Seminary Baptist Book Store, 1972), 39. See also James Leo Garrett, Jr., "John A. Mackay on the Roman Catholic Church," *Journal of Presbyterian History* 50 (Summer 1972): 111, 126.

63. Ira Vinson Birdwhistell, *Southern Baptist Perceptions Of and Responses To Roman Catholicism, 1917-1972* (Ann Arbor: University Microfilms International, 1975), 198, 200.

64. Steve Neil, "First Virginia Baptist-Roman Catholic Dialogue," *Journal of Ecumenical Studies* 14 (Summer 1977): 566-68; Kenneth Stofft, "Midwestern Baptist-Roman Catholic Regional Conference," *Journal of Ecumenical Studies* 15 (Summer 1978): 606-7.

65. "Summary Statement of the Second Triennium in the Dialogue Between Southern Baptist and Roman Catholic Scholars (1982-1984)," *Southwestern Journal of Theology* 28 (Spring 1986): 119.

66. See *Review and Expositor* 79 (Spring 1982).

67. James Leo Garrett, Jr., "Editorial Introduction," *Southwestern Journal of Theology* 28 (Spring 1986), and "The Theology and Practice of Baptism: A Southern Baptist View," *Southwestern Journal of Theology* 28 (Spring 1986): 65-72. Garrett was not involved in the first round of talks, doubtless because he was working in church-state issues at the time of the planning of the dialogues. But he moved back to seminary teaching and played a significant role in the remainder of the discussions.

68. *The Theological Educator* 39 (Spring 1989).

69. James Leo Garrett, Jr., "Understanding the Church: A Southern Baptist Perspective," *The Theological Educator* 39 (Spring 1989), 60-66.

70. Ibid., 66.

71. Fisher Humphreys and Mary Aquin O'Neill, "Introduction," *The Theological Educator* 39 (Spring 1989): 6.

72. "The Scholar's Dialogue: How We Agree/How We Differ," *The Theological Educator* 39 (Spring 1989): 97.

73. "Editorial Introduction," *Review and Expositor* 79 (Spring 1982): 197.

74. At the beginning of the decade, the Baptist World Alliance reaffirmed that one of its major goals was "to increase study and cooperation with other Christian bodies." Carl W. Tiller, *The Twentieth Century Baptist* (Valley Forge: Judson Press, 1980), January 1980, No. 16, 1.

75. "Baptistes et autres chretiens," *Irenikon* 87 (1984): 368. The conferences were projected for five years—to end in 1988.

76. David Russell, "The Extraordinary Synod of the Roman Catholic Church," *The Baptist Quarterly* 31 (April 1986): 295. There were representatives from ten world communions in dialogue with Rome: Orthodox, Coptic, Anglican, Lutheran, Methodist, Reformed, Baptist, Disciples, Pentecostals, and the WCC.

77. Ibid., 298.

18
Modern Roman Catholic Views of the Church

by Doyle L. Young

Introduction

Though the Reformation split the ecclesiastical unity of Europe and established the various major options within Western Christianity, further developments have occurred. This chapter will focus on the most decisive development in the Roman Catholic Church since the Reformation: the Second Vatican Council.[1]

The Historical Background

On January 25, 1959, Pope John XXIII (pope 1958-63) shocked the Roman Catholic world by announcing the convening of an ecumenical council. The announcement, coming only three months after the death of Pius XII (pope 1939-58), came, Pope John believed, by a special inspiration of the Holy Spirit.[2] The council, soon to be called Vatican II, was the Roman Church's twenty-first ecumenical council and the first since Vatican I (1869-70)[3] and only the second since the Council of Trent (1545-63). Pope John's purpose was summarized in the tantalizing Italian word *aggiornamento*. Though never officially translated, the word is usually understood to mean "to bring up to date." In his opening convocation of the Council, John called on the Council Fathers (over 2000 bishops) to take "a step forward," to better present the ancient teachings of the church "in the forms of modern thought."[4] Christopher Butler, auxiliary bishop in Westminster, who attended the Council (then as Abbot of Downside), gleans the Council's meaning of *aggiornamento:* "a recovery of the original gospel, its spirit and purposes, and an adaptation of it which will be at once faithful to the same gospel as originally given and suited to 'the changed conditions of the times.' "[5] This was quite a change for a Church that had since the Reformation evidenced a fortress mentality, emphasizing the Church's authority.

Pope John did not, in announcing the Council, limit the scope of it. He simply wanted to let fresh air into the Church and to avoid making condemnations. Seventy topics were originally proposed for discussion. In the four years of the Council (1962-65), some were dropped, while others were absorbed into related topics. Finally, sixteen documents were presented and approved by the bishops and immediately confirmed by Paul VI (pope 1963-78).

These sixteen documents concerned themselves with three major issues: doctrinal renewal based on the Church and Scripture, issues in modern society (e.g., socialization, affluence and poverty, war and peace), and changes in Church structures (e.g., liturgy, seminaries, ministry).[6]

One should not suppose, however, that radical redirection in thought and practice suddenly appeared *de novo* in 1962. After World War II, particularly in France and Germany, there arose among Roman theologians a "new theology." Though difficult to describe, this new theology was not content to carry on Thomas Aquinas's intellectual achievement of the Middle Ages. These thinkers—Henri de Lubac, Yves Congar, Karl Rahner—called the Church back to biblical and patristic sources. Though the writers were disciplined and even suppressed, the new theology survived. In 1962, then, besides the Thomists and canon lawyers (defenders of "traditional" Roman Catholicism), there were also the new thinkers, who were "in large measure the artificers of the theology of Vatican II."[7]

This new approach showed itself in the first session of the Council (which began October 13, 1962). The bishops rejected by a large majority the first reading of a document on the Church prepared by the papal Curia. Butler comments:

> . . . The council fathers opted for an *aggiornamento* not of the surface but in depth, and even in the fields of biblical scholarship and dogmatic theology. There were many vicissitudes in the subsequent history of the council, but it never looked back from this fundamental option, though, of course, its realisation of its own intentions was only partial.[8]

The relationship of a pope to an ecumenical council should be clarified, particularly since Vatican I (1869-70) declared the pope's infallibility in regard to official statements about theology and ethics. In modern Roman Catholic thought, a council cannot function without a pope. It is the assembly of bishops who are in communion with the pope. Only the pope can convene a council and its decisions must be confirmed by him.[9] But the pronouncements of an ecumenical council have authority. Since the Council of Nicea (325), the Church has ". . . taken for granted that an ecumenical council can both define articles of faith and take practical decisions binding on the whole Church."[10] Though the consensus of the bishops does constitute the ordinary magisterium (teaching office) of the Church, only the extraordinary magisterium (the pope's authority to define doctrine) is infallible. It would be a mistake, Butler observes, to apply the belief in the infallibility of the extraordinary magisterium to the episcopate or the Church at large "without further refinement, criticism, or qualification . . . ."[11]

What authority, then, does the teaching of the Council carry? First, past infallible definitions remain infallible. Second, the Council defined new dogmas. Third, "it made various assertions, of differing quality, on doctrinal issues."[12] Though the doctrinal commission evaded questions about the Council's authority, Butler concludes: "Broadly speaking, one may assume that teaching in exposition of a main theme in a dogmatic constitution has *per se* a greater authority than doctrinal statements in pastoral constitutions, decrees, or declarations.[13]

Dogmatic Constitution on the Church (Lumen Gentium)

The *Dogmatic Constitution on the Church* (referred to as *Lumen Gentium* or by the first two words of the Latin title *De Ecclesia*) is one of only two dogmatic constitutions approved by the Council and pope. It was officially accepted by Pope Paul VI on November 21, 1964, at the end of the Council's third session. Though it is not the longest document accepted by the Council, more time was given to discussion of it than to any other document; of the 168 general congregations (full meetings of the Council for discussion), over thirty were devoted exclusively to this document.[14] Indeed, Butler notes that ". . . the central document of the whole council, and the one which exerted the most pervasive influence on those subsequently debated, was *Lumen Gentium,* the dogmatic Constitution on the Church."[15] Hastings concurs, observing that *Lumen Gentium* represents "the supreme doctrinal contribution of Vatican II, enormously rich both in its central affirmations and in the hints it throws out for further thought."[16]

The *Dogmatic Constitution on the Church* was discussed extensively, with the third draft finally published in eight chapters, containing seventy-six pages of text. The second and third drafts showed the new emphasis.[17]

Chapter 1—The Mystery of the Church

The Church is "in the nature of a sacrament—a sign and instruments, that is, of the communion with God and of unity among men."[18] This is the Church's essential identity; the Church is not first a juridical structure but a sacrament, that is the visible sign and the embodiment of mankind's union with God. Like God, the Church is Trinitarian. *The Father* did not abandon lost mankind but purposed to call together in one body all who should come to faith in Christ.[19] To this end He sent the *Son,* who won our redemption by His obedience and inaugurated the kingdom of heaven on earth.[20] The

Holy Spirit was sent at Pentecost to sanctify the Church continually, guide it into all truth, unify it in communion and works of ministry, bestow "hierarchic and charismatic" gifts on it, direct it, adorn it with fruit, constantly renew it, and lead it to "perfect union with her Spouse."[21]

Christ inaugurated the Church with the preaching of the good news of the coming of the kingdom of God. After Christ died, rose, and poured out the Spirit, the Church received the mission of preaching and of establishing God's and Christ's kingdom, "and she is, on earth, the seed and the beginning of that kingdom."[22] The Council Fathers avoided saying, however, that the Church *is* the kingdom of God. The Church established by Christ is called by many names in Scripture, including the sheepfold, the flock, a cultivated field, the building of God, the Jerusalem which is above, our mother, the spotless bride of the spotless lamb, and an exile.[23]

The most profound biblical image, however, is that the Church is the body of Christ. It is a mystical, sacramental body, though, and not just a social grouping: "for by communicating his Spirit, Christ mystically constitutes as his body those brothers of his who are called together from every nation. In that body, the life of Christ is communicated to those who believe and who, through the sacraments, are united in a hidden and real way to Christ in his passion and glorification."[24] The basis of this body of Christ is clearly sacramental: in baptism, fellowship in Christ's death and resurrection "is symbolized and brought about," and in the Eucharist "we are taken up into communion with him and with one another."[25] Since the Holy Spirit gives gifts to this body, there is a diversity of members and functions. The primary gift given is the apostles. The Spirit also gives unity "both by his own power and the interior union of the members . . . ."[26] It is Christ who provides in His body the gifts of ministries with which the members serve one another and grow. It is the Spirit who gives life to, unifies, and moves the whole body.[27]

So, Christ established and forever sustains His Church "as a visible organization through which he communicates truth and grace to all men."[28] But the mystical, spiritual, sacramental body of Christ and the visible, hierarchical Church are two parts of the same reality, "in a somewhat similar way" to the incarnate Jesus being both human and divine.[29] The divine, mystical fellowship takes on earthly, physical form.

There is no other Church of Jesus Christ than this. "This Church," the Fathers carefully said, "constituted and organized as a society in the present world, subsists in the Catholic Church. . . ."[30] They recognized that there are "elements of sanctification and truth . . . outside its visible confines."[31] Though draft B of the text had said, "This Church *is* the Roman Catholic Church," the final draft says that Christ's Church "*subsists in*" the Catholic

Church.[32] "An exclusive material identification of the Church and the Roman Catholic communion is," Butler observes, "carefully avoided."[33] This tiny change in terminology carried tremendous ramifications, as the *Decree on Ecumenism* will show.

Finally, the mystery of the Church means that the Church is to be, like Jesus, a servant. Though the Church needs money and property to carry out its missions, the Church ". . . is not set up to seek earthly glory, but to proclaim, and this by her own example, humility and self-denial."[34] The Church, "at once holy and always in need of purification, follows constantly the path of penance and renewal."[35] Triumphalism is thus renounced.

Chapter 2—The People of God

Chapter 1 asserted that the Church is not primarily a structure but a mystery, a sacrament. In chapter 2 the Council asserts that a primary metaphor for understanding the Church's nature is that it is the people of God. God did not will to save people as individuals, but to unite saved people into a people. The new race (made up of those in the New Covenant) created by Christ is the people of God. Its head is Christ, their status is the freedom and dignity of the sons of God, its law is the new commandment, its destiny is the kingdom of God. Christ purchased it with His blood, filled it with His Spirit, and provided it with the means for a visible earthly union. It is Christ's instrument for the salvation of the whole world.[36]

Christ has further made this new people of God into a kingdom of priests. All baptized persons are priests, though there is a difference in essence between the "common priesthood of the faithful" and the "ministerial or hierarchical priesthood" of the ordained clergy.[37] "Each," however, "shares in the one priesthood of Christ;" though ministerial priests offer the Eucharist, common priests also participate in the offering of the Eucharist.[38] They are not passive observers. It is through the sacraments that the priestly community receives its sacred character.[39]

But the people of God also share in Christ's prophetic office by spreading a living witness of Him, "especially by a life of love and faith and by offering sacrifices to God."[40] Besides sharing in Christ's priestly and prophetic offices, though, the people of God receive charismata (gifts) individually from the Holy Spirit. It is up to the official authorities to judge the "genuineness and proper use of such gifts."[41] This overriding role of the hierarchy will be explored in the next chapter. All the people of God, even scattered around the world, are in communion with one another through the Holy Spirit.[42]

Finally, who makes up the people of God and how are they incorporated into it? For the Catholic faithful, the Catholic Church is necessary for salvation. Those who know that Christ founded it as necessary and refuse to enter or stay in it cannot be saved. The only members of the people of God who are "fully incorporated into the Church" are those "joined in the visible structure of the Church of Christ, who rules her through the Supreme Pontiff and the bishops."[43] Though this sounds like the juridical definition of the Church again, Hastings notes that, in draft B, the constitution reads that "only Roman Catholics are really incorporated" into the Church. The final draft says that they are "fully incorporated."[44] This advancement on earlier teaching is augmented by the Council's emphasizing that baptized non-Catholics are joined to the Church (the people of God) "in some real way in the Holy Spirit for . . . his sanctifying power is also active in them."[45] Even those who have not yet received the gospel, the Council asserts, are related to the people of God in varying ways.

Chapter 3—The Church Is Hierarchical

It is only after having spoken of the Church as a sacramental mystery and as the whole people of God that the Council turns to the role of the hierarchy. The key concept in this long chapter, longest in the constitution, is the church leadership's *ministry* or *service* to the whole people of God. While pre-Vatican II ecclesiology had emphasized that the Church's leadership was *monarchical,* the Council now affirms that is is more properly *collegial.*[46]

To shepherd the people of God, Christ established in the Church various offices; those who hold these offices "are invested with a sacred power."[47] The chief office in the Church is that of bishop. Christ entrusted His apostles with their mission, and the bishops are their successors. Christ put Peter at the head of the apostles to ensure unity of faith and communion. This apostolic group was established in "the form of a college or permanent assembly," with Peter at the head.[48] The bishops have taken Christ's place to such an extent that "whoever listens to them is listening to Christ and whoever despises them despises Christ and him who sent Christ."[49] Through the bishops Jesus is present among the members of the Church, preaching, administering the sacraments, incorporating new members into His body, directing, and guiding them to eternal life.[50]

But there are limits to the bishop's authority. One is constituted as part of the college only by consecration *and* "hierarchical communion with the head and members of the college."[51] And the college of bishops has no power unless united to the pope, who has full power over the whole Church. The bishops have the same authority over the whole Church, but only with the agreement of the pope. This authority is exercised in a collegial way, whether the bishops are gathered in one place or scattered; but only the pope can convoke and confirm such episcopal decisions.[52]

This collegiate unity is seen further in the relation of the bishop to the individual diocese and to the universal Church. As the pope is the visible source of unity of the whole Church and the whole college of bishops, so the bishop is the visible source of unity in his particular Church (diocese). The individual bishop exercises his pastoral office over his particular diocese, not over other dioceses or the Church universal. But he is to care for the whole Church, for he has the obligation of encouraging and guarding the unity of the Church, as well as upholding the Church's common discipline. He is to teach the faithful to love the whole Church and especially the poor and he is to promote all the active ministries that are common to the whole Church. The bishops, further, are charged to preach the gospel to the whole world. They must, then, support mission work and assist other dioceses in their mission work.[53] But the office committed by Christ to the bishops is a "service, which is called very expressively in sacred Scripture a *diakonia* or ministry."[54]

Among the bishops' important duties, the most important is preaching the gospel. In this "they are authentic teachers, that is, teachers endowed with the authority of Christ."[55] Bishops who teach in communion with Rome are to be revered and honored as teachers of Catholic truth. The faithful are to submit to the decisions of their bishops, and "this loyal submission of the will and intellect must be given, in a special way, to the authentic teaching authority of the Roman Pontiff, even when he does not speak *ex cathedra* in such wise . . . ."[56] The Council reaffirmed Vatican I's teaching on papal infallibility and asserted that, individually, bishops do not share it. They do share infallibility, though, when they teach in agreement with one of the Church's definitive and absolute doctrines or when they teach together in an ecumenical council. In such a council, the bishops are " . . . for the universal Church, teachers of and judges in matters of faith and morals, whose decisions must be adhered to with the loyal and obedient assent of faith."[57] Revealed truth, "the divine deposit of faith," cannot be changed even by pope or council.[58]

In each diocese the fullness of the Church exists and Christ is present. In the diocese the bishop governs "personally in the name of Christ."[59] His authority is subject to the authority of the pope, however, and can be circumscribed by the pope in the interests of the larger Church. Bishops should not, however, be thought of as vicars or representatives of the Roman Pontiff; they exercise their authority in their own right. The bishop should exercise his power as a servant, caring for "his subjects" as for his very own children.[60]

Priests serve in the local parish (congregation) where they preach, shepherd the faithful, and celebrate the Eucharist. The priest is the bishop's "helper," and in the Eucharist the priest acts "in the person of Christ."[61] In the parish the priest "in a certain sense" represents the bishop, and the priests together with their bishop form "a unique sacerdotal college," the presbyterium.[62] The priest should see the bishop as his father "and obey him with all respect;" the bishop should see the priest as his son and friend.[63] It is the responsibility of the priests to unite their efforts and resources under their bishops and the pope "and thus eliminate division and dissension in every shape or form."[64]

Finally, besides bishops and priests, there are deacons in the hierarchical ministry. At the low end of the hierarchy, deacons receive the imposition of hands for ministry, not for priesthood. They may, among other things, administer baptism, distribute the elements at the Eucharist, assist at the blessing of marriages, bring viaticum to the dying, and read the Scriptures in worship. It is their task to perform works of charity and administration. Though the permanent diaconate was not widely established before Vatican II, the Council ordered that the diaconate be restored to its proper and permanent rank within the hierarchy.[65]

Chapter 4—The Laity

The Council next devotes a short chapter to the laity. Everything that has been said about the people of God applies to all—ordained, monastics, and laity—for there is only one people of God. Lay people are due an equal dignity and privilege of faith with ordained or religious. The laity's apostolate or ministry is to share in the Church's redemptive mission; all Christians, the Council Fathers assert, are appointed to this ministry by Christ Himself.[66] But the laity have the special task of making the Church present in places where only they can reach. The hierarchy can also appoint lay people to more direct tasks in the Church. Laypeople share in Christ's priestly office by offering all they have—home, work, family—to God as a spiritual sacrifice. They share in Christ's prophetic office in their proclamation of Christ by word and testimony of life, and their testimony has special power because it is accomplished in the midst of ordinary life. Particularly important is the layperson's role in family life, where he or she can show the love of Christ and teach children how to live. A further crucial role for the laity is in using their technical skills, money, labor, etc., to further Christian ideals and to change the institutions of society. It is primarily laypeople who can bring a sense of moral value to culture.[67]

The Church provides spiritual help to the laity through the sacraments and the Word of God. There are times when, because of their special expertise, laity will be called on to advise the hierarchy on matters concerning the good of the Church. When they do so, however, they must do it only through institutions established by the Church for that purpose, and with reverence and love for the bishops. The laity should "promptly accept in Christian obedience" what the bishops decide, and the bishops should "recognize and promote the dignity and responsibility of the laity in the Church."[68]

Chapter 5—The Call to Holiness

An essential element of the Church's nature is that it is holy. It is holy because Christ was holy and joined the Church to Himself as His body and gave it the gift of the Holy Spirit. All in the Church, then, whether ordained, religious, or lay, are called to holiness. Holiness is devoting oneself wholly to God and the service of neighbors. The Council Fathers give specific instructions to bishops, ministers of lesser rank, married and parents, etc.[69]

Holiness can be cultivated by such means as hearing and reading the Word of God, the sacraments, prayer, self-denial, and acts of service. The highest gift that God can give for the holy life is virginity or celibacy.[70]

Chapter 6—Religious Life

A short chapter on religious (monastic) life notes that Christ gave the example of living according to the three evangelical counsels of chastity, poverty, and obedience. The religious life involves pledging to live by these three principles in a form of life set up by and regulated by the hierarchy. Both ordained and lay can be called to this life.[71]

Chapter 7—The Pilgrim Church

Though the promised restoration of all things has already begun in Christ, it it is not completed. Indeed, the "Church will receive its perfection only in the glory of heaven."[72] Until then, the pilgrim Church awaits the consummation. This pilgrim Church is united to those members already in heaven or being purified and honor should be given to the dead to strengthen this unity. The unity between the pilgrim Church and the dead is best realized in the Eucharist. Though the faithful should invoke the aid and help of those already in heaven, the Council warns against abuses and excesses.[73]

Chapter 8—Our Lady

In the final chapter, the Council Fathers turn to Mary's role in salvation and the Church, though not to a complete discussion of the doctrine of Mary. Catholic faithful should reverence her memory, for she is preeminent and "a wholly unique member of the Church, its type and outstanding model in faith and charity," and she occupies the highest place in the Church after Christ.[74]

According to the Council, though Mary's function in salvation in no way diminishes Christ's unique role as mediator, she did, by her obedience, reverse the work of Eve. Because she cooperated with God in a unique way to bring salvation, "she is a mother to us in the order of grace."[75] In heaven, she still intercedes for us to bring us eternal salvation. So, it is appropriate to call her "Advocate, Helper, Benefactress, and Mediatrix."[76] As the perfect example of virgin and mother, she is a type of the Church, which becomes a virgin (being spotless) and a mother (bringing forth children). Since she has already reached perfection, she is a model for the faithful of virtue.[77] The cult of the veneration of Mary is very ancient and is good, but it "differs essentially" from the adoration of the Trinity.[78] It is to be encouraged and highly valued, but all theologians and preachers should be wary of false exaggeration.[79] Because she is the image and the beginning of the Church as it will someday be perfected in the world to come, Mary is "a sign of certain hope and comfort" to the pilgrim Church, and the faithful should pour out to her urgent supplications for her to intercede with her Son.[80]

Conclusion

In what ways, then, did Vatican II represent "renewal and redefinition" in the Roman Catholic Church? Though the Council declared that it propounded no new dogma, and would argue that it did not depart from authentic Catholic theology, some new emphases are clear:

1. A turn from a structural, juridical, authoritarian view of the Church to a mystical, sacramental one (ch. 1). On earth, however, this Church does have clearly-defined structures and centers of authority.

2. A more inclusive view of the Church that emphasizes not the hierarchy, but the whole people of God (ch. 2). It is a communal, corporate definition, with tremendous ecumenical implications.

3. A turn from a monarchical (papal) view of Church authority to a collegial, shared authority of pope and bishops. Leadership is not a position of prestige, but of service (ch. 3).

4. A new emphasis on the important role and ministry (apostolate) of the laity (ch. 4).

5. A call to all the Church, not just monastics and clergy, to holiness (ch. 5).

6. A turn from a view of the Church as triumphal to a view that the suffering, pilgrim Church faithfully awaits the consummation (ch. 7).

Notes

1. Due to space limitations, this chapter will not treat the myriad of groups that emerged from the radical wing of the Reformation or the sectarian impulse (most seen in America). Though these groups held to a diversity of theological views, they all claimed to be restoring "New Testament Christianity" and thus represent "new" views of the church. Similarly, developments in the mainline Protestant denominations are excluded here, though the ecumenical movement is a distinctly new development in understanding the church.

2. Adrian Hastings, *A Concise Guide to the Documents of the Second Vatican Council,* 2 vols. (London: Darton, Longman, and Todd, 1968), 1:17.

3. On Vatican I, see Hubert Jedin, *Ecumenical Councils of the Catholic Church,* trans. Ernest Graf (London: Nelson, 1960), 187-239, and Philip Hughes, *The Church in Crisis: A History of the General Councils 325-1870* (Garden City, N.Y.: Hanover House, 1961). John Leith, ed. *The Creeds of Christendom,* 3d ed. (Atlanta: John Knox Press, 1982), 447-57 has the text of the decree.

4. Hastings, 1:15.

5. Christopher Butler, *The Theology of Vatican II,* 2d ed. (Westminster, Md.: Christian Classics, 1981), 18. The book was originally published in 1967 and was the theme of the bishop's 1966 Sarum Lectures at Oxford.

6. Hastings, 1:17-18.

7. Butler, 15.

8. Butler, 17.

9. Hastings, 1:20.

10. Butler, 3.

11. Butler, 22. In practice, the Church's theological reflection occurs within a "collective or collaborative climate of opinion" of the *sensus fidelium* ("mind of the Church") and the ordinary magisterium (consensus of the bishops), overseen by the extraordinary magisterium (teaching authority of the pope), 22.

12. Butler, 23.

13. Butler, 23 and 23-24, n. 21. But see Hastings, 1:22, who says one should not distinguish between the different types of documents (dogmatic constitutions, pastoral constitutions, decrees, and declarations). On the authority of the Council's teaching, see *Dogmatic Constitution on the Church,* III:25 and the appendix added by the Fathers to the constitution. The general literature on Vatican II is voluminous, particularly from the years during the Council and just after its close in 1965. A sample includes: Rock Caporale, *Vatican II: Last of the Councils* (Baltimore, Md.: Helicon, 1964), Hans Kung, *The Council in Action: Theological Reflections on the Second Vatican Council,* trans., Cecily Hastings (New York: Sheed and Ward, 1963), and Charles Dollen, ed., *Vatican II: A Bibliography* (Metuchen, N.J.: Scarecrow Press, 1969). Views of Protestants can be found in G. C. Berkouwer, *The Second Vatican Council and the New Catholicism,* trans. Lewis Smedes (Grand Rapids, Mich.: Eerdmans, 1965), Robert McAfee Brown, *Observer in Rome: a Protestant Report on the Vatican Council* (Garden City, N.Y.: Doubleday, 1964), and G. B. Caird, *Our Dialogue With Rome: the Second Vatican Council and After* (London: Oxford University Press, 1967). Each of the sixteen documents of the Council called forth extensive commentary in both journals and books.

14. The other dogmatic constitution is *On Divine Revelation.* Its Latin title is *De Divina Revelatione;* its more common name drawn from the first words of the Latin text is *Dei Verbum.*

15. Hastings, 1:25.

16. Butler, 52. For a chart showing the dependence of other Vatican II documents on *Lumen Gentium,* see Hastings, 1:27.

17. Hastings, 1:95. For the same view, see Herbert Vorgrimler, ed., *Commentary on the Documents of Vatican II,* 5 vols (New York: Herder and Herder, 1966), 1:105. Vorgrimler's work is the classic European Catholic commentary on the documents.

18. For the history of the discussions in the Council and the two major revisions of the docu-

ment, see Vorgrimler, 1:105-37, or for a handier account, see Hastings 1:28-34.

19. *Church,* I:1. The authoritative English text, and the one used here, is Austin Flannery, ed. *Documents of Vatican II* (Grand Rapids, Mich.: William B. Eerdmans, 1975). The format for notation here will come from the document cited *(Church);* the first number refers to the chapter of the document, the second number to the article. In the footnotes, Flannery cites the historical provenance from Catholic history of teachings in the documents.

20. Ibid., I:2.

21. Ibid., I:3.

22. Ibid., I:4.

23. Ibid., I:5.

24. Ibid., I:6.

25. Ibid., I:7.

26. Ibid.

27. Ibid.

28. Ibid.

29. Ibid., I:8.

30. Ibid.

31. Ibid.

32. Ibid.

33. Hastings, 1:38-39.

34. Butler, 61.

35. *Church,* I:8.

36. Ibid.

37. Ibid., II:9

38. Ibid., II:10.

39. Ibid.

40. Ibid., II:11.

41. Ibid., II:12.

42. Ibid.

43. Ibid., II:13.

44. Ibid., II:14.

45. Hastings, 40-41.

6. *Church,* II:15. For a fuller discussion of the Roman Church's new view on its relationship to other Christian churches, see the *Decree on Ecumenism* in Flannery.

47. Hastings, 1:42.

48. *Church,* III:18.

49. Ibid., III:19. The Council Fathers reaffirmed Vatican I's teaching regarding the institution, permanence, nature, and infallible teaching authority of the Roman Pontiff (the pope)—III:18.

50. Ibid., III:20.

51. Ibid., III:21.

52. Ibid., III:22.

53. Ibid.

54. Ibid., III:23.

55. Ibid., III:24.

56. Ibid., III:25.

57. Ibid.

58. Ibid.

59. Ibid.

60. Ibid., III:27.

61. Ibid.

62. Ibid., III:28.

63. Ibid.

64. Ibid.
65. Ibid.
66. Ibid., III:29. For a fuller discussion of the apostolate of the laity, see Flannery, *Documents,*
for the Council document *Decree on the Apostolate of the Laity (Apostolicum Actusoitatem).*
67. Ibid., IV:30-33.
68. Ibid., IV:34-36.
69. Ibid., IV:37.
70. Ibid., V:39-41.
71. Ibid., V:42.
72. Ibid., VI:43-45.
73. Ibid., VII:48
74. Ibid., VII:48-51.
75. Ibid., VIII:52-54.
76. Ibid., VIII:56, 58.
77. Ibid., VIII:62.
78. Ibid., VIII:63-65.
79. Ibid., VIII:66.
80. Ibid., VIII:67.
81. Ibid., VIII:68-69.

Part 4
Contemporary Challenges

In the contemporary mind, "church" has often become associated with buildings, programs, and specific services provided to the community. Yet there are a host of challenges that face the contemporary church, much broader than buildings or programs. This final section addresses seven important issues that have drawn the attention of some of the most prominent thinkers and most capable scholars in American Believers' Church life.

The contribution of the Believers' Church tradition to the matters of separation of church and state are immense and well documented. The issue continues to remain one of primary importance on the contemporary calendar. The relationship of religion and politics has been a growing concern over the past several decades. This seeming inseparable relationship has ironically been coupled with the rising tide of secular thought, blurring many issues thought to have been settled in times past. The "Church and State" issue is pursued with thoughtful reflection by historian William R. Estep, Jr.

Another area of growing interest is the relationship of church to the arts. Reformed and Roman Catholic theologians have given direction to these practical concerns for several generations, but as William L. Hendricks notes, it is a relatively new field for those in the Believers' Church tradition. Hendricks invites the people of God to enhance their appreciation of the arts and the aesthetic nature of theology.

Perhaps no two issues in the church have created as much discussion in recent years as the meaning of ordination and the role of women in the church. Fisher Humphreys and Sharon Hodgin Gritz treat these timely issues from a biblical and theological perspective with irenic spirits and cautious conclusions. Obviously the solutions offered by these two writers do not represent the viewpoints of all major thinkers in the Believers' Church tradition, but their capable handling of these sensitive matters provides more than adequate basis for fruitful dialogue.

Two major thinkers address similar concerns in the essays on "From 'Christendom' to Christian Renewal" and "The Believers' Church and the

Given Church." Franklin Littell, who popularized the term "Free Church" in American church life and who has been one of the leading voices at Believers' Church conferences in recent decades, traces the paths from "Christendom" to Christian renewal in Europe and in America. Harvard University historian George Huntston Williams examines the differences, similarities, and forthcoming challenges facing members of the Believers' Church and the Given Church. A final essay by Dwight A. Moody surveys the theological contributions by "Contemporary Theologians within the Believers' Church."

These concluding essays enable the people of God to speak in an informed fashion to some of the primary challenges facing the contemporary church. In so doing, the people of God can simultaneously celebrate their essential unity in Christ and their diverse expressions of this essential unity.

19
Church and State

by William R. Estep, Jr.

The concept of the separation of church and state embodied in the Constitution of the United States and its First Amendment, once heralded as "America's greatest contribution to civilization," is now the object of relentless attack. Surprisingly, in the front ranks of this new army of discontent are the Protestants, heirs of Luther and Calvin, and others, heirs of the Believers' Church tradition. As with one voice they assail the "wall of separation" as "a myth" and a "judicial nightmare." The "disestablishment of religion" is called "a perverse notion" which only leads to the establishment of "secular humanism" on the "naked public square." It would appear, from these statements, and numerous others that could be cited, that a segment within evangelical Christianity is in essential agreement with the sentiments of Pope Pius IX who, more than a century ago, condemned the separation of church and state as a pernicious error in a papal encyclical, *Allocution "Acerbissimum"* (Sept. 17, 1852), which was included in the *Syllabus of Errors* of 1864.[1] After 200 years under the Constitution and the Bill of Rights in which Christianity and Judaism have flourished as never before, the question arises: "Why and whence this new chorus of discontent?"

A variety of answers has been offered. Richard John Neuhaus suggests that "the naked public square" is the result of the demise of "the mainstream denominations," which has in turn led to the rise of the New Religious Right.[2] Although on the surface of things, this suggested analysis is an oversimplification, it would appear that a marriage between what sociologist Robert Bellah (borrowing the term from Rousseau) has called "Civil Religion" and what might be termed "fundamentalism reborn" can account for the New Religious Right's determination to save America from "secular humanism" and return the country to the "faith of our fathers." Perhaps this helps explain the current disillusionment with religious liberty and the First Amendment.[3]

The sources of the current discontent with the First Amendment and the implied "wall of separation" are varied. Much of it arises from a concept of separation which places religion in a safety deposit box within American life, secure but separated from any meaningful dialogue with or influence upon the political and social life of the nation. Winthrop Hudson makes this point when he cited an editorial in *The New York Times* of April 23, 1960, which read: "We start with the premise, shared by every American who believes in the constitutional principles on which our country is founded, that religion has no proper place in American politics."[4] What was intended was the legal and, therefore, institutional separation of church and state, not the elimination of religion from the life of the nation and its citizens.

There is also a great deal of confusion among Christians in the United States regarding the nature of the state. Is it secular or sacred, or both? If America is Christian, as many preachers and politicians contend, then in what sense can such a position be maintained? Robert Maddox summarized the confused state of affairs when he wrote:

> Now 200 years after Jefferson, the country is gripped in a battle for religious liberty. Through overt and covert means, political and religious leaders want to control religious impulses and reshape spiritual sensibilities. Agencies of the state want to define the church. Politicians want to dictate modes of prayer. Church leaders exhort the government to enforce a religious agenda, though this goal flaunts the principle of religious liberty through separation of church and state (a principle which now sustains attacks as never before in this century).[5]

While most Baptists are ardent patriots and hold many convictions in common with historic fundamentalism, there is a basic distinction that Baptists have made historically between church and state which arises out of their faithfulness to the *witness of the New Testament, the nature of the Christian faith, the Lordship of Christ,* and *the nature of the church.* While the limitations of space do not permit a full review of the Baptist heritage relative to religious freedom and the relation of church and state, an attempt will be made to examine the theological and ecclesiological convictions within the historical context, which have helped to shape the Baptist understanding of the state and its limitations regarding the individual conscience and the church.[6]

The King Is Not God

The first Baptist preacher of record in England died in Newgate Prison. His name was Thomas Helwys. Helwys had studied law at Grey's Inn. Upon his return to London from exile in Amsterdam, he and a handful of followers established their small congregation at Spitalfields, just outside the walls of London. Soon afterwards, Helwys sent a little book to King James entitled *A Short Declaration of the Mistery of Iniquity,* with a handwritten inscription in which he boldly proclaimed:

> The king is a mortal man and not God: therefore hath no power over the immortal souls of his subjects, to make laws and ordinances for them, and to set spiritual Lords over them. If the king have authority to make spiritual Lords and laws, then he is an immortal God, and not a mortal man. O King, be not seduced by deceivers to sin against God whom thou oughtest to obey, nor against thy poor subjects who ought and will obey thee in all things with body, life and goods, or else let their lives be taken from the earth. God save the King. [The words are modernized from a copy with the original inscription in the Bodleian Library.][7]

In this statement Helwys was setting forth the fundamental source of all spiritual and earthly authority as understood by Baptists from the inception of the movement. Every confession of faith from 1609 to 1677 began with a delineation of articles on the nature and redemptive purpose of God. This means that for Baptists, the revelation of God in Christ, as reflected in the Scriptures, provides the Christian with the interpretative key by which the authority of state and its limitations are to be understood. It was clear to Helwys and his brethren that the state had no authority over a person's religious profession or lack of it.

> Our Lord the king is but an earthly king, and he hath no authority as a king but in earthly causes, and if the king's people be obedient and true subjects, obeying all human laws made by the king, our lord and king can require no more: for man's religion to God is between God and themselves; the king shall not answer for it, neither may the king be judge between God and man. Let them be heretics, Turks, Jews or whatsoever, it appertains not to the earthly power to punish them in the least measure.[8]

In these words Helwys was echoing John Smyth, his pastor and mentor with whom he had gone to Holland. Smyth died in August 1612. Apparently, he had written a hundred-article confession of faith in English which his Amsterdam congregation published after his death. There are also two manuscript copies extant in Dutch. In Article 84 of the English version of the confession of 1612, Smyth wrote the often quoted words:

> That the magistrate is not by virtue of his office to meddle with religion, or matters of conscience, to force or compel men to this or that form of religion, or doctrine: but to handle only civil transgressions (Rom. xiii), injuries and wrongs of man against man, in murder, adultery, theft, etc., for Christ only is the king, and lawgiver of the church and conscience (James iv. 12).[9]

It is evident that for Smyth the lordship of Jesus Christ was the ultimate authority for the church and the individual conscience. For this position, Smyth, Helwys, Busher, and Murton, as well as the early Particular Baptists, were dependent upon the New Testament. At one time Smyth, along with other English Separatists, failed to make a distinction between the nature and purpose of the Old Testament and that of the New. However, when

Smyth led his Separatist church, which had been founded upon a covenant after the pattern of the Old Testament "saints," to disband and reorganize upon the basis of individual professions of faith and believer's baptism, the authority had shifted from the Old to the New Testament. Hence it was the New Testament that provided for these early Baptists the authentic (apostolic) witness to the revelation of God in Christ. It was also the New Testament that would henceforth provide the guidelines for their understanding of the church and its relation to the state. The writings of the early English and American Baptist pastors and the early confessions provide ample documentation for this position but none were in a position to implement their teachings until Roger Williams founded Providence.

The Church in the New Testament

Although considered a Calvinist, Williams interpreted the Bible very much like the Anabaptists and General Baptists before him. Therefore, the church, the New People of God, could never be identified with the Massachusetts Bay Colony, as Dr. John Cotton claimed. According to Williams, it included only those who were "born again" through the work of the Holy Spirit. Thus, it transcends national and racial barriers and can never be coterminous with any given nation or race. This concept of the church was based upon the assumption of a completely voluntary act of faith of a mature person and was, therefore, not the result of coercion. He held that compulsion could never produce true conversion—only hypocrites.

> Can the sword of steel or arm of flesh make man faithful or loyal to God? Or careth God for the outward loyalty or faithfulness, when the inward man is false and treacherous? Or is there not more danger from a hypocrite, a dissembler, a turncoat in his religion (from the fear or favor of men) than from a resolved Jew, Turk, or papist, who holds firm unto his principles?[10]

For Williams, the nature of faith and the church demand the separation of church and state, for the state by its very nature, which is secular, is precluded from judging the merits of one's faith or the lack of it. He held that the state's incompetence in the spiritual realm has been demonstrated time and again in both Roman Catholic and Protestant state churches for they have repeatedly mistaken saints for sinners and, therefore, imprisoned and executed multiplied thousands of God-fearing citizens as criminals. Only God is competent to judge between the wheat and tares, and he has reserved the prerogative for himself. However, the state is ordained of God for its God-given function which, according to Williams, is purely secular.

The Christian and the "Civil State"

In addition to the numerous arguments Williams used in *The Bloudy Tenent of Persecution* to establish his case for religious freedom, he clarifies what he means by the "civill" (secular) state and the Christian magistrate's role in government: "All *Civill States* with their *Officers* of *justice* in their respective *constitutions* and *administrations* are proved *essentially Civill*, and therefore not *Judges, Governours* or *Defendours* of the *Spirituall* or *Christian state* and *Worship*."[11] He does not preclude Christian participation in government but forbids a Christian magistrate's use of the state's power to promote his faith. To do otherwise, Williams argued, is to confound the "*Civill* and *Religious*" and deny "the principles of Christianity and civility, and that *Jesus Christ* is come in the *Flesh*.[12]

Williams argued that for a Christian magistrate to persecute even the heretic was a denial of the incarnation. This was a position of a convinced evangelical who set forth the same argument before the Westminster Assembly in 1644. It was also essentially the same argument that Hübmaier enunciated in Article 28 of his *Von Ketzern und ihren Verbrennern (Concerning Heretics and Those Who Burn Them)* in 1524. By this allusion to the incarnation, both Hubmaier and Williams were affirming the voluntary nature of the faith-response to God's gracious offer of salvation in Christ. In other words, for these two "prophets in the wilderness" the proclamation of the gospel was predicated upon an uncoerced response, for Christ came to invite, not to compel, men and women to discipleship. Hence the state, even if staffed by Christian magistrates, remains secular in nature and purpose, not because God does not exist (secular humanism) but because God has so ordered it in His infinite wisdom and according to His sovereign will. Williams, the Calvinist, was instructing his fellow Calvinists more perfectly in the faith, a faith that must be free and voluntary or it is no faith at all. He that would never discriminate against the Jew conceived of his own faith as something other than baptized Judaism, as Perry Miller has suggested.

Regardless of Williams's relationship to the fledgling Baptist movement in the colonies, it was he that introduced to New England the message the Baptists had been proclaiming in old England since their beginning. He and Dr. John Clarke even succeeded in securing a charter from Charles II, giving the citizens of the Colony of Rhode Island the necessary legal right, in the eyes of other colonies in the New World, to "hold forth a lively experiment, that a most flourishing civil state may stand and best be maintained, and that among our English subjects, with a full liberty in religious concernment; . . ." Thus, the colony that the Puritan divines had dubbed "the garbage can" of New England became the prototype of the new nation in the process of birth a century and a half later. Perry Miller said it better than most when he wrote:

> For the subsequent history of what became the United States, Roger Williams possesses one indubitable importance, that he stands at the beginning of it. Just as some great experience in the youth of a person is ever afterward a determinant of his personality, so the American character has inevitably been molded by the fact that in the first years of colonization there arose this prophet of religious liberty.[13]

The Struggle

The century and a half between Williams's exile in the wilderness and the adoption of the First Amendment witnessed a tug of war with the Anglican and Puritan state-church establishments on one side and the Baptists, Quakers, Mennonites, Presbyterians, and Deists on the other. In Massachusetts it was Isaac Backus and the Warren Association that joined battle with the Puritan establishmentarians. Backus never lived to see the victory but John Leland, who had moved back to Massachusetts from Virginia, did. Leland brought with him a backlog of experience from participating in a war of petitions on behalf of the Baptists and others, which finally helped bring about the complete disestablishment of the Anglican Church in Virginia. It was a remarkable development, indeed, that saw these evangelical dissenters, in an alliance with some champions of the French Enlightenment as Jefferson and Madison, achieve a commonly desired goal—religious liberty, complete and unequivocal, established by law.

Exactly 150 years after Roger Williams founded Providence Plantations, Thomas Jefferson's bill for The Establishment of Religious Freedom in Virginia was passed into law. Even though the 1776 Virginia Declaration of Rights called for religious liberty, apparently no one took this aspect of the document seriously. Therefore, Jefferson wrote the first draft of his bill in 1777 and introduced it to the Assembly two years later but, after two readings, it was tabled. Finally after dozens of petitions containing thousands of signatures and Madison's "A Memorial and Remonstrance" had been circulated anonymously throughout the state, Jefferson's almost forgotten measure was resurrected on December 17, 1785, and passed on January 19, 1786. Although by the passage of this Act, religious liberty was established in Virginia, the Episcopal Church was not disestablished. The "Incorporation Act" of 1784 and the possession of the glebe lands seemed to assure a perpetual establishment in spite of article sixteen and the new Act. The Baptists, who had initiated the process of petitioning the House of Burgesses in 1770, continued through sermon and newsprint to agitate the issue of disestablishment. On August 5, 1786, the General Committee asked John Leland

and Reuben Ford to hand deliver to the Assembly a Memorial, asking for a repeal of "the incoporating act." The General Committee also called for a new round of petitions of support.

But now the Baptists, who had succeeded in enlisting the help of the Presbyterians, and after 1784, the Methodists, in the cause of religious freedom found themselves pretty much alone. However, the next year the Assembly did repeal the Incorporation Act, but left intact the glebes, which the Baptists considered public property, since they had been purchased with tax revenues. Finally in 1799 Madison prodded the Assembly into selling the disputed lands. By this time, Madison was well acquainted with the persistent, and sometimes exasperating, Baptists. In the process he had become their staunch and trusted friend.

However, James Madison, the major architect of the Constitution, saw no need for a bill of rights. By 1789 the pressure had mounted and Madison changed his mind. Once elected to Congress, he did not forget his commitment to a bill of rights upon which the Baptists and many others, including Jefferson, had insisted. On June 7, 1789, Madison submitted the first version of the no establishment clause of that which became the First Amendment, "as I considered myself bound in honor and in duty," he explained. The final version of the no establishment clause, in which he also had a hand, read: "Congress shall make no law respecting an establishment of religion, or prohibiting the free exercise thereof." Passed by the House of Representatives in September 24, it was approved by the Senate the next day. Two years later it became the chief cornerstone of the Bill of Rights ratified by the states.[14]

Finally, after more than a century and a half of struggle on the shores of the New World, the institutional separation of church and state, with its constitutional guarantee of religious liberty, had become the law of the land. The Fourteenth Amendment in 1947 made explicit that which had been implicit from the beginning, for the Bill of Rights was a people document, spelling out civil rights for all people in a nation of the free-born. Unfortunately at the time, not all in America were born free, as some Quakers and Mennonites pointed out. But this, too, was to change. Perhaps, Baptists were too preoccupied with celebrating the victory so recently won to launch a full-scale attack upon slavery, as Leland so ardently desired. However, there was much rejoicing in the Baptist Zion as a letter from Madison to Washington, dated November 20, 1789, indicated. "One of the principle leaders of the Baptists lately sent me word," he wrote, "that the amendments have entirely satisfied the disaffeted [sic] of his sect and that it would appear in their subsequent conduct."[15]

Conclusion

As much as Baptist piety propelled the movement toward the Puritan ideal of a sacral society with its inevitable demands for conformity, Baptist principles of ecclesiology have, until recent times, kept this tendency in check. Even when English Particular Baptists adopted The Westminster Confession, to the detriment of their own unique insights, they revised the confession to reflect their quite different ecclesiology with its strong emphasis upon religious freedom and the limitations of the state in spiritual matters (1677).[16]

Too, Baptists have often claimed that unlike some other minority groups, they have not asked for themselves that which they were unwilling to grant to others. From their beginning, they sought freedom for all others, including Jews, Muslims, Catholics, and atheists. Their confessions and published statements on the subject have pretty well substantiated this position. However, not all Baptists have recognized that there is no true freedom *of* religion if there is no freedom *from* religion. This is why Helwys, Williams, Backus, and Leland insisted upon the institutional separation of church and state. Such separation has proved the surest guarantee of religious freedom. It allows the church to be the church and the state to be the state. Unlike some others who hold to the separation concept, Baptists have never interpreted this to mean a withdrawal from social involvement which would effectively limit or even eliminate Christian participation in the political life of a democratic society. By the same token, Baptist confessional statements have always insisted that the gospel is not to be promoted by the arm of the law. To the contrary, the kingdom comes not by the power of the state but by the penetration of the salt, light, and leaven of the Christian witness. Gerhard Oncken stated it well when he said *"Jeder Baptist—ein Missionare."*[17] This is the ideal, for the priesthood of believers surely means as much to Baptists as it meant to Luther, that is, the inescapable social and moral stewardship of the Christian in his calling, whatever that may be.

Perhaps the greatest challenge facing the church today is to produce Christian men and women of integrity who will serve in the political life of the nation with courage and selfless devotion. It is by persuasion through spiritual means that men and women make responsible decisions about the ultimate issues of life. The Christian faith is the fruit of the Word and the Spirit acting upon the conscience to produce a voluntary commitment to Christ as Savior and Lord. Of such is the Kingdom of God and from such come citizens of integrity. The political and social dimensions of this reality do not comprise an American Shintoism. Such civil religion lacks any true transcendence. It too often deifies the state without realizing governments are temporal and finite. The God of Abraham, Isaac, and Jacob, and the Father of our Lord Jesus Christ is not a tribal deity but the Eternal One. Ultimately, the role of governments in the providence of God is a very limited one. Within these limitations they are bound to a higher moral law which recognizes the necessity of religious freedom as that right which is above all others—the right of every person "to obey God rather than men" (Acts 5:29).

Undeniably, the separation of church and state does produce a vacuum in society or a "naked public square." In this fact lies both the glory and the challenge of religious freedom. The so-called mainline denominations are too anemic, theologically, to fill the void and others have failed the crucial test of moral integrity. The times call for a new birth of the Christian faith, possessing both the vision and power of the Holy Spirit to do what no man or government can do. If the Christian faith is unequal to the task, no amount of propping up will do the job. Then, with Thomas Jefferson, I would say, "Let it fall," but with Roger Williams and John Leland, I am convinced it will not, for I am persuaded that "the gospel is still the power of God to salvation" for mankind and nations.

How Christian then is America? Only as Christian as its people—people who are indeed born from above through the power of the Spirit and thereby constitute both the most sensitive conscience and the most balanced critique of the nation. No amount of official public pronouncements or sloganeering can turn a claim into reality. That nation whose people see themselves under the judgment of a just and holy God are the most unlikely to make such a claim. Neither the advocates of a "civil religion" nor the Reconstructionists (the extreme flank of the New Religious Right) are capable of such a role. Only a free church liberated from the entangling alliances of a state church can perform this exacting and necessary task. This set of circumstances only the institutional separation of church and state alone can make possible.

Notes

1. Anne Fremantle, ed., *The Papal Encyclicals in Their Historical Context.* (New York: The New American Library, 1963), 149.

2. *The Naked Public Square* (Grand Rapids: William B. Eerdmans Publishing Company, 1984), 116.

3. Stan Hastey reported that Pat Robertson, a self-declared presidential candidate in 1988, has repeatedly pronounced the separation of church and state a "myth." *Report from the Capital*, October 1982, 8.

4. Winthrop S. Hudson, "The Issue of Church and State" in *Foundations* 13 (April-June 1980): 159.

5. Robert L. Maddox, "Church and State: The Ramparts Besieged," *The Christian Century*, February 25, 1987, 191.

6. See the sermon E. Y. Mullins preached before a World Congress of the Baptist World Alliance meeting in Stockholm, Sweden in 1923, in Walter B. Shurden, editor, *The Life of*

Baptists in the Life of the World (Nashville: Broadman Press, 1985), 57-64, for one of the most succinct and forceful statements of the historic Baptist position relative to religious liberty and its implications for church-state relations.

7. I carefully examined a copy of this little book in 1974 and believe it to have been printed in the Netherlands before Helwys returned to England in 1612. A photostat copy is in the A. Webb Roberts Library, Southwestern Baptist Theological Seminary.

8. Modernized spelling, ibid., 69.

9. William L. Lumpkin, ed., *Baptist Confessions of Faith* (Philadelphia: Judson Press, 1959), 140.

10. Cited in Roland H. Bainton, *The Travail of Religious Liberty* (New York: Harper & Brothers Publishers, 1951), 219, 220.

11. Roger Williams, *The Bloudy Tenent of Persecution* in *The Complete Writings of Roger Williams* (New York: Russell and Russell, 1963), 3:3.

12. Ibid., 4.

13. Perry Miller, *Roger Williams: His Contribution to the American Tradition* (New York: Atheneum, 1962), 254-55.

14. See Edwin S. Gaustad, *Faith of Our Fathers* (San Francisco: Harper & Row, Publishers, 1987), 156-58 for the sequence of events leading to the passage of the First Amendment in Congress.

15. Cited by J. M. Dawson, *Baptists and the American Republic* (Nashville: Broadman Press, 1956), 115.

16. "The Second London Confession" Chap. XXI, art.2. reads: "God alone is Lord of the Conscience, and hath left it free from the Doctrine and Commandments of men which are in any thing contrary to his Word, or not contained in it." Lumpkin, 280.

17. Gunter Balders, ed., *Ein Herr, Ein Glaube, Eine Taufe: 150 Jahre Baptistengemeinden in Deutschland, 1834-1984* (Wuppertal and Kassel: Oncken Verlag, 1985:), 37.

20

The Church and the Arts

by William L. Hendricks

Caricature is an art, at least when done by accomplished artists. In the visual arts one thinks of Honoré Daumier's (1808-79) social and judicial paintings. A century earlier Goya's (1746-1828) caricatures of the wealthy and ecclesiastics come to mind. In oratory Clarence Darrow brought his caricatures and satire to the height of an art in his court cases and his writings. G. K. Chesterton was a literary master of satire, the verbal basis for caricature. I would like to paraphrase an attributed quote from Chesterton as a way of expressing a caricature about Baptists and art. Chesterton is reported to have said that throughout the Middle Ages art was for the sake of God, during the Neo-Classical and Romantic period art was for art's sake (*ars gratia artis*), and in the twentieth century there is no art for God's sake. It is widely assumed about Baptists and among some Baptists that there is no art for God's sake. It is that assumption I would like to challenge by way of providing some examples of Baptist interests in the arts. A caricature is effective only if there is some recognized truth in the portrayal. Certainly Baptists, in their earlier history, have produced neither great artists nor many works of high art. The Anabaptists were generally too busy running to write, and frontier Baptists in America were more given to plowing than painting. Nevertheless, there are notable exceptions to the rules and there are contemporary signs of encouragement.

What Is Baptist Art?

The sectarian question "What is Baptist art?" is a form of the larger discussion of "What is religious art?" or the more specific question "What is Christian art?" Much ink has been used and too little light has been shed on that problem. Is art religious because of the subject matter only? Is art Christian because the artist is Christian? Can secular scenes be sacralized? Can sacred objects be prostituted by poor artistry? Do Christian artists do secular work? Or are religion and art two spheres which overlap but cannot be compared? For example, religion is a system of belief while art is a skill or a product. The question of definition becomes more sensitive in an age of unbelief, which is also an age of "technologized" skills.

The Enlightenment was a revolution in the arts. There was a major shift in the philosophy and the production of the arts when art was no longer done for the sake of God, when art became primarily for humankind's sake. There is even a greater revolution which has occurred in our own time when art is for commercial or investment's sake. In an age which prizes art for its economic value it seems irrelevant to ask if a given artifact is religious or if a building is designed according to Christian sensibilities. The question of Baptist art seems especially vapid or inordinately hubristic. Who cares about a sectarian expression of art? Is a catalog of Baptist artistic endeavors to be used as a keeping-up-with-the-Presbyterians mentality? I trust not. Any given Christian community needs to nurture its adherents. Christian nurture includes a challenge to the full expression of all of the talents of all of its community.

It is axiomatic that humans are artistic. It is consequent that Christians should express their artistic abilities and cultivate their worship through the appreciation for and production of the beautiful. The useful arts of architecture, oratory, and communications should express the distinctiveness of a community's belief no less than the liturgical arts of music and drama and the embellishing arts of painting and sculpture. We need to talk about Baptist arts as art which is expressive of and reflective of Baptist belief. If the title seems less than ecumenical, the intention is thoroughly catholic. It is my conviction that it is precisely in the realm of the arts and their cultivation and appreciation that the people called Baptists will more readily find their relatedness to the whole body of Christ than they have in theological discourse.

There is therefore a deeper purpose to this chapter than that of breaking the stereotype that Baptists are not concerned with the arts and have never produced or fostered them. The deeper intention of the chapter is to encourage an ecumenicity through the arts, an ecumenicity that Baptists have found difficult to accomplish through formal discourse. A third purpose in writing on Baptists and the arts is to issue a call for Baptists to become intensely, even evangelistically, involved in the arts as artists, collectors, patrons, and resource persons. The passion of the Baptist communities for truth (doctrine) has seldom been questioned. There have been Baptists concerned about the good (ethics)—church and state issues, personal morality, the social gospel, etc. There must be a concomitant concern for beauty for the sake of a full-orbed worship and in the recognition of a God who is the Author of beauty as well as of truth and goodness.

These expressions of rationale and purpose have not answered the question, "What is Baptist art?" Is Baptist art that which is performed or executed by Baptist artists? Not necessarily. Is Baptist art about subject matter supposedly sacred to Baptists, that is, baptismal scenes or portraits of Baptist "saints"? Only marginally. I will use both examples of Baptist artists and Baptist subjects, but these only illustrate a broader definition. I would define Baptist art as that exploration and production of beauty in the service of God for the sake of the nurture of the Baptist community with an eye toward its distinctive contributions to and its basic kinship with the body of Christ. In this sense there is also a Roman Catholic art, an Orthodox art, a Methodist art, etc. All of these are aspects of Christian art. Christian art is a necessary way of celebrating the Incarnation of Christ, of worshiping in the body of Christ, and of building a bridge in recognizing the cosmic Christ in all of creation.

Beginnings: Plates and Panes

There were not painters until the Renaissance. Prior to the sixteenth century artists were craftsmen who often did a variety of creative tasks. Certainly the earliest forerunners of Baptist artists were craftsmen also. They were those who made useful objects for everyday life and embellished them. In the 1620s, among Anabaptists coming out of Switzerland into Hungary, was a Habans family who were gifted ceramicists. Habans pottery or ceramics has become a highly prized national treasure in Hungary. One finds copies of it in the museums. The pottery is mostly hard glaze with simple, stylized floral designs. The distinguishing colors of this ceramic ware are deep blue, bright yellow, and pale green on an off-white background. All of the pieces I have seen are ceremonial and of antique usage and patterns. There are tankards, mugs, lavers, chargers, etc. Two factors make this early ceramic pottery a type of Baptist art. The first is the type of pattern and subject matter depicted on the ware. The patterns are basically simple. Human figures are not represented on the early ware, indicative of the iconoclastic religious sentiments of the Anabaptists and the Reformed traditions. These sentiments persist to the present in typical Swiss folk art and the floral and curlique frames of the mottos frequently painted on houses in Swiss villages. One has only to contrast the designs on old houses in villages around the Lake of Thun (Thuner See) with the Roman Catholic adornments in the South German village of Oberammergau to see the startling contrast religious sensibilities played in the folk art of the fifteenth and sixteenth centuries. This contrast is likewise notable in the iconic pictures of Catholic homes placed in the *Herrgottwinkel* (God's corner) and the noniconic embellished mottos of the comparable *Bibelwinkeln* of Lutheran homes. Ervin Beck is certainly correct in saying that ". . . the genre of [of folk arts—paintings on glass is his special reference] as a whole is more important for what it reveals about the sociology, theology and aesthetics of the communities that support the art."[1]

The first factor in describing Hungarian Habans pottery as a Baptist art is that of subject matter and its treatment. The designs demonstrate the simplicity and noniconic subjects. The second factor in styling this ceramic ware as a Baptist art is historical. It was Anabaptists who began this particular artistic craft and produced it for many generations. And to that history is added the significant contemporary affection for and pride in that Anabaptist craft as a symbol of religious freedom and aesthetic production. The Baptists of Hungary today in their immediate past struggles for religious liberty identify, through this artistic medium, with the seventeenth-century Anabaptist originators of this art.

Habans's pottery is a modest but honest Baptist art form. The early history of Baptists (whether one espouses the Swiss or the English theory of origins) was characterized by simplicity. The earliest Baptists were countercultural which, in my opinion, is different from the Philistinism of an anticultural bias characterizing some Baptists in the contemporary scene.[2] In my call for a "Baptist art" it should be made clear that any adequate Baptist art would forbear from being anticultural; for example against classical Catholic art in principle. Nor should a Baptist art be an art of culturization. That is, an appropriate Baptist art should not be accommodated to contemporary architecture, embellishments, and decorations without critical reflection on their secular origins and expressions. We should not build centers of worship without an eye to our theological heritage and our relation to the whole body of Christ.

A second example of Anabaptist art moves us from plates to panes, panes of glass on which painting was done. David Jaris (1501-56), an Anabaptist by religious profession, owed his livelihood to the profession of painting on glass. He was a journeyman in France about 1520 and after study in England he lived and worked in Delft, Holland. Ervin Beck reports a sketch by Jaris in the Albertina in Vienna, and some of his preliminary drawings are in England. Jaris's subject matter was largely biblical scenes. We have the names of two other Dutch Anabaptists who were painters on glass and who are listed among the Dutch Anabaptist martyrs. They were Jan Woutersz and a man named Rommeken.[3] Beck makes loose connections among the Dutch Anabaptists, the German Mennonite and Amish communities, a Mennonite community of Saskatchewan, and contemporary Mennonite communities in Indiana. General characterizations of this group of folk arts and crafts are the Bible verse and moralizing motto motifs which are popular in much pietism and early American Puritan crafts. These paintings on glass also included family records and announcements of rites of passage.

Anabaptist painting on glass and its putative descendants gave appropriate expression to the simplicity and content of their religious beliefs. The beauty of creation, biblical affirmations about God the Creator and the Savior Jesus Christ, moral encouragement, and the significance of family life are threads which bind this line of Anabaptist craft-art to parallel beliefs among their descendants, who include a large number of diverse groups within the "Baptist family."

In addition to the plates and panes of the beginnings of Baptist arts, there are some few other noteworthy examples of Baptist art in Europe from the nineteenth and twentieth centuries. Many Baptists have seen the poignant picture *The Baptism* by a recognized Swedish artist, Gustav Cederstrom (active mid-1800s). The original hangs in the chapel of the Swedish Baptist Seminary in a suburb of Stockholm. Gustav Cederstrom was of the Romantic school, and although not a Baptist, he caught the spirit of Baptist piety in this outdoor baptism in a lake. The painting was created in 1886 from an experience the artist had of coming upon a baptismal service of the Baptists in a remote part of Sweden. The nineteenth-century Swedish clothes common to simple folk, the figure of a woman meditating in the foreground, the pastor in the act of baptizing are features set into a pleasant wooded landscape whose backdrop is a mountain lake, rimmed by mountains in the furthest background. The painting is well known in the Baptist community in Europe. There are numerous small reproductions of it. It is professional artistically and specifically Baptist in reference and subject matter. *The Baptism* shares in the broader community of pietism and serves as a visual witness to the "faith of our fathers" in such a way as to provide a general appeal.

Paolo Paschetto was an Italian artist born in the late-nineteenth century in Val Pellice, Italy. He was the son of a Baptist minister and was active in Italian Baptist circles until his death March 9, 1963. Paschetto was trained at La Academia della Belle Arte in Rome and later returned to the Academy as a professor. Paschetto was an engraver, a book illustrator, and a painter. Much of his work was specifically religious in nature. One of his major contributions was the interior design of the Waldensian Church in Rome, built in 1914. Paschetto planned and oversaw all of the interior embellishments and furnishings including the pulpit, the stained-glass windows, and the light fixtures. On the pulpit are bas-relief carvings of Albegensis, Luther, Calvin, and Savonarola. The ceiling beams are decorated in geometric patterns. The sixteen windows, executed by Picchiarinni, bear biblical inscriptions under visual symbols, including many of the artist's favorite motifs. These motifs include: a stylized, curly wool, prominently embossed, Agnus Dei; lilies; the vine and branches; and the rose of Sharon. This style of Paschatto's work reflects his training as an engraver/illustrator. His overtly religious art is related to the then current international Art

Deco style. His charming landscapes are similar to the neoimpressionist works of Paul Cezanne (1839-1906). Paschetto said that his religious art was a testimony intended to communicate biblical insights, whereas his landscapes were personal expressions of his devotion to God. Paschetto did a series of engravings on Psalm 23. In the office of the Italian Baptist Convention in Rome there is a lovely series of seven paintings based on the phrases of the Lord's Prayer. These express both mystical settings and the social and practical implications of faith, for which the painter and Italian Baptists in general are noted. In 1983 the Baptist community of Italy made a ninety-minute videotape on the life and work of Paolo Paschetto. Some Paschetto designs were chosen by the Italian government as stamp designs.

The mention of postage stamps brings to mind an unusual expression of Baptists in art. A third focus of Baptist art in Europe is on stamps. Professor Klaus Meister of the Baptist Seminary in Ruschlikon, Switzerland, has an extensive stamp collection. The collection is composed of stamps commemorating Baptist individuals and the contributions of Baptists. With this brief and far from definitive overview of the beginnings of Baptist art and some European examples we move to the American scene.

A Singing People

When we turn to the American scene we are faced with a richness and variety of Baptist groups. Doctrines such as the priesthood of all believers and the autonomy of the local church have sometimes led to a fierce and fissiparous spirit. In addition to a major schism among Baptists at the time of the Civil War we must add immigrating groups, language Baptist conventions, and the large and small groups of Afro-American Baptists.

Since it is impossible to be conversant with all of those Baptist bodies, the majority of the illustrations throughout the remainder of this article will be drawn from the group which the author knows best, namely Southern Baptists. Two things may safely be assumed about the source of Baptists counted or uncounted. They have a deep reverence for Scripture and they sing. Baptists are known as a singing people. The art of music is the most prized among us and the skill of music is the most highly developed. There is a Church Music Department which was organized in 1941 at The Sunday School Board of the Southern Baptist Convention, in Nashville, Tennessee. Reports gathered by Southern Baptist statisticians suggest that 1,744,018 Southern Baptists participate in a plethora of choir programs in the churches. There are 4,800 full-time ministers of music in SBC churches and an unreported number of associates, accompanists, volunteer choir directors, and so forth. The Church Music Department (CMD) has edited five major hymnals whose combined sales have been approximately 15 million copies.

The CMD is in the process of editing a new Baptist hymnal which will be issued in 1991.

Moreover the Southern Baptist Convention is heavily invested in music education. Each of the six SBC seminaries has a school or department of church music.[4] Likewise most of the sixty-two Southern Baptist affiliated colleges have departments of music, some of which provide very sophisticated musical programs and performance opportunities in vocal, instrumental, and conducting skills.

There is no standardized music liturgy for Baptists. It is my opinion that musical styles and worship styles are more divisive among Baptists than theological issues are. We have a generally accepted Faith Statement, however diverse the interpretations, but there is no common musical idiom among us. There is a diminishing core of commonly known or appreciated hymns, as illustrated by the survey for the new hymnal conducted by the Church Music Department. Tensions mount when highly trained ministers of music seek to refine or redefine the music tastes of congregations. Gospel songs and praise choruses are desired by some congregations; anthems and classical hymns by others. There are increasing numbers of churches who have both hymnals and gospel songbooks in the music racks of the pews. These enormous diversities are reflected by the choral music performed by the choirs of our churches. Taped musical accompaniments for devotional solo rendering are increasingly prevalent. Through the use of electronic devices the repertoire of even the smallest churches is expanded. Most taped accompaniments relate to contemporary gospel compositions rather than to more formal religious music or classical hymns. One unresolved area in Baptist life is how to relate our academic instruction in music to the less formal music of Baptist congregations. Baptists are still singing, but they are singing more diversely and disparately than formerly. One challenge which lies before us is how to make music, our most skillful and universal art, a unifying rather than a divisive art.

There are several composers of contemporary Christian music among Southern Baptists. Among others, Kurt Kaiser, Ragan Courtney, Ken Medema, Phil Landgrave, and Buryl Red write contemporary Christian music. There is a whole coterie of musical performing artists who earn their living by church concerts and engagements. For example, Cynthia Clawson, whose repertoire and use of varied musical idioms is broader than most gospel singers, has won a coveted Dove award for her gospel music recordings.[5]

"And Ye Shall Build Me a House"

Architecture is sometimes called the oldest art. Many rural Baptist churches in the South in the Colonial period were crude meeting places constructed of logs. As the urban areas prospered, brick churches of some architectural importance and beauty were built. The predominant styles of those pre-Civil War churches was Georgian.

Georgian architecture in a number of variations continues to be the predominant architectural style of Baptist churches in the South. After the Civil War, rural log churches were succeeded by clapboard ones, which, in turn, were succeeded by the small oblong brick houses of worship graced by an entryway steeple. Such are very much in evidence in the countryside today. Currently the Center for Religion and the Arts of The Southern Baptist Theological Seminary is collecting slides and visual histories of Southern Baptist Convention church architecture. Valuable visual representations of stained-glass windows and church buildings are being solicited. Such churches as the Broadway Baptist Church of Ft. Worth, Texas (modified Gothic); the Broadway Baptist Church of Louisville, Kentucky; and the Kirkwood Baptist Church of Kirkwood, Missouri (both modified Georgian); the First Baptist Church of Cleburne, Texas, whose interior art works include impressive wood sculpture; the First Baptist Church of Amarillo, Texas, with its neo-Byzantine interior; and the First Baptist Church of Norfolk, Virginia, which is starkly contemporary, have sent contributions for the architectural archives.

Southern Baptists have given architectural services to their churches since 1910. By 1940, the forerunner of our present Church Architecture Department was organized. The Church Architecture Department of the Baptist Sunday School Board serves approximately 3,600 churches per year with the basic services of plot-development planning, floor-plan studies, interior design, landscaping plans, and master planning.

During the 1970s and 1980s the rapid growth of megachurches made necessary the planning and design of large church building facilities equipped for the multifaceted ministries designed for every service from cafeteria to gymnasiums. Two notable buildings on this greatly expanded scale are the Second Baptist Church of Houston, Texas, and the First Baptist Church of Orlando, Florida.

In the planning of Baptist church structures, function has been more important than aesthetics. Educational and fellowship space has often been equally if not more significant than worship space. Stained glass has been the predominant visual art form in Southern Baptist church buildings. Many stained-glass designs give awareness of biblical and theological details found nowhere else in Baptist churches. In addition to the churches listed above, the biblical-historical windows of the Highland Baptist Church (Louisville, Kentucky), the contemporary faceted glass windows of the St. Matthews Baptist Church (Louisville, Kentucky), and the Tiffany-type windows of the First Baptist Church of Jonesboro, Arkansas, come to mind.

I have a serious theological dilemma about much of the interior design being incorporated in our church buildings today. There are no serious theological symbols included in our interior design aside from certain stained-glass windows. Secular interior designers are using aesthetically pleasant *en vogue* colors and *au courant* furnishings. But such designers, presumably unaware of the visual symbols of the Christian faith, are finishing and furnishing our church interiors in the fashion of television studios, commercial offices, and public buildings. I, for one, find this an inappropriate trend and would like to request our church building committees to think seriously about incorporating appropriate visual symbols of the Christian faith in our churches.

The Paucity of Paintings

The sharpest truths of the caricature about Baptists and the arts is at the point of painting and related visual arts. Apart from rural baptistry art, a genre deserving a full study before it is utterly eradicated, there are few paintings in Baptist churches and virtually no sculpture. We have been rigorous iconoclasts, pictoclasts, symboclasts—all to our detriment. The irony of all of this shying away from visual representations is found in the fact that we have an astonishing predilection for pictures and illustrations in our literature. Since the early part of this century we have had an art and design department at the Baptist Sunday School Board. It is interesting and significant that our best visual art is in children's publications.

The original paintings for children's literature are kept in the art archives of the Baptist Sunday School Board in Nashville, Tennessee. In that respect, it would be important for us all to become children. The often banal illustrations and line sketches of our adult literature need badly to be upgraded to the etching, classic reproduction, full-scale painting stage. One piece of adult literature, *Life Source,* by Avery Willis is to be commended for its Gustave Doré type engravings, nicely reproduced. There are no theological reasons that we should not worship God with our eyes. We whose tradition has often stressed the visual aspects of eschatology would do well to incarnate and encourage appropriate visual aspects in our worship here and now.[6]

Conclusion

These thoughts are preliminary and incomplete. They do not take into account the burgeoning results of the church drama work at the Baptist Sunday School Board. Puppetry is used widely in the children and youth ministries of many Southern Baptist churches. Art teams from Baptist Campus Ministries are cultivating the creative gifts of college students. The Home Mission Board, through its efforts in leisure and resort ministries, uses a variety of artistic media in both seasonal ministries and permanent ministry situations. The Foreign Mission Board has demonstrated interest in the arts by its collections and exhibits of the visual arts and crafts, its encouragement of indigenous artists, and its vigorous program of films and other audiovisual products.

Two encouraging organizations demonstrate a new awareness and interests of Southern Baptists in the Arts. The Center for Religion and the Arts at The Southern Baptist Theological Seminary provides a focal point for gathering materials about Southern Baptists in the arts and for promoting and developing artistic concerns and a theological undergirding and interpretation of the arts. A first National Conference in Religion and the Arts, held in Louisville, Kentucky, September 1989, is evidence of such efforts. In 1989 a group called Churches and Christians in the Arts (CCIA) was organized at the Southern Baptist Convention. All of these are encouraging evidences of Southern Baptist interest and participation in the arts.

It is hoped that this beginning recital of Baptist performances and interests in the arts will at least alter the caricature that Baptists believe there is no art for God's sake. I trust this chapter will constitute a call for awareness among Baptists that we have begun to enjoy and utilize the beautiful in the service of God who is good, and true, and beautiful. Three suggestions are appropriate as we Baptists use the arts. We need to use the arts—from architecture to xylophones—with a theologically critical awareness that asks about the appropriateness of style and content in all our artistic expressions. We need to express in the best artistic manner possible the nuances of our heritage and join them to the worthy artistic expressions of the whole body of Christ. Especially do we need to cultivate and channel the considerable artistic interests and talents of our people so as to claim all of the gifts of God among us. Whether in word or deed, whether in sermon or art, what we do is for the sake of God. Such service is also inevitably a ministry with humankind. There is art for God's sake, and we should be participants in it.

Notes

1. Ervin Beck, "Mennonite and Amish Painting on Glass," *The Mennonite Quarterly Review* (MQR) 63 (April 1989): 115-49. Although this article deals largely with twentieth-century painting on glass, there are also valuable historical materials and comparisons in it.

2. Anticulturalism is also different from a too easy culturalization which characterizes much of contemporary Baptist life. For a theological evaluation of these positions see H. Richard Niebuhr, *Christ and Culture* (New York: Harper and Row, 1954).

3. I am dependent for this information and much of the material in this section on Ervin Beck's article cited above. See also James M. Stayer, "David Jaris: A Prolegomenon to Further Research," MQR 59 (1985): 1.

4. These were established chronologically as follows: The Southern Baptist Theological Seminary; Southwestern Baptist Theological Seminary; New Orleans Baptist Theological Seminary; Golden Gate Baptist Theological Seminary; Southeastern Baptist Theological Seminary; Midwestern Baptist Theological Seminary.

5. I have not given attention to prominent Baptists who perform exceptionally in the broader musical world such as Van Cliburn, the celebrated pianist; Marilyn Mims, who is in her second successful season at the Metropolitan Opera; or Jacob Wil, formerly of the San Francisco Opera, now of the Zurich Opera Company.

6. Statistics were provided by the several departments of the Sunday School Board of the Southern Baptist Convention, Nashville, Tennessee.

21
Ordination in the Church

by Fisher Humphreys

Most Christian churches ordain their clergy. The few who do not, such as the Friends (Quakers), are the small exception which proves the rule. Though the practice of ordination is nearly universal, it is a practice surrounded by questions of meaning, value, biblical basis, historical practice, and other practical matters.

We will begin our effort to respond to these questions by attempting to summarize what the Bible says about Christian ordination.

Biblical Basis

The biblical teaching about ordination is ambiguous. Interpretations of the biblical texts range from the Roman Catholic view that a sacramental understanding of ordination is taught, through the Protestant view that a nonsacramental understanding of ordination is taught, to the radical view of Quakers and Plymouth Brethren and others, that the Bible does not teach anything about ordination and that it is not appropriate even to speak of ordination with reference to the Bible.

I will begin this examination of the biblical teaching of ordination by summarizing a book published in 1982 entitled *Ordination: A Biblical-Historical View* by Marjorie Warkentin.[1] It is the most incisive, analytical, thorough, biblical study on this subject known to me.

Warkentin associates ordination with laying on of hands, a uniquely Jewish-Christian practice. In the Old Testament the laying on of hands had four principal meanings. First, it could be done for blessing. An example of this is the story of Jacob blessing his grandsons (Gen. 48:14). Second, a priest's hands were laid on a sacrificial animal (Lev. 4:4). Third, the Levites were inducted into office when the people of Israel laid hands on them (Num. 8:10). Finally, Joshua was commissioned to leadership when Moses laid hands on him (27:23). In each case except that of the Levites, something sacramental occurred. Jacob actually passed along a blessing to Manasseh and Ephraim; the priest transferred sin to the head of the animal; Moses shared his glory or authority with Joshua. Warkentin believes that the setting apart of Levites and of Joshua were unique events in the history of redemption. They were not repeated in the Old Testament, and they were not repeatable.

Warkentin locates twenty-four occurrences of the phrases "laying on of hands" and "lay on hands" in the New Testament.[2] Most of these usages refer either to blessing (Mark 10:13-16) or to healing (8:23-25), a usage with no Old Testament precedent. Nine other usages occur, one in Hebrews, five in Acts, and three in the letters to Timothy. It is these which must be interpreted in order to understand the New Testament teaching about ordination. Warkentin interprets all nine of them in terms of the Old Testament imposition of hands.

She begins with Hebrews 6:2. Her conclusion is that, in keeping with the book's theme of the superiority of the New Covenant to the Old, the reference is to animal sacrifice; the readers are urged not to offer animal sacrifices in the temple.

The five passages in Acts concern the seven Hellenists (ch. 6), the Samaritans who were baptized (ch. 8), Saul's conversion (ch. 9), the commissioning of Saul and Barnabas (ch. 13), and the twelve converts at Ephesus (ch. 19). Of these five, most discussions of ordination, including most Baptist discussions, ignore Saul's conversion and the baptism of the Samaritans and the Ephesian twelve, simply admitting that sometimes in the early church hands were imposed at baptism. Warkentin does not do this. She insists that they be considered together, because she believes that the writer used the imposition of hands consistently and that he always intended to say something important when he did so.

She suggests that the imposition of hands on the seven Hellenists is to be interpreted in the light of Moses' imposition on Joshua; in each case, men are being set aside for leadership into a new land, Canaan and Hellenism. She interprets the imposition on the Samaritans and the Ephesians similarly. Though involved with baptisms, these events were also important moments in the story of redemption, and the imposition of hands expressed this because it was an allusion to the experience of Joshua.

Saul's baptism is quite different. Warkentin believes that the imposition of Ananias's hands suggests that of the Old Testament priest on a sacrificial animal; Saul is to become a sacrificial offering for the sake of the Gentiles.

The commissioning of Saul and Barnabas to be missionaries was, Warkentin writes, a parallel to the imposition of hands on the Levites; in the experience of Saul and Barnabas as well as that of the Levites, priestly authority is given to mediate a new covenant to the peoples.

Next, Warkentin moves to the pastoral epistles. She leaves unsettled the question of whether 1 Timothy 4:14 and 2 Timothy 1:6 refer to the same event, but she interprets them differently. Second Timothy 1:6 suggests that a unique relation existed between Paul and Timothy, analogous to that between Moses and Joshua, and that Paul passed along his authority to Timothy in something like the way Moses gave his to Joshua. As such, it was a unique event and did not occur in the experience of people other than Timothy. First Timothy 4:14 is similar to the commissioning of Saul and Barnabas recorded in Acts, and it is understood as analogous to the imposition on the Levites. Warkentin admits that 1 Timothy 5:22 is obscure. To the three traditional interpretations—that it refers either to baptism, or to ordination, or to receiving repentant sinners back into church—she adds a fourth. She thinks that Paul was instructing Timothy not to be too quick to put hands on a sacrificial animal, that is, not to be hasty in accepting Jewish cultic requirements.

Warkentin offers some of these interpretations tentatively and others with more confidence. All are given in full awareness of the other available interpretations, and all argued with great care and at great length.

Two of Warkentin's conclusions are important for us. First, in the early church the imposition of hands was a very serious matter, and, except in the case of healing, the New Testament writers always used it in light of Old Testament precedents; in doing so they were interpreting the persons and events of their time theologically. Second, the New Testament provides neither warrants nor precedents for contemporary ordination practices and beliefs. It provides only interpretations of events in its own time, and these are understood as unique moments in salvation history and therefore as being just as unrepeatable as Calvary or Pentecost. All the references to the imposition of hands are descriptive rather than normative.

Where does that leave the current practice of ordination? Warkentin believes that ordination is unnecessary for the church today. It has too many problems to be of service. It divides clergy from laity, violates Jesus' teaching that leaders should be servants, loses sight of the achievement of Jesus as our priest, forfeits the priesthood of believers, and undermines the New Testament teachings that spiritual gifts are given to all Christians and that all are called to ministry. While I do not accept all of her conclusions, I am grateful that she has helped me to look more carefully at ordination in Baptist life.

Meaning

In Baptist life, ordination to the Christian ministry presupposes that the individual has heard and accepted a call from God.[3] So universal is this perception that many Baptists would find it difficult to imagine ordination apart from an individual call.[4] Yet the two are distinct. The call to ministry is given to the individual; ordination, on the other hand, is the community's response to the call which the individual has sensed. If the distinction between call and ordination is clarified, then the importance of their relation will be enhanced.

The distinction might appear more clearly if we acknowledge, quite forthrightfully, that little is said in the Bible to connect them. Let us consider briefly the following facts: the imposition of hands on the Levites and Joshua, two of the Old Testament rites most likely to have been precedents for Christian ordination, do not presuppose a divine call sensed by these men, to which the community was responding. Likewise the imposition of hands on the seven Hellenists and on Barnabas and Saul were not the community's responses to an inner call sensed by these men; at least, no call is mentioned in the texts. Even the most explicitly Christian ordination of a minister, that of Timothy, is not the community's response to an inner call felt by Timothy, for again no call is mentioned. The inner call to an individual and the church's response of ordination are not conflated in the Bible. In fact, the question might seriously be asked whether it is appropriate for the church to understand ordination as its response to a call to ministry felt by an individual.

This raises for us the vital question, "What is the meaning of ordination?" I want to suggest that traditional categories for understanding ordination (sacramental or nonsacramental)[5] are not nuanced enough to provide a clear, helpful interpretation. I propose that the following analysis is more illuminating: (1) ordination as sacrament; (2) ordination as authorization; (3) ordination as installation; (4) ordination as confirmation and blessing.

The first interpretation, the sacramental, is the majority view because it is the official teaching of the Roman Catholic Church as well as the view of some other large Christian bodies. It sees the church as a divinely established institution, entrusted with graces and gifts, which it in turn shares. In ordination an individual receives a sacramental grace which is an indelible character, and he enters an order of priests with special rights and duties.[6] God is thus acting upon him through the ordination.

In defense of this view, it may be said that it takes ordination with profound seriousness, in that it recognizes God's presence and activity therein. It also takes the biblical references to a gift given in ordination (1 Tim. 4:14; 2 Tim. 1:6) in what appears to be their most straightforward meaning. While the fully developed Roman Catholic view goes far beyond the hints given in these two passages, it takes them at what some would call their face value.

This interpretation is finally unacceptable because, we believe, no persons within the church have a grace which can be communicated to others by the imposition of hands. Of course, all Christians may teach and persuade and otherwise influence one another; in this sense they may be channels of blessing to one another, but they do not actually confer gifts from God by means of channels of grace.[7]

The second interpretation, that ordination is authorization, is characteristic of many Protestant churches. Luther and Calvin, for example, retained ordination as a church's conferring of authority to preach the Word and administer the sacraments, with the emphasis being upon the ministry of the Word. Though ordination is to a function rather than an office as in Roman Catholicism, still it is an awesome authority that is given. Though the authority which ordination gives comes through the church, ultimately it derives from God; it is divine authority.

But is even this claim defensible? More precisely, is it the case that only those who are ordained are called to the ministry of the Word, or are all Christians called to be witnesses? Jesus and His disciples were not ordained; were they then not ministers of the Word?

It is possible to make the interpretation of ordination as authorization more defensible by altering the meaning of "authorization." What is done is to say, not that God authorizes ministry by ordination, but just that the church does. In other words, for its own purposes the church may accept as ministers of the Word those whom it ordains, and reject all others. While this interpretation helps remove the anomalies in this view, it is not entirely satisfactory either, for there is no demonstrable connection between the ministry of the Word and ordination, either in Scripture or in experience. If an exact correspondence is affirmed, a church ought logically to ordain all its members, for God calls all Christians to be His witnesses.

The third interpretation of ordination is that it is an installation service. A person who is to take up a new work, for example, in a church or a seminary, may have it inaugurated by a service of dedication. Such a service may include the imposition of hands. This view can claim biblical precedents. Paul and Barnabas received the imposition of hands as the inauguration of their missionary work. The seven received the imposition of hands as the inauguration of their assisting the apostles.

But is an installation an ordination? It is one possible interpretation of the meaning of ordination. It is the widest possible institutional interpretation in the sense that it alone may be acceptable to all Christians. Its importance in the life of an institution lies in its definiteness; a pastor is installed as pastor of this church, precisely; a president as president of this school, precisely. On the other hand, these actions are not necessarily a matter either of a sacramental efficacy or of authorization to the ministry of Word and sacrament.

The primary justification for installing leaders is practical. The church needs ministers, and it needs to signal that their work is beginning; this is a suitable way to do this. Should biblical precedent be claimed for installing a minister? Two things may be said. First, no precedent is needed. The institution is simply signaling that a new minister is in place. This no more requires a biblical precedent than does running a notice in a local newspaper or inviting guests to a reception for the new minister; it is a public notice. Second, Christians have a profound need to find biblical precedents for what they do. Sunday School teachers remember how Ezra and Nehemiah taught the Law. Evangelists identify with the itinerant ministry of Paul. Youth ministers recall that Timothy was told not to allow anyone to despise his youth. Ministers of music love the biblical passages in which Christians are encouraged to sing praises to God. Professors of religion recall with enthusiasm that Jesus taught people. Christians naturally look to the Bible for precedents for their own forms of service. It is no good for a historically alert scholar to point out that it is an anachronism to speak of "professors" or "youth ministers" in the Bible. At an intellectual level this comment is correct, but at the level of lived experience, the need for biblical precedents means that people gain a sense of assurance by identifying themselves with people in the Bible; they find it humanly meaningful to think in terms of biblical precedents; the cash value of this identification is simply this: "God has called me to do my work as a teacher or president or whatever, just as long ago He called those whose stories I read in the Bible." It is psychologically insensitive to deny the appropriateness of such language.

The same is true of ordination. It is not a sacrament with efficacy, and it is not divine authorization. But when it signals the beginning of a person's ministry, it may claim precedents from the Bible. This is true of the imposition of hands; probably its best biblical precedents are Joshua, the Levites, the seven Hellenists, the commissioning of Saul and Barnabas, and Timothy's ordination. What can be said in the case of an installation today and of each of these biblical stories is this: "At this time and in this place, we recognize and acknowledge the beginning of a new service for God on the part of this person (or these persons), and we believe that God is in this."

In Southern Baptist life, the most public example of this reality is the commissioning of persons to missionary service. Another is the inauguration of presidents of academic institutions. But every time a person is ordained to ministry, that, too, is an example of installation.

So far three interpretations of ordination have been suggested. First, it is a sacrament; this view is rejected. Second, it is a divine authorization; this view also is rejected. Third, it is installation; this view is accepted as biblically appropriate and institutionally adequate.

Yet, this view may seem unsatisfactory to many Baptists. They may say, "But ordination is more than installation." And so it is, in a very important sense. But the way in which it is more than installation is not what one might expect. It is not more than an installation in any institutional sense, so far as I can tell. The Bible does not authorize more than this institutionally, because the only other two institutional understandings, as sacrament and as divine authorization, are not defensible. Ordination is more than an institutional installation; it also is a communal confirmation and blessing.

The distinction between the church as an institution and the church as a community of persons has been made many times, nowhere more convincingly than by Emil Brunner in *The Misunderstanding of the Church*.[8] He argued that God's purpose is to create a family of persons who have faith and love and who worship God and serve one another. That is the church; Brunner chose to call it by its Greek name, *ecclesia*. He carefully distinguished the community, *ecclesia*, from the institution we call church, with its buildings, budgets, programs, and organizations. Brunner acknowledged that institutions are inevitable, but he insisted that they are to be the servant of the *ecclesia*, the fellowship of faith. The fundamental reality, the reality that matters, is the community of persons.

In the first three interpretations of ordination—as sacrament, authorization, and installation—we have been thinking of the church as an institution. We have argued that the best institutional understanding of ordination is the third; so far as I can tell, that will suffice for institutional needs, and one is entitled to seek out biblical precedents for it if one wishes.

Now we are proposing that a far more important understanding of ordination is a noninstitutional one, a communal one. It is to see the church acting as a fellowship rather than as an institution. Given this understanding—a family dealing with one of its members—how are we to understand ordination? While several options might be open, I want to suggest that the community is in a position to confirm the sense of call which the individual has and to bless the individual as he attempts to exercise the gifts which God has given him. These activities are entirely familial and interpersonal; they have nothing whatever to do with institutions.

Can ordination, understood as confirmation and blessing, claim biblical precedents? First, it is not necessary to do so. It is entirely appropriate for a family of faith to confirm and support one of its members in what he and they believe to be God's call, and to offer their blessings and best wishes. It may do this in its songs, in its counsel, in its proclamations of faith, in its teaching—and in an ordination service. No biblical precedent is required, other than the general biblical theme that a church should provide nurture for the faith of its members and guidance for their lives.

Second, if God calls persons into special phases of ministry, it certainly is biblical for the church to confirm such a call, and ordination is one way to confirm a member's call. Since these two ideas are not specifically linked in the New Testament—an inner sense of call to special ministry and ordination by the church—two conclusions follow. One is that a church does not have to confirm a call in this way; it may do so in other ways, such as licensing, or simply expressing confirmation of the call verbally. The second is that ordination does not have to wait for an inner sense of call. Surprising as it may appear to many people, the church may be led by God to lay hands on a person who first learned of his call, not from an inner experience, but from the church itself. This was the case with the seven Hellenists and with Paul and Barnabas. Interestingly, it seems sometimes to have been the case in early Baptist life.

Third, when a church expresses a communal blessing by means of the imposition of hands, it has very strong biblical precedents. Jacob blessed his grandchildren, and Jesus blessed children in this way. Would anyone seriously doubt that whenever hands were laid upon a member of the community of faith, a blessing was being given? Sometimes a leader imposed hands (Moses, Ananias, Paul); sometimes a group within the community did it (the elders who laid hands on Timothy, the apostles who laid hands on the seven Hellenists); sometimes the entire community did so (for the Levites, and perhaps for Saul and Barnabas). In any case, a blessing is given by the community together or through its leaders to one of its members. Of course, the community has many other ways of giving its blessing to a member, but this surely is an appropriate one.

In summary, though ordination as a communal confirmation of a member's call and a communal blessing upon him in his service does not require explicit biblical precedents, in fact it has them. Whatever the student of history may conclude about the relationship between the Bible and contemporary church ordination practices and beliefs, a spiritual, religious, theological tie does exist.

Our conclusion, therefore, is that ordination may be regarded institutionally as an installation which meets legitimate institutional needs to signal the beginning of a new work, and communally as a confirmation of a member's call and a blessing upon him and his work.

Our questions about church order and practices usually have been formulated in terms of obligation. "Should we do this—ought we to practice that—what is necessary here?" In view of the fluidity of early Christian practices as revealed in the New Testament, perhaps it would be better to speak of privilege rather than obligation.[9] Perhaps the better question is not "Ought we to ordain?" but "May we ordain?"[10] In other words, may we as

a community of faith call a council, examine a member, recommend ordination, hold a worship service, and lay hands on the member as an institutional installation and a communal confirmation and blessing? The answer,
surely, is "Yes, we may do this."

I do not suppose that this understanding will satisfy all Baptists, let alone
others. I am offering it as an exploratory proposal. As far as I can tell, it is
consistent with the Baptist heritage, and it seems to me to say what needs to
be said. Others will have to decide about that.

Conclusion

God calls all the family of humankind to come to His Son Jesus Christ for
salvation, and He calls all who have faith in Jesus Christ to be His disciples.
Christian discipleship includes both moral obedience and commitment to
service. All Christians are to be servants, that is, ministers.

When a member of a Christian community accepts the call to minister—
in whatever way—the community is free to confirm that call and to put its
blessings upon the member. A Sunday School teacher may be installed; a
ministerial student may be licensed; a summer camp counselor may be inducted; a president may be inaugurated; a dean may receive an investiture; a
summer youth missionary may be appointed; an adult missionary may be
commissioned; a seminary student may be graduated; a family counselor
may be certified; a music minister may be ordained.

The call to individuals may or may not have been specific; what matters is
that they have committed themselves to minister for Christ's sake. The ministry may be lifelong or temporary. The institutional implications of the act
of installation may be limited or extensive. The ministry may involve outstanding leadership, or it may consist of being a loyal follower. The confirmation and blessing may be given with or without the imposition of hands.
If hands are imposed, it may be an entire church or by a representative
group. The church may or may not wish other churches to recognize what it
has done. This may or may not be the only such public act in the life of this
member. These and other matters that are disputed seem to lose their importance when ordination is understood as proposed in this paper.

What, then, is really important in ordination? Ordination is a matter between a church and one of its members. The member is undergoing a passage into a new experience in ministry. Institutionally, the church is providing a signal that one of its members is entering a new phase of Christian
ministry. Communally, the church is confirming this ministry for its member and placing its blessing upon the person and that person's ministry.[11]

Notes

1. Marjorie Warkentin, *Ordination: A Biblical-Historical View* (Grand Rapids: Eerdmans, 1982).

2. Warkentin considers the evidence for first-century rabbinic ordination too undependable to use. Other scholars such as Eduard Lohse and David Daube seem to think that rabbinic ordination was determinative for most of the early Christian ordination practice and beliefs.

3. An extensive literature exists concerning Baptist ordination practices and beliefs. The following items are helpful for gaining an overview:

A paper prepared jointly by the faculties of the Southern Baptist Theological Seminary, Southwestern Baptist Theological Seminary, and New Orleans Baptist Theological Seminary, *The Ordination of Baptist Ministers* (Nashville: Broadman Press, 1954).

H. H. Hobbs, "Ordination: Ministers," *The Encyclopedia of Southern Baptists* (Nashville: Broadman Press, 1958), 2:1056-57.

C. Anne Davis, "Ordination of Southern Baptist Women," *The Encyclopedia of Southern Baptists* (Nashville: Broadman Press, 1982) 4:2557-58.

J. R. Hobbs, *The Pastor's Manual* (Nashville: Broadman Press, 1934), 184-89.

Franklin M. Segler, *The Broadman Minister's Manual* (Nashville: Broadman Press, 1969), 85-94.

Claude L. Howe, Jr., "The Call, Placement, and Tenure of Ministers," *Baptist History and Heritage* (January 1980), 3-13; reprinted in *Glimpses of Baptist Heritage* (Nashville: Broadman Press, 1981).

John E. Steely, "Ministerial Certification in Southern Baptist History: Ordination," *Baptist History and Heritage* (January 1980), 23-29, 61.

The spring 1969 issue of the *Southwestern Journal of Theology* was devoted to ordination; it included valuable articles by W. Boyd Hunt, John J. Kiwiet, J. Ithel Jones, Stewart A. Newman, Porter Routh, and William L. Hendricks, plus shorter items by a number of contemporary Baptist leaders.

The fall 1981 issue of *Review and Expositor* also was on the theme of ordination. Its authors were R. Alan Culpepper, E. Glenn Hinson, J. Robert Wright, Leon McBeth, Raymond Bailey, Daniel Aleshire, and Bill J. Leonard.

The most extensive Baptist study of ordination and guide for the practice of ordination is *Set Apart for Service* by Alton H. McEachern (Nashville: Broadman Press, 1980).

4. Baptists in the past would not all have been surprised. See Claude L. Howe, Jr., *Glimpses of Baptist Heritage* (Nashville: Broadman Press, 1981), 98. Howe's essay includes an exceptionally clear discussion of issues related to the call to ministry, including an analysis of four aspects of the call which was first proposed by H. Richard Niebuhr.

5. See, for example, "Orders and Ordination," *Oxford Dictionary of the Christian Church* (New York: Oxford, 1958), 987-89.

6. Piet Fransen, "Orders and Ordination," *Encyclopedia of Theology* (New York: Burns and Oates, 1975), 1122-48.

7. I am aware that I have asserted but not defended the traditional Protestant rejection of sacramentalism; the arguments are well-known and are too extensive for this chapter. It might be useful to note here that a church's view of ordination is always an integral part of a larger cluster of theological beliefs, especially its beliefs concerning grace and church order. The view of ordination which is espoused in this chapter, for example, is consistent with Baptist church polity as well as with Baptist experience of the divine call.

8. Emil Brunner, *The Misunderstanding of the Church*, trans. Harold Knight (Philadelphia: Westminster Press, 1953).

9. The definitive study of early Christian beliefs about polity is *Church Order in the New Testament* (London: SCM, 1961) by Eduard Schweizer, translated by Frank Clarke. His famous opening sentence, "There is no such thing as *the* New Testament church order," is defended successfully. The view of ordination proposed in this chapter has been offered in con-

scious agreement with Schweizer's work.

10. Neither the Bible, the Baptist heritage, nor contemporary experience mandates ordination. The New Testament contains no command to ordain or to be ordained. The great Baptist preacher C. H. Spurgeon was never ordained. Among recent Southern Baptists, Porter Routh and T. B. Maston, two outstanding ministers, were never ordained.

11. The author is grateful to the Baptist State Convention of North Carolina for permission to use materials here which appeared first in his essay "Call and Ordination: Commissioned to Ministry" which was published in *God-Called Ministry* edited by Morris Ashcraft (Baptist State Convention of North Carolina, 1983).

22
The Role of Women in the Church

by Sharon Hodgin Gritz

The role of women in the church represents "one of the most pressing problems facing believers in the closing years of the twentieth century."[1] Historically, the Free Churches, with their emphasis on spiritual gifts, have allowed opportunities for women in ministry.[2] Those belonging to the Believers' Church tradition have also claimed radical adherence to the principle of *sola Scriptura*.[3] What, then, does God's Word teach concerning the ways women may serve in the church? Specifically, how does one deal with the New Testament materials that offer direct teachings on women and ministry, especially those which appear to restrict their role? This discussion will limit itself to several of the Pauline passages that pose problems and provide principles for dealing with this contemporary issue.

The apostle Paul often serves as a focal point for discussing the role of women in the church. His writings have proved to be controversial, and conflicting interpretations have arisen.[4] For example, some feminists believe that Paul's writings "are distorted by the human instrument [Paul], yet they are instructive in showing us an honest man in conflict with himself."[5] At the same time, others affirm that Paul is "the only certain and consistent spokesman of the liberation and equality of women in the New Testament."[6] Paul's own "mission-praxis" confirms his acceptance of the ministry of women.[7] Nothing in the relevant texts gives any indication that the work of the women was of a subordinate character.[8] The apostle's practice, however, as well as his declaration that in Christ there is no male and female (Gal 3:28),[9] seem to contradict his actual teachings on the role of women in the church. These apparent contradictions derive primarily from three passages: 1 Corinthians 11:2-16[10], 14:34-36,[11] and 1 Timothy 2:9-15.[12]

This essay proposes that Paul's interest in developing, strengthening, and protecting sound family bonds, particularly between the wife and husband, influences his directives on the role of women in the church. The fact that the apostle uses marriage as an illustration of the relation between Christ and the church reflects its high value and the importance of a proper relationship between Christian spouses.

In marriage both partners have responsibilities to one another, responsibilities governed by the concept of mutual submission (Eph. 5:21). Although Paul exhorts wives to be subject to their husbands (vv. 22, 24), this submission stems from their own voluntary initiative[13] and grounds itself in their relationship to Christ. This elevates submission from connotations of docile servility and subservience. The wife submits herself to the husband as her *kephale* ("head").[14] Paul defines this headship in terms of *agape* ("love") and uses the example of Christ Himself for his model. Christ expressed His headship by His total self-giving, cherishing, self-sacrificing, nourishing, and saving rather than through exercising authority, rule, and dominance.[15] Consequently, Christian marriage involves self-giving love and mutual respect and contradicts merely sexual or utilitarian bases for matrimony.

In the New Testament era marriage was the most likely option for women.[16] For this reason, Paul's pronouncements concerning women in the three passages noted above probably were related particularly to wives, with the more general principles applying to all women regardless of their marital status. With this understanding, these passages will now be examined.

1 Corinthians 11:2-16

Both 1 Corinthians 11:2-16 and 14:34-36 occur in a lengthy discussion of pneumatic worship, 1 Corinthians 11—14. The interpretation of the first passage hinges on the understanding of several key words or concepts: *kephale*, head coverings or hair, *doxa* ("glory"), *exousia* ("authority"), and mutual dependence.

Paul uses *kephale*[17] to describe not only the relationship of husband to wife but also of Christ to man and God to Christ. The 1 Corinthians 11 passage does use *kephale* in the literal sense in verses 4-7 and 10. What does the word signify in verse 3? The context here tends to indicate that *kephale* is not confined to "source" alone. One must remember that Paul was writing to a Gentile community in the first century in a time in which marital disintegration through divorce and infidelity was the norm. The church had to reflect a Christian view of family relationships even within the context of worship. For this reason, *kephale* in verse 3 maintains the idea of headship.

Traditionally, exegetes have proposed that Paul refers in verses 4-6 and 13-15 to the custom of women wearing veils.[18] As recent interpreters have convincingly argued, however, the Corinthian women's error lay not in removing veils from their heads but in the manner in which they wore their hair.[19] Respectable fashion dictated that women wear their hair bound in some manner, "la coiffure étant un signe d'honneur."[20] *Akatakaluptos* thus refers in the passage to unbound hair as opposed to uncovered hair.[21] Paul's concern centered in the fact that Christian women should remain distinct from pagan women. Disheveled, unbound hair and wildly tossing heads characterized the veneration of Isis, Cybele, and Dionysius.[22] Evidently some women converts from these pagan backgrounds still had an affinity for their former modes of worship and brought these to the Christian worship setting. This had to stop. Unbound hair to Paul was the equivalent of having a shaved head. This had long signified for Jews grief or disgraceful punishment (for example, for conviction of adultery).[23]

Paul addressed these injunctions concerning hair to men as well (vv. 4,7,14). Evidently the problem in worship involved both sexes. Perhaps some men at Corinth dressed their hair in fashions generally associated with homosexuality.[24] Or, male converts from the pagan priesthood still wore their feminine garb including feminine hair styles.[25] Paul had not eliminated female-male distinctions. Yet, the Corinthians were blurring sexual differences by their unfeminine and effeminate hairdos.[26] Believers were to observe the hair customs that were distinct from pagan ways and appropriate to their sex.

In verse 7 Paul did not deny that women too share in the image and glory of God. He purported to emphasize the proper differentiations between the sexes. Woman was created *dia ton andra*, that is, "because of the man." He needed one corresponding to him. In this sense, woman is the *doxa* of man. In verses 7-9 Paul referred to the Genesis narratives to remind the Corinthian believers of the created differences between females and males. The new creation in Christ did not abrogate these sexual distinctions. Furthermore, women's worship demeanor includes their own *doxa*, their hair (v. 15).

Because women and men alike are to worship in a manner consistent with their sex, women should have *exousia* on their heads "because of the angels." Most exegetes assume that *exousia* signifies veil.[27] The discussion above, however, shows that the head-covering issue actually concerns hair style. How does this symbolize power or authority? The interpretation that best represents the active force of *exousia* is the authority which woman herself possesses.[28] The New Testament does not use this word in a passive sense.[29] The proper hair style marks a woman's authority, power, or license to participate in the public worship of God.[30] This verse gave Jewish women converts a freedom in worship hitherto unexperienced. It reminded their Gentile counterparts of the need for propriety in Christian worship.

Verses 11 and 12 form a theological climax for Paul's argument. Here he affirms the equality and mutual dependence of woman and man. Though man preceded woman in creation, he depends on her subsequently for birth. The two sexes are interdependent. Paul gives this counterbalance to check male abuse arising from a dominating headship and to reaffirm the unity of woman and man despite their sexual differences.[31]

In summary, 1 Corinthians 11:2-16 deals with the demeanor of both women and men during public worship. Believers should worship decently and in order (1 Cor 14:40). Women should worship as women, and men should worship as men. This principle would apply to married and single believers alike. Equality in Christ does not obliterate sexual distinctions. Nor does equality in Christ dissolve the wife-husband relationship in the Christian congregation. The husband remains the *kephale* of the wife despite her participation and equal standing in worship.

The entire discussion above has assumed what the passage itself assumes, namely "that Paul here quite clearly allows women the right of active participation in the gatherings of the local church."[32] Specifically, Paul allows women to pray and prophesy publicly. With the pneumatic gift of inspired speech, women could teach and build up the Corinthian congregation. Thus, Paul writes in 1 Corinthians 11:2-16 that women and men who have the endowment of prophecy exercise that gift decently and in order.

1 Corinthians 14:34-36

"Let the women keep silent in the churches" appears to conflict on the surface with 1 Corinthians 11:2-16 where Paul permitted women to speak by praying and prophesying.[33] The better efforts at resolving the apparent disagreement between the two passages attempt to determine the particular form of participation or speaking to which Paul referred, since he had already permitted praying and prophesying. One must start with the broader context. First Corinthians 14:26-36 gives rules for church worship. Verse 26 serves as an introduction and expresses the principle that all things should be done for edification. Verses 27-28 deal with regulations for tongues; verses 29-33, for prophets; verses 34-36, for wives.[34] Two clues in these verses point to the fact that Paul addressed wives here. The most obvious clue is the reference to the husbands of these women, *tous idious andras*. The second concerns *hupotassesthosan* ("let them submit themselves"). This voluntary submission characterizes the wife-husband relationship.

Why does Paul desire wives to be silent and to question their husbands at home? In the verses immediately preceding these injunctions for wives, Paul has given instructions for prophets and prophesying in worship. This part of worship included the evaluation and exploration of the prophets' messages. At this point wives should be silent.

> I Corinthians 14:34-5 represents the application, in a particular cultural context, of an order of the present creation concerning the conduct of a wife *vis-à-vis* her husband. It reflects a situation in which the husband is participat-

ing in the prophetic ministries of a Christian meeting. In this context the co-participation of his wife, which may involve her publicly "testing" (*diakrinein*, 14:29) her husband's message, is considered to be a disgraceful (*aischron*) disregard of him, of accepted priorities, and of her own wifely role. For these reasons it is prohibited.[35]

The prohibition has nothing to do with ecclesiastical authority.[36] Paul's concern here centers in maintaining the wife-husband relationship even when both spouses participate together in worship. Wives should exercise their gifts in a way that does not involve the violation of their husbands' headship.[37] In the particular instance here, this means their silence while their husbands' prophecy was being discussed and tested. Consequently, *sigatosan* does not refer to complete silence on the part of wives or women in general but to the testing of the prophets.[38]

Paul's appeal to the law (v. 34) may not have had a specific text in mind, although most commentators see it as pointing to the Genesis narratives.[39] The Old Testament pattern affirmed the husband as the head of the family. The apostle addresses the rhetorical questions of verse 36 to the entire congregation, demanding that they recognize his instructions as words from the Lord. Worship should be done properly and in an orderly manner (v. 40). It should not disrupt family relationships. Not surprisingly, similar problems to those in Achaea developed later in the principal Pauline church on the eastern side of the Aegean Sea—Ephesus.

1 Timothy 2:9-15[40]

1 Timothy 2:9-15 implies that some women were teaching in public worship in the Ephesian church.[41] Such activity must have taken place, or Paul would not have forbidden it.[42] How then did Paul perceive women teachers in the Ephesian church? Did the apostle have more concern with suppressing the deception of false teachers than with defining the role of women during worship?[43] Did Paul's injunctions concerning women teachers apply only to the first-century church in Ephesus because of the problem there with heretics?

A reading of the adjacent parameters of 1 Timothy 2:9-15 (1 Tim. 1 and 3) discloses a context which relates to the heretical elders in Ephesus.[44] First Timothy 1 includes a statement of the problem of false teachers and ends with the mention of Paul's excommunication of two of these. First Timothy 3 contains descriptions of several church leaders—*episkopos, diakonos,* and *gunaikes*. These delineations detail qualifications of character which stand in sharp contrast to all that the Pastorals say about the false teachers. Within these boundaries of counter-heretical admonitions rests chapter 2.

The opening paragraph of 1 Timothy 2 provides guidance for prayer. One can understand these instructions as responses to the presence of errant elders in the church. These teachers promoted an elitist or exclusivist mentality among their followers. Consequently, Paul taught that Christians should pray for *all* people (vv. 1-2). A tranquil and quiet life results from such praying (v. 2*b*). The false teachers did not promote tranquility but turmoil and strife. The theological basis for prayer centers in a gospel which is universal in its scope (vv. 3-7). Again heretical notions of exclusiveness stand refuted.[45] Finally in verse 8 Paul depicted the manner in which men ought to pray, "without wrath and dissension," that is, without the characteristics of the false teachers.

Therefore, 1 Timothy 2:1-8 appears to relate directly to the heretical controversy. This paragraph on prayer also establishes the context for the following paragraph on women. Paul continues to deal with worship.

Verses 8 and 9 take a standard feature of the household chores, the pairing of *andres* and *gunaikes*, and develop it in the new context of church worship.[46] Thus, the passage combines rules for conduct in worship services with rules for daily life.[47] Even with the utilization of traditional materials[48] from the household tables, a specific purpose related to public worship exists for the content and inclusion of this paragraph on women in 1 Timothy.

Demeanor in Worship (vv. 9-10)

The false notions circulating in the Ephesian church which prompted Paul to offer some correctives for prayer (vv. 1-8) led him to consider the behavior of women in worship. He used a series of descriptive words and phrases to delineate how women should participate in worship. They should adorn themselves with "proper [deportment]" (*en katastole kosmio*).

The apostle further clarified the general principle above. Women should deport themselves outwardly by dressing "modestly and discreetly" (*meta aidous kai sophrosunes*). Greek literature often pairs *aidos* and *sophrosune* as virtues of women who exhibit proper reserve and self-control in sexual matters.[49] The force of these two words encourages modesty and chasteness in dress on the part of believing women. The use of these words, however, implies that some very inappropriate behavior had taken place in the church at Ephesus. The sexual nature of this unbecoming dress would appear natural in the religious milieu of Ephesus with its Artemis fertility cult. Such enticing dress, though, is not natural for a Christian worship setting and should be avoided.[50] Self-control evidently represented a problem for some women in the Ephesian congregation as well. Some felt "sensual desires in disregard of Christ" (5:11) and were "led on by various impulses" (2 Tim.

3:6). The sensuous clothing of some women probably caused male worshipers to lust rather than to adore God.[51] Consequently, Paul encouraged the women to exercise good judgment and decency about their clothes.

Verse 9 contains a further specific definition about modest attire: "not with braided hair and gold or pearls or costly garments." Hair style again becomes a matter of concern in the church. The terminology used indicates the styles which characterized fashionable, wealthy women of the first century.[52] The condemnation of the focusing on outward attire by these women is essential. In addition to the possibility of arousing male worshipers and manifesting misplaced priorities, such ostentation might have made the poorer members feel inconsequential.[53]

In contrast Paul presented in verse 10 the positive and more important adornment for women—Christian character. Women should not depend on externals for their decoration. Good works stand as the means by which believing women should clothe themselves—*di' ergon agathon*.

Paul's whole effort in verses 9-10 pertains to the demarcation of Christian women from pagan. Women who confess the Christian faith must substantiate this confession with their good works.[54] Belief and practice go together. The instructions of these verses also have relevance beyond the role of women in public worship. Modest and decent dress, which reflects only one aspect of a godly life, should characterize both women and men on all occasions.[55] The problem at Ephesus centered in the worship setting where some women's demeanor caused disruptions. For Paul, purity and propriety inherent in the profession of the gospel should not be compromised by inappropriate dress or other external behavior.

Participation in Worship (vv. 11-12)

The verb *manthaneto* ("let a woman continue learning") presupposes that women already participated in public worship. These women were to continue to study the truths of the Christian faith. A command for women to learn which even acknowledged that this was already occurring indicates an advancement beyond Judaism. Some of the male Jewish converts may have called for the omission of women from doctrinal instruction. Paul opposed this non-Christian conservatism with his command.[56]

Paul qualified the manner in which women should learn: *en hesuchia* ("with quietness") and *en pase hupotage* ("with all submission"). The repetition of *hesuchia* in verse 12 makes this qualification an important one. Women should learn with a quiet demeanor. A calm spirit signifies an attitude of receptivity. It implies learning with respect for the teaching one hears and the teacher who instructs. In verses 11-12 *hesuchia* does not mean "not speaking." If Paul sought to silence women completely, he would have used *sigao*. Instead *hesuchia* defines the spirit required of a learner.

Learning should also take place "with all submission." To whom is this submission given? Perhaps *hupotage* does not refer to a person—such as a husband—at all. The context deals with how women should learn. They should learn with a quiet attitude. They should learn with submission to *what is taught*. Since the verb form does not appear here, *hupotage* best relates to the truths which leaders in the congregation taught.[57] Learning involves submission to the sound teaching that Paul promoted as opposed to the errant notions of the false teachers.[58] The apostle wanted to stem heresy and the conduct it produced on the part of some women.[59] Women must exercise restraint even when they seek instruction.[60]

From the positive command to learn in verse 11 one moves to the negative statements of verse 12. For the first time in this passage since Paul has turned his attention to women, a form of *gune* (*gunaiki*) is paired with a form of *aner* (*andros*). This usually indicates a reference to the wife-husband relationship.[61] The numerous similarities between this verse and 1 Corinthians 14:34-36, in particular a specific prohibition for wives, again reinforce the interpretation that Paul now directed his attention not to women in general but to wives in particular. Given the problems caused in Ephesus by disruptive women, the apostle wrote to qualify further the ministry of married women. He gave two prohibitions here: wives were not *didaskein* ("to teach") or *authentein* ("to exercise authority over") their own husbands in the worship setting.

False teaching and straying elders figure as one of the problems in the church at Ephesus (1 Tim. 1:3; 6:3). Paul ranked the teaching ministry as one of the preeminent gifts (1 Cor. 12:28-29; Eph. 4:11; Rom. 12:7). As a charismatic function any believer—female or male—could receive this gift (1 Cor. 12:11). Women too received the charisma of teaching in the early church. To assume that Priscilla's teaching of Apollos in Ephesus represented an exception challenges the obvious intentionality of the Acts account. Women participated vocally in mixed worship assemblies in an authoritative manner as prophets (1 Cor. 11:5). Both the prophet and teacher in early Christianity possessed authority.[62]

Why, then, did Paul issue this prohibition here? As indicated earlier, women had apparently become involved in the unorthodox teachings.[63] Some had failed to grasp Christian truth and maintain sound doctrinal balance. They were creating confusion.[64] Marriage represented one area under attack by the heretical elders (1 Tim. 4:3). Paul reminded women of the importance of the marital bond between wife and husband. Being a Spirit-endowed teacher did not negate marital responsibilities. Wives still were to recognize their husbands as *kephale* and submit themselves accordingly.[65]

Thus, married women should not teach in public worship when the exercise of that ministry interfered with their relationship to their husbands.[66]

Paul also prohibited wives from *authentein* their husbands. Numerous articles have analyzed this New Testament *hapax legomena*.[67] The preferred translation is "to have authority over." Verse 12 links this term, as well as *didaskein*, with *hesuchia*, implying that disruptive behavior was taking place in Ephesus. Just as Paul prohibited wives from teaching their husbands in public worship, so he also forbade them to have authority over their husbands in that same context when such an exercise might fracture their marital bond. Wives, therefore, should participate in worship in a manner consonant with their marriage responsibilities.

That Paul found it necessary to give these directives must mean that the opposite behavior was taking place in Ephesus among some believing wives. At this point one can see the relationship between *didaskein* and *authentein*. Teaching in the first century did contain the idea of authority for both Jews and pagans. For wives to teach their husband gave the impression that they were "lording it over them."[68] The problem intensified in Ephesus because of the arrogant and highhanded attitude of the false teachers.[69] Some women, including wives, unfortunately had adopted this unchristian disposition. A further complication resided in the fact that the heretics evidently forbade marriage. As a result, some wives publicly demeaned their husbands. Some Ephesian Christian wives had overstepped their bounds.[70] This behavior had to cease. Paul's instructions in this entire passage reveal his pastoral concern at this point to maintain not only order in church worship but also healthy family relationships in an environment hostile to such ties.

Verse 12 affirms the same principle underlying 1 Corinthians 14:34-36: a wife's marital obligations qualify her ministry in the church. The verse is best translated "I do not allow a wife to teach or exercise authority over her husband but to remain quiet." This is not to say, however, that this verse prohibits all women from ever teaching or having authority over men.[71] Biblical precedents, such as Deborah, Huldah, Phoebe, and Priscilla, refute this view.

Theological Bases for Participation in Worship (vv. 13-14)

In verses 13-14 Paul expressed the theological bases for his directives. He began by pointing to the creation account as recorded in Genesis 2. Why did Paul employ *protos* ("first") and *eita* ("then"), thus emphasizing the creation order? The context offers a clue. All of the topics in 1 Timothy 2 have been given as correctives—the correct objects, basis, and manner of prayer; the appropriate dress and demeanor of worship; the proper attitude for learning; and maintaining the legitimate marital relationship in the exercise of gifts in worship. Does the rationale in verse 13 also serve as a corrective to false understandings in Ephesus? Some wives' disregard of their marriage roles as well as their adoption of the haughty attitudes of the heretics necessitated a firm reminder of their duties in marriage. In a religious environment saturated with the "feminine principle" due to the Artemis cult, attitudes of female exaltation or superiority existed. Verse 13 attempts to correct such an emphasis. God formed Adam first, then Eve. This truth would certainly deflate ideas of female superiority. Also, the myths of Cybele and Attis from which the Ephesian Artemis sprang emphasized the creation of the goddess first, then her male consort.[72] Paul could be affirming the historical truthfulness of the biblical narratives to expose the fiction-based nature of the *Magna Mater* myths.

Next the apostle turned to the account of the fall in Genesis 3. In Romans 5:12-21 Paul placed the responsibility for the fall on Adam. First Timothy 2:14 does not exculpate Adam but shows that the man deliberately chose to sin.[73] "Adam was not deceived" provides the contrast for what is now stated about Eve.

The apostle's use of two forms of *apatao* ("deceive") shows a focus on deception. Deceitfulness characterized the false teachers in Ephesus (2 Tim. 3:13; Titus 1:10). Some women had been led astray by the wayward elders. Paul pointed to Eve's deception because it illustrated the problem among the Ephesian believers.[74] Wives who did not submit to sound doctrine but espoused unorthodox notions and so instructed their husbands in public worship reenacted Eve's misbehavior. Paul wanted to break this sinful pattern at Ephesus.[75]

Positive Encouragement (v. 15)

Verse 15 begins with a contrast to verses 13 and 14 due to the use of the adversative *de* ("But"). Eve's prominent place in the fall presents a dismal, hopeless view of the spiritual condition of women. But—*de*—Paul contended that their situation does have hope. The promise of this verse alleviates the severity of verses 13-14. Women do have the hope of salvation.

What does "she shall be saved through bearing children" mean?[76] The entirety of 1 Timothy 2 up to this verse has aimed itself at correcting abuses and errors of the wayward elders. One must also see verse 15 in this light. It too serves as a corrective. This verse contradicts the ascetic, antisexual beliefs of Paul's opponents who have rejected marriage (1 Tim. 4:3). The heretics proclaimed the evil nature of marriage, sexual intercourse, and procreation.[77] Verse 15 refutes these heretical ideas. It promises Christian women—wives—that bearing children and, by implication, sexual relations do not endanger their own salvation in Christ. Some wives needed this corrective and encouraging word.

Verse 15 rectifies any misunderstanding of salvation that verse might convey. In essence it states, "Provided of course that she is already a truly Christian woman."[78] Childbearing itself neither procures salvation nor hinders it. Faith serves as the means of salvation. Verse 15 ends where verse 9 begins—the need for *sophrosune* ("deportment," author's translation). The word again reminds the Christian wives in Ephesus of areas in which they needed to exercise self-control as believers. Paul urged them to persevere in the Christian faith. By implication, they should stop following the heretics and return to those beliefs and behavior which not only foster healthy marital relationships but which also reflect positively on the household of God.

Conclusion

What principles related to the role of women in the church can be derived from these passages? First Corinthians 11:2-16 teaches that women who participate in worship, including the use of spiritual gifts such as prophecy, should do so in a decent and orderly manner that does not disregard sexual distinctions or deny marital roles. The prohibitions voiced in 1 Corinthians 14:34-36 and 1 Timothy 2:9-15 are given to protect marriage relationships from possible disruptions resulting from the exercise of the wife's spiritual gifts during worship. Both of these passages respond to specific problems in the early church. At Corinth wives were participating in the public evaluation of their husbands' prophecies. At Ephesus the involvement of some wives with the false teachers and their heresies disrupted marital relations. These behaviors had to stop. Paul's directives to wives did not contradict his practices concerning their participation in the life and work of the churches.

The normative principle underlying these passages is that marriage qualifies a married woman's ministry. A wife's commitment to her husband and family should shape her public ministry.[79] By implication, this should also apply to husbands. This principle does imply that single women may have greater opportunities in ministry (1 Cor. 7:32-33).

After examining these problematic passages, one may ask, "Does the New Testament suggest limitations for women's roles in the churches?" In my opinion, ministry is servanthood (Mark 10:45), and God does call women to serve Him. The form that service or ministry takes depends on the woman, her spiritual gifts, and her family relationships.

Notes

1. Bonnidell Clouse and Robert G. Clouse, *Women in Ministry: Four Views* (Downers Grove, Ill.: InterVarsity, 1989), 20.

2. See Ruth A.Tucker and Walter L. Liefeld, *Daughters of the Church: Women and Ministry from New Testament Times to the Present* (Grand Rapids: Zondervan, 1987).

3. Walter L. Liefeld asks whether the rejection of the ministry of women as teachers embodies a defection from the Protestant principle of *sola Scriptura*. "Women and the Nature of Ministry," *JETS* 30 (1987): 59.

4. See Richard Boldrey and Joyce Boldrey, *Chauvinist or Feminist? Paul's View of Women* (Grand Rapids: Baker Book House, 1976).

5. Virginia Ramey Mollenkott, *Women, Men and the Bible* (Nashville: Abingdon Press, 1977), 104.

6. Robin Scroggs, "Paul and the Eschatological Woman," *JAAR* 40 (1972): 283.

7. E. Earle Ellis, *Pauline Theology: Ministry and Society* (Grand Rapids: Eerdmans, 1989), 65-66. For further discussion of Paul's women coworkers see Sharon M. Hodgin Gritz, "A Study of 1 Timothy 2:9-15 in Light of the Religious and Cultural Milieu of the First Century" (Ph.D. diss., Southwestern Baptist Theological Seminary, 1986), 113-22.

8. Elisabeth S. Fiorenza, "Women in the Pre-Pauline and Pauline Churches," *USQR* 33 (1978): 156; Scroggs, "Paul and the Eschatological Woman," 294. Wayne A. Meeks describes women's roles as nearly equal to those of men. *The First Urban Christians: The Social World of the Apostle Paul* (New Haven/London: Yale University, 1983), 81, 161.

9. On Galatians 3:28 see Ellis, *Pauline Theology* 78-85; Ben Witherington III, "Rite and Rights for Women—Galatians 3:28," *NTS* 27 (1981): 593-604; and Gritz, 122-27.

10. This discussion accepts Pauline authorship of 1 Corinthians 11:2-16 and rejects the theory that it represents a post-Pauline interpolation. No manuscript evidence indicates that this was an interpolation. For those advocating the passages's non-Pauline, interpolated character, see William O. Walker, "1 Corinthians 11:2-16 and Paul's Views Regarding Women," *JBL* 94 (1975): 94-110; Lamar Cope "1 Corinthians 11:2-16: One Step Further," *JBL* 97 (1978): 435-36; John P. Meier, "On the Veiling of Hermeneutics," *CBQ* 49 (1978): 212-26; and Garry W. Trompf, "On Attitudes toward Women in Paul and Paulinist Literature: 1 Corinthians 11:3-16 and Its Context," *CBQ* 42 (1980): 196-215. For a refutation of this view, see Jerome O. Murphy-O'Connor, "The Non-Pauline Character of 1 Corinthians 11:2-16?" *JBL* 95 (1976): 615-21.

11. This essay accepts Pauline authorship. E. Earle Ellis believes 1 Corinthians 14:34-35 to be a marginal note by Paul himself. See "The Silenced Wives of Corinth (1 Cor. 14:34-5)," in *New Testament Textual Criticism: Its Significance for Exegesis*, ed. Eldon Jay Epp and Gordon D. Fee (Oxford: Clarendon, 1981), 213-20. For a review of the arguments contending that 1 Corinthians 14:34-36 represents a non-Pauline interpolation, see André Feuillet, "La dignité et le role de la feme d'apres quelques textes pauliniens: comparaison avec l'ancien testament," *NTS* 21 (1975): 162-70.

12. Though cognizant of the historical, doctrinal, linguistic, and ecclesiological difficulties posed by Pauline authorship of the Pastorals, this discussion accepts their inclusion in the Pauline corpus. For a refutation of the view that assigned the Pastoral Epistles to a post-Pauline period as well as an argument that Paul utilized preformed traditions in these writings, see E. Earle Ellis, "Traditions in the Pastoral Epistles," in *Early Jewish and Christian Exegesis: Studies in Memory of William Hugh Brownlee*, ed. C. A. Evans (Decatur, Ga.: Scholars, 1987), 148-53.

13. Paul used the middle voice of *hupotasso* ("submit").

14. Ephesians 5:23; 1 Corinthians 11:3. *Kephale* has three possible meanings: (1) the literal, anatomical meaning, "head"; (2) "first" in relation to time, beginning, or source; or (3) "chief among," or "head over," connected with the idea of priority. Stephen Bedale, "The Meaning of *Kephale* in the Pauline Epistles," *JTS* 5 (1954): 212-14. Those advocating that *kephale* means

"source" include: Scroggs, "Paul and the Eschatological Woman," 300-01; Fred D. Layman, "Male Headship in Paul's Thought," *Wesleyan Theological Journal* 15 (1980): 56; Boldrey and Boldrey, *Chauvinist or Feminist?*, 34. Those who believe that the use of *kephale* sets forth a hierarchical social structure in God's economy based on the order of creation include: Bruce K. Waltke, "1 Corinthians 11:2-16: An Interpretation," *BSac* 135 (1978): 48; Noel Weeks, "Of Silence and Head Covering," *WTJ* 35 (1972): 21-23; James Hurley, *Man and Woman in Biblical Perspective* (Grand Rapids: Zondervan, 1981), 167. Had Paul wanted to emphasize "source" only, he could have used *arche* ("first"). Had he desired to stress authority or a "chain of command," he could have used *archon* ("ruler") or *kurios* ("lord"). *Kephale* allows the expression of the unity of the wife-husband relationship while permitting the concept of submission as well. William H. Leslie, "The Concept of Woman in the Pauline Corpus in Light of the Social and Religious Environment of the First Century" (Ph.D. diss., Northwestern University, 1976), 97-100.

15. Layman, "Male Headship," 54.

16. See Sarah B. Pomeroy, *Goddesses, Whores, Wives, and Slaves: Women in Classical Antiquity* (New York: Schocken, 1975), and Fritz Zerbst, *The Office of Woman in the Church: A Study in Practical Theology* (St. Louis: Concordia, 1955), 33-35.

17. See n. 14 above.

18. See F. W. Grosheide, *Commentary in the First Epistle of the Corinthians, NICNT,* ed. N. B. Stonehouse (Grand Rapids: Eerdmans, 1953), 252-53; F. F. Bruce, *1 and 2 Corinthians, The New Century Bible* (London: Oliphants, 1971), 104-5; Scroggs, "Paul and the Eschatological Woman," 301; Feuillet, "La dignité et le role," 159-62. The only word approaching veil in meaning occurs in verse 15, *peribolaiou* ("covering") in the construction *he kome anti peribolaiou*. This phrase affirms that women have their hair instead of or as a substitute for headcoverings. In verses 4,5,6,13, where interpreters also have believed Paul refers to the veiling custom, other expressions are used: *kata kephales echon* (literally "having down from the head" or "having the hair down"), *akatakaluptos* ("uncovered"), and *katalupto* ("cover").

19. See James B. Hurley, "Did Paul Require Veils or the Silence of Women? A Consideration of 1 Corinthians 11:2-16 and 1 Corinthians 14:33b-36," *WTJ* 35 (1973): 191-204; Jerome Murphy-O'Connor, "Sex and Logic in 1 Corinthians 11:2-16," *CBQ* 42 (1980): 482-500; and S. A. Reynolds, "On Head Coverings," *WTJ* 36 (1973): 90-91.

20. Annie Jaubert, "Le voile des femmes (1 Cor. 11: 2-16)," *NTS2* 18 (1972): 425.

21. Murphy-O'Connor, "Sex and Logic," 489; Hurley, "Did Paul Require Veils?," 197-99.

22. Jaubert, "Le voile," 424; Richard Kroeger and Catherine Clark Kroeger, "An Inquiry into Evidence of Maenadism in the Corinthian Congregation," *SBLASP* 14 (1978) 2:332-34. See also Fiorenza, "Women in the Pre-Pauline and Pauline Churches," 159; and Bruce, *1 and 2 Corinthians,* 104-5.

23. Hurley, *Man and Woman,* 171.

24. J. Keir Howard, "Neither Male Nor Female: An Examination of the Status of Women in the New Testament," *EvQ* 55 (1983): 35; Layman, "Male Headship," 58.

25. For instance, the priests of Cybele adopted female attire and wore long hair. E. O. James, *The Cult of the Mother-Goddess* (New York: Frederick A. Praeger, 1959), 168.

26. See Murphy-O'Connor, "Sex and Logic," 490; James G. Sigountos and Myron Shank, "Public Roles for Women in the Pauline Church: A Reappraisal of the Evidence [1 Cor. 11:2-16; 1 Cor. 14:33-36; 1 Tim. 2:15]," *JETS* 26 (1983): 284; Robin J. Scroggs, "Paul and the Eschatological Woman Revisited," *JAAR* 42 (1974): 536; Layman, "Male Headship," 56-59.

27. Morna D. Hooker presents a common view of those following the "veil" interpretation. The veil which depicts "the effacement of man's glory in the presence of God" enables the woman also, with the glory of man hidden, to reflect the glory of God. "Authority on Her Head: An Examination of 1 Corinthians 11:10," *NTS* 10 (1964): 413-16.

28. Ibid., 416; Feuillet, "La dignité et le role," 160.

29. Leslie, "Concept of Woman," 110.

30. G. B. Caird, "Paul and Women's Liberty," *BJRL* 54 (1972): 277.

31. Scroggs, "Paul and the Eschatological Woman," 302. See Ellis's discussion of equality/subordination and unity in diversity. *Pauline Theology*, 57-65.

32. Howard, "Neither Male Nor Female," 33.

33. One solution contends that 1 Corinthians 14:34-36 represents a non-Pauline interpolation. See n. 11 above. Or, 1 Corinthians 11:2-16 does not give women permission to speak, so no conflict exists. Noel Weeks, "Of Silence and Head Covering," *WTJ* 35 (1972): 26. Chapter 11 refers to private services while chapter 14 refers to public services. Grosheide, *First Corinthians*, 341-42. First Corinthians 14:34-35 represents a quotation from the letter Paul is answering. It expresses the mind of the men Paul chides in verse 36 and not the opinion of the apostle. Neal M. Flanagan, "Did Paul Put Down Women in 1 Corinthians 14:34-36?" *BTB* 11 (1981): 10-12. Montgomery translates verse 34 with quotation marks and bracketed words as follows: "In your congregation" [you write], "as in all the churches of the saints, let the women keep silence . . . . " None of these options deals with the text and its context adequately.

34. See Elisabeth S. Fiorenza, *In Memory of Her: A Feminist Theological Reconstruction of Christian Origins* (New York: Crossroad, 1983), 230; Hurley, *Man and Woman*, 189-90.

35. Ellis, "Silenced Wives of Corinth," 218.

36. Contra Hurley's view. *Man and Woman*, 190-91.

37. Ben Witherington III, *Women in the Ministry of Jesus: A Study of Jesus' Attitudes to Women and Their Roles as Reflected in His Earthly Life* (New York: Cambridge University, 1984), 129; see also Sigountos and Shank, "Public Roles for Women," 284.

38. Other uses of *sigao* in this passage (vv. 28,30) also refer to specific situations and not silence in other ways of participating in worship.

39. For example, see Bruce, *1 and 2 Corinthians*, 135-36.

40. For a more detailed examination of this passage, see the exegesis in Gritz, 177-230.

41. David Verner, *The Household of God: The Social World of the Pastoral Epistles* (Chico, Calif.: Scholars, 1983), 171.

42. Douglas J. Moo denies the possibility that any women were teaching at Ephesus, especially in light of the church's Jewish constituency or element. "1 Timothy 2:11-15: Meaning and Significance," *Trinity Journal* 1 (1980): 82.

43. Leslie, "Concept of Woman," 292-93.

44. See Gritz, 149-76 for a discussion of (1) the purpose of the Pastoral Epistles concerning how Christians should conduct themselves and the need to refute false teaching and (2) the nature of the heresy attacked in the Pastorals. These factors are essential for understanding 1 Timothy 2:9-15. The heresy Paul confronts in Ephesus represents a syncretistic tendency—a gnosticizing form of Jewish Christianity which reflects affinities with the Artemis cult. Some women among the Ephesian believers had become involved in this heretical movement. See 2 Timothy 3:6-7; Gritz, 162-69; David M. Scholer, "1 Timothy 2:9-15 and the Place of Women in the Church's Ministry," in *Women, Authority and the Bible*, ed. Alvera Mickelsen (Downers Grove: InterVarsity, 1986), 195-200.

45. Gordon D. Fee, *1 and 2 Timothy, Titus: A Good News Commentary* (San Francisco: Harper and Row, 1984), 25-28.

46. Verner, *Household of God*, 166.

47. Martin Dibelius and Hans Conzelmann, *The Pastoral Epistles*, in *hermeneia* (Philadelphia: Fortress, 1972), 5, 48.

48. Ellis notes the similarities between 1 Corinthians 14:34-35 and 1 Timothy 2:11-3:1a. This suggests the indebtedness of both passages to a common tradition or existing regulation as opposed to a direct literary relationship to each other. "Silenced Wives of Corinth," 214-15. See also idem, "Traditions in the Pastoral Epistles," 242. The appearance of words in 1 Peter 3:1-5 which parallel those in 1 Timothy 2:9-15 also support the use of a preformed tradition.

49. Verner, *Household of God*, 168; Grant R. Osborne, "Hermeneutics and Women in the Church," *JETS* 20 (1977): 346.

50. Norbert Brox, *Die Pastoralbrief, RNT* (Regensburg: Friedrich Pustet, 1969), 132.

51. Osborne, "Hermeneutics and Women," 346.

52. See Alan Padgett, "Wealthy Women at Ephesus: 1 Timothy 2:8-15 in Social Context," *Int* 41 (1987): 23.

53. Leslie, "Concept of Women," 272.

54. *TDNT*, s.v. *"theosebes,"* by George Bertram, 3 (1965): 126.

55. See B. W. Powers, "Women in the Church: The Application of 1 Timothy 2:8-15," *Interchange* 17 (1975): 57.

56. Don Williams, *The Apostle Paul and Women in the Church* (Glendale, Calif.: Regal Books, 1977), 111-12.

57. Dibelius and Conzelmann, *Pastoral Epistles*, 47. Padgett concludes the submission was to teachers. "Wealthy Women at Ephesus," 24.

58. See Moo, "1 Timothy 2:11-15," 64. Moo thinks the word possesses a dual reference: submission to sound teaching and submission to men.

59. Leslie, "Concept of Woman," 284.

60. *TDNT*, s.v. "manthano," by Rengstorf, 4:410.

61. See Gritz, 196, n. 77.

62. Sigountos and Shank, "Public Roles for Women," 286.

63. See n. 44 above.

64. S. Scott Bartchy, "Power, Submission and Sexual Identity among the Early Christians," in *Essays in New Testament Christianity: A Festschrift in Honor of Dean E. Walker*, ed. C. Robert Wetzel (Cincinnati: Standard Pub., 1978), 73-74.

65. Ellis notes that Paul interprets submission Christologically. Submission does not negate a wife's equality with her husband but rather manifests it. *Pauline Theology*, 61.

66. See N. J. Hommes, "Let Women Be Silent in Church: A Message concerning the Worship Service and the Decorum to Be Observed by Women," *Calvin Theological Journal* 4 (1969): 13-14.

67. Catherine Clark Kroeger, "Ancient Heresies and a Strange Greek Verb," *Reformed Journal* 29 (1979): 12-15; Armin J. Panning, *"AUTHENTEIN*—A Word Study," *Wisconsin Lutheran Quarterly* 78 (1981): 185-91; Carroll D. Osburn, *"AUTHENTEO* (1 Tim. 2:12)," *Restoration Quarterly* 25 (1982): 1-12; George W. Knight III, *"AUTHENTEO* in Reference to Women in 1 Timothy 2:12," *NTS* 30 (1984): 143-57; and L. E. Wilshire, "The TLG Computer and Further Reference to *AUTHENTEO* in 1 Timothy 2:12," *NTS* 34 (1988): 120-34.

68. Grant R. Osborne, "Hermeneutics and Women in the Church," *JETS* 20 (1977): 346.

69. See Bartchy, "Power, Submission and Sexual Identity," 74.

70. Osburn, *"AUTHENTEO,"* 11.

71. Philip B. Payne, "Libertarian Women in Ephesus: Response to D. J. Moo's Article, '1 Timothy 2:11-15: Meaning and Significance,' " *Trinity Journal* 2 (1981): 175.

72. See Grant Showerman, *The Great Mother of the Gods* (1901; reprint, Chicago: Argonaut, 1969), 20-24.

73. See Payne, "Libertarian Women," 189; Moo, "1 Timothy 2:11-15," 70.

74. Fee, *1 and 2 Timothy*, 40.

75. Spencer, "Eve at Ephesus," 219.

76. Commentators have offered at least five interpretations of this statement. This verse could signify (1) a reference to Christ's birth; (2) a reference to physical deliverance during childbirth; (3) an affirmation that the Christian woman still receives salvation from the eternal judgment against sin in spite of experiencing the temporal judgment of the curse; (4) an affirmation that childbearing counterbalances man's prior creation, that is, the woman's ability to give birth cancels the ramifications of her being created second; (5) an affirmation that woman will be saved and will find her greatest fulfillment by faithfulness to her proper role—motherhood. For a discussion of these views and the relevant literature, see Gritz, 221-28.

77. Bartchy, "Power, Submission and Sexual Identity," 74; Hommes, "Let Women Be Silent," 21. The Artemis cult in Ephesus encouraged sexual continence. See Gritz, 45, 62.

78. Fee, *1 and 2 Timothy*, 38.

79. Biblical models for women in ministry, specifically in leadership roles of teaching or exercising authority, do include married women—Deborah, Huldah, and Priscilla.

23

From "Christendom" to Christian Renewal

by Franklin H. Littell

As this chapter was being written, the relation between church and state in Eastern Europe was undergoing a radical convulsion. In Poland, certain elements in the Roman Catholic Church had been active in support of the trade union movement "Solidarity," and had given their imprint to the movement for political liberation. In the German Democratic Republic, some leaders of the Protestant Church—in East Germany chiefly Lutheran—also made their parishes the centers of the quest for political liberation.

In both Poland and the GDR, the ideological establishment of Marxism— which for decades functioned like a state church of the most primitive kind— has had to make room for older systems of being. In the Soviet Union itself, Jews, Muslims, and dissident Christians have been given spiritual breathing space denied them since the revolution of 1917.

Is there any hope that the traditional religions, having wintered through the decades of oppression by the Marxist establishments, will have learned some important lessons? For instance, will they abandon the pattern of establishment for one that affirms religious liberty as well as political freedom?

In Poland and East Germany, the churches have survived for fifty-five years under the establishment of "substitute religions" (*Ersatzreligionen*) that made their members pay the many social, economic, and political dues exacted of second-class citizens. In Soviet Russia, the time span has been more than seventy years. Will they, along with other freed churches in the Marxist empire, simply revert to the style of life of the earlier Christian empire *(corpus Christianum)*? Or will they have gained creative insights into a healthier relation of church and state that will point them toward renewal rather than restoration?

Christianity or "Christendom"?

After World War II, one of the striking contrasts between the two Germanies was the status of the formerly established churches. The Protestant establishments, since the early-nineteenth century more clearly defined by

315

political circumstance than the Roman Catholic communion, were especially vulnerable to government intervention during the Hitler years. Yet by
and large, in spite of the heroic opposition to statist idolatry raised by the
Barmen Synod (May 1934),[1] after the collapse of the Third Reich there was
little push to go free. In the West another choice was made, and in the East
no choice was offered.

Even during the church struggle itself, the "Ten Theses for a Free
Church" presented by Franz Hildebrandt were rejected. The majority of
the Confessing Church took the position that the collaborators with Hitler-
ism *(Deutsche Christen)* who had captured key ecclesiastical posts represented no true church: the Confessing Church represented (was *stellvertre-
tend fuer)* the true church. After the collapse of the Third Reich, with the
reconstitution of the Protestant church establishments, the Protestant ecclesiastical map of the German states was an almost exact overlay of the geographical pattern of the *Landeskirchen* following the Congress of Vienna
(1815).

Most of the collaborator bishops were sent to rule parishes (but not all),
and the most unsightly collaborating theologians were removed from their
faculty posts (but not all),[2] but in the West the Protestant territorial churches took the path of return to the model of Christendom rather than going
forward through radical internal reform. In East Germany, churchmen
found themselves in a new arena of the church struggle *(Kirchenkampf).*

Considering the unquestioned courage and spiritual energy of the men of
Barmen, their apparent naivete in respect to the importance of structures
seems doubly pathetic. That naivete had been evident from the beginning of
the confrontation with Nazism. In a pre-Barmen confrontation between
Karl Barth and Martin Niemoeller, which the latter—vastly more astute
politically—won, Barth argued that as opponents of the *Deutsche Christen*
takeover they should appeal directly to the *Fuehrer.* Their appeal should be
to the *Fuehrer* "to give the church back her freedom, and allow a new decision without duress from the Party."[3] Niemoeller's position was that they
should concentrate on splitting the *Deutsche Christen* front.

What was the vaunted "freedom" of the church to which Barth referred?
It was the benign structure of the union of throne and altar, the *landesherr-
liche Kirchenregiment* which—in spite of the revolutions of 1848 and
1919—had seemed to function so comfortably until the coming of the Nazi
style of church politics. It did not then occur to Barth that the problem
posed by the church collaborators with Nazism was structural rather than
personal.

Franz Hildebrandt's "Ten Articles"

Hildebrandt, a close friend of Dietrich Bonhoeffer in the illegal Finken-walde seminary, put a strong case for the Christian resistance to Nazism to go free. The Articles run as follows:

1. The way to the Free Church can only be justified as the path of faith; therefore the question about whether it will work or not is basically irrelevant.

2. Anxiety about "achieving" nothing, [anxiety that] "nothing" will happen, is no reason to stick to that which cannot survive.

3. To wait for "the right moment" is either illusion or tactic and is the root of all the compromises of the church struggle; the moment is ripe when faith is present, not the reverse.

4. To retreat to the parish is to abandon the church—[the tactic] that is the guarantee of all ecclesiastical confusions.

5. With the event at Ulm,[4] schism has been declared; however, the legitimate church does not get outside the manifesto itself, as long as in actual practice openings are given to the Mueller Church, to the order and rule of the heresy of Jaeger.

6. The so-called *Volkskirche* ("people's church") has no validation in the Bible, no fulfillment in history, and in the contemporary scene no significance.

7. In the choice between State Church and Free Church—there is no third choice any more—the one appears to be without means and prospects and the other without Gospel and Confession of Faith.

8. According to the Augustana Confession we are ordered to the office of preaching, but not to the parish office; at all costs the church of the Gospel, but not at all costs the *DEK* (institutional church), the parsonages and the church buildings. (Luther had to give up the priestly robe and the Scottish Free Church had to give up church property; [they had to do it] and they were able to do it.)

9. The service of the Confessing Church is not primarily for the sake of the victors but rather for the victims of the Church Struggle, who—outside the church—have already been waiting for it for a long time.

10. Only a Free Church is in condition to give this service, [one that] no longer uses its strength for ecclesiastical politics but truly and solely for the care of souls.[5]

Racially tainted under the Nazi Aryan decrees, Franz Hildebrandt survived the war in exile and spent his prime years in distinguished teaching at Drew Theological Seminary. His theses were rejected at the time of struggle, even by the Christian resistance itself.

Will the East German Church Go Another Way?

In the most intense period of the church struggle with the Marxist establishment in the German Democratic Republic, the Barmen resistance to Nazism provided an important model. In the 1950s the struggle was concentrated on the youth, with the Communist government deliberately setting youth events to conflict with church programs. Moreover, the Party instituted a Youth Dedication Service *(Jugendweihe)*, required of all who hoped to go forward in school and in the professions, to replace Christian confirmation.

In the midst of the confrontation between state and church, at an Extraordinary Synod called in 1956, a superintendent in the DDR put the implications of the church struggle for church/state relations very clearly:

> To alert minds, the situation of Christendom in contemporary Europe is defined by the fact that the end of the Constantinian era has arrived.
>
> The Theses of Barmen, in which all hyphenated Christianity is repudiated through proclamation that Jesus alone is Lord, remain significant as the documentation of the emancipation of the Biblical message from a Babylonian captivity.
>
> After the end of illusions about the Constantinian era, and with return to the Early Christian witness, we no longer have the right to call upon the state to support the Gospel by privileges and monopoly.[6]

We shall learn, perhaps soon, whether the churches of Eastern Europe, having suffered under two ideological establishments hostile to Christianity, have now come to understand the mortal danger in a Constantinian pattern. Whether a government patronizes or persecutes, the danger is there, but it can perhaps be more clearly seen at a season of persecution.

The Decisive Year: 1848

In 1848, before the democratic revolutions across Europe had failed, a German Baptist spoke up for liberty and self-government. Julius Koebner understood the connection between liberty, conscience, and popular sovereignty.

> When Almighty God broke the chains of your civic servility, there was also cast aside that invention that had earlier bound your tongue. Today the defenders of your rights are rejoicing that they may speak political truth. And there is rejoicing also among those of your fellow citizens whose heart beats even more warmly for God than for political freedom, that they may speak Christian truth, no longer crippled by a control system which limited the Word to a monopolizing churchianity alone—so that there was eternally hidden from you the truth that Christianity and state-priesterdom are just as different from each other as Christ and Caiphas.

Koebner also understood clearly the difference between religious liberty and toleration—a difference many do not distinguish even today:

> We claim not only *our own* religious freedom. We urge it for *every* person who inhabits the earth of the Fatherland. We urge it to the same degree for all, whether they are Christians, Jews, Mohammedans or something else. We not only say that it is a very un-Christian sin to lay the fist of violence upon any

person's honoring of God: we also believe that any advantage to any party qualifies as an equal entitlement for all. If one or more than one remain in possession of special privileges, they will always be tempted to use the worldly apparatus left to them to lift themselves up and push others down.[7]

In the Europe of the "Holy Alliance," with one of the most reactionary Popes in history in the Vatican, with a flow of repressive measures decreed by authoritarian rules "by divine right," with secret police terrorizing democratic movements, with the despots of Protestant Prussia and Roman Catholic Austria-Hungary and Orthodox Russia cooperating in the suppression of republican initiatives of any kind, Koebner's message had no chance.

Within the *Landeskirchen* the message of enlightened leaders had no chance either. In 1848, the year of the *Communist Manifesto*, a leader in the German Protestant establishment issued a timely warning. Johann Hinrich Wichern declared at the Leipzig *Kirchentag* of that year that unless the established churches turned around, they would lose the people. In the following century and a half, the churches did indeed lose both the working class and the professionals to other creeds and systems of being.

Although the fiction of "Christian nation" was maintained, and the facade of blended patriotic and Christian liturgies was kept up on the appropriate calendar days, the signs of Christendom's disintegration were everywhere. The tax rolls continued to show an overwhelming majority of the populations still formally "Christian," while in truth the substitute religions (*Ersatzreligionen*) such as Marxism and later Nazism, infiltrated the parishes and seduced the baptized.

Modern German Apologists for "Christendom"

The blissfulness of the theologians of the establishment was well represented by Karl Holl of Tübingen, who vigorously attacked what he called the "sect-influenced Anglo-Saxon view of the Church" and termed the sixteenth-century Christian revolutionary Thomas Muentzer the spiritual ancestor of such *Schwärmerei*. He accused the Free Churches of mixing religion and politics, but even after the First World War he never noticed how seriously his own binding of the church to this world's princes and powers had damaged the power of the gospel.

Holl's *Gesammelte Aufsätze zur Kirchengeschichte* are still cited with approval by conservative American theologians—including his strictures against the "Anabaptist" Müntzer—as well as by state church scholars in West Germany today. Few voices, including Free Church voices, have been raised against him in Germany, even though the promiscuous policy of church adherence which he defended until his death in 1926 later threw the door wide open to the hyphenated loyalties of the *Deutsche Christen*.[8]

Holl's postwar, stubborn, orthodox defense of the establishment never reached the euphoria of two "liberal" professors at the turn of the century. Addressing the fifth Evangelischer Sozialkongress, they exuberated:

> It is not long since culture, rights and human dignity were the monopoly of some few thousands amongst all the inhabitants of Europe, while the great masses of people lived dreary lives under tyrannous oppression, possessing neither rights nor education, their whole existence being one long misery. Today, on the contrary—at least in our own country, and among many other kindred nations—all citizens are equal in the eyes of the law; all enjoy the same legal protection; slavery and serfdom are things of the past; a fair amount of knowledge and education are within the reach of all; and labor is respected. Liberty, Equality and Fraternity are in many ways no mere empty words, but the real framework of the building we are raising. All this has been accomplished in the life-time of a few generations, and it is absurd to question the fact of progress, amidst improvements so obvious and immense.
> Retrogression is no longer possible for us.[9]

Defense of civil religion (*Kulturreligion*) was less ecstatic after World War II, but the basic accommodation was seldom challenged. Between the wars the church triumphantly held its public ground.

In July 1939 the present writer had the opportunity to meet with Bishops John L. Nuelsen (American) and Otto Melle (German) of the Central European conference of the Methodist Episcopal Church (*Bischoefliche Methodistenkirche*). Otto Melle was a good, old-fashioned Methodist preacher—president of the German Temperance Society (*Blaue Kreuz*), champion of lesser moralities. He told our American student group how during the 1920s German youth had been going to the devil—drinking, smoking, dancing, and staying out late nights. Then along came a man of miracles (*Wundermensch*), who inspired the youth and lifted them out of their dissipation and gave them discipline and the willingness to make sacrifices for the people (*Volk*). Melle ended with an affirmation that has haunted me for more than fifty years: "Hitler is God's man for Germany!" No state church leader could have made a more reckless identification of politics and religion.

Russian Apologists for "Christendom"

The malaise in Eastern Orthodoxy was as serious as it was in the West. The Russian Church became the chief center of Orthodox Christianity after the fall of Constantinople in 1453, and the Constantinian pattern prevailed. The education of the masses was neglected, while the hierarchs cultivated intimacy with a viciously exploitative ruling class. Marxism came upon the scene as a superior system of being, threatened the economic and religious status of the Holy Russian Empire with its capital, Moscow—the "Third

Rome" of Orthodox poets and theologians.

The answer of Konstantin Pobedonostsev—chief constitutional adviser to the last Tsar, presiding officer of the Holy Orthodox Synod—was to augment the work of the secret police and encourage anti-Semitic demonstrations. He it was who offered the famous tsarist solution to "the Jewish problem": one third will be forced to convert, one third will be driven into exile, and one third will be killed. The answer of Russia's alienated intellectuals was bloody revolution, dictatorship, and a crusade against religion.

Like those who live near a fertilizer plant or an oil refinery, the European church leaders who had grown accustomed to the nauseous odors of a decaying Constantinian establishment failed to perceive how greatly the spiritual and ideational atmosphere had been penetrated by dangerous elements. Antisemitic, anti-Christian and antihumanistic thrusts penetrated the church establishments and captured political centers of power.

European Christendom Today

By and large, the facade of "Christendom" remains even though the reality has long since fragmented and eroded away. This generalization is true even after the collapse of the Third Reich, even among those who honor the heroes of the church struggle. Once in a while governments succeed in passing laws against "cults and sects" in the name of Christian principles. From time to time there are overt incidents of anti-Semitism or even minor right wing political party platforms where anti-Semitism is justified by traditional Christian dogma. But in spite of feverish flurries of Christian nationalism, a quick review exposes the fact that behind the false front there is no more to be seen than behind the false front of a Hollywood set for a grade-B cowboy movie.

The encyclopedias and almanacs, like the church statistics and tax rolls, tell the official and less important side of the story. Take Italy, said to be 99.2 percent Roman Catholic. The Church's own studies show only 11 percent of Italian men making one confession and mass a year, the minimum set at the Fourth Lateran Council (1215 C.E.) to avoid automatic excommunication. Italy has for long boasted the strongest Communist Party in the Free World. The mayor of Rome himself is a Communist. Take Spain, which was not only Roman Catholic but medieval until a few years ago. A study by Spanish Jesuits shows only 17 percent of the population with any connection to the Church.

Take Sweden, where the Riksdag has just voted that everyone is automatically a Lutheran (whether baptized or not) unless he takes official exception to the designation. The official figure, for tax purposes, is 96.4 percent; the truthful figure is 3.6 percent adherence. In Denmark, also state church

Lutheran, the figures are 96% and 3.4%. In Hamburg, the largest city in West Germany, the figures show 84.5 percent paying church taxes, with 3.5 percent in any effective connection.

Whether Roman Catholic, Orthodox, or Protestant, the Constantinian establishments are today what is left in the bottom of the barrel. Even the signs of new life, such as the *Deutscher Evangelischer Kirchentag* and *Evangelische Akademien* in Germany and the *Vormingszentren* in the Netherlands, cannot disguise the true nature of the crisis. Europe is missionary territory, just as the Free Church fathers proclaimed in the sixteenth century—when the first fissures and evidences of a shattering to come were becoming evident to sensitive Christian consciences.[10]

Statistics do not tell the whole story, of course, and neither does the fact of legal privilege. There are on the American scene disturbing indications that the great American Free Churches, long used to enjoying social acceptance as well as legal protection in the free exercise of religion, are developing some of the danger signs of establishment. And there is one area important in the post-Auschwitz era where almost all the Free Churches share with the European establishments the need painfully to review and redirect their actions. That area is the relationship to the Jewish people.

"Jews and Heretics"—Victims of "Christendom"

Even though the Free Church fathers dated "the fall of the church" from the point of the Constantinian establishment—with its union of church and state, its baptism of infants, its enthronement of bishops and doctrinal dominance of theologians, its pridefulness in place of Christian humility, etc. — strangely they seldom noted that the Jews commonly suffered the same fate as "heretics" in Christendom. In fact, most repressive laws named the two elements together.

The French historian Jules Isaac, who lost his family in the Holocaust, noted the same turning point in the nature of the Christian religion as did the Anabaptists. Author of the great study *Jesus and Israel* (French: 1948), he later wrote," . . . after very deep historical research, I say and maintain that the fate of Israel did not take on a truly inhuman character until the 4th century A.D. with the coming of the Christian Empire."[11]

Even though neither Christian nor Jewish historians have noticed it, the same seasons that have produced cruel persecution of the Jews have also produced cruel persecution of Christians who dissented from the dominant state church. The parallels are striking:

Nicaea—public decrees against Jews	Also against "heretics"
	Crusades—butchery of Jews in Europe
Internal crusades against Waldenses, Albigenses, Bogomili	
Iberia—expulsion of Jews	Inquisition against evangelical Christians
Luther—hatred of Jews	Death to Anabaptists, Schwenkfelders
Tsarist Russia—pogroms	Savagery toward "Old Believers," Stundists
Soviet Russia—against Soviet Jewry	Also against Pentecostals, Baptists, and others
Third Reich—Holocaust	Also against "sects & cults"

The Jews could not escape Hitler, Himmler, Heydrich, Eichmann, and their associates. Sixty percent of all European Jews were murdered—one third of all the Jews then in the world. The crime was committed by baptized Christians, by what the Free Church fathers of the sixteenth century called *getauftes Heidentum*.

A Way Forward

There are two major elements required for a new offensive of gospel Christianity. The first is a recovery of the genius of the early church. The second is the aiming and aligning of that gospel to a post-Holocaust world. The Holocaust is a formative event, a watershed in history, an event of impact like that of the exodus of old.

The directions for the first of these turnings are known. The pilgrim church is not to be laid in chains, not to any government agency, and not to any secular way of life or "spirit of the times."

The directions for the second are being wrestled out, like Jacob wrestling with the angel through the long night, by post-Holocaust theologians and preachers. Among the better impulses to prayer and discussion, affirmative action has been given by the Protestant Church of the Rhineland—under the leadership of Heinz Kremers and Eberhard Bethge, persons deeply influenced by the church struggle, and especially by the witness of the Christian martyr Dietrich Bonhoeffer and by the Association of German Baptists, under the leadership of Erich Geldbach of Bensheim and Marburg—well known for his articles and books on religious liberty and Free Church history.

For such radical conversions to occur, for legal European "Christendom" and American social "Christendom" to be turned around in their preaching and teaching, we must open again and read. The books are those the Free Church fathers, who expected great and dramatic things of God, called a book "sealed with the seven seals" (Rev. 5:1). The books are the Book of Life (the Bible), and second to it the Book of History. The first place of the Scriptures is important, but so is the willingness to dialogue with the past.

Notes

1. Translation of the Six Articles in Franklin H. Littell, *The German Phoenix* (New York: Doubleday & Co., 1960), Appendix B; the full theological discussion is by Arthur C. Cochrane: *The Church's Confession Under Hitler* (Philadelphia: Westminster Press, 1962), Appendix VII; Rolf Ahlers has recently published a source study and critical edition: *The Barmen Theological Declaration of 1934: The Archaeology of a Confessional Text* (Lewiston & Queenston: Edwin Mellen Press, 1986).

2. See the new study by Robert P. Ericksen: *Theologians Under Hitler* (New Haven: Yale University Press, 1985). Gerhard Kittel never returned to Tübingen, and was denied a pension; Emanuel Hirsch escaped retribution by managing a timely retirement for medical reasons; Paul Althaus was returned to Erlangen in 1947 and continued to teach until retirement, preaching and publishing until his death in 1966.

3. Klaus Scholder, *Die Kirchen und das Dritte Reich, I: Vorgeschichte und Zeit Der Illusionen, 1918-1934* (Berlin: Propylaen Verlag, 1980), 707.

4. On 22 April 1934 Bishops Wurm of Württemberg and Meiser of Bavaria joined forces in a church service at Ulm to which other Confessing Churches were invited to send representatives. They came, and a ringing manifesto was read which condemned the attempt of a false church regime to take over properly constituted church governments. Ludwig Mueller was Hitler's appointee as head of the National Church; August Jaeger was the newly appointed Nazi administrator of the National Church.

5. In Dietrich Bonhoeffer, *Gesammelte Schriften, I: Kirchenkampf und Finkenwalde*, ed. Eberhard Bethge (Munich: Christian Kaiser Verlag, 1959), 167-68.

6. Guenter Jacob, "Der Raum fuer das Evangelium in Ost und West," in *Bericht ueber die ausser-ordentliche Synode der evangelischen Kirchen in Deutschland: 1956* (Hannover-Herrenhausen: Evangelischer Kirchnakanzlei, 1956), 17-29.

7. Quoted by Erich Geldbach in "Religioese Polemiken gegen 'neue Religionen' im Deutschland des 19. Jahrhunderts," in Johannes Neumann and Michael W. Fischer, eds., *Toleranz und Repression: Zur Lage religioeser Minderheiten in modernen Gesellschaften* (Frankfurt/M: Campus Verlag, 1987), 193-94.

8. Karl Holl, "Luther und die Schwärmer," in *Gesammelte Aufsaetze zur Kirchengeschichte* (Tübingen: J. C. B. Mohr, 1932), 1:466; for abundant detail on the scurrilous traditional definition of "sects" (including both Methodists and Baptists), see my "Church and Sect" (with special reference to Germany)," in *The Ecumenical Review* (1954) 3:262-76.

9. *Bericht ueber die Verhandlungen des 5. Evangelischen Sozialkongresses . . .* (Berlin: Rehtwitsch & Langewort, 1894), 136-73.

10. Cf. Franklin H. Littell, "The Great Commission," Chapter IV in *The Anabaptist View of the Church*, 2d ed. (Boston: Beacon Press, 1958).

11. Jules Isaac, *Has Anti-Semitism Roots in Christianity?* (New York: National Conference of Christians and Jews, 1961), 45.

24

The Believers' Church
and the Given Church

by George Huntston Williams

The first Believers' Church Conference met at Louisville, Kentucky, in 1967. The chairman of both The Southern Baptist Theological Seminary committee and the interdenominational planning committee that was responsible for this conference was James Leo Garrett, Jr. The papers from this conference were edited by Garrett for a symposium on *The Concept of the Believers' Church*.[1] This generic term, coined by Max Weber, was first used prominently at this time to embrace the several communities of Christians who, in distinction from, but not over against, both classical Protestant and Catholic understandings, define membership by "insistence on the indispensability of voluntary churchmanship in its many implications.[2] The term recognizes the difference between the ecclesial status of "birthright" progeny (to pick up a phrase from the Quakers; their counterpart term being "convinced" Friends) and that of informed and explicit believers.

For many of the conveners, this terminology represented a conscious effort to adapt Ernst Troeltsch's tripartite ecclesiological typology of "church," "sect," and "mystical type" to the American denominational setting. The conveners wished to impart fresh contour and substance to an identifiable segment of American Protestantism in order to mark off, and hence to establish, a recognizable form of the "sect" on American soil. Here Troeltsch's European constructs of "sect" and "church" function alike in that they are both constitutionally separate from the state, not at all territorial, but wholly voluntary. At the same time, with this fresh designation the conveners upheld the plenary ecclesial character of such denominations of informed and self-disciplined believers.[3]

In the preface to the published papers of the Louisville conference, Garrett indicated his awareness of the possibly invidious inference for other Christians of the term *Believers' Church*, and he insisted:

> The term must . . . never be understood to imply any denial of true Christian believers in other Christian traditions or to signify the primacy of belief in its most creedal sense.[4]

Having first made the appropriate irenic gesture, in his supplementary phrasing, Garrett was also prudent to protect the Believers' Church from critique for not having a consensus creed. Such a critique might well come from the representatives of Troeltsch's ideal church type who, for the most part, do preserve confessionally, or at least liturgically, the four ancient symbols of the undivided church (*Apostolicum, Nicaenum, Athanasium,* and *Te Deum Laudamus*) and uphold as well the newer territorial Protestant confessions (Augsburg, Heidelberg, Westminster, and so forth).

The non-creedal character of much of the exposition of faith within the Believers' Church, an exposition most commonly expressed and renewed in covenants or simple professions, spontaneous declarations, and statements of faith from a converted heart, was affirmed. On this covenantal view, the act of yielding oneself to the waters of baptism is as important as any creedal formulation of the faith that impels one so to submit to Christ. These affirmations express a new mind and heart, not articulate in the venerable words of former epochs.

Baptists have been the most conspicuous and steadfast in opposing on principle the profession of formal creeds, preferring assent to a statement of Baptist faith and message. This evangelical stance has its apostolic—and indeed scriptural—sanction (among other Gospel *loci*) in the simple profession of faith on the part of the converted chamberlain of the Ethiopian queen Candace who, on coming to an understanding of the text, was forthwith immersed by Philip the Evangelist. The Ethiopian official was, of course, already a Jewish believer, having in fact gone up to the temple in Jerusalem to worship (Acts 8:27), but he had never before, on his own testimony, understood Isaiah on the suffering servant. To this day, for most converts but certainly not for all, the meaning of Jesus Christ as the Christ is, as for the Ethiopian, most fully understood in the setting of the Old Testament. In the sixteenth century, even for the most radical of the pacifistic Anabaptists, this remained an empowering part of their Bible.

Today, however, it is no longer clear to what extent the Law must also be proclaimed as the foil of the gospel. To what extent is Jesus accepted by converts (believers) in the conviction that He is the foreseen Christ (Messiah) of the Old Testament? To what extent does conversion to, or confirmation in, the Christian faith and disciplined churchmanship occur from one's overwhelming awareness of the meaninglessness, emptiness, or dissipation of certain received formularies of faith? To what extent does the convert (or awakened Christian) seek and find an experiential Christ nurtured primarily by the substance of the four Gospels on their own, as evangelically proclaimed? It is indeed no longer clear in the global Christian mission in the last half of the twentieth century how to present the Old Testament or Hebrew Bible alongside, and then above, the venerable claims of other religions and traditions, with their own institutions and cultural achievements. The Believers' Church, as much as the "Given Church" of the various great traditions, faces a theological challenge in their formative and fundamental claim to a continuity with, or supersession from, the People of the Old Testament and their claim to be heirs to the ancient promises. In a world where the State of Israel regards the Hebrew Bible as the chronicle of its earliest prehistory; where the Christian conscience, along with that of the Jews, must probe ever freshly the roots and consequences of the Holocaust; where the Hispanic southern hemisphere is undergoing something comparable to the upheaval of the Reformation era and where many sectors of that society are appropriating the Old Testament witness against the corruption of the ordained powers; where the nations most affected by the original Reformation are now largely secularized—in such a world of nationalistically reclaimed faith and abandoned faith—the Believers' Church has a distinctive mission and discipline alike on the older terrains of Christendom and the Second and Third Worlds.

The terms "Given Church" and "Gathered Church" were first proposed by the Methodist theologian Harris Franklin Rall in an earlier effort to accommodate the tripartite Troeltschian ecclesiological typology to the America scene.[5] Professor Rall, of what was then the Garrett Biblical Institute in Evanston, was conscious of how his own Methodist Episcopal Church of the United States was continuous with the class meetings from within and beyond the structures of the Established Church of England (of which John Wesley to the end remained a priest). Now Rall's helpful term, *Given Church*, might be used for the first time as the foil, or the benignly intended antonym, for there was never any intention of the conveners of the Believers' Church Conference in 1967 to think of their opposite as the Unbelievers' Church!

Rall thought of the Given Church as corresponding to Troeltsch's "church" (Catholic and territorial Protestant), but at the same time he ascribed the plenary ecclesial character to both models and recognized that the sect/Gathered Church, like his own Methodist Episcopal Church, might indeed, in the fullness of time, take on many or all those features, responsibilities, and civic and social dispositions that constitute the American equivalent of a regional, territorial, socially privileged, established church. This might become so even in a pluralistic form, as is the case with several of the British and other European churches on Canadian soil. Rall's term, Given Church, proposed long ago, thus applied at once to the established, tax-supported *Landeskirchen* of Troeltsch's Germany and to the "mainline" pedobaptist denominations of the United States, from Catholics up to, but not including, Believers' Baptist churches. This was true even for localities where, for example, Southern Baptist churches effectually occupy the social space, exert the cultural pressures, and shape the social expectations in ways almost comparable to those of an established church, say, of a canton of Switzerland.

The leadership of the denominations of what we are pleased to call generically, or ideally, the Believers' Church will certainly wish to find ever-fresh ways to encapsulate in affirmations of their faith the sense of our Old Testament as embodying, at once, venerable faith and the foil of our faith.[6] In deep ways, not wholly understood, over against the Given Church of Christendom in the sixteenth century and even as reformed and altered into the territorial and sometimes national churches of classical Protestantism in Britain, Scandinavia, Germany, Swiss cantons, and elsewhere—over and against these Given Churches, at once confessional and territorial—are the (ecclesiologically) Gathered churches, (theologically) conceptually the Believers' Church, examples of which were the sixteenth-century Anabaptists and the seventeenth-century General and Calvinistic Baptist separatists from the Established Church of England (whether Episcopal, Presbyterian, or pedobaptist Independent/Congregational).

As for this last it is noteworthy that among the territorial, or Given, churches of Britain and overseas, the Puritan Independent Congregationalists of the Massachusetts Bay Colony, pedobaptist though they were, regarded themselves as the Given, the established, form of Reformed Protestantism in their ever-enlarging New England. Since the Baptists in America and their widely accepted New Hampshire Confession of 1832 owe much to the New England setting, it is worthy of note that Bay Colony Puritan Congregationalists, like the pedobaptists, fully Separatist Congregationalists of the neighboring Pilgrim Plymouth Colony, used the term "gather" for the constitution of their territorial, town-by-town congregations/churches. The establishment of these churches was done with the approval of the central religio-political body of each colony: in Massachusetts, the General Court and Assembly. The formative New England Puritan Congregationalists were thus semi-Erastian, although they eschewed the term themselves.

The protesting Baptists of New England, Roger Williams foremost among them, broke away from every vestige of this Congregational territorialism linked to magistracy. Of even greater interest, therefore, to adherents of the Believers' Church is the well-known fact that the New England Congregationalists of the Standing Order, both Separating and Non-Separating, centered respectively in Boston and Plymouth, avoided the use of any creed. For both groupings, however, their church and town covenants often included some biblical phrasing. In due course they came to accept the Westminster Assembly formularies for substance of doctrine, if not for polity. They never, however, used the Westminster Confession in the act of owning church membership by the profession of saving faith. As for the evolving congregational polity, the rural Massachusetts Congregationalist preacher, Nathaniel Emmons (d. 1840), completed for his denomination the process by which both the aristocratic and territorial local congregation of the founding fathers of the New England Way became a "pure democracy," the pastor a "mere moderator."[7] At the same time he recognized and confirmed the increasingly gathered, not territorial, and lay character of his whole denomination, traits which persisted until its merger to form the United Church of Christ in 1957. New England Congregationalism, as far as its once mighty regional stream still flows within the new denomination, thus bears some of the traits of the denominations of the Believers' Church in being congregationally gathered, in convenant, and in not observing a liturgical or constitutive creed.

A full classical Protestant ecclesiology of whatever tradition, whether Anglican, Lutheran, or Reformed, must continuously relate itself symbiotically to Rome, itself ever undergoing its own concurrent reforms because of its own wounds, self-clarifications, and renewals partly in reaction to the Protestant Reformation and the ongoing theological impact of world Protestantism in all its forms.[8]

Likewise, a full Believers' Church ecclesiology must recognize the ongoing importance of always rethinking the relation between the congeries of denominations that group themselves as the Believers' Church and the other denominations that are more directly the New World continuation of the Classical or Magisterial Protestant Reformation. Yet the "Landmark" presumption in many denominational traditions of the Believers' Church, for example the Hutterite, Mennonite, Baptist, "Arian" Polish Brethren, and the Campbellite traditions, is that there was a continuous trickle of faithful witnesses from the Apostolic Age to the onset of their particular community of faith. While this presumption has been historiographically resourceful, it has, even in more sophisticated modalities, insulated or distorted the theological and ongoing church historical task of relating the Believers' Church to the Given Church.

One of the disadvantages of Rall's pair of terms, and a possible explanation of why his suggestion has not been widely accepted, is that many of the denominations he embraced as Gathered are for the most part worshiping in stately urban edifices, though the buildings by now are often oversize for the remnant still gathering for Sunday worship. In the global perspective, there has emerged a new kind of Christian Polity, identified by Henry Pitt Van Dusen after a world tour in 1958, as "The Third Form." To that, one would today add the possibly quite new form of Latin American "community of base" and in the age of global televangelism, also the quite massive electronic church of extraordinary face-to-face intimacy and yet remoteness of membership (or auditorship) control apart from voluntary contributions by mail.

One may perhaps usefully employ the term Given Church in order to make again the point that as the third millennium of Christianity approaches we shall more and more think of ourselves, together with our heirs and successors, as members of the Believers' Church of Jesus Christ, who through the Holy Spirit gathers into His fold ever new believers from out of the nations, the old nations of Mediterranean Christendom as well as new recruits of the people of God under the lordship of Christ from all nations and cultures, at all latitudes and longitudes, from around our endemically pluralistic globe.

The Church of Pentecost and the churches of the Ante-Nicene world were at once Given and Gathered, for the Given "Church" was Israel, the community of the covenant in later Christian terms, at once "civil" and "ecclesiastical." Indeed, many in the early church considered themselves as constituting the New Israel, even a Third Race, neither Jewish nor Hellenistic. Yet, except for the Gnostics among them, who were basically dualistic, the early Christians made the claim that they were the true heirs of Israel. In a process facilitated by their almost exclusive use of the Hellenistic Jewish translation of the Old Testament into Greek (the Septuagint), they made a claim unique in the history of religions: that they were, to the exclusion of the lineal descendants of the original people, the sole proper interpreters of their ancient books of divine revelation. Gentiles gained access to the nurturing sap from the venerable winestock of the Lord into which they were grafted by their eventual exclusionary belief in the ancient promises: in part fulfilled, yet to be fulfilled eschatologically. In due course their Christendom, Latin and Byzantine, became levitical, hierarchical, and sacrally ruled. In the ferment of Luther's Reformation, in his humanistic return to the original sources of the faith in Greek and Hebrew and, therewith, the renewed emphasis on divine election, the new territorial reformed churches could understand themselves as inwardly gathered by faith alone, as indeed believers' churches with new confessions made up of adherents who had gone through something like the change of heart of which Luther's own conversion in the tower was the prevailing paradigm, scripturally reinforced by that of Paul on the road to Damascus. But just as Paul propagated the gospel in the synagogues of the diaspora, so Luther and his followers of

Renaissance Christendom spread their liberating doctrine of salvation by faith alone from within the venerable Romanesque and Gothic churches. Transformed by gospel faith and preaching, the old parish edifices continued to serve as the places of evangelization. Only those radicals whom Luther generically (and condescendingly) called *Schwärmer* (1520), whom Troeltsch classified sociologically as sectarians (1912/31), whom John T. McNeill and Roland Bainton called the Left Wingers of the Reformation (1940/41), whom Franklin Littell called Restorationists (1956), and whom the present writer called the Radical Reformers (1959/62) in allusion to the intended break from medieval Christendom by the willed exit from the very edifices, parishes, and ordained institutions of the old order—only they sought in various old and new ways to restore the more intimate, self-disciplining fellowships of the ancient Church. In the mid-1960s the Given (Protestant) Church was composed primarily of the mainline churches. These churches tended to be the self-conscious bearers of the values of the Republic (Richard Neuhaus). The Roman Catholic Church, a "Given Church" only in the Southwest, where it is grounded in the Spanish heritage, was no longer primarily an ingathering of various ethnic groups. First under the French, then under largely Irish episcopal leadership, on the margins of mainline Protestantism, it had taken over enough of the American lay spirit and enterprise to have been falsely charged in Rome with a condemned deviation (Americanism). Yet its bishops had shown their loyalty and their mettle at Vatican I, and it had come to express itself politically in the majority party in the uncomfortable coalition of Southern whites, northern urban blacks, and ethnic blue-collar workers.

Now in the fullness of time, with the displacement of the earlier mainline Protestants by the Evangelicals and others at the fore in the public domain, with new political coalitions formed since the rise of the Moral Majority (1979-89), the Catholic Church, and particularly its episcopal leadership, finds itself much closer than ever before in the United States to the erstwhile "mainline" churches on some public policies—notably in regard to foreign policy and the social consequences of managerial capitalism—while on family issues and biomedical ethics it often finds itself making common cause with Conservative and Evangelical Protestantism and Eastern Orthodoxy.

As we are now witnessing an epochal shift within and among the Christian bodies in the American body politic, it is imperative to reexamine the Believers' Church as a body ecclesiastic in relation to the ongoing Given Church of antiquity. This reexamination and redefinition of the role and distinctive mission of the Believers' Church today is undertaken in the context of the "Given Church," whatever that may prove in the circumstances to be—whether it be the Given Church of post-Vatican II Roman Catholicism caught up in the polarization between its centralist, conservative, restorationist, authoritarian modalities and historic commitments; or the Given Church of cultural Protestantism in general; or the Given Church represented by the "mainline" Protestant denominations (grouped with the Orthodox) in the National Council of Churches, itself seeking fresh identity and mission; or the national transculturation of the Southern Baptist Convention; or another kind of perhaps providential givenness within the American psyche and society.

Notes

1. James Leo Garrett, Jr., ed., *The Concept of the Believers' Church* (Scottdale, Pa.: Herald Press, 1969). Garrett has been identified from the beginning of his academic ministry with the life, thought, and discipline of the Believers' Church.

2. Ibid., 5. The first use of "voluntary church" may be in the Hutterite *Chronicle* for 1570.

3. More recently, and as it happened, felicitously, in the *Festschrift* for the present writer in 1980, Garrett reached back from the transformative sixteenth century to formative ancient Christianity to examine systematically, for the first time, the patristic witness to the adherence to the belief of the priesthood of all believers from the First Epistle of Peter (2:9), through Tertullian, up to Bishop Cyprian of Carthage, who first used *sacerdotum* exclusively for the ordained clergy, especially for the bishops [in *Continuity and Discontinuity*, eds. F. Forest Church and Timothy George (Leiden: Brill, 1979)]. Garrett had earlier explored the scriptural antecedents of the priesthood of all Christian believers in his article, "The Biblical Doctrine of the Priesthood of the People of God," in *New Testament Studies*, eds. Huber L. Drumwright and Curtis Vaughan (Waco, Tex.: Baylor, 1975).

4. See Philip Schaff, *Creeds of Christendom*, IV (1939; reprint ed., Grand Rapids, Baker, 1977), 164-73.

5. Garrett, *Believers' Church*, 5.

6. Cf. ibid., 322-23 for the eight-point "Summary of the Believers' Church Affirmations."

7. Quoted by Franklin Littell in ibid., 19.

8. This interconnection has been recognized by James Leo Garrett in his welcome of the stage of "irenic dialogue" between Protestants and Catholics. Garrett's second doctoral thesis, for the Ph.D. at Harvard, was on Protestant writings between 1870 and 1965 in the United States on Roman Catholicism. It was an analysis and critique in view of what he construed as the opening of a new phase in American society of the Protestant "confrontation" evolving from "anti-Popery," through efforts at conversion, to irenic dialogue. This last he especially welcomed, having studied for a semester at Catholic University of America (1963) and having attended, as guest observer, the last session of Vatican II (1965), which issued among its decrees the decisive declaration on religious freedom of conscious and there incorporated (by way of Father John Courtney Murray, S.J.) the very essence of the "free exercise" clause of the American Constitution and its consequent radical separation of church and state.

As a theologian and historian of the generic Believers' Church, working from a pastoral, professional, editorial, and administrative base within America's largest Protestant denomination, the Southern Baptist Convention, Garrett felt called upon to interpret the relationship in the United States between Protestant apologists of disparate denominations, organized since 1908 within the Federal and now National Council of Churches, and the most cohesive Christian community in the land under its National Conference of Catholic Bishops with their link to the Holy See through the Apostolic Delegate (now Pro-Nuncio) in Washington, D.C.

25
Contemporary Theologians Within the Believers' Church

by Dwight A. Moody

Introduction

The Believers' Church tradition is broad, varied, and not easy to define. It is easier to name those included than to explicate what fundamental similarities bind them together. The conference on the Concept of the Believers' Church, held in 1967 at The Southern Baptist Theological Seminary in Louisville, Kentucky, attempted to explore this genre of Christianity.[1]

However elusive may be a definition of "Believers' Church," there is one significant characteristic of those within the Believers' Church movement, namely, the reticence to write and publish systematic theologies. While such communions as Presbyterian, Lutheran, and Catholic have a long and rich history of systematic theology, most Believers' Church groups have produced very few theologians and even fewer books of theology.[2] It is often pointed out that the Believers' Church segment of Christianity is more interested in the *practice* of the faith than they are in the *explanation* of it. Most of these groups have emerged as common folk movements established as alternatives to the more established, and learned, churches. Schools and scholars have been few and far between. The theories and doctrines of the Christian religion have not occupied the attention of this tradition as much as the very issue of survival.[3]

Given this background, it is remarkable that there seems to be a veritable renaissance of systematic theology from one branch of the Believers' Church, namely, the Baptist. During the last fourteen years, no less than seven full-scale systematic theologies have been launched into publication. These include: *God, Revelation and Authority* by Carl F. H. Henry,[4] *The Christian Story* by Gabriel Fackre,[5] *The Word of Truth* by Dale Moody,[6] *Systematic Theology* by Thomas Finger,[7] *Christian Theology* by Millard Erickson,[8] *Systematic Theology* by James McClendon,[9] and *Integrative Theology* by Bruce Demarest and Gordon Lewis.[10] All of these save one are multivolume works; as of this writing four of the seven have been published in their entirety.

At least two others have been accepted for publication. James Leo Garrett, Jr., of Southwestern Baptist Theological Seminary, is publishing a two-volume systematic with volume 1 in process;[11] and Wayne Grudem of Trinity Evangelical Divinity School is writing a one-volume systematic, tentatively titled *Systematic Theology: An Introductory Course.*[12]

This is not the first time Baptist theology has come ashore in waves. A century ago, three prominent Baptist theologians published the fruit of long and thoughtful careers. In 1886 A. H. Strong, professor of theology and later president of Andover Newton Theological School, published his multivolume *Systematic Theology.*[13] One year later, the president and professor of theology of The Southern Baptist Theological Seminary in Louisville, Kentucky, James P. Boyce, published the single volume *Abstract of Theology.*[14] In 1898 William Newton Clarke published his *Outline of Christian Theology.*[15] Clarke was a prominent Northern Baptist pastor and theologian who concluded his ministry with eighteen years of teaching at Colgate Theological Seminary. These three works were dominated by the issues and answers of the classical Protestant tradition and, in turn, dominated the training of Baptist ministers for half a century. They continue to exert influence among some segments of the Baptist denominations.

Thirty years later a second wave of theology textbooks swept through Baptist schools and churches. Walter Rauschenbusch, Baptist pastor and later professor of church history at Rochester Theological Seminary, climaxed his career with the influential *A Theology for the Social Gospel* in 1917.[16] E. Y. Mullins, another president and professor of theology of The Southern Baptist Theological Seminary, published his innovative *The Christian Religion in its Doctrinal Expression* in 1917.[17] Douglas C. Macintosh, a Baptist teaching at Yale University, shared Mullins's interest in experientially based religion. His contribution, published in 1919, was entitled *Theology as Empirical Science.*[18] In 1924 W. T. Conner, of Southwestern Baptist Theological Seminary, published his first book of theology, *A System of Christian Doctrine.*[19] A few years later came his *Christian Doctrine.*[20] It is hard to overestimate the influence of these books in the training of generations of Baptist ministers and, in the case of Rauschenbusch, in the shaping of American Protestant religion.

Some seventy years have passed since the last wave of systematic theologies from the Baptist perspective. But today, from Massachusetts to California, from Minnesota to Texas, theologians are writing and publishing what surely is the most significant wave of Baptist systematic theology of this century, perhaps even in the history of the Believers' Church tradition. It is the purpose of this chapter to introduce these writing theologians and to describe this resurgence of systematic theology among Baptist peoples.[21]

Carl F. H. Henry

Carl F. H. Henry was the first of the current Baptist theologians to launch into the publication of a systematic theology. He may also be noted as the most prolific, for by the time he brought this project to a close, it numbered 2,765 pages, considerably longer than he anticipated.[22]

Henry is without doubt the most well known of the seven men reviewed in this chapter, and indeed, may be the most famous living theologian in America. He grew up in what he describes as a neopagan environment, even though he was confirmed in the Episcopal Church.[23] As a young newspaperman in New York City, he was converted, and soon thereafter headed west to Wheaton College. While there, he was attracted to Baptist principles and was immersed and received into the membership of a Baptist congregation. After graduating from Wheaton, he took two degrees at the Northern Baptist Theological Seminary, the Bachelor of Divinity and the Doctor of Theology, and in 1947 was awarded the Doctor of Philosophy degree from Boston University.

Henry has maintained his roots in the Baptist heritage, primarily through membership in Baptist churches (currently in Arlington, Virginia, where he now resides) and by serving as professor-at-large at Eastern Baptist Theological Seminary in Philadelphia. Nevertheless, Henry's chief focus, and the primary avenue of his notoriety, has been within that religious and theological coalition known as the Evangelical movement. He has been associated with six major components of that movement: Wheaton College, Fuller Seminary, *Christianity Today*, World Vision International, the Chicago Conference on Biblical Inerrancy, and the Lausanne Conference on World Evangelization.

The six volumes of *God, Revelation and Authority* cannot really be termed a systematic theology. Ostensibly, it addresses only the first two (revelation and God) of the customary eight to ten doctrinal subjects. Some topics, such as Christology, ecclesiology and eschatology, receive an introduction of sorts in the three-volume doctrine of revelation, and others, such as creation and humanity, are treated as part of the two-volume doctrine of God. In many ways, the entire six-volume set is an extended introduction to systematics. It is prolegomena. It is a detailed and learned dialogue, not so much with Scripture or the Christian tradition or even the human experience, but rather with the intellectual exponents and organizers of modern secular thought, many of whom Henry would describe as semi-Christian thinkers.

The introduction to the prolegomena consumes volume 1. There, Henry articulates his threefold concern for, first, the search for truth, second, the value of revelation, and third, the capacity of human reason to comprehend revealed truth. He states his thesis in these words:

> The task of Christian leadership is to confront modern man with the Christian world-life view as the revealed conceptuality for understanding reality and experience, and to recall reason once again from the vagabondage of irrationalism and the arrogance of autonomy to the service of true faith.[24]

Volumes 2, 3, and 4 address the epistemological question by expounding fifteen theses concerning divine revelation. He begins volume 3 with these words: "Nowhere does the crisis of modern theology find a more critical center than in the controversy over the reality and nature of divine disclosure."[25] Henry enters the controversy with the following fifteen affirmations.

1. Revelation is a divinely initiated activity, God's free communication by which he alone turns his personal privacy into a deliberate disclosure of his reality.
2. Divine revelation is given for human benefit, offering us privileged communion with our Creator in the kingdom of God.
3. Divine revelation does not completely erase God's transcendent mystery, inasmuch as God the Revealer transcends his own revelation.
4. The very fact of disclosure by the one living God assures the comprehensive unity of divine revelation.
5. Not only the occurrence of divine revelation, but also its very nature, content, and variety are exclusively God's determination.
6. God's revelation is uniquely personal both in content and form.
7. God reveals himself not only universally in the history of the cosmos and of the nations, but also redemptively within this external history in unique saving acts.
8. The climax of God's special revelation is Jesus of Nazareth, the personal incarnation of God in the flesh; in Jesus Christ the source and content of revelation converge and coincide.
9. The meditating agent in all divine revelation is the Eternal Logos—preexistent, incarnate, and now glorified.
10. God's revelation is rational communication conveyed in intelligible ideas and meaningful words, that is, in conceptual-verbal form.
11. The Bible is the reservoir and conduit of divine truth.
12. The Holy Spirit superintends the communication of divine revelation, first, by inspiring the prophetic-apostolic writings, and second, by illuminating and interpreting the scripturally given Word of God.
13. As bestower of spiritual life the Holy Spirit enables individuals to appropriate God's revelation savingly, and thereby attests to the redemptive power of the revealed truth of God in the personal experience of reborn sinners.
14. The church approximates the kingdom of God in miniature; as such she is to mirror to each successive generation the power and joy of the appropriate realities of divine revelation.

15. The self-manifesting God will unveil his glory in a crowning revelation of power and judgment; in this disclosure at the consummation of the ages, God will vindicate righteousness and justice, finally subdue and subordinate evil, and bring into being a new heaven and earth.[26]

Volumes 5 and 6 focus on the doctrine of God, with extensive discussions on the divine attributes, the Trinity, creation (including evolution and creationism) and evil, as well as shorter treatments of election, providence, and the Holy Spirit.

Gabriel Fackre

The second contemporary Baptist theologian to launch into the publication of a systematic theology may well be the last to finish. The first edition of *The Christian Story* by Gabriel Fackre was issued in 1978. It was revised and reissued in 1984. Volume 2 of the series, which Fackre calls 'a pastoral systematics,' was issued in 1987 with the subtitle *Authority: Scripture in the Church for the World*. Volume 3 of a projected eight-volume series is in preparation and will deal with revelation.[27]

Gabriel Fackre is a Baptist theologian in the sense that he was raised and trained in the Baptist tradition, in the sense that he teaches at a seminary related to a major Baptist denomination, and in the sense that much of his theological vision is influenced by those ideas and experiences typical of a Believers' Church tradition.

Fackre gives a good introduction to all of these influences in the introduction to volume 2 of his systematic.[28] He grew up in the Hanson Place Baptist Church of Brooklyn, New York, a congregation influenced by the fundamentalism of its long-term pastor, A. C. Dixon. He attended two Baptist Schools, Bucknell University and the Divinity School of the University of Chicago. His experience with both fundamentalism and liberalism left a decided distaste for the Baptist tradition, and he took his degree and headed east to Pittsburgh seeking an avenue less sectarian and more socially active. He found this in the Evangelical and Reformed Church, which ordained him to the ministry and provided him with a two-church ministry among mill town families in the steel-producing Monongahela Valley of western Pennsylvania.

Fackre began his teaching career in the middle of Pennsylvania Dutch territory at Lancaster Theological Seminary, a school affiliated with the Reformed wing of the Evangelical and Reformed Church (later to become part of the United Church of Christ). Shortly after moving to Pennsylvania, he finished his graduate work and was awarded the Doctor of Philosophy degree by the University of Chicago Divinity School. His ministry in Lancaster (1961-71) spanned the decade of social change in America and immersed him in a steady stream of social and political causes. His move to Newton Centre, Massachusetts, to teach at Andover Newton Theological School solidified his connections with the United Church of Christ. This seminary was created in 1962 when the Baptist-affiliated Newton Theological Institute merged with the UCC-related Andover Seminary, creating an institution with a broad base in the Believers' Church tradition. However, it is the ecumenicity of his own pilgrimage, of the school in which he is now teaching, and of the theological atmosphere of Boston in general that has been his chief orientation during these last two decades.

The Christian Story is subtitled 'A Narrative Interpretation of Basic Christian Doctrine.' It is an effort to retell the story associated with the Christian tradition; namely, creation, fall, covenant, Christ, church, salvation, consummation, with their prologue and epilogue, God. It is, furthermore, an effort to tell this story from both an ecumenical and a contemporary perspective. Fackre is ecumenical in the sense that he recognizes and incorporates the biblical and theological contributions of most branches of the Christian Church. For instance, he advocates the implementation of all three forms of church government, congregational, presbyterian and episcopal.[29] While the work is transparently Protestant by virtue primarily of what it omits, it is nonetheless generically Protestant, providing few hints (other than the introduction autobiographical section) of Fackre's own denominational heritage. (It is true that only two volumes of a projected eight have been published and that his denominational loyalties may be more pronounced in future volumes.) Fackre is contemporary in that he incorporates, for instance, the rather modern understanding of salvation as release from social and political oppression as well as the more traditional understanding of salvation as release from sin and death. His chapter on "Salvation" is divided into discussions of "Salvation from Sin," "Salvation from Evil" and "Salvation from Death." He concludes with this statement: "The Good News of salvation Now is a *word of faith* about the mercy offered to us on Calvary that covers our sin and guilt, a *work of love* that keeps company with the Presence in the world, and a *vision of hope* of a future opened by the risen Christ.'[30]

Volume 2 of *The Christian Story* was intended to focus on both authority and revelation, but the contemporary debate on the nature and use of Scripture dictated that more attention be given to the matter of authority.[31] Thus, Fackre develops a detailed analysis of the sources of authority (Scripture, Christ, church, world, and various combinations of these) and, in the end, presents a concept of authority which honors "the insights of our worldly setting . . . while at the same time taking as its measure the biblical source and Christological norm and the church and its tradition as its guide."[32] Fackre focuses on the Bible as "the text of authority" and describes how it is to be interpreted through the use of common sense, critical sense, canonical sense, and contextual sense.[33] The volume is, in reality, a strong defense of the primacy of Scripture in the life of the church and an able and attractive description of how the Bible is, in fact, used by most pastors and teachers today.

Dale Moody

In 1981 Dale Moody released his *The Word of Truth: A Summary of Christian Doctrine Based on Biblical Revelation* and thus continued the tradition of his predecessors at The Southern Baptist Theological Seminary, James P. Boyce and E. Y. Mullins, both of whom taught theology at that school and published influential textbooks of systematic theology. The significant differences in the theologizing of these three men illustrate the diversity inherent in Baptist life and thought.[34]

Moody has spent his life with one foot in Texas and one in Kentucky.[35] Texas provided a birthplace, religion, and education. He was born in Jones County, was converted and baptized through the ministry of the United Baptist Church of Grapevine, and graduated from Baylor University. Kentucky offered him a place to study and teach. He earned the Master of Theology and the Doctor of Theology from Southern Seminary. From Louisville, he traveled to Basel, Zurich, New York, Oxford, Rome, and Jerusalem, learning and teaching, and earning a Doctor of Philosophy degree from Oxford University. From 1945 to 1983 he taught theology at his alma mater in Kentucky.

The outline of *The Word of Truth* is in the classical Protestant tradition: Introduction, Revelation, God, Creation, Man, Sin, Salvation, Christ, the Church, the Consummation. But while the organization of this systematic theology may be predictable, the same cannot be said for the use of Scripture. Moody offers a unique blend of criticism and biblicism that, shaped by his creative mind and wide learning, presents a formidable case for the revision of some aspects of his Southern Baptist theological heritage.

In the first place, *The Word of Truth* is full of detailed and scholarly exegesis. Scripture references are not simply provided in parentheses to indicate biblical support for a given statement or doctrine. Much of the material in the book is actually the type of writing that one normally finds in a commentary. Furthermore, Old Testament materials have a far more significant role to play in the shaping of the doctrine than is customary among Baptist theologians, who have traditionally relied almost exclusively on New Testament teaching.[36]

Second, Moody warmly embraces the modern critical approach to Scripture study. He writes in the preface: "Those who fear that using the findings of . . . the critical-historical method of Bible study is inevitably uncongenial to a strong view of biblical authority will, I hope, find the explorations of this book a pleasant surprise."[37] Thus, in developing his ideas of, especially, God, creation, the church and the consummation, Moody is not afraid to allow the reconstructed literary history of the biblical text to influence how he presents the theological material.

Most importantly, Moody emphasizes the role of Scripture as an authority by which tradition, even his own Baptist tradition, is to be held accountable. He writes: "What really makes the difference is the fidelity with which the authority of Scripture is elevated above ecclesiastical traditions."[38] Moody elsewhere claims that the chief distinctive of the Baptist tradition is the supremacy of Scripture,[39] and Moody uses the Scriptures freely and forcefully to critique some prominent elements of the Southern Baptist tradition, such as dispensationalism, Landmarkism, fundamentalism, and Calvinism. Concerning the consummation, Moody inveighs against "the deviations of Dispensationalism," whose theory of the rapture has "not one word (of support) in Revelation 7 or at any other place in the Bible" but nevertheless "has captured the imagination of many uncritical people."[40] On Landmarkism and its denial of the universal church, he writes: "Many Southern Baptists, unaware of the facts of Southern Baptist history and unmoved by the plain teachings of the New Testament, have followed the innovations of Landmarkism which infiltrated the South from the North through such personalities as J. R. Graves and J. M. Pendleton."[41] And on the issue of creation, Moody turns his guns on those who propose the well-known catastrophic view of earth origins. "It is neither good science nor good theology to claim that God created the world 'which had an appearance of age' that in reality does not exist."[42] There is, he says, "no going back to a precritical and prescientific posture in Christian theology."[43]

Much of his criticism of traditional Baptist theology is directed against Calvinism. On the issues of Dort, Moody is a thoroughgoing Arminian, and it was his treatment of "Salvation and Apostasy" that provided the chief battleground throughout his career. He concludes that chapter with these words:

> It is indeed time to put the plain teachings of Scripture above all traditions, for, as The Baptist Faith and Message of 1963 does rightly say, the Scriptures "will remain to the end of the world, the true center of Christian union, and the supreme standard by which all human conduct, creeds and religious opinions should be tried." To this I fully subscribe.[44]

Thomas Finger

Thomas Finger is both the youngest and perhaps the least known of contemporary Baptist theologians. He teaches at the Eastern Mennonite Seminary in Harrisonburg, Virginia. For ten years, Finger taught systematic theology at Northern Baptist Theological Seminary in Lombard, Illinois. Volume 1 of his two-volume systematic was published in 1985. The second volume was issued in 1989.

Finger was raised in what was essentially a nonreligious home but was converted at the age of twenty-one.[45] He graduated a few years later from Wheaton College, from what was then Gordon Divinity School, and finally from Claremont Graduate School where he was awarded a Doctor of Philosophy degree. The Baptist connections of these schools introduced him to the thought and practice of the Believers' Church. But it was at his first teaching position at Eastern Mennonite College (1973-76) that he encountered the radical Anabaptist tradition. This came through the reading of two books, *The Theology of Hope* by Jürgen Moltmann[46] and *The Politics of Jesus* by John Howard Yoder.[47] These books set his mind toward the combination of ethics and eschatology as the starting point of theology. This was, certainly, in the best tradition of the Believers' Church movement.

Finger's eschatological approach to systematic theology arises from his desire to abandon the traditional effort to write theology from the standpoint of any one denomination or tradition, including that of the Believers' Church. He writes: "Given the normative status certain biblical events have always had for faith we must seek to begin from the original message. In accordance with common theological usage, we may call that message the 'Kerygma.' "[48] Later, he provides a brief summary of the eschatological bent of this kerygma:

> Christ's life, death, resurrection, ascension had inaugurated a new age. The ascended Christ was Lord of the Universe. From on high he sent the Holy Spirit, who restored and energized life at the deepest levels. . . . The earliest proclamation of the resurrection and the new lifestyle that went with it were rooted in the joyous conviction that the final age of history had arrived. This final age, however, was present in a somewhat paradoxical manner. On one hand, the earliest Christians were convinced that it was "already" present. On the other, since Christ was still to return, it was "not yet" consummated. . . . In this sense the outlook and lifestyle of the earliest Christians were saturated by eschatology.[49]

Finger uses this future-oriented proclamation of the early Christians to give form and structure to his theological system. Thus, he begins with extensive discussions of the future hope, namely, resurrection, judgment, heaven, hell, and the millennium. This eschatological revelation leads naturally to consideration of other dimensions of revelation: personal, historical, and propositional.[50] Volume 1 concludes the presentation of the "objective" side of our hope by systematic consideration of the life, death and resurrection of Jesus Christ.[51] "The kerygma is grounded in and points toward 'objective' acts of God, yet it arouses intense 'subjective' hope."[52] Following this simple outline, volume 1 focuses on the objective dimensions of our eschatological hope and volume 2 deals with the "human and contextual side of things."[53] In so doing, he offers a good illustration of what he means by doing theology from an eschatological perspective.

Finger begins with an extensive discussion of "anthropology" in which he rejects the creation narratives of Genesis in favor of the life of Jesus as the starting point for describing human nature. "Genesis 1—2 affords a fairly slim foundation for such detailed anthropologies."[54] Jesus is then interpreted as the person oriented toward and obedient to the coming kingdom of God, characterized by obedience, servanthood and stewardship in response to the call of God.

His treatment of "sin" follows the same path, reviewing the "history of resistance to God's kingdom which climaxed against Jesus."[55] He concludes:

> Sin is a massive corporate power, or interweaving of interrelated powers, which opposes God on all social, religious, and personal levels, seeking to bring all creation under the dominion of death.
>
> For humans, sin is turning the heart from God, turning back from the future which God promises . . . .[56]

When Finger turns from anthropology to soteriology, he gives even more evidence of his creative use of the eschatological perspective. Salvation is, first of all, justification, but not in the static and traditional Protestant sense of "imputing" a foreign righteousness to the sinner. Rather, it is the imputation to them of a righteousness that they will one day actualize in their own life.

> It is the eschatological contrast between the *already* and the not yet. When sinners surrender themselves authentically to the dynamism of God's righteousness, that righteousness already takes them up decisively into its flow. . . . Such persons are righteous in the sense of being caught up into that righteousness which will inevitably transform them entirely.[57]

These examples are sufficient to demonstrate how the eschatological angle of Finger's thinking shapes his theological system. Both the structure and the substance of his two-volume systematic is the result of his concentrated focus on Jesus and the kingdom of God. In many ways, Finger breaks out of the tracks of traditional Protestant, Catholic or even Mennonite theologizing to offer a way of thinking that is an attractive contribution to the renaissance of Baptist theology.

Millard J. Erickson, Jr.

Millard J. Erickson is vice-president, dean, and professor of theology at Bethel Theological Seminary of St. Paul, Minnesota. Erickson grew up as a Baptist of the Swedish variety. After graduating from the University of Minnesota (Phi Beta Kappa) in 1953, he attended Bethel Seminary and then graduated from Northern Baptist Theological Seminary. After two pastorates, Erickson joined the faculty of Wheaton College, and then, in 1969, returned to Bethel Seminary as professor of theology.[58]

The three volumes of Erickson's *Christian Theology* were published in 1983, 1984, and 1985. A one- volume edition was released in 1986. By 1990 it had become perhaps the most widely used textbook of Baptist theology in America.[59]

The popularity of Erickson's *Christian Theology* is in large measure attributable to three things. First, it is quite comprehensive. This no doubt is due to its intended use as a classroom textbook for beginning theology students.[60] The 1,247 pages of systematic theology follow the classical format of the Protestant tradition. There are twelve sections: Studying God (prolegomena), Knowing God (revelation), What God Is Like (the attributes of God), What God Does (creation and providence), Humanity, Sin, The Person of Christ (Christology), The Work of Christ (atonement), The Holy Spirit, Salvation, The Church and the Last Things (eschatology). In treating these theological subjects, Erickson assumes of the reader only a knowledge of the Bible and church history.[61] This assumption allows Erickson to introduce carefully and systematically each theological topic, to survey the various options in dealing with the topic, and, finally, to state his own position. This is an attractive format for students being introduced to the history and method of systematic theology.

Second, a mild and tolerant tone pervades the work. Erickson is on no crusade to right wrongs, defeat enemies, or save Christendom. Balanced and respectful presentations characterize the discussions of such controversial matters as biblical criticism, apostasy, glossolalia, inerrancy, and millenarianism. In the chapter on human origins,[62] to take one example, Erickson asks the question about the historicity of Adam and Eve as recounted in Genesis chapters 1 and 2. With a fair and unbiased spirit, he presents Emil Brunner's position as an example of those who reject the historicity of the narratives. Then, rather briefly, Erickson states his own positive view of the historicity of this passage, based primarily on two passages in the New Testament, Romans 5:12-21 and 1 Corinthians 15:21f,45. Even in disagreeing with Brunner, there is no spirit of condemnation. When next he asks how the human race developed from one couple, he surveys the various options (naturalistic evolution, fiat creationism, deistic evolution, theistic evolution, and progressive creationism) and concludes with this conciliatory word:

> Given the assumptions and tenets of this book, the two most viable options are theistic evolution and progressive creationism. Both have been and are held by committed Bible-believing scholars, and each can assimilate or explain both the biblical and the empirical date.[63]

Erickson then turns to the question of the age of the human race. His treatment of the subject is but one of many examples of how his spirit of toleration expresses itself in a synthetic affirmation of what are often considered opposing, even contradictory, positions. In this particular section, he sets the tone for his conclusions with an anecdote about acorns growing into trees. Then he writes:

> Fundamentalism has sometimes seemed to require immediacy of action. . . . Liberalism, on the other hand, stresses process. . . . What is at stake in the difference between these two views is actually our understanding of God and his relationship to the world. Fundamentalism stresses that God is transcendent and works in a direct or discontinuous fashion. Liberalism, on the other hand, emphasizes that God is immanent and works through natural channels. Each view regards the other as inappropriate. Since God is both transcendent and immanent, however, both emphases should be maintained, that is, to the extent they are taught in the Bible.[64]

Third, Erickson's theological positions can best be described as moderate, traditional, and even predictable. There are few, if any, surprises. It is a mild (or "diluted")[65] brand of Calvinism in the Baptist tradition with an orientation toward the issues and affirmations common within that broad coalition known as Evangelicalism. A few examples will suffice. Revelation is divided into general and special, with Jesus Christ being the final and complete revelation.[66] The original writings of the Bible are inerrant.[67] Election is of individuals to salvation.[68] The fetus is regarded as a human person and should be treated so by Christians.[69]

It is true that Erickson does introduce into the subject matter of systematic theology a number of items normally ignored. Among these are racism,[70] ecumenism,[71] the administration of the Lord's Supper,[72] and the social and corporate dimensions of sin.[73] And on more than one issue, his moderate and accommodating inclinations allow him to stretch the limits of his conservative Baptist traditions. Examples are the use of literary criticism in interpreting the Bible,[74] a rather positive evaluation of general revelation,[75] and, as mentioned above, the reasonableness of theistic evolution.[76]

James William McClendon, Jr.

James William McClendon was reared in the Baptist heartland of the American South.[77] He attended college at the University of Texas, graduated from Princeton Theological Seminary, and completed formal theological studies at Southwestern Baptist Theological Seminary with a Bachelor of Divinity degree in 1950 and a Doctor of Theology in 1953. He moved immediately to the faculty of Golden Gate Baptist Theological Seminary near San Francisco where he stayed for ten years. Even with all of this Baptist influence in his life and work, it was not until he was forty years old that he experienced a "conversion" to Baptist theology. In the preface to his *Ethics: Systematic Theology, Volume I*, dated Thanksgiving Day 1985, McClendon writes these words:

> Nineteen seventy-four, I believe, was the year I read John Yoder's *Politics of Jesus*. I was then a professor in the Church Divinity School of the Pacific, a Baptist from the South teaching in an Episcopal seminary in an ecumenical setting, the Graduate Theological Union in Berkeley. I am still there, but that book changed my life. In it, I discovered, or rediscovered, my own profound roots in the Anabaptist (or as I now prefer to write it, baptist) vision. . . . It became clear to me that while other traditions, Reformed and Catholic and Lutheran and Anglican, had enjoyed a rich development, my own had not, or not enough. So in about 1980 I resolved to write . . . a 3-volume systematic theology "in the light of the baptist vision," the whole to appear in the order I, Ethics; II, Doctrine; III, Fundamental or Philosophical Questions. This is the *Ethics*. . . . So in 1981 . . . I set out to visit twenty-five centers of current "baptist" thought and life, from Walla Walla College in Washington to the Interdenominational Theological Center in Atlanta, from Fort Worth, Texas, to Elkhart, Indiana, laying my plans before scholars and students in many places and asking their counsel. . . . Not that I have found universal consent so far! Some have thought my basis mistaken; they said I should start from Calvin, not Anabaptism; others have urged me not to be identified with any particular standpoint, indicating as they did so the catholicity of the drafts I had to show. Each had a point, and I believe I really listened to all, but I have come out here. There is indeed this "free church" or "believers' church" or *baptist* style of Christian thought that is widely displayed but only haltingly voiced. Not until it has sounded its own note can there be full and fair conversation in our times between it and other voices, other styles in the one kingdom of Christ.[78]

Some things have changed since 1985. The *Ethics* book was published in 1986; the *Doctrine* volume is being written; volume 3 has been tentatively renamed *Theory*; and McClendon left the Church Divinity School of the Pacific after two decades on the faculty. But some things have not changed, and chief among these is McClendon's fundamental commitment to the writing of systematic theology rooted in the "baptist vision." Thus, he takes his place as a rightful and respected participant in the current resurgence of Baptist theology.

McClendon begins his innovative approach to systematic theology by seeking "to give an adequate explanation for the scarcity of baptist theologies, and to show how the scarcity may be overcome."[79] After surveying several proposals for explaining this "scarcity," he concludes:

> The baptists in all their variety and disunity failed to see in their own heritage, their own way of using Scripture, their own communal practices and patterns, *their own guiding vision*, a resource for theology unlike the prevailing scholasticism round about them.[80]

And again, after discussing the suggestions of others, McClendon offers his own suggestion as to what exactly is this "baptist vision."

> The role of Scripture is indeed the clue. . . . Scripture . . . effects a link between the church of the apostles and our own. . . . So the vision can be expressed as a hermeneutical motto, which is shared awareness of *the present Christian community as the primitive community and the eschatological community*.[81]

In other words, Baptists see themselves in the narrative of Scripture, utilizing the hermeneutic expressed in the biblical phrase "this is that."

This commitment to finding oneself in the Scripture stories naturally emphasizes the role of Christian living (ethics) over Christian confessing (doctrine) and Christian thinking (theory). This is the pattern of theologizing McClendon finds in the life and work of Origen "in the earliest Christian 'theological seminary.' "[82] This is also the one he proposes for authentic Baptist theology. Christian living, or ethics, is described by McClendon as having three dimensions: the natural, the social and the eschatological.[83] This judgment becomes the organizing principle of his volume of systematic theology.

McClendon presents the notion of natural, or body, ethics by telling the story of Jonathan and Sarah Edwards.[84] This little-known story about the well-known New England theologian focuses attention upon their married life, especially the romantic and sexual dimensions. In this way, the natural environment of the human person is explained and affirmed. The social dimensions of Christian ethics arise out of this question: "Can any general account of social relations be offered that will first (and primarily) do justice to the biblical and Baptist vision, while at the same time offering insight into the life of the people of God in the most varied circumstances of their social and political life . . . in which tomorrow's Christianity is now being formed anew?"[85] McClendon answers yes, and offers the life story of Dietrich Bonhoeffer as an illustration.[86] And finally, the resurrection of Jesus becomes the final arbitrator and vindicator of Christian living. Resurrection ethics, what McClendon calls "the sphere of the anastatic," is presented through the life and ministry of Dorothy Day.[87]

All of this is a very different way of doing theology, also of doing ethics. No doubt we can expect more such creative thinking when the other volumes are published. In an unpublished and preliminary paper entitled "Toward a Conversionist Spirituality" McClendon sketches out his search "for a form of the church that will nurture both formation and transformation." It involves four transformative elements of Christian living with a corresponding feature of community life: Preparation (catechesis), conversion (baptism), discipleship (Eucharist) and an unpredictable element (prophetic discernment).[88]

Bruce Demarest and Gordon Lewis

The most recent contribution to the new wave of Believers' Church theologies is that being written by two professors at Denver Conservative Baptist Seminary, Bruce Demarest and Gordon Lewis. Demarest was raised in an independent Baptist church in Flushing, New York. His education was at Wheaton College, Trinity Evangelical Divinity School, and the University of Manchester, where he earned a Doctor of Philosophy degree in biblical theology under the direction of F. F. Bruce. Much of his theological orientation was shaped by ten years of overseas mission work.[89]

Gordon Lewis, also a native of New York, was educated at Baptist Bible Seminary and Gordon College, then at Faith Theological Seminary (Master of Divinity) and finally at Syracuse University (Master of Arts and Doctor of Philosophy). From his first teaching days at Baptist Bible Seminary, Lewis has been interested in apologetics. He has continued this ministry through more than thirty years on the faculty of Denver Seminary, currently as Professor of Systematic Theology and Christian Philosophy. He is a member of a Baptist church.[90]

How do two people produce one systematic theology? Demarest and Lewis answer this question in the preface to volume one:

> After the authors agreed on the basic approach and the issues, Bruce Demarest contributed the first half of each chapter, defining the problem, surveying the historical views, and summing up the relevant biblical evidence. Gordon Lewis contributed the second half of each chapter, formulating the doctrine systematically, defending it, and applying it to life and ministry. Then we interacted with each other's materials and with several readers' and editors' suggestions, making revisions accordingly.[91]

This paragraph gives us an introduction to the basic design of *Integrative Theology*. Demarest and Lewis utilize what they call "a new paradigm for doing theology."[92] This paradigm is different than (1) confessional theology that describes and defends the theological tradition of a particular denomination or school of theology; (2) fideistic theology that declares truth from a position of assumed authority; and (3) traditional systematic theology that fails in the areas, particularly, of objectivity, biblical exegesis, and relevance to life and ministry.[93] This leads Demarest and Lewis to what they term the "verificational" approach to theological thinking composed of six distinct steps.

> (1) defining and distinguishing one distinct topic or problem for inquiry; (2) learning alternative approaches to it from a survey of Spirit-led scholars in the history of the church; (3) discovering and formulating from both the Old and the New Testament a coherent summary of relevant biblical teaching by making use of sound principles of hermeneutics, worthy commentaries, and biblical theologies; (4) formulating on the basis of the relevant data a cohesive doctrine and relating it without contradiction to other biblically founded doctrines and other knowledge; (5) defending this formulation of revealed truth in interaction with contradictory options in theology, philosophy, science, religion, and cults; and (6) applying these convictions to Christian life and ministry in the present generation. These six steps provide the outline for each of the following chapters: The Problem; Historical Hypotheses; Biblical Teaching; Systematic Formulation; Apologetic Interaction; and Relevance for Life and Ministry.[94]

Each section concludes with the same list of "Review Questions" and "Ministry Projects."

This decision to include major sections of the history of dogma, biblical exegesis, apologetics, and the practice of ministry creates a theology book that is far more comprehensive in intent than traditional systematic theologies. By incorporating these elements into one writing project the amount of space and attention given to the "systematic formulation" of the doctrine is thereby reduced. Demarest and Lewis acknowledge this limitation, insisting that other dimensions of truth and learning, such as sociology and psychology, need to be heard from in the development of Christian theology.

Even with the addition of these new elements in the process of systematic theology, the conclusions affirmed are remarkably familiar: a distinction between general and special revelation, with the latter essential for salvation;[95] an inerrant Bible containing both historical and propositional revelation;[96] God as triune, self-existent, eternal, unchanging, omniscient, omnipotent, just and loving;[97] conditional reprobation of all to damnation and the unconditional election of some unto salvation.[98]

Conclusion

By the time Martin Marty wrote of the "baptistification" of American religion in 1983[99] eight books of Baptist theology by Henry, Fackre, and Moody were well into circulation. Since then another nine volumes of Baptist theology have been written, and yet another twelve are planned for publication. It is reasonable to conclude that this wave of systematic theology is part of that larger social and religious trend which Marty describes as "the most dramatic shift in power style on the Christian scene in our time, perhaps in our epoch."[100] If so, they function to provide the intellectual and theological dimension of this movement in American Christianity.

Those of us within the movement can be encouraged by this theological activity as yet another sign of the health and vitality of our religious tradition. It is not just the sheer volume of systematic theology that is encouraging, but it is both its creativity and diversity. The books by Fackre, Moody, Finger, McClendon, and Demarest/Lewis make a conscious and explicit effort to bring fresh ideas and methods to the Baptist tradition. Among the most appealing and potentially productive aspects of these theologies are the interaction with nonreligious disciplines (such as psychology, anthropology, geology, etc.) by Moody and Finger, the experiment with multiple authorship by Demarest and Lewis, and the use of narrative, both biblical and biographical, by Fackre and McClendon. It perhaps goes without saying that innovations in the substance and structure of Baptist theology result from significant and sustained interaction with non-Baptist traditions, both sacred and secular. And this is certainly apparent from the testimonies these men provide of their own intellectual journeys. It is precisely this openness to dialogue with and influence from non-Baptists that has made this group of theologians of tremendous potential influence far beyond their Baptist heritage.

Even though these men all identify with the Baptist tradition, care must be taken not to neglect the diversity among them. Attention has already been drawn to the variety of structures employed. There are also significant differences in mood. Henry, Moody, and Demarest/Lewis are polemical and, on occasion, contentious. Erickson and Fackre are congenial, even accommodating. These theologies are oriented in different directions: Henry, Erickson, and Demarest/Lewis toward the evangelical community; Moody, Finger, and McClendon toward narrower denominational constituencies; and Fackre toward the broad ecumenical scene. Theologically, Erickson and Demarest/Lewis favor the Calvinistic wing of the Reformed tradition, while Moody and Finger are Arminian. Henry is a classic rationalist while McClendon is experientialist. And it is clear that the works of Moody,

Erickson, and Demarest/Lewis arise out of the classroom situation, where-as Henry and McClendon, especially, are largely independent of that environment.

But make no mistake, even with these differences these men are Baptist. Indeed, the diversity may itself be a chief distinction of the Baptist tradition, witnessing as it does to the notion of freedom imbedded so deeply in the Baptist consciousness. Furthermore, there is remarkably little notice given to the creeds and confessions of faith of the Christian (or Baptist) tradition. Above all, Scripture is the focal point of their theological work. Most of these books can be classified as compendiums of Bible teachings on various topics. Systematic theology is obviously understood as the effort to discern, describe, and defend what the Bible has to say about certain religious topics. This is especially true of Finger, Erickson, Demarest/Lewis, and Moody. Henry is no exception even though his orientation is overtly philosophical rather than biblical. Fundamentally, his system is an effort to describe and defend the biblical world view against its modern competitors. And in that sense, he also is rooted and grounded in the Bible.

Henry does, however, lead the way as to another aspect of the biblical orientation of these theologians, and that is the theological question of Scripture and its ancillary issues of revelation and authority. Fully one third of the total pages written by these seven men address this matter, including four of Henry's six volumes and two of Fackre's projected eight volumes. Granted, this reflects the status of revelation and Scripture as the chief theological issues of the entire Christian community of the twentieth century. But for Baptists, who represent the ideology of biblical restorationism, this is of natural and traditional concern.[101]

Once upon a time, this Baptist vision of biblical restorationism was a radical alternative to the prominent models of Christian living. But not even the strong element of creativity mentioned above can alter the essentially conservative nature of these seven systematic theologies. This may be a commentary on the success of the Baptist movement itself. Or it may be a witness to the triumph of the confessional approach to exegesis and theology. Whatever the reason, Henry, Fackre, Moody, Finger, Erickson, McClendon, and Demarest/Lewis, when placed within the wide spectrum of contemporary Christian theology, are decidedly on the conservative end. There is nothing here that can legitimately be called liberal, even if occasionally one differs with a traditional Baptist formulation of a specific doctrine. A prominent sign of this conservatism is the low level of concern for many of the chief issues that face the church today. Examples include: ecology, bioethics, charismatic renewal, ecumenism, family life, gender identity and roles, Catholicism, religion and politics, economics, and world religions.

While all seven mention some of these matters in passing, only Erickson approaches adequacy in this regard, and that may help explain the popularity of his work. Furthermore, Erickson joins forces with the other six men to reject many of the more significant (and liberal) theological proposals of the twentieth century, including process theology, universalism, relativism, and, for the most part, liberation theology and biblical criticism. And, sadly, there is little evidence that these theologians have been influenced by the way Christianity is thought and lived in the Third World. Surely these seven theologians cannot be mistaken for those "reformation radicals" one recent writer thought he saw riding across the theological landscape.[102]

Nevertheless, this wave of theology is a welcomed addition to the life and work of Baptists. The completion of those projects already begun by Fackre, McClendon, and Demarest/Lewis and the publication of those in process by Garrett and Grudem will further strengthen that wing of the church of Christ known as the Believers' Church. They will do so, not because they merely research and repeat the elements of our noble heritage, but because they use the Baptist vision to explain the Christian's experience of the risen Lord and to shed light upon the way Christians are called to live in the world today.

Notes

1. James Leo Garrett, Jr., ed., *The Concept of the Believers' Church* (Scottdale, Pa.: Herald Press, 1969). There have been seven more conferences on the Believers' Church tradition held periodically since 1967, the most recent in February 1990 on the campus of Southwestern Baptist Theological Seminary in Fort Worth, Texas.

2. Ibid., 6f.

3. Thomas Finger, *Christian Theology: An Eschatological Approach* (Nashville: Thomas Nelson, 1985), 84-85; James Wm. McClendon, Jr., *Systematic Theology: Ethics* (Nashville: Abingdon, 1986), 36-37.

4. Six volumes (Waco, Tex.: Word, 1976-83).

5. Two volumes (Grand Rapids: Eerdmans, 1978 [and revised in 1984] and 1987). Six more volumes are planned.

6. Grand Rapids: Eerdmans, 1981.

7. Volume 1 (Nashville: Nelson, 1985; reprint, Scottdale, Pa.: Herald Press, 1987) and volume 2 (Scottdale, Pa.: Herald Press, 1989).

8. Three volumes (Grand Rapids: Baker, 1983, 1984, 1985 with a one-volume edition in 1986).

9. Nashville: Abingdon, 1986. Two more volumes are planned.

10. Two volumes (Grand Rapids: Zondervan, 1987, 1990). A third volume is to be published.

11. Phone conversation, James Leo Garrett and Dwight A. Moody, February 24, 1990.

12. Phone Conversation, Wayne Grudem and Dwight A. Moody, February 22, 1990.

13. Philadelphia: Judson Press. Later, a one volume edition was issued. For biographical sketches on the following Baptist and Methodist theologians see Daniel G. Reid, ed., *Dictionary of Christianity in America* (Downer's Grove, Ill.: Inter-Varsity Press, 1990).

14. Philadelphia: American Baptist Publication Society, 1887. F. H. Kerfoot, Boyce's successor in the chair of theology, issued a slightly revised edition of the volume in 1892. The

Christian Gospel Foundation of Pompano Beach, Florida, reprinted the original edition, omitting the preface.

15. New York: Scribner's Sons, 1898.

16. New York: Macmillian, 1917.

17. Philadelphia: Judson Press, 1917.

18. New York: Macmillan, 1919.

19. Nashville: Broadman, 1924.

20. Nashville: Broadman, 1927.

21. See the interesting statistics and comments of Thor Hall in a study entitled *Systematic Theology Today: The State of the Art in North America* (Washington, D.C.: University Press of America, 1978), 33-35. His work can be summarized in these words: "these calculations show that two denominational 'families,' namely the Baptist and the Methodist, are under-represented in the community of systematic theologians, while several other traditions, notably the Presbyterian, the Episcopalian, and the United Church of Christ, are markedly over-represented. . . . No one will begrudge these denominational 'families' their theological strength, of course. It is nevertheless to be regretted that the Baptist and Methodist traditions do not show the same level of concern for making contributions to the discipline of systematic theology at the present." Ibid., 35. Perhaps the current renaissance of Believers' Church theology will go a long way toward correcting this statistical imbalance.

22. Henry, *God*, 1:12, 2:7, 3:7.

23. Biographical information is readily available in his own autobiography, *Confessions of a Theologian: An Autobiography* (Waco, Tex.: Word, 1986). See also Bob Patterson, *Carl F. H. Henry*, (Waco, Tex.: Word, 1983).

24. Henry, *God*, 1:43.

25. Ibid., 2:7.

26. Ibid., 2:8-16.

27. Fackre, *Story*, 2:347; phone conversation, Gabriel Fackre and Dwight A. Moody, February 25, 1990.

28. Ibid., 3-41. Information for this section was also derived from a personal letter, Gabriel Fackre to Dwight A. Moody, November 2, 1989, and a personal conversation, Gabriel Fackre and Dwight A. Moody, January 25, 1990.

29. Fackre, *Story*, 1:182-84.

30. Ibid., 1:195-218.

31. Ibid., 1:vii; 2:vii, 168-69, n. 12.

32. Ibid., 2:156.

33. Ibid., 2:chapter 3, "The Text of Authority," 157-210 and chapter 4, "The Context of Authority," 211-53.

34. Timothy George, "Systematic Theology at Southern Seminary," *Review and Expositor* 82 (Winter 1985): 31-47.

35. Dale Moody and Clifton D. Harrison, "A Texas Tumbleweed," *Elm Fork Echoes*, 9 (April 1981): 10-15; Dwight A. Moody, "Doctrines of Inspiration in the Southern Baptist Theological Tradition" (Ph.D. diss., The Southern Baptist Theological Seminary, 1982), 179-81.

36. Dan Stiver, "Dale Moody: Rightly Dividing the Word of Truth" in the forthcoming book *Baptist Theologians*, ed. David Dockery and Timothy George (Nashville: Broadman, 1990).

37. Moody, *The Word of Truth*, xi.

38. Ibid., 47.

39. Dale Moody, "The Inspiration of Holy Scripture," (unpublished manuscript edited by Dwight A. Moody, Boyce Centennial Library, The Southern Baptist Theological Seminary, 1981).

40. Moody, *The Word of Truth*, 539.

41. Ibid., 441.

42. Ibid., 142.

43. Ibid., 23.

44. Ibid., 365.

45. Phone conversation, Thomas Finger and Dwight A. Moody, February 10, 1990.

46. New York: Harper and Row, 1967.

47. Grand Rapids: Eerdmans, 1972.

48. Thomas Finger, *Christian Theology*, 1:36.

49. Ibid., 100f.

50. Ibid., chapter 8 (135-54) and chapter 9 (155-76).

51. Ibid., chapter 10 (177-94), chapter 11 (195-212) and chapter 12 (212-34).

52. Ibid., chapter 15 (277-302), chapter 16 (303-24), chapter 17 (325-48) and chapter 18 (349-64).

53. Ibid., 2:11.

54. Ibid., 2:13.

55. Ibid., 2:102, 139.

56. Ibid., 2:147.

57. Ibid., 2:159f.

58. Ibid., 2:193f.

59. Biographical information on Erickson is derived from Leslie R. Keylock, "Evangelical Leaders You Should Know: Meet Millard J. Erickson," *Moody Monthly*, June 1987, 71-73. A good evaluation of Erickson's theology and influence is David S. Dockery, "Millard J. Erickson: Baptist and Evangelical Theologian," *Journal of the Evangelical Theological Society*, 32 (December 1989): 519-32. This article will also be published in the book of essays edited by Dockery and Timothy George entitled *Baptist Theologians* (Nashville: Broadman Press, 1990).

60. According to information supplied by Baker Book House, some 25,000 copies of the individual volumes have been printed and the one volume edition is now in its 6th printing with 30,000 copies in print. Erickson's systematic may be in use by more than 70 colleges, universities and seminaries. Personal correspondence, Allan Fisher to Dwight A. Moody, February 23, 1990. See also Keylock, "Erickson," 71.

61. Erickson, *Christian Theology*, 1:11.

62. Ibid., 1:12.

63. Ibid., 2:473-93.

64. Ibid., 2:482.

65. Ibid., 3:1105. Another good example is in the matter of "Christology from above" versus "Christology from below." See ibid., 2:662-75.

66. Ibid., 1:153-92.

67. Ibid., 1:221-40.

68. Ibid., 1:345-63; 3:907-28.

69. Ibid., 2:553-56.

70. Ibid., 2:542-49.

71. Ibid., 3:1129-46.

72. Ibid., 3:1124-27.

73. Ibid., 2:641-58.

74. Ibid., 1:81-104. He writes: "It should be apparent that biblical criticism need not be negative in its results." And again: "Biblical criticism, then, if carefully used and based upon assumptions that are consistent with the full authority of the Bible, can be a helpful means of shedding further light on the meaning of Scripture." (104) This is evidently what he means by his statement in the preface to volume 1: "In particular, I attempt to approach the Scriptures postcritically rather than critically, or precritically, or uncritically" (12).

75. Ibid., 1:153-74.

76. Ibid., 2:473-87.

77. Sources for biographical information include: Personal correspondence, James Wm. McClendon, Jr., to Dwight A. Moody, December 11, 1989; Curriculum Vitae: James William

McClendon, Jr., October 1989; phone conversation, James McClendon and Dwight A. Moody, February 15, 1990.

78. McClendon, *Ethics*, 7-8.

79. Ibid., 21.

80. Ibid., 26.

81. Ibid., 31.

82. Ibid., 43.

83. Ibid., 62-67.

84. Ibid., 110-55.

85. Ibid., 159.

86. Ibid., 187-239.

87. Ibid., 276-98.

88. James Wm. McClendon, "Toward a Conversionist Spirituality" (unpublished paper in the files of Dwight A. Moody, Pittsburgh, Pennsylvania, no date).

89. Sources for biographical information include: Personal correspondence, Bruce Demarest to Dwight A. Moody, January 26, 1990; personal conversation, Bruce Demarest and Dwight A. Moody, February 25, 1990.

90. Sources for biographical information include: Personal correspondence, Gordon R. Lewis to Dwight A. Moody, January 25, 1990; "Gordon R. Lewis," biographical information sheet supplied by Lewis, now in the files of Dwight A. Moody, Pittsburgh, Pennsylvania.

91. Demarest and Lewis, *Integrative Theology*, 1:13.

92. Ibid., 1:7.

93. Ibid., 1:8-9; cf. 23-28.

94. Ibid., 1:26.

95. Ibid., 1:72-78.

96. Ibid., 1:148-65.

97. Ibid., 1:231-40, 270-80.

98. Ibid., 1:310-22.

99. Martin E. Marty, "Baptistification Takes Over," *Christianity Today*, September 2, 1983, 33-36.

100. Ibid., 33.

101. It remains to be seen how McClendon, the most explicitly anabaptistic writer of the seven, will handle Scripture, in theory and in practice, beginning as he has with ethics and planning to end with theory.

102. Charles Scriven, "The Reformation Radicals Ride Again," *Christianity Today*, March 5, 1990, 13-15.

Scripture Index

Person Index